THE SUNDAY TIMES

GREAT
SPORTING
MOMENTS

THE SUNDAY TIMES

GREAT SPORTING MOMENTS

Edited by Alan English

HarperCollins*Publishers*

Published in 2001 by
HarperCollins*Publishers*
77-85 Fulham Palace Road
London W6 8JB

First published in 1999 as *The Sunday Times Sporting Century*

British Library Cataloguing in Publication Data:
A catalogue record for this book is available from the British Library

Printed and bound in Great Britain by the Bath Press Ltd

ISBN 0 0071 3245 X

ACKNOWLEDGEMENTS

When the series "50 Stories of the Sporting Century" first appeared in *The Sunday Times*, in January 1999, letters and e-mails from readers lobbying for the inclusion of their favourite sporting moments arrived quickly and in great quantities. If many will be disappointed that their nominations have failed to make the cut, they at least have our gratitude for making their cases so eloquently.

Jeremy Bayston on *The Sunday Times* picture desk, assisted by Lawrence Smith, performed wonders of research and, from the graphics department, John Smith, Julian Osbaldstone and Clare Harrison helped us to do justice to several of the stories. Immense gratitude goes to Thomas Cussans and Philip Parker at HarperCollins, whose enthusiasm matched our own. No less professional were the book's designers, Paul Calver and Roger Hammond.

Many people helped us to tell these 50 stories, some of them major figures of the sporting century, others less well known but important witnesses none the less. All of them have our thanks.
Alan English

CONTRIBUTORS

ALAN ENGLISH was deputy sports editor of *The Sunday Times* until 2000. He began his career at the Limerick Leader in Ireland and his favourite sporting moment is the Clay-Liston fight at Miami Beach in 1964, followed by the 1974 Ali-Foreman contest in Zaire

BRIAN GLANVILLE was football correspondent of *The Sunday Times* for 33 distinguished years, between 1958 and 1991. He is the author of many books. He returned to *The Sunday Times* in 1998

DAVE HANNIGAN was Irish football correspondent of *The Sunday Times* until 2000. His first book, *The Garrison Game*, a study of Irish football, was published in 1998

IAN HAWKEY joined *The Sunday Times* fresh from award-winning coverage of the transition to democracy in South Africa. He took his first steps in sports journalism on the programme at Fulham FC, and regrets only that he left before Mohammed Al Fayed arrived to adjust the club's wage structure

STEPHEN JONES, *Sunday Times* rugby correspondent, won the 1994 William Hill Sports Book of the Year award for his account of the changed rugby landscape, *Endless Winter*. He was Sports Correspondent of the Year in 1998 and in a short but eventful rugby career was sent off six times (once, he claims, through mistaken identity)

JOE LOVEJOY, football correspondent of *The Sunday Times*, is the author of *Bestie*, the authorised biography of George Best published in 1998 and widely regarded as the definitive account of that legend's life

HUGH McILVANNEY is the outstanding sports journalist of his generation. Sports Writer of the Year seven times, he is also the only sports journalist to have been voted Journalist of the Year. He has published collections of his work

on boxing, football and horse racing and his collaboration with Sir Alex Ferguson, *Managing My Life*, became a bestseller in 1999

NICK PITT writes mainly on golf, tennis and boxing and is a former sports editor of *The Sunday Times*. His account of the relationship between Naseem Hamed and his trainer Brendan Ingle, *The Paddy and the Prince*, was published in 1998

JONATHAN POWELL, *Sunday Times* racing correspondent until 2001, is also well known to BBC racing viewers for his on-course interviews. He is the author of five books. *Champion's Story*, his bestselling biography of Bob Champion, was made into a film starring John Hurt

ALASDAIR REID has written for *The Sunday Times* for more than 10 years, most recently as a golf correspondent. He has never, he says, won a damned thing in his life

DAVID WALSH was British Sports Writer of the Year in 2001 and also in 1997. He was Irish Sports Journalist of the Year four times and is the author of several books, including *Inside the Tour de France* and a biography of Sean Kelly

DENIS WALSH writes mainly for the successful Irish edition of *The Sunday Times* and is a former Sports Journalist of the Year in Ireland. Although he writes about a range of sports, his first love is hurling

KEITH WHEATLEY was a Fleet Street gossip-columnist until he ran away to sea, lured by the romance of the America's Cup. He has been *Sunday Times* sailing correspondent since 1985 and is the author of four books on nautical matters

SIMON WILDE, *Sunday Times* cricket correspondent, is the author of four books on the sport. Two of them – *Ranji: A Genius Rich and Strange* and *Letting Rip* – were shortlisted for the William Hill Sports Book of the Year award

CONTENTS

INTRODUCTION

Why is sport important? The American writer Dan Jenkins tells a story about a fellow toiler who once found himself among a group of distinguished academics on a panel debating the issue. For several hours the dons droned on about the convergence of sport and society until, finally, it was the sportswriter's turn to speak. Why did he think sport mattered? "I really don't know," he said. "Can I go home now?" This book, an updated version of the volume originally published as *The Sporting Century*, seeks more to tell stories than interpret their significance. It is both a journey right to the heart of the events that have made the biggest impression on lovers of sport and a celebration of the men and women whose brilliance left so many indelible memories and brightened so many lives.

If some of the more illustrious players in the sporting pantheon are missing from the 50 stories here, then that is because ours has not been a technical exercise in saluting the greatest accomplishments in sports history. You may disagree with our choices, but pleasing everybody was never a possibility. Why choose Red Rum's first Grand National win over his historic third? Because the 1973 race gave us Crisp, a runner-up so valiant that his courage will always be remembered by all those who love the great race.

Some of sport's biggest heroes have helped us to revisit their finest hours and, in many cases, bring fresh perspectives to familiar stories. One man makes two appearances. We meet him first in Miami as a 22-year-old rank outsider called Cassius Clay and, a decade later, on an unforgettable African night, as Muhammad Ali. His claims to the title of greatest sportsman of the 20th century were already strong before his eighth-round defeat of George Foreman in Zaire; after it, they were beyond dispute. If she is lucky, Shirley Babashoff will merit a mere footnote in the sporting history books. Babashoff won six Olympic silver medals and was four times beaten by East German swimmers who were systematically doped by the state. The problem of drugs in sport has never been more acute and Babashoff may be the most cheated athlete of all time. Her story, and that of the ill-fated British cyclist Tom Simpson, may have nothing of the feelgood factor we associate with memorable sporting moments, but both have much to tell us about the forces that drive sport in the 21st century. Gripping narratives also secure them their places alongside the coruscating deeds of Bannister and Botham, Pele and Piggott and many more.

Alan English
September 2001

7

THE TEN GREATEST SPORTING YEARS

1 1953

- The Matthews FA Cup final
- Gordon Richards wins the Derby at 28th and final attempt
- England reclaim the Ashes after 20 years
- Dazzling Hungarians rout England at Wembley
- Ben Hogan wins three Major titles – the Open, the US Open and Masters
- Maureen Connolly wins first women's tennis Grand Slam

2 1981

- Botham's Ashes
- Between them, Sebastian Coe and Steve Ovett break world mile record three times in nine days
- Phenomenal Shergar leaves opposition in his wake in the Epsom Derby
- Liverpool win third European Cup
- Bernard Hinault wins third Tour de France
- Bob Champion and Aldaniti overcome the odds to win the Grand National
- Ricky Villa classic wins FA Cup for Spurs
- Tempestuous John McEnroe takes Bjorn Borg's Wimbledon title

3 1973

- Red Rum beats Crisp in unforgettable Grand National
- Gareth Edwards scores wonder try for Barbarians against All Blacks
- Johnny Miller shoots record 63 to win US Open at Oakmont from six shots back
- George Foreman beats Joe Frazier in Zaire; Muhammad Ali loses to Ken Norton
- Sunderland beat Leeds in fairytale Cup final
- Jan Tomaszewski, so-called clown, denies England
- Billie Jean King beats Bobbie Riggs in Battle of the Sexes

4 1958

- Garry Sobers scores 365 not out for West Indies against Pakistan, a new record
- Arnold Palmer wins the Masters, the first of four Augusta titles
- Brazil, inspired by 17-year-old Pele, win their first World Cup
- Sugar Ray Robinson wins his sixth world crown
- Mike Hawthorn shades Stirling Moss to win F1 world title

5 1970

- Pele and the masterful Brazilians win their third World Cup
- Doug Sanders misses short putt on 18th at St Andrews and loses Open to Jack Nicklaus
- After a 3½-year enforced absence, Ali returns with a vengeance against Jerry Quarry
- Nijinsky wins the Triple Crown
- Margaret Smith Court wins Grand Slam

6 1974

- First Ali beats Frazier, then he shocks George Foreman in Zaire
- Willie John McBride's Lions are undefeated in South Africa
- Eddie Merckx wins record-equalling fifth Tour de France
- Johan Cruyff's Holland, playing Total Football, beaten in World Cup final by West Germany
- Brian Clough sacked by Leeds after 44 days in charge

7 1975

- The Thrilla in Manila – exhausted Ali prevails over Frazier
- Underdog Arthur Ashe beats Jimmy Connors at Wimbledon
- Billie Jean King wins sixth Wimbledon title
- West Indies win cricket's first World Cup
- Tom Watson wins first of his five Opens, at Carnoustie
- Grundy beats Bustino in so-called Race of the Century

8 1986

- Nicklaus wins Masters at 46
- Diego Maradona wins World Cup for Argentina
- Kenny Dalglish leads Liverpool to the Double
- Greg LeMond denies Hinault sixth Tour de France victory
- Mike Tyson becomes youngest world heavyweight champion

9 1908

- Jack Johnson becomes first black world heavyweight champion
- Dorando Pietri disqualified in London marathon for accepting help to finish
- WG Grace retires and Jack Hobbs celebrates his Test debut with 83 against Australia
- Signorinetta, only filly in race, wins the Derby

10 1977

- Red Rum wins third Grand National
- Liverpool win their first European Cup
- Tom Watson and Jack Nicklaus in classic duel at Turnberry
- Virginia Wade wins Wimbledon in Jubilee year
- Kerry Packer's circus rocks cricket establishment
- Geoff Boycott scores his hundredth hundred

Carl Lewis, Los Angeles 1984

The listings on this page have been chosen by a panel of *Sunday Times* journalists

THE TEN GREATEST SPORTING MOMENTS

1. Rumble in the Jungle – Muhammad Ali v George Foreman, 1974

2. Roger Bannister breaks the four-minute mile, 1954

3. Bob Beamon shatters world long-jump record, 1968

4. Jack Nicklaus wins his sixth US Masters title, 1986

5. Jesse Owens wins four gold medals at the Berlin Olympics, 1936

6. Botham's Ashes, 1981

7. Brazil win the 1970 World Cup

8. Cassius Clay beats Sonny Liston, 1964

9. Manchester United win the European Cup, 1999

10. Bjorn Borg wins his fifth Wimbledon title, beating John McEnroe, 1980

Michael Jordan, Seattle 1987

THE TWENTY GREATEST SPORTS FIGURES

1. Muhammad Ali
2. Pele
3. Jack Nicklaus
4. Jesse Owens
5. Don Bradman
6. Diego Maradona
7. George Best
8. Lester Piggott
9. Michael Jordan
10. Garry Sobers
11. John McEnroe
12. Billie Jean King
13. W G Grace
14. Tiger Woods
15. Carl Lewis
16. Fanny Blankers-Koen
17. Juan Fangio
18. Babe Ruth
19. Joe Louis
20. Ayrton Senna

Athletics

Steven Downes

THE TEN GREATEST MEN

marathon. It was his debut at the distance. His grimacing, front-running style was popular with fans, as he went six years unbeaten at 10,000m.

5 Paavo Nurmi

Twelve Olympic medals, nine of them gold, and 20 world records put this Flying Finn in a class of his own. Winner of the Olympic 10,000m in 1920 and 1928; in 1924, Nurmi won the 1500m and 5,000m

1 Jesse Owens

Best remembered for his unsurpassed four Olympic golds at Berlin in 1936 (100m, 200m, long jump and 4x100m relay). But Owens's greatest athletic achievement came a year before the Games, when he produced four world-record perfomances within an hour. His victories in both the 220-yard sprint and 220-yard hurdles also gave him new world records at the slightly shorter 200m distance – making six in all.

2 Carl Lewis

At the 1984 Los Angeles Olympics, Lewis emulated Jesse Owens's achievement in Berlin, winning four gold medals. At his last Games, in Atlanta in 1996, he emulated Al Oerter's feat of winning an event at four successive Olympics when he took gold in the long jump. In all, Lewis won nine Olympic golds and eight world championships and set nine world records.

3 Daley Thompson

The greatest competitor ever. From 1978, when he finished second in the European championships at the age of 20, Thompson went unbeaten in the decathlon until 1987. He won two Olympic gold medals and broke the world record four times.

4 Emil Zatopek

A real-life legend. Zatopek had won his first Olympic gold at 10,000m in 1948, but it was in Helsinki, four years later, that he would make history. After retaining the 10,000m, he went on to win gold at 5,000m and then, uniquely, also won the

Paavo Nurmi, Antwerp 1920

golds within just 90 minutes. Made his last Olympic appearance as the torchbearer at the 1952 Helsinki Games.

6 Sebastian Coe

The only man ever to win back-to-back Olympic 1500m titles, in 1980 and 1984, when he also won silver medals at 800m. Britain's most prolific world-record-setter, with nine outdoors and three indoors. His 800m record was unbeaten for 16 years.

7 Haile Gebrselassie

By the age of 26 the little Ethiopian had broken 15 world records. World champion at 10,000m in 1993, 1995, 1997 and 1999, he also won the Olympic title in 1996 and 2000. Gebrselassie displayed tremendous range by winning the 1500m and 3,000m world indoor titles in 1999, becoming the first man ever to achieve such a double. Finally beaten at 10,000m in the 2001 world championships.

8 Al Oerter

When Oerter won his third consecutive Olympic discus gold medal for America in 1964, he was already acclaimed as the greatest thrower the world had seen. In 1968, he won his fourth consecutive title (a feat only Carl Lewis in the long jump has emulated). The first man to throw beyond 200ft, Oerter broke the world record four times.

9 Sergei Bubka

Unparalleled dominance saw the Ukrainian win the pole vault at the first six world championships (1983–97), win Olympic gold (1988), and break 35 world records, in the process becoming the first to clear 6m (1985) and 20ft (6.1m) in 1991. He finally retired in 2001.

10 Edwin Moses

Between August 1977 and June 1987, nobody beat Edwin Moses in a 400m hurdles race – establishing the longest unbeaten streak in the sport, 122 successive races. He won Olympic golds in 1976 and 1984 (the US boycott of Moscow denied him in 1980) and held the world record for 15 years.

THE TEN GREATEST WOMEN

1 Fanny Blankers-Koen
Having survived the privations of the War, and competing at a time when women's sporting opportunities were limited, the Dutch housewife's four golds at the 1948 London Olympics (100m, 200m, 80m hurdles and 4x100 relay) is an achievement latter-day, professional athletes still dream about. Also set world records for the high jump, long jump and pentathlon.

2 Wilma Rudolph
Born the 17th of 19 children in Tennessee, Rudolph said she learned to run fast because she needed to get to the dinner table first. Paralysed at four, she only learned to walk normally at seven. Her style and grace in winning 100m, 200m and sprint relays at the 1960 Olympics endeared her to generations of fans.

3 Babe Didrikson
The all-round sportswoman of the century (inset illustration above left). Broke her first world record (javelin) at 16, and two years later won gold for 80m hurdles and javelin at the 1932 Olympics. She was denied high jump gold because the judges disapproved of her head-first style. What she might have achieved can only be guessed at: Didrikson then turned to golf, winning the British women's championship and three US Opens.

4 Grete Waitz
The first woman to win the world title at the marathon (1983), Waitz did much to popularise women's distance running. The Norwegian's long track career was stifled by the maximum distance in the championships being restricted to 3,000m, but on the roads she seemed unbeatable. Won New York marathon nine times and took world cross-country title a record five times.

5 Ingrid Kristiansen
Winner of 13 major marathons, including London four times, she is the only athlete to hold world records at 5,000m, 10,000m and marathon at same time, and to be world champion at track, road and cross-country. A former cross-country skier (placed 21st in 1978 world championships), the Norwegian's 2hr 21min 6sec stood as the marathon world best from 1985 to 1998.

6 Iolanda Balas
The first woman to high-jump six feet, which she accomplished 50 times in a career that included two Olympic golds (1960 and 1964) and 14 world records. The Romanian's hold on the record lasted from 1956 to 1971, when her 1.91m world best, set in 1961, was finally beaten.

7 Marion Jones
A former basketball player at North Carolina, Jones turned to the track in 1997 with devastating effect, winning the world title at 100m and the sprint relay. She retained that title in 1999 and won five medals at the Sydney Games in 2000, including golds at 100m, 200m and the 4x400m relay. Lost her world 100m title in 2001 but took gold in the relay and the 200m.

8 Irena Szewinska
Won her first Olympic gold at 18 as part of the Polish sprint relay team at the Tokyo Olympics, where she also won silver at long jump and 200m. Broke the world record to win gold at 200m in Mexico City four years later. In Montreal in 1976, she won gold at 400m at the age of 30. The first woman to break 50sec for 400m.

9 Florence Griffith-Joyner
Flamboyant and controversial, Flo Jo's four medals at the 1988 Olympics (100m, 200m and 4x100m golds, silver at 4x400m) is a record for a woman. Her world records of 10.49sec for 100m and 21.34 for 200 remained out of reach for a decade until her premature death in 1998 at the age of 38, further fuelling allegations that she had used banned drugs.

10 Marita Koch
Another tainted athlete, but one of the tragedies of 20th-century sport is that we cannot know who was clean and who used drugs. Possibly the most successful product of the East German athlete factory. Olympic gold medallist at 400m in 1980, Koch also set 11 world records.

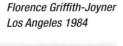

Florence Griffith-Joyner Los Angeles 1984

THE TEN GREATEST ATHLETICS FEATS

1 Paavo Nurmi winning 1500m and 5,000m titles within 90 minutes at the 1924 Olympics

2 Jesse Owens's 8.13m long jump (and five other world records in the day), 1935

3 Bob Beamon's 8.90m long-jump world record at 1968 Olympics

4 Emil Zatopek's three gold medals at the 1952 Olympics

5 Roger Bannister breaking the four-minute mile in 1954

6 Herb Elliott's 1500m in a front-running world-record 3:35.6, 1960 Olympics

7 Al Oerter's fourth gold medal at four different Olympics, 1968

8 Steve Cram beating Sebastian Coe and breaking world record by more than a second in the 1985 Dream Mile in Oslo (3min 46.32sec)

9 Mike Powell breaking Beamon's long-jump world record (with 8.95m) to beat Carl Lewis and win the world title in Tokyo in 1991

10 Jonathan Edwards's 18.16m and 18.29m world records at the triple jump in the 1995 world championships

Boxing

Hugh McIlvanney

THE TEN GREATEST BOXERS

1 Sugar Ray Robinson

Most people with a worthwhile opinion agree that Sugar Ray Robinson (originally Walker Smith Jr) was the most accomplished boxer ever to step through the ropes. He was the fighter with everything: lightning speed applied with inspired timing, a dazzling range of skills, a solid punch, stamina and a warrior's instinct. He won the middleweight championship on five separate occasions between 1951 and 1958 but it was as a welterweight (world champion 1946–51) that he best demonstrated his unrivalled quality.

2 Muhammad Ali

Ali was not only the greatest figure in the history of boxing but, to my mind, the most remarkable phenomenon ever produced by any sport. Technically, he had obvious flaws but the power of his will and the scope of his imagination combined so irresistibly with his speed and athleticism that at his best (which means before his three and a half years of enforced exile began in 1967) he looked superior to any heavyweight who ever fought.

3 Joe Louis

Whatever the claims of other outstanding heavyweight champions such as Jack Johnson, Jack Dempsey and Rocky Marciano, for the purposes of this list Louis (illustration left) must join Muhammad Ali in representing the most glamorous division. He was the dominant presence in boxing from the 1930s into the 1950s. Economy of movement and explosive punching made him a great champion. Natural grace outside the ring made him a hero who was loved rather than merely applauded.

4 Henry Armstrong

At his peak "Homicide" Henry Armstrong appeared in the ring more often than some modern fighters show up at the gym. He fought and won 27 times in 1937 alone, using relentless pressure and deadly punching to stop 26 of his victims. During 1938 he held the featherweight, lightweight and welterweight world titles simultaneously – a phenomenal feat in an era when there were only eight weight classes.

5 Archie Moore

Archie Moore's record total of 141 knockout victories is surely unassailable. No fighter these days would dream of a career stretching across 27 years, as Moore's did between 1936 and 1963. Racism and fear of his talent denied him proper reward for the superb strike-without-being-struck technique that persuaded admirers to call him "The Mongoose". Being the light-heavyweight champion from 1952 until 1961 was barely adequate testimony to his worth.

6 Sandy Saddler

One of the roughest (some would say dirtiest) fighters of the modern era, and so formidable that no featherweight in history could have been backed with confidence to beat him. He had exceptional height (5ft 8½in) and reach (70in) for a 9st man and hit hard enough to knock out 103 opponents. His body-punching was brutal.

7 Benny Leonard

Leonard, lightweight champion from 1917–23, was such a consummate boxer that awed tributes to his skills still reverberate through the mythology of the ring. But this product of New York's East Side ghetto also had an anaesthetising punch. His reputation is reinforced by the standard of opponents he faced. They included Freddie Welsh, Jack Britton and Ted "Kid" Lewis.

Archie Moore, New York 1958

8 Jimmy Wilde

None of the fanciful nicknames that abound in boxing was more justified than that given to Wilde, who was known as "The Ghost with a Hammer in His Hand". With his skeletal frame often weighing less than 7st, he proved himself a miracle of destruction against bigger men. He lost only three of more than 140 fights and held the world flyweight title from 1916 until 1923. Heavyweight Gene Tunney called him "the greatest fighter I ever saw".

9 Ray Leonard

The second Sugar Ray (background illustration below) had film-star looks and his smile could light up a town but in the ring he was an artist with a mugger's malice. The economical grace of his boxing – particularly his ability to slide fluidly in and out of punching range – combined with ferocity of intent and destructive power to make him a truly great welterweight in the 1970s and early 1980s.

10 Carlos Monzon

The statistics of Carlos Monzon's career overwhelm the jibe that he held the middleweight championship when there was a dearth of distinguished challengers. The Argentine lost only three of his 100 fights, was never knocked out and was undefeated from 1964 until he retired in 1977. I saw him fight and he was a wonder in the ring. Outside it, his life was a disaster. In 1988 he was convicted of murdering his estranged lover and he died in a car crash in 1995.

THE TEN GREATEST FIGHTS

1 Muhammad Ali v George Foreman

KINSHASA, ZAIRE, OCTOBER 30 1974. Many would rate Ali's first fight with Joe Frazier in Madison Square Garden or their third meeting, the Thrilla in Manila, above this collision in the middle of an African night. But the setting and the circumstances (Foreman came into the showdown as an unbeaten and apparently unbeatable ogre) made Ali's eighth-round triumph the most dramatic sports event I have ever reported. (*See page 140*).

2 Jack Dempsey v Luis Firpo

NEW YORK, SEPTEMBER 14 1923
In the wildest first round ever produced by any title fight, Dempsey knocked down his Argentine opponent seven times and was twice lifted off his feet by Firpo's furious retaliation. One of those assaults sent Dempsey sprawling through the ropes and on to the press tables. The violence had a more rational pattern in the second round as the champion battered Firpo, forcing him to take a count of five and then knocking him out with a short-arm right.

3 Joe Louis v Max Schmeling

NEW YORK, JUNE 22 1938
It lasted just one round but its violent decisiveness and its implications ensured that it will never be forgotten. Two years earlier Schmeling, carrying the Aryan banner of Hitler's Germany, had knocked out the great black champion in the 12th round. In front of a crowd of 75,000 at Yankee Stadium, Louis annihilated Schmeling's resistance in 124 seconds.

4 Ray Leonard v Thomas Hearns

LAS VEGAS, SEPTEMBER 16 1981
In the greatest fights, fortunes fluctuate and as the rounds pass it seems that first one man and then the other is likely to win. That is how it was when the second Sugar Ray and "Hit Man" Hearns met in their welterweight prime. Unrelentingly fierce and highly skilful, the battle remained close until Leonard (ludicrously scored in arrears on all three judges' cards) stopped Hearns in the 14th.

5 Willie Pep v Sandy Saddler

NEW YORK, FEBRUARY 11 1949.
Pep suffered inside-the-distance losses in three of his four viciously contested matches with Saddler. But in the second of the series, at Madison Square Garden, Pep refused to be discouraged by cuts over each eye and on both cheeks and his brave application of fluent skills brought him a points success at the end of 15 rounds.

6 Jack Dempsey v Gene Tunney

CHICAGO, SEPTEMBER 22 1927.
"The Battle of the Long Count" can still stir arguments 70 years after it took place before 102,000 spectators at Soldier Field. Tunney had taken the heavyweight title from Dempsey with a 10-round points win in 1926 but in the seventh round of the rematch the new champion was dropped on his back near the ropes. Unfamiliar with Illinois rules, Dempsey failed to go to a neutral corner, the count was delayed and Tunney was given 14 seconds to rise. It is often forgotten that on his way to another points victory Tunney floored Dempsey briefly in the eighth.

7 Marvin Hagler v Thomas Hearns

LAS VEGAS, APRIL 15 1985
This was another reminder that brief wars can be unforgettable. It is doubtful that the pace and intensity of the first round have been equalled in any other three minutes of a championship fight. To those of us at ringside, the mutual bombardment seemed to have lasted half an hour. Hagler kept his middleweight crown by hammering Hearns into helplessness in the third round.

8 Alexis Arguello v Aaron Pryor

MIAMI, NOVEMBER 12 1982
Although Pryor had an advantage in age (27 to 31) and may have been naturally stronger at 10st than Arguello, who campaigned for years at lighter weights, these two undeniably great fighters provided a classic. For much of the fight, Arguello's tactical brilliance more than answered Pryor's aggressive surges and his devastating gift for finding the target from almost any angle. But Pryor pounded the Nicaraguan so cruelly in the 14th that the referee mercifully intervened.

9 Wilfredo Gomez v Lupe Pintor

NEW ORLEANS, DECEMBER 3 1982
Having gone to New Orleans to cover a junior-middleweight championship fight between Thomas Hearns and Wilfredo Benitez, I found myself writing instead about the junior-featherweight heroics of Gomez and Pintor. A Puerto Rican against a Mexican in that division was almost a guarantee of class but their see-sawing struggle was so rich in technical excellence and competitive fire that by the time the magnificent Gomez had settled it in the 14th I knew I was having one of the great boxing experiences of my life.

10 Sugar Ray Robinson v Jake LaMotta

CHICAGO, FEBRUARY 14 1951
The last of Robinson's six fights with LaMotta (Sugar Ray won five and lost one) occurred on St Valentine's Day and it was punishing enough to invite Chicagoans to talk of a massacre. However, not all the suffering was on one side. After eight rounds, LaMotta led on two cards and Robinson on one. From the ninth, Robinson assumed control and LaMotta was a bleeding, staggering wreck when rescued by the referee in the 13th.

Cricket

Simon Wilde

THE TEN GREATEST BATSMEN

1 Don Bradman

The greatest run-maker there has ever been. His figures speak for themselves: a Test average of 99.14 where the next best figure is 60.97; a first-class average of 95.14 against the next best of 71.22. He scored a century every third time he went out to bat and was perhaps the batsman who had the fewest spells of bad form.

2 W G Grace

By playing the game on an hitherto unseen plane, Grace spectacularly broadened cricket's appeal. The image is of a portly, avuncular figure, but in his 1870s pomp he was tall, strong and thought nothing of belting fast bowlers operating on rough pitches to all parts. Averaged 50 when the next best mustered half that.

3 Viv Richards

Like Bradman, he was mentally extremely resilient, despite playing in an era when bowling was as consistently hostile and intimidatory as at any time in history. Richards set himself to take on and beat the most threatening bowlers – and usually came out on top. His badge of pride was to never wear a helmet.

4 Jack Hobbs

The most prolific scorer of runs and centuries in history, and one of the most durable batsmen England has possessed. He was her leading batsman from 1909 until 1928, during which period he averaged more than 50 in 10 out of his 11 Test series. The complete player, a master of all conditions and bowling.

5 Len Hutton

Hutton carried England's batting for the best part of 10 years after the Second World War, when they were faced by a powerful Australia side led by two tremendous fast bowlers in Ray Lindwall and Keith Miller. After an aberrant selectorial decision to drop him in 1948, he scored 1,200 runs against this pair in 12 Tests.

6 Garry Sobers

Easily the best batsman of his day in the world and arguably the best left-hander ever. Sobers was a wonderfully instinctive player, who had no problem against any particular type of bowling, and who was impossible to keep quiet once set. Fast bowlers could not ruffle him, though he often ruffled them, as Fred Trueman could testify.

7 Wally Hammond

Hammond was a majestic batsman who, had Bradman not played at the same time, would have enjoyed even greater celebrity. England's greatest batsman between Hobbs and Hutton, his four double-centuries against Australia are unmatched, and his 231 at Sydney in 1936 and 240 at Lord's two years later rank among the greatest-ever Test innings.

8 Denis Compton

Touched with genius, Compton (inset illustration above) was one of the greatest of entertainers, whose gift for strokeplay and improvisation disguised a fundamentally sound technique. His big-match temperament was revealed when he scored a hundred in his first Test against Australia at 20. His 3,816 runs and 18 centuries in 1947 are both records which still stand.

9 Sachin Tendulkar

Tests and one-day matches combined, Tendulkar has scored more international hundreds than any player in history – and had done so by the age of 25. The most precocious batsman the game has known, he played his first Test at 16 and had seven Test hundreds to his name by the time he was 21. No bowling troubles him; perhaps only the expectations of a billion Indians.

10 Victor Trumper

Many Australians thought Trumper a more gifted and certainly more exciting player than the relentlessly efficient Bradman. He was an adventurer who could destroy bowling in any conditions. He was one of the first to master googly bowling and in the wet English summer of 1902 showed his skill on rain-affected pitches with 11 hundreds.

Viv Richards, May 1991

THE TEN GREATEST BOWLERS

1 Sydney Barnes

His contemporaries agreed that he was the greatest bowler they had ever seen and his record supports the case that there has never been one better. Operating at medium-pace, and capable of cutting and swinging the ball both ways, Barnes took 189 wickets in 27 Tests and a staggering 6,229 wickets in all competitive cricket.

2 Dennis Lillee

From the mid-1970s until the early 1980s, Lillee was the supreme fast bowler in an age dominated by them. He scarcely had a bad Test match in all that time or during his two years playing for Kerry Packer. Inspired a whole generation of bowlers across the world. A record 163 wickets in Ashes Tests.

3 Shane Warne

Leg-spinners have had more variations than Warne, but none has had the power to turn his leg-break such prodigious distances, an asset that made Warne the most effective and influential spin bowler of the modern age. Phenomenally accurate for his type, he was the first leg-spinner to take 300 Test wickets.

4 Bill O'Reilly

Bradman rated him the best bowler he faced and O'Reilly gave Hammond more trouble than anyone. O'Reilly purveyed a unique mixture of leg-spinners, top-spinners and googlies with all the aggression of the most ferocious fast bowler. When he died in 1992, *Wisden* described him as "probably the greatest spin bowler the game has ever produced".

5 Malcolm Marshall

Having learned the arts at the knee of Andy Roberts, Michael Holding and Joel Garner, Marshall was the leading West Indies fast bowler when they were at their absolute height. Between 1982 and 1989, he claimed 292 Test wickets at 19.23 apiece and was never on the losing side in a Test series. Amazingly versatile and durable.

6 Richard Hadlee

Hadlee was Marshall's main rival as the world's best bowler in the 1980s, not as quick but with an equally sophisticated armoury and an encyclopaedic knowledge of opponents. Between 1982 and 1989 he took 227 Test wickets at cheaper cost than Marshall and was the leading wicket-taker in 11 out of 15 series.

7 Ray Lindwall

Like Marshall, Lindwall was the complete fast bowler, capable of moving the ball around at great speed. Many contemporaries thought him technically the best they had seen. Formed legendary new-ball attack with Keith Miller that was the scourge of England in the post-War era.

8 Wasim Akram

A magician with the ball and the greatest left-arm fast bowler in history. Swings the ball both ways at speeds that subtly vary but are always fast enough to examine a batsman's technique. He may well retire as the most prolific wicket-taker in Test history.

9 Fred Trueman

Trueman was the cutting edge of England's attack in the late 1950s and early 1960s, genuinely fast and possessing a deadly late outswinger that brought him many of his 307 Test wickets, a world record until 1976. He was effective in conditions all round the world.

10 Michael Holding

One of the most graceful fast bowlers the game has seen and perhaps second only to Jeff Thomson for speed in the modern age. Holding took 14 wickets on an unhelpful Oval pitch in 1976 and bowled an over to Geoff Boycott in Barbados in 1981 that is still spoken of with awe. Rivalled Lillee for quality in the early 1980s.

SIMON WILDE'S BEST XI

1 Len Hutton

2 Jack Hobbs

3 Don Bradman

4 Viv Richards

5 W G Grace

6 Garry Sobers

7 Ian Botham

8 Alan Knott

9 Shane Warne

10 Dennis Lillee

11 Sydney Barnes

12th man Wasim Akram

Sydney Barnes, 1910

Football

Joe Lovejoy

THE TEN GREATEST PLAYERS

1 Pele

The undisputed No 1. Edson Arantes do Nascimento starburst upon the international firmament when Brazil won the World Cup in 1958. Blessed with adhesive close control, and remarkably good in the air for a man of only 5ft 9in, Pele scored more than 1,000 goals, mostly for Santos. He was at his stratospheric peak when Brazil were at theirs, in 1970.

2 Diego Maradona

The Argentinian's performance against England at the 1986 World Cup was a microcosm of his career. The infamous "Hand of God" goal marked him out as a cheat, his slaloming second as a genius. Maradona (illustration above) featured in four World Cups – some would say too many after his expulsion for drug-taking in 1994; others too few, for he was good enough at 17 to have made the 1978 squad.

3 George Best

Pele acclaimed Manchester United's errant Irishman as the world's best: George wouldn't argue. He never got the chance to prove it in a World Cup, but as United's David Sadler said: "You could have put George in just about any position in our 1968 team, and he would have been better than the person playing there."

4 Tom Finney

The "Preston Plumber" could play anywhere across the old five-man forward line. As a winger, he was good enough to displace Stanley Matthews in the England team, as a goalscorer he knocked in 30 in his 76 international appearances, and, at 38, 17 in 37 League games in his last season in the old First Division.

5 Franz Beckenbauer

The "Kaiser" all but invented the position of sweeper in its modern, playmaking form. A midfield player in the 1966 World Cup, he moved back to become probably the most accomplished defender of all time. Captain of West Germany's 1974 World Cup-winners, he was a world champion again as manager in 1990.

6 Alfredo di Stefano

Goal-scoring focus of the fabled Real Madrid team of the late 1950s, Di Stefano was the complete centre-forward – strong in the air, technically adept and a devastating finisher. An Argentinian, he switched his allegiance to Spain but never took part in the finals of a World Cup.

7 Ferenc Puskas

Has there ever been a more potent left foot? The "Galloping Major" was a ball player of wondrous dexterity, who scored 85 goals in 84 games for Hungary and was just as prolific for Real Madrid. Captain and inspiration of the Hungarian team that humiliated England 6-3 at Wembley in 1953.

8 Michel Platini

The most gifted and aesthetically pleasing playmaker of them all who could shoot, as well as pass, the opposition to death. In his first season at Juventus he scored 16 goals – a staggering return for a midfield player. His myriad skills and footballing intelligence illuminated three World Cups, and were crucial in helping France win the 1984 European Championship.

9 Johan Cruyff

Nominally a winger but the athletic Dutchman was just as elusive in midfield or in the penalty area: the prime example of Holland's Total Football of the 1970s. Typically Dutch, too, in that he was something of an individualist, but as such he was good enough to be European Footballer of the Year three times.

10 Ruud Gullit

This dreadlocked son of Surinam was equally comfortable at sweeper, orchestrating the midfield or in attack. Clever, strong and blessed with all-round vision and a laser-guided pass, "Rudy" was the shining star of Holland's 1988 European Championship winners. Even when his knees went, he was still formidable.

George Best, 1972

THE TEN GREATEST TEAMS

1 Brazil, 1970

There are plenty of pleasing Brazilian teams to choose from, but these World Cup winners were surely the best. Pele was at his peak, Tostão the perfect foil, Jairzinho a goalscoring sensation on the right wing and Rivelino and Gerson were both virtuoso performers in midfield. *La crème de la crème.* (*See page 120*).

2 Real Madrid, 1960

You could pick any one of the Real teams that monopolised the European Cup for its first five years, but in Glasgow in 1960 their cosmopolitan parts gelled so sumptuously that they beat Eintracht Frankfurt 7-3 in the final. Puskas ("all left foot", the Germans sneered) scored four, Di Stefano the other three.

3 Ajax, 1972

Holland's finest were European champions for three years, from 1971–3, and it was in the 1972 final, when they beat Internazionale 2-0, that Total Football had total victory over the total boredom the Italians called *catenaccio*. Johan Cruyff scored twice, handsomely supported by Krol, Neeskens and Haan.

4 Brazil, 1958

The Brazilians' youth and experience made them favourites for the first time, but they had terrible trouble overcoming Wales 1-0, with what Pele has described as the most important goal he ever scored. After that he added a hat-trick against France and two more in the final against Sweden.

5 Hungary, 1953

It is impossible to overstate the impact on the game everywhere of Hungary's 6-3 triumph over England at Wembley (*see page 68*). England were totally bewildered by the Hungarians' innovative formation, which amounted to 4-2-4, with the centre-forward, Hidegkuti, withdrawing into midfield. The 6-3 was no fluke. Hungary won the return 7-1 six months later, and beat Germany 8-3 in 1954.

Real Madrid, 1960

6 England, 1970

The World Cup holders were even stronger four years on, with Banks, Moore and Hurst better than ever and Cooper, Mullery and Lee substantial reinforcements. England qualified comfortably for the last eight, despite an epic 1-0 defeat by Brazil, and would surely have beaten the Germans in the quarter-finals but for Alf Ramsey's ill-judged substitutions of Charlton and Peters.

7 Liverpool, 1984

They had already won the European Cup three times, not to mention eight League titles in 11 years, but defeating Roma in Rome had to be the Everest of Liverpudlian success. Souness can never have played better, dominating Brazil's Falcão and Cerezo and the Italians, like everybody else, got little change out of Lawrenson and Hansen.

8 France, 1984

Granted, they had home advantage when they won the European Championship, but what a *belle* team. Michel Platini, at his awesome best, made up for the lack of a prolific striker by scoring nine times from a musketeering midfield in which his all-for-one-one-for-all partners were Giresse and Tigana. It was sweet compensation for their exit in the semis in the 1982 World Cup.

9 Bayern Munich, 1974

The Bundesliga's best were to win the European Cup three times in a row, but their first victory was probably the best, and certainly the most exciting. The original match against Atletico Madrid was a 1-1 draw, necessitating a replay two days later, when the Germans did full justice to the talents of Beckenbauer, Breitner, Muller and Hoeness, winning 4-0.

10 Celtic, 1967

A surprising choice, perhaps, but a worthy one on two grounds. In the mid-1960s, the defence-orientated football played by the Italians was gaining ground because of its success in Europe. Jock Stein's Lisbon Lions halted the trend by having a go at Internazionale, and winning 2-1. Celtic deserved great credit for the fact that their players were all drawn from the Glasgow area. (*See page 100*).

JOE LOVEJOY'S BEST XI (4-4-2)

1 Peter Shilton

2 Carlos Alberto   **4** Daniel Passarella   **5** Franz Beckenbauer   **3** Giacinto Facchetti

11 Tom Finney   **6** Johan Neeskens   **8** Michel Platini   **7** George Best

9 Diego Maradona   **10** Pele

Golf

Nick Pitt

THE TEN GREATEST PLAYERS

3 Bobby Jones

His greatest achievement was the Grand Slam, the winning of the Open and British amateur championship as well as the US Open and amateur championships in 1930. Although he never turned professional, he won four US Opens and three Opens before retiring at 28 (illustration left).

4 Ben Hogan

Success came late to the great perfectionist, who by force of will made himself a great ball-striker. He won four US Open titles, three of them after a near-fatal car crash. He won the US Masters and the USPGA twice each, as well as the Open, at Carnoustie, on his only visit to Britain.

5 Harry Vardon

His record of six Open championships remains. He also won the first US Open of the century. Perhaps the straightest hitter who ever lived, he battled against illustrious contemporaries such as James Braid and J H Taylor, all of whom acknowledged him as the master.

6 Arnold Palmer

On the charge, with Arnie's Army under his spell, he was irresistible, a hero-figure who did more than anyone to popularise the game as it entered the television age. His Major titles as a professional comprised four US Masters, one US Open and two Opens.

7 Walter Hagen

In 15 years from 1914, he won 11 Major championships, more than any professional except Nicklaus – and all this before the Masters had been launched. Saying that he didn't want to be a millionaire but wanted to live like one, he more than anyone raised the status of professionals.

8 Byron Nelson

A wonderful shotmaker and, at his peak, in a class of his own. In 1945 he won 11 tournaments in a row at an average of just over 68 strokes a round. During that period he played 19 consecutive rounds under 70. But for the War, would have won more than his five Majors.

9 Young Tom Morris

Assessing just how good was Young Tom Morris, and just how good he might have become, is impossible. But few have ever dominated their rivals so completely. The youngest-ever winner of the Open, he won four titles in a row, and won the 1870 championship by 12 strokes, before he died at 24.

10 Seve Ballesteros

The greatest of the modern Europeans; passionate, imaginative, brave and with a wonderful touch: the most compelling figure in the game since Palmer. The price of his refusal to compromise was heavy, for only five Major titles (two US Masters and three Opens) was a poor reflection of his genius.

1 Jack Nicklaus

With 18 Major titles as a professional, Nicklaus's record is in a category of its own. He was an incredibly consistent player, a big hitter, a wonderful iron player and a great putter under pressure. But perhaps most pertinently, he had the best of all golfing brains.

2 Tiger Woods

By winning three Majors in the year 2000, and subsequently holding all four at one time, Woods fulfilled his prodigious talent and proved himself head and shoulders above his contemporaries, both as a shotmaker and competitor. One question remains: can he sustain it and replace Nicklaus as the best ever?

Seve Ballesteros, Spain 1994

Horse Racing

Jonathan Powell

TEN GREATEST FLAT HORSES

1 Sea-Bird II
Greatest Derby winner of the 20th century (1965). Annihilated one of the finest fields ever in the Arc.

2 Brigadier Gerard
By-word for excellence and versatility with a sequence of 15 victories in the highest class.

3 Mill Reef
Jaunty little bay with a superb attitude. Won the Derby, King George and Arc with impressive ease.

4 Shergar
The 10-length margin of his win in the 1981 Derby may never be equalled. A colossus.

5 Nijinsky
The last colt to claim the Triple Crown (1970). Scored a memorable victory in the King George.

6 Secretariat
31-length win in the Belmont Stakes (1973) was possibly the single greatest performance of the last century. The final leg of a superb Triple Crown.

7 Ormonde
The greatest horse of the 19th century, Ormonde won the 1886 2,000 Guineas, Derby and St Leger and was never beaten.

8 Pretty Polly
Chestnut filly with wings on her heels who set the standard for the 20th century in 1904 by achieving the Triple Crown.

9 Sceptre
A remarkable mare. Her 1902 record of four of the five Classics will never be equalled.

10 Ribot
The best racehorse bred and raced in Italy. Unbeaten in 16 races, won the Arc twice and the 1956 King George.

TOP 10 FLAT JOCKEYS

1 Lester Piggott
2 Gordon Richards
3 Fred Archer
4 Steve Donoghue
5 Willie Shoemaker
6 George Fordham
7 Charlie Elliott
8 Charlie Smirke
9 Pat Eddery
10 Yves Saint-Martin

TOP 10 JUMP JOCKEYS

1 Fred Winter
2 Tony McCoy
3 John Francome
4 Richard Dunwoody
5 Peter Scudamore
6 Tim Molony
7 Dick Rees
8 Josh Gifford
9 Jonjo O'Neill
10 Bryan Marshall

TEN GREATEST NATIONAL HUNT HORSES

1 Arkle
The finest chaser ever to see a racecourse. Won 22 of his 26 races over fences, including three consecutive Gold Cups.

2 Golden Miller
Only horse to win the Gold Cup and Grand National in the same year (1934). Five consecutive Gold Cups (1932-6).

3 Easter Hero
1929 Gold Cup winner and second in the National the same year. Claimed a second Gold Cup in 1930.

4 Red Rum
Stands alone as the only horse to win the Grand National three times (1973, 1974 and 1977).

5 Dawn Run
The only horse to win jump racing's two championship races, the Champion Hurdle (1984) and the Gold Cup (1986).

6 Night Nurse
Arguably the finest hurdler in a golden age, winner of successive Champion Hurdles (1976-7).

7 Monksfield
Two-time Champion Hurdle winner (1978-9). Shared unforgettable dead-heat with Night Nurse at Aintree in 1977.

8 Persian War
Claimed a hat-trick in the Champion Hurdle (1968-70) and a gallant second at his fourth attempt .

9 Mill House
Won the 1963 Gold Cup but was overshadowed by Arkle in subsequent years.

10 Flyingbolt
Won Two Mile Champion Chase (1966) and finished third in the Champion Hurdle next day. Won the Irish Grand National under 12st 7lb.

Fred Winter on Kilmore, Aintree 1962

Rugby union

Stephen Jones

THE TEN GREATEST PLAYERS

1 Gareth Edwards
Scrum-half who re-wrote the record books – and the manual on rugby's possibilities. Brilliant sprinter, devastatingly hard for his relatively small frame and almost impossible to tackle near the line. Huge pass, a complete range of kicks. Scored 20 tries in 53 internationals for Wales. The springboard for the '71 and '74 Lions.

2 Colin Meads
The archetypal All Black, and the greatest-ever forward. Talisman for his team in three decades, a fine footballer and a granite-hard worker in the tight. The harsh edges to his game cowed many an opponent lacking the same mental steel.

3 Sean Fitzpatrick
The most influential player of his generation as New Zealand's hooker and captain. An implacable opponent, hard-edged and fierce and the inspiration behind a front five which was rarely bettered. Perfectly combined intelligence, power and skill.

4 David Campese
Leading try-scorer in Test history (64) and the most dramatic figure in the Australian team that won the 1991 World Cup. Brilliant entertainer, outspoken character and, on the field, a chancer. But he took his chances on a bedrock of skills and fitness and a glorious instinct for the try-line.

5 Serge Blanco
Mesmeric, dark and aloof at the back but a devastating, loping runner in attack and nothing short of a genius with the ball in hand. Only Campese and Rory Underwood scored more Test tries, even though he was supposed to be a defender.

6 Lucian Mias
Fine French forward and rugby philosopher who dragged French rugby, kicking and screaming, into the 20th century. Did more than any one individual to raise the profile of rugby in France; in 1959 led his country to their first outright triumph in the Five Nations.

7 Gerald Davies
At the end of his career, as rugby became more pragmatic, he was wasted by Wales. Greatest attacker of his generation, with a slashing sidestep which ensured he was rarely tackled by the first opponent. Yet still hard enough to finish movements in the zone of pain by the corner flags.

8 Kenneth MacLeod
MacLeod, the Scottish three-quarter, was such a brilliant schoolboy player that his headmaster was approached about his availability to play for Scotland when he was only 15. He was eventually capped against the 1905 All Blacks, still only 17.

9 Dave Gallaher
Led the 1905 New Zealand tour of Britain, where their revolutionary play and Gallaher's demeanour – leather-shin guards outside his socks – so shocked British rugby that disbelieving papers printed the first result (a 55-4 defeat of Devon) as 5-4.

10 Wavell Wakefield
England captain and rumbustious forward in the 1920s who made his mark on the game by ushering in forward specialisation by insisting on fixed scrummaging positions rather than those arriving first forming the front row, and so on. (Illustration above left.)

STEPHEN JONES'S BEST XV*

15 Serge Blanco (France)
14 Gerald Davies (Wales)
13 Frank Bunce (New Zealand)
12 Jeremy Guscott (England)
11 David Campese (Australia)
10 Jonathan Davies (Wales)
9 Gareth Edwards (Wales)
1 Gerard Cholley (France)
2 Sean Fitzpatrick (New Zealand)
3 Ken Gray (New Zealand)
4 Colin Meads (New Zealand)
5 John Eales (Australia)
6 Abdel Benazzi (France)
8 Mervyn Davies (Wales)
7 Michael Jones (New Zealand)

* limited to players he has seen

Serge Blanco, Paris 1991

Rugby league

David Lawrenson

THE TEN GREATEST PLAYERS

1 Ellery Hanley
The complete rugby league player. Won international honours in four different positions – wing, centre, stand-off and loose forward – and was a prodigious try-scorer. Ruthless professionalism and unflinching self-belief made him a legend.

2 Alex Murphy
The quintessential rugby league scrum-half (illustration above), with pace, skill and strength. Made his mark with Great Britain in Australia at just 19, then shone for St Helens in the early 1960s. As player/coach turned Leigh and later Warrington into Challenge Cup winners.

3 Harold Wagstaff
"Prince of centres" and youngest-ever professional when he signed for Huddersfield at 15. Leading light in the "team of all talents", he was a sublimely gifted threequarter and inspirational captain who led Great Britain to an heroic series victory in Australia in 1914.

4 Reg Gasnier
An early Australian superstar, a magnificent centre and a wonderfully balanced runner with exceptional pace. Picked for Australia after just a handful of club games, he tortured Great Britain, scoring a hat-trick in his first international against them in 1959 and another at Wembley in 1963.

5 Billy Boston
Welsh wing of awesome power and pace, snapped up by Wigan before he had established himself in rugby union. Two months later he was in Australia with Great Britain, where he scored 35 tries. Won every honour at Wigan in the 1950s and 1960s. Virtually unstoppable in full flight.

6 Tom Van Vollenhoven
After scoring a hat-trick for South Africa against the British Lions in 1955, St Helens convinced the dynamic wing to switch codes. He proved an instant success, scoring 397 tries in 10 years. Blindingly quick, with a brilliant sidestep and swerve.

7 Brian Bevan
Amassed 796 touchdowns in 20 years. An Australian, he signed for Warrington in 1945. Boasted lightning speed and a fabulous sidestep. Balding, gaunt and swathed in bandages, he was an unlikely sight – yet a genius with ball in hand.

8 Vince Karalius
A fearsome loose forward for St Helens and later Widnes. Nicknamed "The Wild Bull of the Pampas" by the Australians in 1958 when he toured with Great Britain. A ferocious tackler, he was also a creative ball player and one of the first to recognise the importance of physical fitness and conditioning.

9 Wally Lewis
A portly figure, thinning hair and lack of pace disguised a brilliant rugby brain and dazzling ball skills. Among the all-conquering Australians of the 1980s, Lewis was king. First player to be paid £1,000 a game when he played 10 times for Wakefield Trinity in 1983.

10 Mal Meninga
Huge presence in the centre for Australia. Came to prominence on the 1982 tour of Great Britain. Immensely powerful runner with great ball skills and a stunning turn of pace.

DAVID LAWRENSON'S BEST XIII

1 **Jim Sullivan** (Great Britain)
2 **Billy Boston** (Great Britain)
3 **Mal Meninga** (Australia)
4 **Reg Gasnier** (Australia)
5 **Tom Van Vollenhoven** (South Africa)
6 **Wally Lewis** (Australia)
7 **Alex Murphy** (Great Britain)
8 **Cliff Watson** (Great Britain)
9 **Benny Elias** (Australia)
10 **Artie Beetson** (Australia)
11 **Mark Graham** (New Zealand)
12 **Dick Huddart** (Great Britain)
13 **Ellery Hanley** (Great Britain)

Ellery Hanley, 1991

Tennis

Richard Evans

THE TEN GREATEST MEN

1 Lew Hoad
It wasn't just that he won the French over Sven Davidson in 1956 on no sleep – he had been up all night drinking vodka with some Russians – more that this taciturn Australian with the looks of a Greek god had every shot in the book and continued to beat top players – including Rod Laver – when his chronic back made him half the player he had been.

2 Rod Laver
A wonderful attacking player (illustration above) with a big-match temperament to complement his flair, Laver achieved the Grand Slam in 1962, turned pro and then did it again in 1969 when the game went open. Compensated for a moderate serve with great volleys and the first truly great left-handed backhand.

3 Pete Sampras
Still no French title and that prevents Sampras from being ranked higher, although he has done everything else to suggest he might be the best of all. Exceptional serve, razor-sharp volleying, unwavering concentration. Awe-inspiring in winning a seventh Wimbledon.

4 John McEnroe
Although his record – just seven Slams with no Australian and no French – works against him, no one has been able to do more with a tennis ball. Sublime instinctive skills, the greatest pair of hands, devastating leftie serve and that ferocious commitment suggest he would have handled anyone, any time.

5 Andre Agassi
No argument now – the little Las Vegan thrust himself into this list by winning the French in 1999, joining an elite quintet who have won all four Grand Slams. To have done it on four different surfaces makes it a greater achievement than in the days of Perry and Emerson, when grass was used in three out of four.

6 Bjorn Borg
Five consecutive Wimbledon titles by an essentially back court player? Phenomenal. But although the US always eluded him, it was the way Borg guarded his kingdom of clay that made him so exceptional. Six French titles and virtually unbeatable in Europe during that time, the Swede was a born winner.

7 Don Budge
The first man to achieve the Grand Slam, this tall American also proved, in a short amateur career, that he could win big Davis Cup matches. Budge had one of the great backhands and would have won countless titles had he not turned pro in 1939.

8 Jimmy Connors
If Agassi has under-achieved, no one ever said the same about this feisty lightweight who punched well above his avoirdupois. An astounding 109 career titles – nobody else is close – including five US Opens among his eight Slams were earned off the back of a superb counter-punching game and snarling commitment.

9 Ken Rosewall
This little Australian could be blown away by the big guns but a Grand Slam-winning record spanning 20 years, plus an appearance in a Wimbledon final – one of four that he failed to win – at the age of 39 make Rosewall one of the wonders of the game. As was his backhand. Exquisite.

10 Stefan Edberg
There are four other candidates for the tenth spot – Fred Perry, Roy Emerson (both of whom won all four Slams), Bill Tilden and Boris Becker, who won Wimbledon at 17. Edberg not only won three Slams twice each, he also reached the final of the French – and remained totally unspoilt.

Lew Hoad, 1963

THE TEN GREATEST WOMEN

1 Steffi Graf
Has anyone loved the game more or played it with greater panache? The 1999 French Open brought Graf her 22nd Grand Slam title after a three-year hiatus. Injuries and family tragedy had interrupted the flow of that forehand but, after achieving the Grand Slam in 1988, there was never any doubt this superb athlete would dominate her era. Retired in 1999, having done it all.

2 Martina Navratilova
Took tennis into the gym and emerged to set new standards for athleticism in the women's game. Extended Evert's career through the challenge she presented and the pair created one of the longest-running rivalries in sport. Nine Wimbledons, 18 Grand Slam singles in all.

3 Margaret Smith Court
An amazing reach at the net and exceptional power for her day enabled this great athlete to win 24 Grand Slam singles titles, still a record. Interestingly she won more French titles (5) than Wimbledons (3) and if winning the relatively weak Australian 11 times dilutes her achievement, there is no arguing with a remarkable 62 Grand Slam titles in all, including doubles.

4 Chris Evert
The ultimate clay court champion. Evert won the French Open seven times and was good enough to adapt her baseline game sufficiently to claim three Wimbledons. An icon from the moment she burst onto the scene at 16, Evert never let the mask drop on court, keeping her acute sense of humour for more private moments.

5 Helen Wills Moody
It was front page news when Wills lost to Suzanne Lenglen in a much-hyped confrontation in Cannes, but that was before the lady with the sunshade went on to dominate the game in extraordinary fashion – eight Wimbledons between 1927 and 1938; seven US and four French. And barely a smile for the cameras. Miss Poker Face, they called her.

6 Suzanne Lenglen
Like Billie Jean King decades later, Lenglen liberated women through her tennis, throwing away corsets with much the same abandon as she swept regal forehands past overwhelmed opponents. Six Wimbledon titles was only the half of it. Until Helen Wills arrived, nobody could touch her.

7 Maureen Connolly
Little Mo might have gone on to become the greatest winner of all if she hadn't fallen off her horse. Before her accident, this teenage prodigy had won nine Major titles and, in 1953, became the first woman to complete the Grand Slam.

8 Monica Seles
It wasn't Seles's fault that someone stabbed her in the back in 1993 when she was threatening to eclipse Graf as the player of decade. Who knows how great that rivalry might have been had she not subsequently been kept off court for two years? Courage enabled her to add to her eight

Steffi Graf,
Wimbledon 1993

Grand Slams by winning Australia for the fourth time in 1996.

9 Billie Jean King
A dynamic competitor whose effervescent teenage personality soon hardened into a crusading leader for women's rights, King won all four GS titles in the 1960s including an unmatched 20 titles at Wimbledon – six singles, 10 doubles and four mixed.

10 Martina Hingis
No player who dominated the game at the age of 16 at a time when women's tennis has never been stronger can be excluded from this list. Became the youngest player to win a Grand Slam this century when she triumphed at Melbourne in 1997 and the youngest to defend a Slam title the following year. In March 1997 she became the youngest player ever ranked No 1.

The man who won – and lost

Already in the stadium and with only 300 yards to run, Dorando Pietri, clear leader in the 1908 London Olympic marathon, repeatedly collapsed before being helped over the line by officials. Such a clear violation of the rules could only mean his disqualification. But his plight excited passions everywhere and helped spark the original marathon craze.

DENIS WALSH

It was after five o'clock on an oppressively humid July afternoon when the Olympic marathon of 1908 lurched and veered towards its resolution. In London's White City stadium a crowd of nearly 70,000 waited. Ten minutes before the leaders reached the track it was announced by megaphone that they had come into sight. When they passed the last station on the route, a gun-blast relayed their progress. So close now, anticipation dulled the noise of the crowd. The expectation carried no sense of what would soon pass before their eyes. How could it?

At last, a runner staggered down the incline towards the cinder track. It was the little Italian, Dorando Pietri. He wore a white vest and red knee-length trousers. His hair was white with dust, his senses scrambled from exhaustion. Pietri stood for a moment, seemingly dazed. A red cord had been drawn around the track, directing runners to turn right, but he turned left. Officials raced on to the track to make him turn back, but in his delirious state he thought they were trying to deceive him and began to argue. Finally he relented and returned to the course as best as his embattled spirit would propel him.

"He staggered along the cinder path like a man in a dream," reported *The New York Times*, "his gait being neither a walk nor a run, but simply a flounder, with arms shaking and legs tottering. People lost thought of his nationality and partisanship was forgotten. They rose in their seats and saw only this small man with his head so bent forward that the chin rested on his chest." At the turn of the track he dropped to the ground for the first time. Only 300 yards separated him from the finishing line, but an abyss lay in his path and he was powerless to skirt it.

Pietri was not one of the favourites for the marathon. He had taken up athletics, as a

Tottering into history: Pietri finally makes it over the line supported by officials. Pietri's claim after the race that he could have finished unaided persuaded no one. It is probable that his collapse was partly brought on by strychnine. (Above) with the cup presented by Queen Alexandra.

"He staggered along the cinder path as best he could, his gait being neither a walk nor a run but simply a flounder"

19-year-old, only four years before, having stumbled upon his talent. Working in a pastry shop in the north Italian town of Carpi he was sent one day to post a letter. Pietri didn't return for four hours and the temper of his boss, Signor Melli, rose to boiling point. He was about to deliver his reprimand when Pietri explained that he had delivered the letter himself, running the round trip of 50 kilometres.

A few weeks later Pericle Pagliani, Italy's most famous long-distance runner of the time, visited Carpi for a 10km exhibition run around the town's main square. As Emanuele Carli, Pietri's biographer, told it: "Pietri left the pastry shop, rolled up his apron and followed the Roman champion, hanging on his heels until the end."

Two years later, in 1906, he attempted his first marathon, in Rome, and won easily. The performance earned him a place on the Italian team for the intermediary Olympics in Athens that summer. Pietri was forced to retire from the race, but came back to win Italian titles at two distances the next year. Approaching the 1908 Olympics his form was in spate. Seventeen days before the Games he broke the Italian 40km record, a distance just 2.2km short of the marathon.

In New York an Irish-American called Johnny Hayes was also preparing for the biggest race of his life. Hayes worked in the Bloomingdales department store, where his employers were so committed to his athletics career

1

that they built him a cinder track on the roof and gave him leave with full pay to attend the Olympics. Having finished second in the Boston marathon that year, a mere 20 seconds behind the winner, he travelled to London with more than hope.

Like many of the events at the Games, the marathon was widely expected to be a duel between the US and Britain, with Britain fancied to produce the winner from their nine-man team. An American, Thomas Hicks, had won the 1904 marathon at the St Louis Games, a race that ended in farce. Fred Lorz, another American, finished first, only to be disqualified for covering part of the course in a truck. Hicks ran the closing miles fuelled by strychnine, eggs and brandy. In the final stages he suffered hallucinations and could scarcely lift his legs. Second over the line behind Lorz, he was awarded the gold medal.

Photographs of Hicks in the final miles show him being helped by two men running at his side, but when a protest was lodged it was that he had been paced by an automobile. The protest was thrown out; the drugs and physical assistance ignored. In time, Hicks's finish wouldn't seem so bad.

"It seemed inhuman to leave Dorando to struggle on unaided and inhuman to urge him to continue"

From the beginning, the London Olympics were riven by hostility between the US team and the organisers. The Americans were incensed that their flag was missing from those decorating the stadium and responded with insolence. In the opening parade, the US flag-bearer, Martin Sheridan, refused to dip the Stars and Stripes when he passed King Edward VII's box. "This flag dips to no earthly king," Sheridan said.

The track and field events saw repeated American protests against the British judges, reaching a head in the final of the 400m. When one of the Americans ran wide in the final stretch to avoid being passed by a British runner, the officials broke the finish-

ing tape to declare the race void. It was to be re-run two days later but the three American finalists boycotted what had only been a four-man final. Wyndham Halswelle ran the race alone to take gold. It was against this background of distrust and argument that the marathon was run.

The race began at Windsor Castle, the required 26 miles from the White City stadium, but for royal convenience the course was extended by 385 yards. As one of Princess Mary's daughters was having a birthday party, it was agreed the start would be under the windows of the nursery. The finish, however, was still to be opposite the royal box in the stadium. After the 1908 Olympics the extra distance became enshrined in the marathon. On the start-line Pietri, like the others, would have thought nothing of it.

Over the first 18 miles, the lead changed repeatedly. Some of the early leaders went too fast and fell victim to the muggy conditions. Then the South African, Charles Heffernon, hit the front, holding a four-minute lead at the 20-mile mark. Pietri had moved steadily through the field and was now the closest challenger.

As Pietri started to reel Heffernon in, both made critical mistakes. "With Pietri closing the gap, Heffernon accepted a drink of champagne from a spectator," wrote marathon historian Charlie Lovett. "Less than a mile later he was suffering from stomach cramps and dizziness. For his part, Pietri, encouraged by the cheering crowds, picked up his pace too much and too soon, running the risk that he would exhaust himself. Further ahead, the crowd was now slapping Heffernon on the back over and over in an effort to encourage him. This show of goodwill only served to further exhaust the spent runner. A half-mile from the stadium Pietri passed Heffernon and moved into the lead."

Behind the leaders the Americans Hayes, Joseph Forshaw and Alton

The final stretch of the race and Pietri is out on his own. But his misjudgement of the pace meant he had already taken too much out of himself. The drama was at hand.

Welton were running strongly, eroding the gap. When Hayes reached the long straight at Wormwood Scrubs, a mile and a half from the finish, he could see Heffernon and Pietri up ahead, bent from the effort. Hayes knew he had more in reserve. He had not eaten or drunk anything during the race but had bathed his face with Florida water, gargled with brandy and kept going at a steady pace.

Pietri, though, had conserved nothing. He entered the stadium a shell of the man who had left Windsor Castle. When he fell for the first time the rules decreed that doctors should have taken him away but in their sympathy officials helped him to his feet and put their hands to his back in support.

"It seemed inhuman to leave Dorando to struggle on unaided," reported *The Times*, "and inhuman to urge him to continue. It did not seem right that thousands of people should witness a man suffering as he did. It seemed hard that he should lose the victory after having reached the stadium so long before anyone else. And yet, after all, the race was not to the stadium entrance but to the finish in front of the royal box."

He collapsed three more times before his agonies came to an end. Steps from the finish, on the point of collapse again, race organiser Jack Andrew took Pietri by the arm and helped him across the line. Hayes was now in the stadium, less than a minute behind, but with the crowd so distracted by Pierti his arrival drew no more than a muted reception.

The Americans immediately lodged their protest. It is not known whether the British judges recalled the assisted victory of Hicks in St Louis four years earlier but in any case they didn't use it as a mitigating precedent. The race was awarded to Hayes, with a winning time of 2:55.18. As Pietri recovered on a stretcher, the Italian flag was lowered and replaced by the Stars and Stripes.

After a fraught Games, American gratification at the victory was undiminished by the circumstances: "Wasn't it great?" said the US manager, "we not only won the big race of the Olympic Games, but also got third, fourth and ninth places. Well, we can forget what has gone before, although we will always feel that we have been unfairly treated."

Sympathy for Pietri, however, ran deep. At a banquet that night it was announced that Queen Alexandra wished to present him with a cup similar to the one Hayes received for winning the race. The idea, it is thought, came from the writer Arthur Conan Doyle, who had been one of the officials cradling Pietri on the track.

On the night of the race, when Pietri had recovered his strength, he tried to rationalise what had happened, but his story bore no relation to reality: "I felt all right until I entered the stadium. When I heard the people cheering and knew I had nearly won, a thrill passed through me and I felt my strength going. I never lost consciousness and if the doctor had not ordered the attendants to pick me up I believe I could have finished unaided."

In defeat Pietri became a celebrity. Irving Berlin wrote a song about him, the tenor Enrico Caruso drew a cartoon about his countryman for an Italo-American paper. In his home town a collection raised nearly 1500 lira, a princely sum at the time.

The impact of Hayes's victory in America was significant, too, prompting the original marathon craze. Hayes and Pietri both turned professional and in November 1908 a rematch was staged at Madison Square Garden in New York; 261 laps of the track. The public's imagination was fired. At $10, tickets were 10 times the price of the best seats at a baseball match, but crowds were locked out. Pietri won by 45 seconds. In the following six months he ran 22 races in North America over distances from 10 miles to the marathon and won 17 of them. During that time he beat Hayes twice more and in their final meeting early in 1910 he beat him for a fourth time.

Against Hayes, his honour was satisfied. "I'm not the winner of the Olympic marathon," Pietri said, "but as the English say, I'm the guy who won and lost his victory." The sum of his defeat exceeded what victory could ever have been.

The eventual winner, Johnny Hayes. Pietri beat Hayes all four times they raced after the London Games. But it was intelligent race tactics that won Hayes his Olympic medal, not talent by itself.

December 1908

The ring's original genius

Against a background of undisguised racial hostility, in 1908 Jack Johnson was at last allowed to challenge for the heavyweight crown. His humiliation, evidence of the white man's superiority, was eagerly anticipated. But Johnson not only won, he won overwhelmingly – and changed boxing for ever.

NICK PITT

An old bedsheet had been hung up to serve as a screen. A projector whirred and the film began. It was early cinema, a silent movie with figures jerking like puppets: two men fighting in a boxing ring long ago. "Jack Johnson," said Muhammad Ali, intoning the name with reverence.

It was around lunchtime on October 26 1970, the day Ali returned to the ring after an absence of three and a half years. Ali sat on a sofa in a cottage in a suburb of Atlanta, killing time before his fight that evening against Jerry Quarry. Jim Jacobs, who owned the biggest collection of boxing films in the world, and who would later manage Mike Tyson, had brought the film. It featured the first world heavyweight title fight to be won by a black man: Johnson against Tommy Burns in Sydney on Boxing Day 1908.

The quality of the film was exasperatingly poor but Johnson's boxing style and dramatic presence were unmistakable. Springing from an age when crude assumptions and brute force held sway, he was a student of applied psychology, a master of movement and defence. He liked to catch his opponent's punches with an open glove, as nonchalantly as if they were butterflies. He also liked to enrage his man by voice and gesture.

Up on the bedsheet, Johnson grinned and taunted Burns. "He's something else," said Ali. Johnson waved goodbye to Burns at the end of a round. "Look at that," said Ali. "He's saying, 'See you later, partner'. I believe I'll do that with Quarry tonight."

The parallels between Johnson and Ali are striking: both were hate figures who refused to compromise and suffered exile; both elevated their sport by crossing the boundary between the athletic and artistic; both inspired their race. "Jack Johnson was the most influential person in my career," Ali once said. "He did things in the ring defensively that I saw on film and tried

"All coons are yellow". Burns was convinced his superior stamina would show up the flashy black man. Rarely can a fighter's hopes have been more completely dashed.

to copy. He came along at a time when black people felt they had nothing to be proud of, and he made them proud." That evening in 1970, as Ali tricked and battered Quarry to defeat in three rounds, his irrepressible trainer and sidekick, Drew "Bundini" Brown, chanted: "Ghost in the house! Ghost in the house! Jack Johnson's here."

Rain fell in Sydney on Christmas night 1908, an unwelcome nuisance for the thousands who had camped out around the specially constructed arena at Rushcutter's Bay. The fight was not due to start until 11am, when the light would be right for filming, but queues began to form well before dawn. When the gates opened at 7am, 5,000 people rushed in. They were followed by another 15,000, with an estimated 30,000 left outside.

Johnson entered the ring first, according to his custom. Wearing a dressing gown and cap, he was greeted by boos and shouts of "coon" and "nigger", which, as usual, he ignored. He smiled his famous golden smile, the product of a wide mouth, gold-filled teeth and immense confidence. When the fight was over, he had predicted, he would be off to the races while "poor Tommy" recovered in bed.

Burns, a 7-4 on favourite in the betting, received a champion's welcome. But he carried himself like an underdog. Over his trunks, he wore an old blue suit. He carefully removed and folded the suit and placed it in a

wicker suitcase. Jack London, the novelist, adventurer, socialist and racialist who was covering the fight for *The New York Herald*, noted that Burns was "pale and sallow, as if he had not slept all night, or as if he had just pulled through a bout with fever".

Perhaps Burns knew that his game was up. Born in Canada, and originally named Noah Brusso, at 5ft 7in he was the smallest of all world heavyweight champions, though his reach was uncommonly long, his chin sound and his punching powerful. A good businessman who never had a manager and never needed one, he won the title in 1906 by defeating Marvin Hart, who had assumed it on the retirement of the formidable Jim Jeffries. Burns made 10 defences in the next two-and-a-half years, all against white challengers.

Meanwhile, Johnson, who was born into poverty on the waterfront in Galveston, Texas, had proved himself the best fighter in the world. He had beaten not just every black heavyweight of note but every white heavyweight who would fight him.

As a public figure, Johnson was already reviled for his refusal to accept inferior status; his delight in being insufferable to white society; and his displays of defiance, which took the form of fine clothes, fast cars and, most dangerously, white women. But as a boxer, he was widely recognised as innovative, scientific and formidable. Gunboat Smith, a white fighter of distinction who sparred with him, recalled that "Johnson was a fellow that used to stand flat-footed and wait for you to come in. And when you came in, he'd rip the head off you with uppercuts, cut you all to pieces. That's the way he fought." Like most great boxers, rather than sluggers, Johnson

"Why aren't you fighting Tommy? Find that yellow streak." Johnson infuriated white supremacists not just because he was black, nor just because of his undoubted boxing ability. It was his arrogant self-confidence and his refusal to be cowed that most enraged – and unnerved. His humiliation of Burns set off a long and largely futile search for the Great White Hope to teach the black man his lesson.

2

When Johnson entered the ring, he was greeted by boos and shouts of "coon" and "nigger"

exercised control through wonderful defence and counter-punching. No black man, however, had been able to fight for the world heavyweight crown. Outstanding candidates such as Peter Jackson and Sam Langford were denied their chance as the early champions, John L Sullivan, Jim Corbett and Jim Jeffries, drew the colour bar.

When Burns toured Europe, defending the title in London, Dublin and Paris, Johnson followed him to press his claim. Burns declared he was prepared to fight Johnson, but his price was $30,000. Johnson had hardly arrived in London when Burns decamped to Australia. After two fights in Plymouth, Johnson followed.

In Australia, Burns had joined forces with Hugh D "Huge Deal" McIntosh, the first of the impresario-entrepreneur promoters who would control boxing through the century. McIntosh realised the opportunity presented by the coincidence of a frontier society with a wild enthusiasm for gambling and fighting and two antipathetic antagonists. He signed up the fighters, Burns for $30,000 guaranteed, Johnson for $6,000, and built his own stadium.

As the first bell clanged, Johnson continued smiling as Burns moved forward in his distinctive crouch. Burns feinted, out of range, as if shadow boxing. "Come on Tommy, you've got to have it," Johnson said as Burns closed. He caught Burns with a punch to the ribs, but Burns bulled forwards to fight inside. He was met by Johnson's trademark punch, a right uppercut to the chin. After 20 seconds, Burns was on the canvas.

He rose at the count of six, weathered the immediate storm and settled for a war of attrition. It was a common myth – and one subscribed to by Burns – that negro fighters suffered two physiological disadvantages: they could not take shots to the stomach; and they lacked stamina. Furthermore, it was believed, as Burns himself put it, that "all coons are yellow".

Burns attacked to the body. Johnson, who had trained seriously, tightened his stomach muscles and allowed Burns to hit him at will before cuffing him contemptuously away. "Good boy, Tommy," Johnson remarked. "Good little boy."

All Burns's hopes were futile. There was no abdominal weakness. There was no lack of stamina. And in strategy and composure, as well as speed, strength and skill, Johnson was embarrassingly superior. He smiled the golden smile as he chided Burns: "Why aren't you fighting, Tommy? Come, I'll show you how."

Burns answered in fury. "You cur. You big dog. Come and fight, nigger. Fight like a white man." But his rushes into range, arms flailing, were as futile as his words.

As Johnson wrote in his autobiography, "I found my opponent easier than I had anticipated. My defence completely baffled him. I led brisk lefts and rights to his body and face, and administered an awful punishment to him. I kept up a continual conversation with Burns and with those at the ringside. Once, with my hands at my side, I extended my chest and chin, inviting Burns to hit me. I made openings for him and called his attention to them. 'Find that yellow streak,' I told him. 'You have had so much to say about it – now uncover it'. At first, Burns tried to answer my sallies, but he soon desisted, his remarks being scarcely audible."

After a few rounds, Burns's only available ambition was to prove his bravery. He fought on. By the 13th round, Burns's blood-spattered body and mis-shapen face presented a grotesque contrast to the golden smile. Spectators, all for Burns and all certain of the outcome, shouted for the fight to be stopped. After the 13th, the police entered the ring and spoke to McIntosh, who was the referee as

The colossus: the world had never seen a black man with the confidence and charisma of Johnson, a man who so decisively refused to play his allotted humble role in society.

Johnson was unapologetic in his pursuit of the good life – and fast cars figured high on his list. Here he is ticketed for speeding. In 1946, he died from injuries suffered in a car crash.

well as the promoter, and Burns was urged to give in. He refused.

In the 14th, with Burns incapable, Johnson attacked full out, striking Burns at will until he sank to the canvas. The count reached eight and Burns rose once more, but stood as if helplessly drunk. Police entered the ring again and McIntosh signalled the fight over. Johnson was champion.

Like many celebrated writers who would turn their hand to fight reporting during the century, Jack London reached for images by the fistful. "The fight, there was no fight. No Armenian massacre could compare with the hopeless slaughter that took place in the Sydney stadium today. The fight, if fight it could be called, was like that between a pygmy and a colossus. It had all the seeming of a playful Ethiopian

at loggerheads with a small white man – of a grown man cuffing a naughty child – of a monologue by Johnson who made a noise with his fist like a lullaby, tucking Burns into a crib – of a funeral, with Burns for the late deceased, Johnson for the undertaker, grave-digger and sexton, all in one.

"So far as damage was concerned, Burns never landed a blow. He never fazed the black man. He was a glutton for punishment as he bored in all the time, but a dewdrop had more chance in hell than he with the Giant Ethiopian. But one thing now remains. Jim Jeffries must now emerge from his alfalfa farm and remove that golden smile from Jack Johnson's face. Jeff, it's up to you. The White Man must be rescued."

London's appeal launched the first search for the Great White Hope. Several inadequate contenders were easily dismissed by Johnson before Jeffries, who had retired unbeaten six years earlier, agreed to

return to the ring. Johnson and Jeffries fought in Reno on July 4 1910, in the first contest to be billed as "the fight of the century". When Johnson won – once again with contemptuous ease – race riots broke out across the United States, with at least 14 deaths directly resulting. As one popular ballad put it:

The Yankees hold the play,
The White Man pull the trigger,
But it makes no difference what
  they say,
The world champion's still a
  nigger

Johnson never claimed leadership of his race. He was not politically conscious, but his insistence on behaving as he pleased, his personal refusal to submit to the colour bar, and his winning of the greatest prize in sport had incalculable effects. Great white fighters such as Jack Dempsey and Rocky Marciano would play their part, but the heavyweight championship during the century was largely dominated by black fighters, all of whom owed a debt to Johnson. A couple of them, Muhammad Ali and Joe Louis, were arguably superior as boxers, but none had the influence of the ring's most original genius, Jack Johnson.

Burns's blood-spattered body and mis-shapen face presented a grotesque contrast to Johnson's golden smile

The greatest athlete in the world

Jim Thorpe remains a compellingly tragic figure. His pentathlon and decathlon golds at the 1912 Olympics brought worldwide fame. Six months later, his medals were stripped from him when it was discovered he had played semi-pro baseball. Whatever sporting success he later enjoyed, his life had somehow lost its meaning.

DAVE HANNIGAN

At the junction of Joe Boyle Circle and Route 903, three flags stand over the tomb of Jim Thorpe. On each side of a rectangular mausoleum hewn from 20 tonnes of russet granite, images echoing the cadences of his life are carved. Amid the poses of an athlete running, hurdling, jumping and throwing, there is a baseball player, an American footballer and an Indian in feathered head-dress astride a horse. Beneath them runs the legend: "Sir, you are the greatest athlete in the world – King Gustav V, Stockholm, Sweden, 1912 Olympics".

This rustic corner of north-eastern Pennsylvania is the final resting place of Jim Thorpe, gold-medal winner in the decathlon and pentathlon at those games, outfielder on the New York Giants team that lost the 1917 Baseball World Series, storied contributor to what is now the National Football League and American Indian. When the Associated Press held a vote in 1950 to establish the athlete of the half-century, Thorpe polled nearly twice as much as his nearest challengers, Babe Ruth and Jack Dempsey. In the pantheon, this is the kind of company he keeps, but his legend has a lustre all its own.

The monument makes clear the range of his prowess but not the tumult of his existence. Six months after the Swedish monarch's sweeping encomium (Thorpe's reply was a simple and

charming, "Thanks, King") it emerged that Thorpe had flouted the Olympic amateur ideal, and he was stripped of his medals. It would take until 1983 to have his good name restored, 30 years after his death as an alcoholic, living in a California trailer park.

Even his posthumous 2,500-mile journey cross-country from the West Coast to this grave at the southern edge of the Poconos Mountains was besmirched by controversy. After a couple of failed negotiations, Thorpe's third wife, Patricia Askew, sold his remains to the twin communities of Mauch Chunk and East Mauch Chunk for cash and an assurance that they would commemorate him suitably. The towns amalgamated, rechristened their new conurbation Jim Thorpe and hoped their investment in a famous corpse and a resonant name would prove a tourist attraction.

This particular muggy Thursday in high summer, there are no other

daytrippers to puncture the calm surrounding the plot, just the nagging, intrusive thought of Indian folklore. According to Sac and Fox tradition, Thorpe will never be at peace until his body is buried, attended by appropriate ceremony, in his native Oklahoma. Until then, his soul is doomed to wander, his spiritual dislocation one more metaphor for his troubled life.

On a May morning in 1887, moments after giving birth to the first of twin boys, Charlotte Vieux Thorpe watched the sun streak through her family's one-roomed hickory cabin and named her son Wa-Tho-Huck. "A bright path lit up at night by a bolt of lightning," the lyrical translation of his Indian appellation was perhaps already a portentous sign about the child the rest of the world would come to know as James Francis Thorpe. His father Hiram, grandson of an Irish immigrant, married an Indian, peddled whiskey, traded horses and turned his hand to whatever else he could to keep his family. In the Oklahoma Territory of the time, theirs was a typical frontier subsistence.

From an early age, the precocious Jim mastered the lassoe. At 15, it was said there was no wild horse he could not catch, saddle and ride. Reared on a diet of trapping and hunting, his preference for the outdoors over the classroom at the local Indian agency school brought him into constant conflict with his father. When his twin brother Charlie died of pneumonia in

Commemoration – of a sort. Jim Thorpe's tomb in the re-named town of Jim Thorpe in Pennsylvania. On it are inscribed King Gustav's eloquent words of praise.

1898, Jim tried to eschew formal education altogether and throughout his teens he spent intermittent spells running away from home until his father eventually enrolled him at Carlisle Indian College in faraway Pennsylvania.

Under the stewardship of Lieutenant Richard Henry Pratt, Carlisle was a strict institution, the expressed purpose of which was to teach a new generation of Indian children the ways of the white man. In doing so, they sought to eradicate as much of the Indians' native heritage as they could. It was here that Thorpe's athletic promise, which had first presented itself in impromptu games of prairie baseball back on the reservation, came to prominence.

His lithe frame and blinding speed made him an instant track and field star, the unorthodox way of his youth lending itself to his new career. Every Indian hunter developed the ability to mimic the physical movement

of a prey and Thorpe merely reapplied this talent to his new pursuits, throwing a javelin to Olympic standard after just a couple of hours studying others do it.

Having made his name in athletics, Thorpe took up American football, conquering the discipline with such elan that he turned Carlisle into something of a powerhouse. To underline his versatility, he spent his summers playing baseball in Rocky Mount, East Carolina, for $2 a game. It was normal practice for college athletes to dabble in semi-pro competitions but most had the wherewithal to preserve their amateur status by doing so under assumed names. Thorpe's failure to adopt a pseudonym was to prove the mistake which defined his life.

The adulation he received in Rocky Mount during the baseball season persuaded him against returning to school in the autumn of 1909. It was now, too, that the problems that would dog his later years first appeared. During that

3

winter back in Oklahoma, he began drinking. Cut off from the discipline provided by Carlisle, he started to drift. Eventually, his coach Pop Warner lured him back with the prospect of more football campaigns. His athletic career, too, gathered momentum. By the summer of 1912, he was in the American team heading to Sweden for the Fifth Olympiad.

The journey to Stockholm highlights how hard it is to separate myth from truth in Thorpe's life. According to some eye-witnesses, Thorpe was the most diligent athlete on the USS *Finland*, pounding his way round the cork track that had been laid on the ship's deck. Yet in the newspapers of the day, there are reports of Thorpe whiling away the trip in his hammock, reluctant to let overuse dissipate his natural gifts.

Whatever the truth, Thorpe arrived in Sweden in the condition of his life, and put down a marker on his first day of competition. The fame afforded by his achievements with the Carlisle football team had burdened him with a favourite's tag that he was anxious to justify. The pentathlon began with the running broad jump and Thorpe leapt 23ft to an easy victory. He recovered from a less impressive fourth place in the javelin to win the 200m dash by the narrowest of margins, and from that point on he was peerless. He hurled the discus over 116ft, three feet farther than his nearest challenger, before cantering to victory in the 1500m.

His appetite for competition wasn't sated by taking gold, and he used his rest days before the start of the decathlon to participate in the high jump and long jump, finishing a creditable fourth and seventh in both events. Perhaps it was fatigue due to his over-ambition, or maybe the incessant rain that fell on the first day of the decathlon, but Thorpe struggled in the opening two events. Third in the 100m, he was more disappointed by his second in his specialty running broad jump. It took a momentous shot putt of more than 42ft to re-establish his supremacy, and that first

Thorpe's career as a full-time professional both in baseball and American football was startlingly successful. But it never quite seemed to compensate for his lost medals.

place meant he started the second day 245 points ahead of the field.

With the weather improving, Thorpe reached new levels of consistency. He was first in the high jump and fourth in the 400 metres while no Olympic decathlete would come close to matching his winning time of 15.6sec in the 110m hurdles until 1948. Second in the discus, third in the javelin and third in the pole vault, the gold was his even before he shaved four seconds off his pentathlon time for the 1500m in the final discipline. He had scored 8,412 points out of a possible 10,000, 700 clear of the second-placed man, the Swede Hugo Weislander. Along with his second medal, he was was given a bust of King Gustav, a silver chalice from the Czar of Russia and a worldwide reputation.

On his return to America, Thorpe received a letter of congratulation from the White House, and, ignoring myriad offers from professional sports franchises, he returned to school for the greatest football season of his college career. Bulwarking Carlisle on the way to victories over more established schools like Brown and Syracuse, it was after a triumph over West Point that *The New York Times* dubbed him "the athletic marvel of the age". One particularly deft Thorpe sidestep that December afternoon caused two Army players to collide, one of them, Dwight D Eisenhower, breaking his nose. The year Thorpe died of a heart attack, Eisenhower became president.

A couple of days after the Army game, Thorpe was spotted in training by a coach from the old Carolina League who mentioned his semi-pro baseball past to a reporter called Roy Johnson. For weeks, Johnson sat on the story before breaking it in January 1913. That Thorpe was guilty of the same offence as hundreds of other amateur athletes proved no defence. He was immediately ordered to hand back his medals and the gifts lavished on him in Sweden. "I was simply an Indian schoolboy and I did not know about such things," wrote Thorpe in a letter of appeal Pop Warner is alleged to have dictated to him. "I did not know I was doing wrong because I was doing what I knew several other college men had done."

"My dad was never a great talker but it was obvious for sure the medals thing always hurt him"

The letter effectively absolved Thorpe's coach, his school and the Amateur Athletic Union of blame. To some, the Indian was a convenient scapegoat, his guilt making unnecessary the sort of further investigation which might unearth a host of other transgressions.

A lucrative professional baseball contract with the New York Giants broke Thorpe's initial fall from grace but it was American football where he would make the biggest splash. He played until he was 42, his influence such that at the American Football Hall of Fame in Canton, Ohio, a statue of Thorpe is the first thing a visitor sees on entering the building. Once that career had ended, however, he led a rootless existence. He went through three marriages and a succession of jobs, from being in charge of casting Indian characters in Westerns to digging ditches. He sold

By 1931, Thorpe was working as a labourer, one of a host of occasional jobs, in Los Angeles. Sporting glory was long past him. An increasingly shiftless life beckoned.

the film rights to his life story for $1,500, and even did a stint in the merchant navy, perhaps to find again the discipline he had enjoyed at school.

"My dad was never a great talker but it was obvious for sure the medals thing always hurt him, sometimes you could just see the sadness in his eyes," says Grace Thorpe. "He had his problems with alcohol and despite all the sporting glory, he did have a very unhappy personal life. Losing his twin brother affected him so badly that he always claimed he had inherited some of his energy and strength from Charlie. Then, both his parents died while he was still a teenager and his own first child, Jim Junior, died at two. His life was something of a Greek tragedy."

The Thorpe campaign to get their father's Olympic medals back and his records restored culminated in a moving ceremony at a Los Angeles hotel in 1983. For decades, their cause had been obstructed by the autocratic Avery Brundage, the long-time president of the International Olympic Committee, who was reckoned to hold a grudge against Thorpe since he himself had finished a disappointing sixth in the 1912 pentathlon. Having seen the power of concerted effort then, Grace Thorpe has taken up the cudgels again. She divides her time between working to keep nuclear waste off Indian land and campaiging to have her father voted athlete of the century. Age and ill-health have forced her to cut back on travelling, so she has taken her electioneering to the Internet. Already, there have been resolutions moved on Thorpe's behalf in both the US Senate and House of Representatives.'

"I just want people to remember him because he was a very special person," says Grace Thorpe. "Six months before he died, I left him at a bus-stop near my home in New York City. He was standing in front a cinema under a sign advertising the film *Jim Thorpe, All-American*, starring Burt Lancaster. Dad was wearing a cowboy hat, a suede jacket with tassles on, and he had an old, scarred leather satchel over his shoulder. Everyone was staring at him but then everyone was always staring at him for one reason or another."

With the slightest catch in her voice, she spoke his epitaph.

Shame of the Black Sox

In 1919, eight members of the Chicago White Sox with links to organised gambling threw the World Series. Though all received life bans, only seven confessed their guilt. One – Joe Jackson – would maintain his innocence for the rest of his life. Innocent dupe or active conspirator? The controversy continues.

DAVE HANNIGAN

In the folk memory, this is how the story goes. Having spent two hours testifying before a Grand Jury about the fixing of the 1919 baseball World Series, Shoeless Joe Jackson emerges from Chicago's Criminal Courts flanked by two bailiffs, their presence evidence of the threats against his life. As he pushes through the baying crowd to his car, his progress is checked by a child. "Say it ain't so, Joe." implores the kid. "Yes, boy, I'm afraid it is," replies the fallen hero. In that simple exchange, every nuance of the scandal is captured, the plaintive voice of the little boy echoing the sound of a nation being stripped of one more layer of innocence.

Except there was no such kid that September afternoon in 1920. Reports exist of a similar incident outside Comiskey Park some time that week but relocating it to the Cook County judiciary at the precise moment when Joe Jackson effectively made his exit from baseball was mere mythmaking by a fanciful journalist seeking to

The White Sox on the eve of the World Series. Chick Gandil, instigator of the scam, is in the back row, seventh from the left, Joe Jackson is in the front row, second from the right. (Right) Jackson at the plate.

invest the occasion with added pathos. The truth was much less evocative.

As the 32-year-old Chicago White Sox left-fielder, the man with the third-best betting average of all time and the proprietor of the fabled glove where triples went to die, strode the gauntlet, he maintained a dignified silence. Apart from agreeing to give a deputy sheriff a lift to the south side of town, he said nothing. Decades later, Jackson recalled: "The only guy who spoke was a guy who yelled at his friend: 'I told you the big son of a bitch wore shoes'."

Even that pointed up more fallacy. Once, early in his career as a minor leaguer, Joseph Jefferson Wofford Jackson had been troubled by blisters as he broke in a new pair of shoes. As his club had a limited roster, he couldn't afford a rest day to cure the problem so he played one game in his stockinged feet. Nobody noticed until he hit a triple in the seventh inning. As he reached third base, a voice from the bleachers cried: "You shoeless son of a gun you!" Jackson never played without shoes again but the legend had been created. In time, people would believe that major league scouts dis-

covered him playing barefoot in the boondocks of South Carolina. It was just another half-truth he spent a lifetime trying to dispel.

I n so many ways, 1919 had been a baseball season to remember. The previous year, America's involvement in the First World War had curtailed the fixture list while the absence of key players on military assignment diminished what spectacle remained. With peace restored, life reverted to familiar rhythms. In baseball, too, normal service was resumed. Champions in 1917, the Chicago White Sox began to reassert their status as the most powerful team of the day. The absence during the War of Jackson and other stalwarts such as Eddie Collins, Swede Risberg and Lefty Williams had hampered the team's attempts to win consecutive titles. But with those key players back on board, the White Sox cruised to a World Series showdown with the Cincinnati Reds.

The Reds were a gripping narrative in their own right. Before the season, it emerged that their manager, Christy

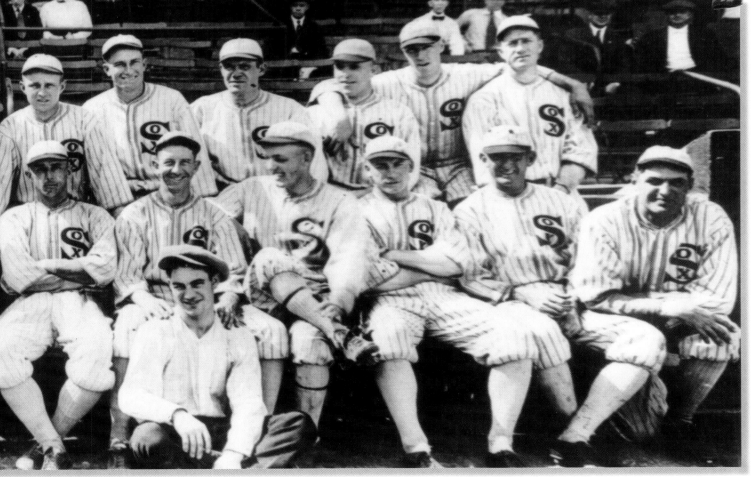

4

Mathewson, was missing in action in Europe, and Pat Moran was appointed in his place. Although Mathewson eventually turned up, his health had been seriously damaged by the mustard gas of Flanders. By then Moran had in any case transformed a team of journeymen into genuine contenders. Boasting just one major star in centre-fielder Edd Roush, their emergence captured the imagination of a nation sold on the idea of the plucky outsiders putting one over on Chicago's celebrated team of all the talents.

The White Sox' prolific record that season disguised a club riven by discord. The players were divided into two camps headed respectively by Chick Gandil and Eddie Collins. Despite playing in close proximity to each other at first and second base, Gandil and Collins hadn't spoken for two years, and their two factions divided accordingly. Gandil's clique was predominantly rural, lacking in formal education and given to a work-hard, play-hard philosophy. Collins's group were more urban: some boasted college degrees, all subscribed to the disciplined lifestyle of a professional athlete.

The locker room probably only ever really united in its antipathy to the club's owner, Charles Comiskey. Notoriously mean, he had reneged on a promised cash bonus after the 1917 World Series, instead handing his players a crate of champagne. "It tasted like stale piss," said Ring Lardner, one of the predominant journalists of the era. In fact, if

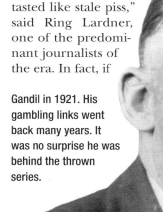

Gandil in 1921. His gambling links went back many years. It was no surprise he was behind the thrown series.

Comiskey had the most gifted squad around, it was also one of the worst paid, the penurious owner keeping their daily expense allowance on the road well below the league average. He even charged them for laundering their uniforms, a practice that earned them the name Black Sox long before the team was tarnished by allegations of wrongdoing. Early in the 1919 season, the players had tried to bargain with Comiskey for better pay. His refusal even to discuss the subject was perfectly in character.

Baseball had been linked with gambling since its emergence as an organised sport

From its beginnings as an organised sport in the 1870s, baseball had been linked with gambling. In the first two decades of the new century, stories of bribery abounded. Clubs would often not announce their starting pitchers until just before a game to prevent their being got at by interested parties. In 1917, even the all-conquering White Sox were alleged to have been involved in a particularly dubious double-header against the Detroit Tigers,

At a time when players, newspapermen and gamblers drank in the same saloons and moved in the same circles, those in the know would have had ample opportunity to exploit the discontented White Sox. When it came to fixing America's greatest sporting event, the White Sox in 1919 amounted to nothing less than laboratory conditions for fomenting corruption.

Arnold "Chick" Gandil, the tough but average first baseman described by his peers as a "professional malcontent", knew that better than most. Gandil was friends with a bookmaker called Sport Sullivan, for whom he would often ferret out information on the form of certain players. Knowing the bitter reaction of some of his colleagues to Comiskey's refusal to rene-

gotiate, Gandil saw his opportunity. Three weeks before the series, Gandil and Sullivan hatched a plan. In return for persuading enough White Sox players to throw the World Series, Gandil would receive $80,000 for distribution among his co-conspirators.

Eddie Cicotte was first on board. An ace pitcher nearing the end of an illustrious career, Cicotte had taken out a huge mortgage on a farm and Gandil played on his financial worries to lure him in. As the probable starting pitcher in two games of the best-of-nine series, he was an essential recruit. Gandil then made his way through the rest of his coterie. Swede Risberg and Fred McMullin were easily convinced, Lefty Williams thought it over before enlisting. Then, at the Ansonia Hotel in New York, Buck Weaver and Happy Felsch opted in.

That Shoeless Joe Jackson never attended the meeting in New York, nor another in Cincinnati before the opening game, is the cornerstone of the continuing campaign to have him exonerated. Twice in the lead-up to the first encounter with the Reds, Gandil approached Jackson to join the consortium. Rebuffed, Gandil increased the offer to $20,000 but Jackson still would not bite. "Joe, it's going to happen with or without you," said Gandil in parting. "You don't have to do too much."

By now, the rumours were beginning to circulate, a massive surge of late money on the underdogs fuelling public suspicions. The White Sox' performance in losing the first game at Cincinnati's Redland Field by 9-1 did little to quell concerns. During a game-turning fourth inning when the sides were level at 1-1, Cicotte gave up five hits for five straight runs, repeatedly ignoring the signals from his catcher, Ray Schalk. Schalk, from Eddie Collins's side of the clubhouse and fully aware of the gossip surrounding the series, almost came to blows with Cicotte in the locker room afterwards.

That night, Kid Gleason, the White Sox manager, went to Comiskey's hotel room to voice his disquiet. Clutching a batch of accusatory

The strong arms of the law: the hard-pressed Kid Gleason, manager of the White Sox, with Judge Landis, the man who threw out the eight White Sox players. On the right is John McGraw, manager of the New York Yankees.

telegrams, Gleason alarmed Comiskey, who sought the assistance of John Heydler, president of the National League. Together, they went to Ban Johnson, president of the American League. Johnson dismissed the idea of a fix out of hand, describing Comiskey's allegations as "the whelp of the beaten cur". Next day, Lefty Williams turned in an erratic pitching display, his failure to obey crucial instructions from his catcher mirroring Cicotte's performance in the first game, handing the home side a 4-2 victory and making a fool of Johnson.

Back in Chicago for game three, Dickie Kerr hurled a three-hit shutout, and a 3-0 win allowed the favourites to claw back to 2-1 in the series. Cicotte pitched again in game four, but the most crucial play of that day came in the field, Cicotte deflecting a Jackson throw to allow Pat Duncan home for Cincinnati. The visitors followed up that 2-0 triumph with a 5-0 walloping of the White Sox, the latter pockmarked by Lefty Williams's poor pitching and some questionable fielding by both Felsch and Jackson.

Another controlled display by Kerr ensured the Sox won game six. Bucking the

trend, Cicotte then pitched wonderfully in the next game to leave the series finely poised at 4-3. But Williams had received a warning from the gamblers the night before game eight, and he adhered to the original script, offering up three runs off his first 15 pitches, sending Cincinnati on the way to a 10-5 win that clinched the series.

That evening, Williams went to Jackson's hotel room with an envelope containing $5,000. Jackson refused to take the money. Williams threw it at his feet. Thereafter, its whereabouts are unknown. Jackson contended he was prevented from immediately delivering the money to Charles Comiskey by the owner's secretary. After his death his supporters say a similar sum was bequeathed to a cancer facility in his will. For others, that he kept the money at all is proof enough of his guilt.

After almost a year, the constant drip-feed of innuendo about the 1919 series became a torrent when Billy Maharg, a small-time hood

aggrieved at being cut out of the deal, confessed all to a Philadelphia-based sportswriter. On the somewhat double-handed advice of Comiskey's lawyer, Jackson, Cicotte and Williams told the grand jury all they knew. In tandem with Maharg's evidence and that of another gambler, Bill Burns, their confessions formed the central plank of the case against the eight players charged with conspiracy to defraud the public, the clean White Sox and the business of baseball.

On August 1 1921, a jury spent two hours and 47 minutes deliberating before finding the cabal not guilty. After Sport Sullivan's initial involvement, the plot had widened to encompass a host of minor villains, while behind them all loomed the black hand of Arnold Rothstein, the biggest mob financier of the age. Given the labyrnthine dimensions of the intrigue, there was never really going to be any other verdict. But if the civil courts were inhibited by such a cast of duplicitous characters, Judge Kenesaw Mountain Landis had seen enough. In his inaugural act as baseball's first czar, he issued life bans against each indicted player. Eight men were out.

Of them, only Jackson remains a *cause célèbre*, his legion of defenders basing their claims on his performance in the series and the belief he was an illiterate exploited by other, more worldly, men. According to the statistics, the *aqua vitae* of so much American sport, Jackson batted an excellent .375, led both teams with 12 hits and notched the only home run in the series. His detractors cite the fact he hit only two from 10 with runners in scoring positions, and ask how such a supposed dumb jock could later carve out an impressive business career.

Moments before Jackson's heart finally gave out at his home in Greenville on December 5 1951, his wife Katie called his brother David to his bedside. Joe took David's hand in his, and whispered: "I'm going to meet the greatest umpire of all and he knows I'm innocent." Eighty years after the event, so many other juries remain out.

"Joe, it's going to happen with you or without you. You don't have to do too much"

Thunder Down Under

In 1932 England faced an Australian team dominated by a one-man run-machine, Donald Bradman. To counter him, England unleashed an endless series of fast balls aimed directly at the batsman: Bodyline. The tactic provoked outrage and came close to rupturing diplomatic relations between the two countries.

SIMON WILDE

November 19 1932 fractured the worlds of Don Bradman and cricket. At 24 Bradman, the cold-blooded destroyer of bowling who had stepped from New South Wales into stardom, could have anticipated years of uninterrupted record-breaking. But Bradman had upset the balance of international cricket as no player had ever done. That day, in front of 54,000 startled Australians at the Melbourne Cricket Ground, the grim reckoning dawned.

There had already been suspicions about the tactics England's battery of fast bowlers would use. Now, with only two weeks until the first Test, suspicion became certainty. Douglas Jardine, MCC's equally cold-blooded captain, intended to neuter Bradman with fast, short-pitched bowling aimed at the batsman's body and with a ring of leg-side fielders. Australia's batsmen were being asked to choose between physical wellbeing and safeguarding their wickets. By the end of the first Test this brand of leg-theory – an old tactic pursued with uncompromising ruthlessness – had a name. Bodyline.

Even before Bradman batted that day, Bill Woodfull, Australia's captain, had been hit above the heart by Harold Larwood, England's spearhead without whom Bodyline could never have been put into practice. Larwood was extremely fast and accurate – and

Bodyline made the super-human Bradman seem mortal after all

speed and precision were essential to Bodyline's success. Nonetheless, Bodyline was a huge gamble, so much so that Jardine was not even there to supervise its baptism; perhaps for tactical reasons, he had gone fishing. He left it to his deputy, Bob Wyatt, to move the slips one by one to the leg side for Larwood and Bill Voce as the new ball lost its shine. By the time Bradman came in Larwood was bowling to three short legs and a man on the boundary for the hook. Larwood bowled exceptionally fast, dismissing Bradman for 36, but it was the disruption to Bradman's normally serene methods that grabbed the headlines. He played some extraordinarily bad strokes, getting into such a tangle against Bill Bowes that he fell over, his bat over his left shoulder, the ball striking it for a single. It was the most undignified run he ever scored.

"They attacked him remorselessly," Leo O'Brien, the batsman at the other end, said, "and he was certainly upset." In the second innings Larwood got him again, bowled for 13 trying to cut a ball on off stump, a "wild swing" the bowler called it.

Larwood knew he had achieved a significant victory. "I had Don on the run," he wrote in his autobiography. "I

Larwood bowls, Woodfull ducks: the fourth Test, Brisbane. By now, with no fewer than six close fielders on the leg-side and Larwood rampant, Bodyline had undermined Australian resistance.

had upset his equilibrium ... Leg theory had succeeded far better than I expected. Don, caught in two minds by the leg trap, had jumped out of the way to avoid rising balls over the leg stump, at times using his bat with a clubbing action that would have done credit to a wood-chopper."

The *Evening Standard* predicted: "Provided that Larwood retains his present demon speed, the Bradman problem has been solved. Bradman dislikes supercharged fast bowling." The *Manchester Guardian* was equally euphoric: "Bradman is a mortal after all." When, in the following game between New South Wales and MCC, Bradman scuttled to the off side and

was bowled by Voce, the English thought he "would never be the same man again"; when he missed the first Test through ill health, it was rumoured his withdrawal was diplomatic.

At this stage, Jack Hobbs was one of the few to anticipate the troubles ahead: "The bowling looked very dangerous stuff. The newspapers will have very unpleasant things to say about these undoubted shock tactics." But the Australian press was not yet united in condemnation, even though it had no reason to love Jardine, whose dislike of foreigners was plain and who made it clear he would not put himself out for reporters. MCC had been dismissed for 60 by the Australian XI and

few doubted Bradman would clear this latest hurdle as he had every other. "Nobody wishes to cast any unsportsmanlike epithets in the direction of England," declared the *Melbourne Truth*. "If that's her idea of cricket, good luck to her."

A few highly charged weeks put an end to that sort of tolerance. The temperature began to rise in the first Test, in Sydney, which England won easily thanks to Larwood and Voce's pace. Larwood claimed 10 wickets and was the chief object of derision for the barrackers on the Hill. Larwood played them at their own game, giving them V-signs and thumb-

Agents of destruction: Larwood (far left) and Voce. Larwood was small for a fast bowler but very powerfully built and with exceptional stamina. (Below) Bradman, the phenomenon, the man Bodyline was intended to stop. In 1930, on his first tour of England, Bradman had all but destroyed England's bowlers.

ing his nose, but it was given and taken in good part. But Bodyline drew the crowd's ire. "Every time I dropped one short they erupted like a human Krakatau," Larwood recalled. "You could feel the tension of the crowd. From the time Jardine switched the field over to the leg side they didn't stop yelling."

England were again surprised at the success of their tactics. With the notable exception of Stan McCabe, the Australian batsmen, normally ready to hook, were more intent on ducking out of the way than trying to score. McCabe made a superbly defi-

To *Wisden*, the third Test was "probably the most unpleasant ever played"

ant 187 that showed that with courage and first-class batsmanship Bodyline bowling could be scored off, even if he did have several slices of luck. Larwood said he felt sure Jardine would have abandoned leg-theory had all the Australian batsmen battered it as McCabe did in that game. As it was, even with Bradman absent, the English were uncertain whether it would pay off.

All soon became clear. To his first ball in the second Test, back at Melbourne before a crowd of 64,000 that cheered his every step to the wicket, Bradman skipped across and

lashed out with a hook, dragging the ball into the leg stump. It had not bounced as much as he expected. "A hush fell on the ground," Jack Fingleton, one of the Australian team, wrote, "an unbelievable hush of calamity, for men refused to believe what their eyes had seen." In the words of Bowes, the bowler, Jardine, normally so reserved, started "jigging around like an Indian doing a war dance".

Bradman's response was to produce one of the innings of his life second time around. Under extreme pressure after a string of failures, he showed he had devised a method of dealing with Bodyline by scoring an unbeaten 103 that enabled Australia to level the series. To balls on leg stump, he either stepped back to cut or shovel them through the off or went across and swiped them down through the leg side.

But the Melbourne pitch was slow and on quicker surfaces even his eagle eye could not save him for long. In the three remaining Tests, he passed 40 four times but never made more than 76 – and only once stayed more than two hours. He scored most runs in the series but Woodfull, McCabe and Fingleton batted longer.

Bradman's batting not only disheartened his team, it played a vital part in shifting opinion against Bodyline. "Don's antics in

Melbourne in jumping about the crease made spectators think I was deliberately trying to knock his head off," Larwood wrote. "Bradman and Woodfull were the only ones who used to 'show' a little when they got out of the way of a rising ball. Their mannerisms made the crowd think I was trying to kill them." In fact, Larwood hit Bradman only once in the series.

After Melbourne, Bradman wrote a letter to the Australian Board of Control that was released to press. It said: "I do not know of one batsman who has played against fast bodyline bowling who is not of the opinion that it will kill cricket if allowed to continue." This helped fuel debate about the merits of Bodyline, a debate that gathered pace with reports of dissension in the English camp. Gubby Allen, the one amateur fast bowler in the party, refused to bowl Bodyline, partly it was suspected because he was not accurate enough to do so. The effect was to make the strategy look more and more like Jardine's own. With his silk scarf and Harlequins cap, Jardine became an intolerably provocative figure to Australians recalling past grievances at the hands of the Mother Country.

By the third Test, in Adelaide, public feeling had turned against

England to such an extent that the South Australian government, still nervous after street battles during the Depression, put the cricket ground under police siege. This did nothing to lighten the mood of a match described by *Wisden* as "probably the most unpleasant ever played".

There were two flashpoints. The first was when Woodfull was again hit over the heart by Larwood: he dropped his bat and staggered from the wicket, clutching his chest as though shot. Within earshot of Bradman, Jardine aggravated the situation by saying to Larwood: "Well bowled, Harold." Moments later, Jardine indulged in more psychological warfare, halting Larwood in his run-up and assembling the leg-trap. Larwood was jeered all the way to the wicket. His next ball knocked Woodfull's bat out of his hands.

The crowd erupted; the police, fearing the pickets would be stormed, moved in. An English fielder said to umpire George Hele: "If they come over the fence, leave me a stump." Hele replied: "Not on your life. I'll need all three myself." Though a riot was averted, both Bradman and McCabe fell to the leg-trap as England moved to an easy victory.

That evening the dispute gained a political dimension. Plum Warner and Richard Palairet, MCC's joint managers, went to the Australian dressing room to enquire after Woodfull. The response was curt: "Mr Warner, there are two teams out there on that field and one is playing cricket and the other is not. That's all I have to say to you. Good afternoon." Warner turned on his heels, in tears.

Matters got worse with the second incident, when Bert Oldfield suffered a cracked skull as he mishooked Larwood, who again was not bowling Bodyline at the time. It was simply a bad shot but the crowd, in no mood for reason, once more came near to rioting.

The barracking alarmed the English

Patrician, disdainful, ambitious: Jardine sits serenely among his team. Larwood is in the back row, third from the right.

party: "I thought they were going to come at us," Larwood recalled. "I felt that one false move would bring the crowd down on me." Maurice Tate, sitting in the enclosure, withdrew to the dressing room saying: "I'm getting out of here – somebody will get killed."

News of the Woodfull-Warner exchange leaked out, leaving the Australian Board of Control either to drop Woodfull or support him. It supported him, sending a cable to the MCC in London which read: "Bodyline bowling has assumed such proportions as to menace the best interests of the game ... This is causing intensely bitter feeling between the players as well as injury. In our opinion it is unsportsmanlike. Unless stopped at once it is likely to upset the friendly relations existing between Australia and England."

The cable provoked uproar. To Englishmen denied a first-hand view of events, it looked like whingeing, while the suggestion that a team led by three Oxford-educated amateurs, Warner, Palairet and Jardine, could conduct itself in an unsportsmanlike manner was an affront. In fact, Warner was as hard-nosed a competitor as Jardine and drew vehement criticism from the Australian press for refusing to rein in his captain despite previously condemning leg-theory in print.

For three weeks

the tour hung in the balance as cables flew between London and Melbourne. Ties of Empire were stretched taut and it was only when government officials in both countries, including prime ministers, stepped in that the dispute was resolved.

There could only be one result: the day before the fourth Test, in Brisbane, the Australian Board, forced into a humiliating volte face, withdrew its charge. They assumed their climbdown meant England would modify their bowling. But there was no change and England, inspired by Larwood in Brisbane's oppressive heat and Bradman's shaken nerve, went on to win the last two games and to regain the Ashes.

Though MCC won the war, it lost the peace. A year later, with Australia threatening to abandon their tour of England, it accepted that Bodyline bowling was "an offence against the spirit of the game". A few weeks before Woodfull's team arrived, Jardine announced he had "neither the intention nor the desire to play cricket against Australia" and when Larwood was asked to apologise for the way he had bowled in Australia he refused – and never played for England again. He emigrated in 1950 – to Australia.

"I thought they were going to come at us. I felt that one false move would bring the crowd down on us"

Black day for Hitler

The Berlin Olympics were intended to trumpet Hitler's Germany, above all the prowess of its "racially pure" athletes. But in perhaps the most celebrated Olympic feat of all, it was a black man who emerged as the hero of the Games – Jesse Owens. His achievements remain an object of wonder.

NICK PITT

Jesse Owens had one long jump left. If he fouled again, or failed to leap the qualifying distance of 23ft 5in, he would miss the final.

It was a cold, damp morning, Tuesday, August 4 1936, the third day of competition in the Berlin Olympics, the Nazi Olympics. For two days, Owens had breezed towards glory. On day one, Sunday, he won his first 100m heat in 10.3sec, equalling the world record; he won his quarter-final in 10.2sec, which would have improved the record except that officials claimed there was a following wind (though the flags high above the sta-dium were still); and he won his semi-final in 10.4sec.

On day two, he merely won the 100m gold medal, again matching the world record. As Peter Wilson of the *Daily Mirror* noted: "Owens's legs never seemed to be coming down on to the cinder track, always lifting from it. He was handsome in an uncompli-cated way, his face scarcely distorting even in the throes of the most desper-ate competition, and he had the most perfect body of any track and field ath-lete I ever watched."

Day three promised to be busier. Owens had started well, breaking the Olympic and world records in his first 200m heat before making his way to the long-jump pit for the qualifying competition. He measured his run and tried it out. Still in his warm-up sweater, he ran to the take-off board and through the pit, making no attempt to jump. In America, a pre-competition run-up practice was allowed. In Europe, it wasn't. The red flag was raised – one no-jump. The flag was raised again next time, when Owens leaped far beyond the qualify-ing mark but stepped fractionally beyond the take-off board.

Which left one jump. In later years, Owens would build a fable from the rare moment of crisis. Lutz Long, the blond German jumper who appeared the physical personification of the Nazis' Aryan ideal, approached Owens and told him in faltering English that he himself had once had the same problem of overstepping. He had solved it by taking his mark back six inches and taking off from well behind the board. According to Owens, Long even placed his hand-kerchief behind the take-off board as a guide for Owens.

Like other reminiscences by Owens, it made a good story. But Grantland Rice, a veteran American sportswriter, saw events differently. "With his third and final chance to qualify coming up, I watched Jesse from the press box with a pair of pow-erful glasses," he wrote. "I was search-

Despite nearly failing to qualify for the final, Owens won the long jump – and his second gold – with a leap that would not be improved for 24 years. Hitler may have regarded Owens as scarcely human, but Lutz Long, the blond German hero beaten into second place, recognised him as an extraordinary athlete.

ing for some tell-tale sign of emotion. Calmly, he walked the sprint path into the take-off board and then retraced his steps. Studying the situation for a moment, the American athlete anteloped down that runway and took off at least a foot behind the required mark, but qualified!" Owens had taken off a foot behind the board, but landed two feet beyond the qualification mark.

After lunch, Owens ran his quarter-final of the 200m, winning again and equalling his morning's world record, before switching back to the long

The year before the Berlin Games, Owens had set three world records and equalled one in the space of an hour

jump, for the final. Effectively, it was a two-man battle. Owens took the first-round lead with 25ft 10in. Long matched that mark exactly with his second-round jump, and Owens responded by producing the first 26ft jump in Olympic history.

Long could not improve with his final jump, which left Owens assured of gold with one leap remaining. Owens broke the Olympic record once more – "He seemed to be jumping clear out of Germany," Rice wrote – with a mark of 26ft 5in that would not be bettered until the 1960 Games in Rome.

It was at this point that Owens and Long first conversed. Long rushed up to Owens to congratulate him. Under the gaze of Adolf Hitler, they walked off arm in arm.

That evening, Owens sought out Long in the Olympic village. They drank coffee and spoke as best they could, discovering that they had much in common. Both were born to poor rural families who had moved to cities to find work. Owens was born in Alabama in 1913, the son of a share-cropper and descendant of slaves. His family moved to Cleveland in 1922. Both Owens and Long were married with one child. Both were essentially apolitical, "two uncertain young men in an uncertain world", as Owens later put it. They agreed to correspond.

Long, a loyal German but no Nazi, recognised the genius in Owens. In one day, Owens had broken or equalled Olympic records four times and world records twice. It was not the first time he had produced such stupendous feats of repeated brilliance. Indeed, he exceeded his Olympic day of days on a warm Saturday in May 1935, an occasion justifiably described as "the greatest single day in the history of man's athletic achievements".

Representing Ohio State University at Ferry Field, Ann Arbor, Michigan, Owens equalled the world record for 100 yards (American competition distances remained imperial), broke the world record

for 220 yards by almost half a second, broke the world record for the 220 yards low hurdles and broke the world record for the long jump. Three world records set, one equalled, and all within an hour. But what he did in Berlin, both on that extraordinary Tuesday, and in the days preceding and following it, was made infinitely more important by its context.

Hitler intended the Games to be a demonstration of German superiority and Nazi organisation. The stadium, holding 110,000, was the largest in the world. For the first time, there was photo finish and rudimentary television. The official film was directed by Leni Riefenstahl, who had 80 cameramen at her disposal.

The Olympic village was far in advance of any accommodation provided at any previous Games. Masterminded by Captain Wolfgang Fürstner, who was in charge of the German army's sporting programme, it set a standard for the remainder of the century. For the men's teams, 160 homes were built in an area landscaped within a birch forest. Each housed 24 athletes in double rooms with a washbasin, shower and lavatory. Stewards who spoke the appropriate language were provided, and food was tailored to national tastes. The British team was provided with Horlicks.

Fürstner was a brilliant organiser – and a Jew. Already deprived of German citizenship by law, he was replaced as director of the Olympic village shortly before the Games and dismissed from the army.

The German leader attended the stadium daily. He was observed at close quarters by Martha Dodd, the daughter of the American ambassador. "He watched day by day the marvellous performance of American athletes," she wrote. "The winner of whatever event was on usually went up to his box to be

"He had the most perfect body of any track and field athlete I ever watched"

congratulated; however, when Owens or other coloured competitors from America won, he was conveniently out of his box. One day the American flag went up at least five times. Hitler saluted with arm outstretched and with a dour expression on his face. However, if a German would win, his enthusiasm and good humour were boundless and he would spring to his feet with wild and childish joy. In him, in his face and bearing, there was not the slightest indication that he knew what good sportsmanship meant, or had any appreciation of sport for its own sake."

"As smooth as the west wind", wrote American Grantland Rice of Jesse Owens. Here he powers to gold in the 200m.

For Hitler, the Games would also display the superiority of the Aryan race, which in Nazi terminology meant whites, apart from Jews. Blacks were regarded as subhuman. "It was the Nazi attitude, which I once heard expressed by a supposedly intelligent assistant of Joachim von Ribbentrop [who had just been appointed ambassador to London], to consider negroes as animals, and utterly unqualified to enter the Games," Dodd wrote. "This young man elaborated his thesis, saying that, of course, if the Germans had had the bad sportsmanship to enter deer or another species of fleet-footed animal, they could have taken the honours from America in the track events."

The official Nazi newspaper, *Der Angriff*, also refused to regard the black Americans as authentic competitors, referring to them as "black auxiliaries". But the huge crowds that filled the stadium on every day of competition took a different view. Owens, whose previous feats were well known, received an ovation every time he entered the stadium.

Unremarkable elsewhere in life, once he was engaged in athletic competition his grace and easy, unassuming superiority were unmistakable. Like few others – Sobers, Pele and Ali spring to mind – there was majesty about him. "He had great power in his legs, he had blinding speed and his style was flawless, with no sign of extra effort," Rice wrote. "Jesse was as smooth as the west wind."

To begin with, Hitler's expectations were gratified. On the first day of competition, Hans Wöllke, a shot-putter, won Germany's first-ever Olympic gold medal in track and field. Wöllke, a policeman, was led to Hitler's box to be congratulated and was said to have left it three ranks higher. That afternoon, two German medal winners in the women's javelin, and the three Finns who finished first, second and third in the 10,000m, were also presented to Hitler.

But the black contingent that for the first time formed the core of the American Olympic team soon made its mark. Owens was scheduled only to run heats on the first day, but another black American, Cornelius Johnson, won the high jump, with David Albritton, a close friend of Owens, second. Hitler ignored them.

Hitler was informed by the president of the International Olympic Committee after the first day that he must either invite all winners to his box or none. From day two, he no longer received athletes in his box. Therefore, the suggestion that he specifically snubbed Owens, first made by the American press but later endorsed and embellished by Owens himself, was incorrect. If anybody was snubbed, it was Johnson.

In fact, Owens was quite unconscious at the time either of a snub, or of the political portents, or of the moral import of his victories. "When I passed the chancellor, he arose, waved his hand at me and I waved back at him," Owens said. "I think the writers showed bad taste in criticising the man of the hour in Germany."

When Grantland Rice encountered Owens in the Olympic village, he found he had no feelings at all about Hitler. "I haven't even thought about it," Owens told him. "I suppose Mr Hitler is much too busy a man to stay out there for ever. After all, he'd been there most of the day. Anyway, he did wave in my direction as he left and I sort of felt he was waving at me."

Owens was an athlete, whose only purpose in Berlin was to run and jump. Although the deeper impact of his achievements may have been unwit-

In one day, Owens had broken or equalled Olympic records four times and world records twice

ting, they were real. Owens must be chiefly credited with foiling the Führer's purpose, exposing Nazi theories to ridicule and giving satisfaction if not hope to those marked first as inferior, thereafter as victims.

By lunchtime on Wednesday, August 5, five American gold medals had been won, four of them by black athletes, two of them by Owens. Once again, it was drizzling as Owens dug his starting holes from the wet, red cinder track with the trowel provided. Normally a slow starter, he tore into the lead, as he had in the 100m final, and stretched away to another gold medal and another world record, 20.7sec. As Owens crossed the line, the drizzle turned to a downpour. An American novelist sitting near Martha Dodd in the diplomatic box let out a whoop of triumph. "Hitler twisted in his seat, looked down, attempting to locate the miscreant, and frowned angrily," Dodd wrote.

Owens would rub it in with one further gold medal, and world and Olympic record, in the 4x100m relay. Nobody since the 1900 Games had won three golds in track and field. Owens had won four. Over five days of competition, he raced 10 times in the 100m, 200m and 4x100m relay. He jumped twice in long-jump competitions. He won them all. He, rather than Hitler, was the object of wonder in the Olympic stadium. The question hardly needed to be put: where now was the much-vaunted superiority of the Aryan?

Owens was just 23, but when the Games were over so, too, was his athletic career. Trying to cash in on his fame, he was declared a professional, ineligible for Olympic or any other serious competition. Owens's loss was the world's loss. For others, the Nazi Olympics marked the end of the future. The Jewish builder of the village, Captain Fürstner, anticipating the inevitable, killed himself with a single shot. Lutz Long, a decent man, became a soldier and was killed in Sicily in 1943. Theirs were just two lives destroyed, among the many millions.

WHATEVER HAPPENED TO BERLIN'S MIRACLE MAN?

After the 1936 Olympics, Jesse Owens joined the American team on a tour of Europe to raise funds for the American Athletic Union, which had overspent on the trip to the Games. He was among the most celebrated people in the world. He was inundated with offers from impresarios, including one of $25,000 to appear on stage in California with an orchestra for two weeks. He was also broke.

On August 15, he ran his last race as an amateur, at the White City stadium in London, taking one leg of a relay. But his heart was not in it. Preferring to return early to the United States rather than continue, he was in any case banned from amateur competition in the United States.

Once home, Owens found that most of the offers were illusory. He made money quickly but not always with dignity. A week after his return from Europe, Owens embarked on a tour to persuade black voters to support Alf Landon's Republican presidential campaign. He was paid $10,000. Endorsements for food and clothing and appearances at banquets and concerts brought in further amounts.

Owens's athletic appearances were restricted to gimmick races against horses, cars, trucks, baseball players and Joe Louis, the heavyweight boxing champion.

He later started a dry-cleaning business, which failed, and worked as an assistant coach at his old university. After the war, he was a personnel officer for the Ford Motor Company. Although never wealthy, he was able to buy himself a new car every year for the rest of his life.

A heavy smoker in his later years, Owens retired to Scottsdale, Arizona, and there, on March 31 1980, he died from lung cancer. Two of his grandchildren helped to carry the Olympic torch on its way to the Atlanta Games in 1996.

The flying Dutchwoman

The Dutch mother-of-two was too old to win gold medals, said the experts. They were wrong. In the first post-War Olympics, held in London in 1948, Fanny Blankers-Koen entered four events and won them all. Not only did she transform perceptions of women in sport, her record of four golds in one Games has never been equalled.

DAVID WALSH

Fanny Blankers-Koen lives alone in a fourth-floor apartment at Hoofddorp, not far from Amsterdam. Now in her ninth decade, she has moved feistily into the autumn of her life. Her laughter is irreverent, the memories self-deprecating and innocent, but it is her zest for life which is remarkable.

"Don't move," she says, "there are so many doors, the elevator is hard to find. I'll come and get you." Maybe so, but it seems a ruse to allow a more personal welcome. She comes down the lift and into the hallway: "You're welcome, please come this way." Inside her apartment, she cannot do enough for her guest. "May I take your coat?" she says. "Sit wherever you wish. Would you like tea now or later?"

It is the home of any elderly woman. Little ornaments, well-tended plants that breathe life, a television guide open on today's date. But as your eyes wander, they pick up traces of her former life. Here in a glass case a steel sculpture with the five Olympic rings, there a photograph of a younger Fanny being decorated by Holland's Queen Juliana. Another a montage of Fanny the athlete: running, hurdling, straining, winning.

But nothing reflects the achievement of her athletic career as much as the framed print of a Dominican Republic postage stamp which has Fanny in full

The 200m and Fanny's third gold. Persuaded to run only by her husband's cajoling, she won the race, run on a sodden track, by the widest margin in Olympic history.

flight. Why should a little country, so far away, honour Fanny Blankers-Koen? On a coffee table sits today's post. It has brought a request from two sisters, Y and P Anttila from somewhere called Torslanda, for an autograph. More than 50 years after her gold medals at the London Olympics, the fan letters continue to arrive.

As a teenager, no matter what she entered, she won

There isn't a hint of fragility. She doesn't so much walk to the kitchen to make tea as bound there and back. "God, you're still a fit woman." "Not as good as you think," she says, as she rubs the hip she hurt at tennis and complains it has slowed her down.

The strength that was such a part of her running is evident in her lean and upright physique and in the sureness of her step. Her power, she says, was always in the arms and legs. Not like other girls who had it in their shoulders and thighs, who were a little more, let us say, masculine. She stretches an arm and pulls up the right leg of her fawn trousers. The leg is still muscular and shapely, the skin smooth and taut – it looks like the limb of a 25-year-old.

Her four gold medals at the 1948 Olympics have never been equalled in women's athletics. More important was the legacy of Blankers-Koen's success. It changed attitudes towards women in sport, earning them a respect they had been denied previously.

Such was the impact of her success, Blankers-Koen would soon tour America and Australia to speak to high-school girls about the possibilities for women in sport. She became something more than a heroine, rather a symbol for female potential. To understand how she got to this pedestal, it is necessary to understand where she started from.

Leap of faith: Britain's Maureen Gardner pushed Fanny all the way in the 80m hurdles. It was her toughest race. After it, she was determined to go home.

"I was brought up on a farm, a simple country girl." Arnold and Lena Koen had five children: four boys and Francina. They called her Fanny. Arnold loved sport, and Fanny alone shared his passion. He would watch her leave the house, always running, never stopping to open the garden gate but hurdling it. He brought her to local meetings and no matter what she entered, she won.

He also saw something in her spirit. Everyone disliked the whale-liver oil he believed essential for good health

7

but Fanny took her spoonful each day, wincing as she swallowed. Although Arnold suspected Fanny was good, he had no real idea until his 17-year-old daughter joined a proper athletics' club in Amsterdam. Within months she was the best athlete in Holland. A year later she competed for her country at the Berlin Games of 1936.

It was her first time outside Holland; she ran the relay, competed in the high jump and shivered with excitement when Adolf Hitler entered the arena and the German crowd rose in acclamation. What did she know of the war to come? She left Berlin with nothing more than Jesse Owens's autograph and sharpened ambition. But all that soon seemed irrelevant; Europe went to war, Germany invaded Holland and life changed.

Fanny married her coach, Jan Blankers, in 1940 and bore their first child a year later. A boy, Jantje. Five years on a daughter, Fanneke, arrived. Mum might have given up running but Jan coached other women and she yearned to be among them.

"What will happen to my milk supply if I train and race?" she asked her doctor. "You won't know until you try," he said. Back in training, her milk increased. "I would bring my girl in a basket to the changing room and feed her between races."

Through the war there was no international competition, but, racing at home, Blankers-Koen set world records in the 100 yards, 80m hurdles, long jump and high jump. While she trained at the stadium in Amsterdam, Jantje and Fanneke played in the long-jump sandpit.

Mothers didn't win gold medals. Fanny herself believed that if she could get to one final it would be enough

The cancellation of the 1940 and 1944 Olympics meant her name was barely known outside Holland . When London agreed to host the Olympics in 1948, Blankers-Koen was 30. In most eyes, that was too old. Mothers didn't win gold medals. Fanny herself believed if she could get to even one final, it would be enough. Jan Blankers thought his wife could do better. He wouldn't allow her to walk in the opening parade. "Too tiring," he said.

Blankers-Koen's memories of those London Olympics are sharp. The Dutch women boarded with four other teams at St Helen's School in Northwood, took a train to Wembley and then walked to the stadium. In her first race, a 100m heat, she ran hard, won easily but came away with the impression that her rivals were saving themselves for the final.

She won the semi-final comfortably and still believed the others were holding back. Although nervous at the start of the final, she made a good start and knew immediately she would win. For her, this was a strange feeling because she had always been afraid of losing and here, at last, she felt she could win. Fanny beat the Englishwoman Dorothy Manley by three yards.

Golden memories: half a century on, Fanny Blankers-Koen revisits Wembley Stadium, scene of her extraordinary triumphs.

For her, it was enough. At St Helen's School that evening, she said: "I don't want to run anymore, I don't want to do the 80m hurdles tomorrow." At that moment, her husband and coach walked into the room. "What are you doing?" Jan asked. "I am an Olympic champion and I don't want to run anymore ... I am so happy I want to have a party." 'Tomorrow," Jan said, "you have the heats for the hurdles. Go to bed, get a good night's sleep."

She had seen the British athlete, Maureen Gardner, at the warm-up track. Gardner came with her own hurdles to practice technique and at 19 was one of her country's most talented athletes. A ballet teacher, she was also a striking-looking young woman.

The final became the fiercest battle. Blankers-Koen started badly and then had to run too fast to catch up. "When I ran all out in this event, the distance between the hurdles wasn't sufficient for my long stride. I hit the second hurdle, stumbled over the fifth and just leaned forward enough to get in front of Maureen. I leaned so low, the tape cut my neck and the blood trickled onto my vest."

Thinking she had won, Gardner jumped for joy. Blankers-Koen thought she had just won but didn't dare to presume it. King George VI entered the stadium, God Save The King was played on the public address and the Dutchwoman, unaware of the King's arrival, feared this signalled victory for her rival. She was wrong.

After the hurdles win, Blankers-Koen wanted to return to Jantje and Fanneke in Amsterdam. All the warm-ups, the practice, the heats and the finals had drained her. Next morning she sat in the dressing room unable to go to the start for the heats of the 200m. Jo Pfann, the ladies team manager, tried to talk her into competing but without success. Seeing Fanny sobbing, the lady who stood sentry on the door called for Jan Blankers. In normal circumstances coaches were not allowed into the changing room but this was different.

"I can't do it, I don't want to run anymore, I want to go home." "You don't have to run," Jan said. "You can go home if you wish. But in time you will be sorry. Just go out there and try to make the final, that will be enough." Maybe it was Jan's sympathetic response that caused Fanny to cry uncontrollably. Once it subsided, she felt better and ready to run. She won the 200m by the widest margin in Olympic history.

By then Fanny needed to party. Jan brought her to the West End that evening and treated her to a glass of wine. He also agreed she could go shopping the next morning, as long as she returned in plenty of time for the 4x100 relay.

Many of the women who came to London for the 1948 Olympics did not know what it was like to shop for non-essential goods. Given the opportunity, they bought towels and raincoats. It took Fanny time to find the raincoat of her choice, a beige man's coat that sat magisterially on her angular frame. Time had passed quickly, the streets were busy, the trains crowded and when she got to Wembley Stadium, the Dutch team had already finished their warm-up for the relay.

THE RATION-BOOK OLYMPICS

The 1948 Olympics were the Games nobody wanted to stage. With Europe laid waste by six years of war and London pockmarked by the Blitz, even the concept of sporting festivals seemed crass at a time when there was not enough to eat.

When the first post-War congress of the Olympic Committee was staged in 1946, it was agreed to go ahead with the Games of the XIV Olympiad, and London volunteered. No other European city was capable of staging the first Games for 12 years.

The decision was not without opposition. London's *Evening Standard* complained: "A people which has had its housing programme and food imports cut ... may be forgiven for thinking that a full year of expensive preparation for the reception of an army of foreign athletes verges on the border of excessive."

But the mood was modified when the foreign teams arrived with their own food and donated the surplus to local hospitals. The excitement of the event could not be contained, either, especially as these were the first Games to be widely televised, taking the performances beyond the 80,000 spectators who daily filled Wembley Stadium. They became known as the "ration-book" Games.

The total cost of the London Games amounted to less than £600,000.

"Where have you been?" Jan asked. "You said I could buy a raincoat." "Yes, but not for the entire morning." Fanny saw the disappointment in the faces of her team-mates and felt she had let them all down. If ever there was an occasion to run fast, this was it. Nobody considered the Dutch team fast, but with Fanny, who could predict the outcome? She, of course, would race the anchor leg and she prayed that the race wouldn't be over when she got her chance.

She returned home to an extraordinary welcome. She thought the fuss would soon die. It never did

Dutch newspaper reports of the time said that Blankers-Koen was sixth and last when she took over from team-mate, Gerda van de Kade. "My first thought was that I had no chance to win. I was so far back. Joyce King, from Australia, was in front. She had red hair. 'I could never win this,' I thought, 'never, never, never'. Then with 50 metres to go, I thought, 'Maybe. I have a chance, I have a chance'. I ran faster then than I had ever run, getting closer all the time, until a couple of metres from the line, I passed her."

She returned to an extraordinary welcome in Amsterdam the next day and thought the fuss would soon die down. It never did. On those tours to Australia and America, she began to understand what she had done. Before a room full of high-school girls, the head teacher would say "This is Fanny Blankers-Koen who got married, had two children and then won four gold medals at the Olympics." Her success freed women from the presumption that motherhood and athletics could not be combined. Fifty years ago, that was quite a realisation.

It is now getting towards the end of a long, absorbing afternoon at her apartment in Hoofddorp. Three sessions of tea and plain biscuits have satisfied her need for niceties. "Like a beer?" she asks, and noting her visitor's reticence, adds: "I'm having one anyway." So we share a beer and Fanny gets a little philosophical. She laments Jan's death in 1977. He died too soon.

In a different way, she regrets calling their daughter Fanneke. A supremely talented young athlete, Fanneke became known as "Fanny". The little Fanny Blankers-Koen. She heard adults whisper: "This is Fanny Blankers-Koen, she will win" and at the age of 12 the girl told her mother she never wanted to race again. She never did. Mother understood.

Then the telephone rings. She picks it up. An Italian journalist wants to come to interview her next month and she says why not? He agrees to ring next week with details. Pleased, she hangs up. "All these years, there have been many journalists from Holland, many from England, the US, France and Belgium. But never before one from Italy. Now, at last, I'm going to get my Italian boy." Life for Fanny Blankers-Koen goes on.

Turpin's night of glory

Randolph Turpin's defeat of Sugar Ray Robinson in 1951 was one of the most sensational upsets in sporting history. It was widely believed that Turpin would be just another scalp for Robinson, the most feared – and glamorous – boxer in the world. But however deserved, Turpin's fame was to prove ephemeral. Tragedy awaited.

NICK PITT

"Who is this guy Turpin?" asked Sugar Ray Robinson on his grand tour of the Continent during the summer of 1951.

Actually, he was the European middleweight champion, but Robinson could be excused his ignorance for he inhabited a different world. At 30, he was acknowledged to be the best pound-for-pound boxer alive, probably the best who had ever breathed. He had lost only once, on points eight years earlier, in 133 professional fights. He travelled like a film star or potentate, with a 10-man entourage that included a trainer, a secretary, a golf professional, a barber and a midget to play the medieval fool.

And when, after completing his series of exhibitions and non-title fights in Paris, Zurich, Antwerp, Liege, Berlin and Turin, Robinson headed for England with a week to prepare to defend his world middleweight title, his chief concerns were domestic. Could he get his pink Cadillac convertible across the Channel? Where could he stay when the Savoy asked him to leave because the crowds of gawpers were making the running of the hotel impossible? How could he kill time down at his new pre-fight headquarters, the Star and Garter pub in Windsor?

Turpin shared a priceless asset with Robinson: he never worried about a fight

It was at the weigh-in, held at the Piccadilly Circus offices of the promoter, Jack Solomons, at lunchtime on July 10, the day of the fight, that Robinson first saw Randolph Turpin. He realised he might have a problem. When Turpin stripped and stepped on to the scales, Robinson found it hard to believe that such a physique could be accommodated within the 160lb limit. Turpin was 5ft 11in and broad-shouldered. He looked like a cruiserweight. "Right there, Turpin impressed me," Robinson admitted in his autobiography. "His torso was like an oak tree. If he could box even a little bit, I was going to be in trouble."

Sweet success: (above) Turpin savours his victory. (Right) he ducks to avoid a left from Robinson. Turpin was fitter, faster and better prepared than the champion: his success was never a matter of luck. It was his enduring misfortune that after the fight his career began an inexorable decline.

Turpin could box more than a little bit, and while Robinson had been swanning around Europe, Turpin had been training for the fight of his life. More importantly, he shared with Robinson one priceless asset: he was never worried about a fight, or who he fought.

That morning, while Robinson's Cadillac led the procession from the Star and Garter to Solomons's office, Turpin, with his brother Jackie and his manager, George Middleton, took the train from his home town, Leamington Spa. "How you feeling, Kid?" Jackie Turpin asked his brother. "Great." "You're not worried?" "No, I'm not bothered."

When they arrived in Piccadilly, the streets were so crowded that mounted police kept order. There were well-wishers for Turpin, but most wanted a glimpse of the fabulous Robinson. Turpin made his way down an alley at the back of Solomons's office and sat quietly in the shade. Robinson arrived at the appointed time, and was escorted through the crowds and up the stairs for the weigh-in. Turpin was missing. "Where's Randy?" Middleton asked Jackie Turpin. "Solomons is going mad. Go and find him, for God's sake." Jackie found Randolph with a group of boys, reading comics.

After the weigh-in, Randolph and Jackie Turpin and George Middleton went to the cinema. Randolph, who that evening would be fighting the greatest boxer in the world, slept through the film. They arrived at the Earl's Court Arena in the early evening. In the dressing room, Randolph made himself comfortable on the physio's table. "Wake me up when it's time to put me gear on," he said before falling asleep.

Jackie Turpin, the last survivor of the three fighting Turpin brothers, and one of the few still alive intimately acquainted with Randolph's triumph and tragedy, sits in his favourite armchair in a basement flat in Warwick. He is hardly resting; his eyes are alive, his hands move fast – now the open palm, now the closed fist – and the words spill out.

Their mother Beatrice was a local woman whose father had been a bareknuckle fighter who fought in the stables at the Woolpack Inn. Their father, Lionel, was West Indian. He had fought in the Great War, was wounded and poisoned by gas. He had died when Randolph was still a babe in arms. The three Turpin boys were the only blacks in Leamington but they rarely suffered for their colour. It was a tough but happy childhood.

Jackie became a featherweight of near championship class who had more than 140 fights as a professional (more than his brother Randolph and Dick combined). Dick, the eldest, was the first black to win a British title after the Boxing Board of Control's shameful colour bar was lifted. Randolph, the youngest, was a natural athlete, the gifted one.

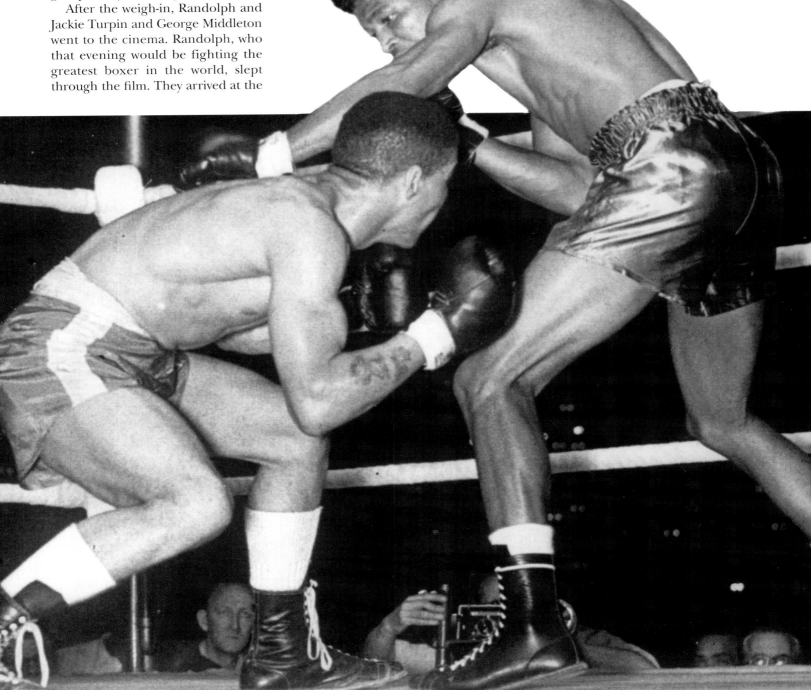

Jackie's stories career around chronologically, from the early days to the glory days, to the dark later days that still seem unbelievable. But now Betty, his wife for more than 50 years, and another of those few who knew Randolph really well, is laughing. Jackie has started on a story she knows all too well, but it's one of the best.

"It was a month before the first Robinson fight, and Randy was training at Gwrych Castle in Wales," Jackie says. "There were four sparring partners, a heavyweight and middleweight and then Stan Parkes, who was a lightweight, and myself. Stan and I were there to give Randy speed work. We were all getting regular beatings, getting mangled. It wasn't much fun for us, and it wasn't good for Randy because he was too far ahead of himself, too fit too soon, and I thought I must do something.

"One day, I went into the town with Stan and we went into Woolworth's. I went to the ladies lingerie counter and bought a bra and bloomers. Then I asked the assistant for some fancy garters. She looked at me oddly, but I got those and then I bought some lipstick and powder. We went back to the castle and I hid all the stuff in the toilet.

"We always used to get dressed in the flat in the castle before going down to the sparring, which was open to the public. I put all my gear on and went down wrapped in a dressing gown, keeping my head down. First in with Randy that day was the middleweight and he got a licking. He was ready to

Few thought Turpin could last long against Robinson's fluid skills

pack it in after a couple of rounds.

"Then it was my turn. I took off the dressing gown and climbed into the ring. I had on my bra, bloomers and garters, and across my stomach I had written in lipstick: Do Not Strike Here. On my forehead I had written: Out Of Bounds. For once, he couldn't hit me for laughing. I said to him afterwards that it was for his own good, that he was way over with a month to go."

Turpin entered the Earl's Court ring around nine o'clock. He sat on a stool in his corner as

Family affair: Randolph Turpin (centre) with his brothers Dick (left) and Jackie.

Robinson made his entrance. The monarch's retinue had assumed their roles for fight-night: one to smooth down his hair, one to hold the satin-covered water bottle, one for the spittoon, another to handle the champion's gumshield and the midget to prance about and wish his master luck.

Turpin's cornermen formed a screen around him so that he wouldn't be affected, but Turpin wanted to see what was going on. "Move out of the way," he said. "It doesn't scare me. Let me see the circus."

Eugene Henderson, the referee, gave his instructions and Turpin jogged back to his corner. "I was looking after his bottle and bucket," Jackie Turpin recalled. "Randy had this habit of kicking up his heels and shrugging his shoulders just before the first bell to make himself loose. Then he went straight out and boom, boom, boom, he threw three left jabs as if to say, 'It's Ray Robinson, but who's Ray Robinson?'."

In fact, the grainy black-and-white shows that Robinson threw the first punch, a jab that missed, but Turpin was soon making his strength and condition tell. According to Robinson's autobiography, Turpin had "a ruffian style developed as a cook in the British navy". Turpin may not have been blessed with the dancing feet and loose-limbed grace of Robinson, and he may have been a regular at fairground booths, taking on allcomers, but he was no crude slugger.

He was somewhat like John Conteh – hard and fast, an all-round fighter in the American style. He was the youngest-ever winner of a full Amateur Boxing Association title and the first black ABA winner. At 23, after five years as a professional, he had become the British and European champion, the most formidable fighter produced in Britain.

Yet such was Robinson's reputation that hardly anybody gave Turpin a chance. The bookmakers had Robinson favourite at 7-2 on. The boxing writers concurred. Peter Wilson of the *Daily Express* found it hard to believe that Turpin could survive a quarter of an hour of combat with a man whose fluid skills masked a dreadful brutality.

Gradually, the plain fact and incredible thought began to dawn. Turpin was holding his own. No, he was doing better than that. He was on top, for the moment. No, he's really on top. Betty Turpin, sitting a few rows back from the ring, described it as a kind of murmur: "People around me were saying, 'He's going to win this, he's going to win'."

For Wilson, no less astonished, the decisive moment came in the seventh round. "The two men's heads came together – the fault of neither – with a sickening click like two billiard balls colliding," he wrote. "Turpin came away unmarked but Robinson was so badly gashed that after the fight his doctor had to insert 14 stitches near his left eye."

Turpin, whose fitness gave him even greater domination in the later stages, kept to his plan. He did not try to knock out Robinson, but controlled him with his jab and flurries of hooks. During the 14th and 15th rounds, most of the 18,000 present were on their feet, many singing "For he's a jolly good fellow". When the final bell rang, the result was beyond doubt, even for Robinson, who accepted the truth without dissent as the referee raised Turpin's hand. Turpin's finest hour was also the greatest upset in a British ring, and the greatest achievement by a British boxer. If only his story could have ended there.

Sixty-four days later, as per contract, Turpin met Robinson in a return fight, at the Polo Grounds, New York. It was a dull contest, with Robinson impressing early on but Turpin growing stronger round by round, until the 10th, when a clash of heads sliced open a cut on Robinson's forehead. Most saw the clash as accidental. But not Robinson. "Turpin butted me again and I felt the blood oozing out of the scar from the first fight," he said.

Blind in one eye as it filled with blood, and with the referee peering at him as if minded to stop the contest, Robinson attacked in desperation. He caught Turpin with a long, optimistic right-hand punch, hurling him into the ropes, hurt. Another right dropped Turpin for a count of nine. When he rose, Robinson attacked mercilessly and without reply, until, with eight seconds of the round remaining, the referee stopped the fight.

Many argued that the stoppage was premature, that it had been prompted by excessive caution because a recent fight in New York had led to a boxer's death. But the controversy was irrelevant, for Turpin after his 64-day blaze of glory was already in decline.

"When we were kids, he always said he would be the best in the world, and he had achieved that," said Jackie Turpin. "He had nothing more to reach for. And the second Robinson fight came much too soon for him. Randy needed to reach a peak, come down and then climb another."

Two years later, after Robinson had retired, Turpin returned to New York to fight Carl "Bobo" Olson for the vacant world title. On the *Queen Mary*, Randolph and Jackie did their roadwork by running around the upper deck. Jackie noticed that Randolph was wandering to the left and sometimes bumped into him. Later, in the ship's gym, he confronted his brother. "There's something wrong with your eye, isn't there?" "No," said Randolph, "and if you say anything, I'll break your bleeding neck."

The Olson trip was a microcosm of what was to come. There were divisions in the training camp (and precious little training), tax demands, a wretched defeat over 15 rounds and an arrest after allegations of assault made by a woman Turpin had met when he was training for the second Robinson fight.

How the mighty are fallen: washed up as a fighter, his fortunes declined. Turpin took a series of ever-more demeaning jobs. By the late 50s he was working in a scrap-metal yard. Worse was to come.

As his health deteriorated, so Turpin's mind became dark and troubled

Already partially deaf from a childhood accident, Turpin's sight deteriorated and his tendency to withdraw became more marked. After retiring from boxing, he invested badly, lent money to friends, became a wrestler to pay the bills, was bankrupted and ended up as the cook in a transport cafe run by his second wife in Leamington. "Randy would never cry or let himself go," said Jackie. "People wanted to help him but he wouldn't let them."

Turpin enjoyed one more gala night. He was invited to New York, all expenses paid, to attend a farewell salute to Robinson at Madison Square Garden in December 1965. Robinson greeted Turpin like a long-lost brother and noted that he was still fit enough to box. But by now Turpin's mind was dark and troubled. Nobody can tell us why Turpin acted as he did five months later. The deed was too awful. On May 17 1966, Turpin led one of his daughters, Carmen, aged 17 months, upstairs to a bedroom above the transport cafe. He shot her twice before turning the gun on himself. She survived. He did not.

Zatopek supreme

Emil Zatopek dominated middle-distance running after the War. 10,000m champion at the London Olympics, his crowning achievement came at the Helsinki Games in 1952. As expected, he won both the 5,000m and 10,000m. And then he won the marathon, a distance he had never run before.

ALASDAIR REID

On a sultry afternoon in summer, the tree-shaded house in the northern suburbs offers a cool retreat from the fierce Prague heat. An elderly lady, bustling with attentive welcomes, places a jug of iced water on the table, fills her husband's glass and settles it close to his right hand. He smiles. His left arm, almost ineffectual after two strokes, hangs by his side. There is an air of quiet forbearance about him. Even with his good arm, it is an effort to raise the glass to his lips. You want to help, but you hold back, unwilling to intrude on his dignity. When he talks, the words are slow and deliberate, and you have to restrain yourself from finishing his sentences.

You feel awkward because you knew the bare bones of his life before you arrived. You knew that he was not only a giant of sport, but a towering symbol of defiance in other spheres. You knew of the remorselessness of his training, the agony he endured to set countless records and collect four Olympic golds, of how he stood before the Russian tanks in Prague's Wenceslas Square, a brave emblem of his people's desire for freedom. And you find yourself faced with a frail, stoop-shouldered man in a pullover. Mortality was the last thing you expected of Emil Zatopek.

He wasn't particularly interested in the race. Had the low-key 1500m event through the streets of Zlin, eastern Moravia, not been sponsored by the shoe company where he worked, the 18-year-old Zatopek would not have taken part. As a child, he had always enjoyed running, but it was its freedom he relished, not the discipline of competition.

So Zatopek ran, finishing second in a field of 100 youths, many of whom had trained hard for the event. The year was 1940, when central Europe was in the grip of German occupation, and Zatopek found release in the offer of coaching that his surprise success brought. Two years later, a fortnight short of his 20th birthday, he made his major debut, finishing fifth in the 1500m at the Czech national championships.

His aspirations, though, were as a distance runner. Ambivalent as he had been about his initial involvement in

Zatopek produced a devastating surge to win the 5,000m in Helsinki. Mimoun and Schade are left struggling, Chataway sprawling. (Above) Zatopek and Dana, his wife.

athletics, Zatopek grew fixated by the achievements of Paavo Nurmi, the original flying Finn, who had dominated the sport in the 1920s. He modelled his own preparations on Nurmi's training technique, the so-called interval method in which sprints over 200m and 400m were interspersed with lighter jogs over the same distances.

"People became very interested in how I trained, but it was really very simple. I would run 200m as fast as I could, 200m slowly, then 200m very fast again. I would repeat that 20 times then run 400m fast, 200m slow, 20 times as well. Then more 200s fast and slow. Distance running is all about speed of recovery, that is the one thing you always need to do well."

But Zatopek's methods were frowned upon by Czech coaches, who preferred the disciplined drudgery of sustained runs over long distances. Increasingly, he worked alone, building strength, stamina and speed. Another consequence was that his distinctively inelegant running style, with excessive shoulder movement, lolling head and agonised grimace, was never coached out of him either. Gradually, his times improved and, in 1944, he broke the Czech records at 2,000, 3,000 and 5,000 metres.

Training as relentlessly as ever, he began to win international events. In 1946, he won cross-country races in Germany, Belgium and England. The following year,

The 10,000m and Zatopek's first gold at Helsinki. He made it look easy yet still knocked 42sec off his Olympic record.

events. What I did there would not have been possible at other Games."

Zatopek's modesty is still astounding. When he arrived in Helsinki for the 1952 Olympics, he was one of the biggest names in sport. An army captain, he was also a prize asset of the Czech government in an era when athletes were just beginning to be used as the standard-bearers of communism. Zatopek, however, was no dupe.

He had inspired a generation of young Czech athletes, among them Stanislav Jungwirth, a talented 1500m runner. Jungwirth was easily good enough to make the Czech team for Helsinki, but was left out of the squad because his father, a dissident, had been imprisoned for anti-government activities. His omission infuriated Zatopek, who presented the Czech authorities with an ultimatum: "I told them that if Jungwirth did not go then I would not go either."

His brinkmanship continued until he knew for sure that his protégé had arrived in Finland. Two days before the games, he left for Helsinki, arriving for the opening ceremony. The centrepiece of the occasion was the lighting of the Olympic flame by Nurmi, an unannounced yet wildly acclaimed moment. Within eight days, however, Nurmi's reputation as the greatest-ever distance runner had been eclipsed.

he beat Viljo Heino, the Finn regarded as the inheritor of Nurmi's mantle, by a fraction of a second in a sensational 5,000m race in Helsinki. In 1948, in his preparations for the London Olympics, he set the fastest times in the world at 5,000m and 10,000m.

Zatopek was still little-known, but he demolished his anonymity on the opening day of the London Games. In the 10,000m, he led from the tenth lap, measuring his pace against signals from a Czech coach in the crowd to hold a target speed of 71 seconds a lap. After four kilometres, he blasted out a 30-metre lead and held it to the end. Heino, the world-record holder, wilted in the stifling conditions and dropped out.

Zatopek's win installed him as the favourite for the 5,000m as well. But the heats were scheduled for the day after the 10km and he had to endure a sapping race to qualify for the final two days later. Conditions relented for the race, which was held in persistent rain,

but despite a dramatic surge towards the end he could finish only second, two strides behind Gaston Reiff, the Belgian. He had been denied the double – but an even greater achievement lay over the horizon.

Zatopek demolished his anonymity with his 10,000m win at the London Games

"Even now, I still give thanks to the organisers for the way the [Helsinki] Games were scheduled. In London, it would have been almost impossible to win two golds, but the people of Helsinki knew more about distance running and appreciated the needs of the athletes. The races were spaced out in a way that allowed recovery time between

The starter's shot rang out at 6.13pm on Sunday July 20, releasing a field of 33 runners for the first track final of the Helsinki Games, the 10,000m. Zatopek, now 30 and at the height of his powers, settled into the pack as Les Perry, a stocky Australian, and Gordon Pirie of Great Britain made early, fruitless breaks.

Relentlessly, the Czech clocked up his laps at a steady 71sec, reining in a succession of challengers, until only Alain Mimoun, the Frenchman who had finished second in London in 1948, could stay with him.

"I had no real problems in that race. Mimoun was good, but I always knew I could beat him," he remembers. That he did so even without the trademark injection of pace at three-quarter distance merely emphasised his command. Five laps from the finish, he drew away. His time of 29min 17sec bettered his own Olympic record by more than 42 seconds.

Crossing the line to win the marathon, Zatopek raised his arms and smiled

So relaxed had he looked that the double was talked of as a foregone conclusion. Zatopek, however, knew better. The field for the 5,000m was far better than it had been in London, with Reiff, the reigning champion, Herbert Schade, the German who was fastest in the world that year, and Britain's Chris Chataway all in contention. He also had to get through his heat on the Tuesday, two days after the 10,000m final. Remembering his efforts in London, he relaxed in the early laps. On the sixth circuit, he and four others broke away. "Only five runners would go into the final," he recalls. "Once we had made the break, I realised it was useless to race against each other, so I held up five fingers and shouted, 'We are five, we are five'. There was no reason to push harder."

The final was scheduled for the Thursday, the same day as the women's javelin. In 1948, Zatopek had married Dana Ingrova, the Czech javelin champion, also in the Czech team in Helsinki. If it was a remarkable coincidence that both were chasing medals on the same day, it was all the more so that both achieved their goals.

Emil's came first. At 4.40pm the field set off, the first, jostling lap in 65.8sec, and the four subsequent circuits producing almost identical times, around 68 seconds a lap. Thereafter, Zatopek and Schade shared the lead, before pulling away after 3,000m, drawing Reiff, Chataway, Mimoun and Pirie in their wake.

All six were in contention at the bell: "I thought I would have a comfortable lead at that point, but I had misjudged things. When we started the last lap I was fourth and thought I was out of the medals. But in long-distance running it is always dangerous to start too soon. Luckily, I was able to get past them."

Luck was not what the crowd saw. At the final bend, Chataway led, but in the space of 100m, the order changed completely. Schade and Mimoun moved past the Englishman, who stumbled on the kerb and fell. Then Zatopek, his features locked in a gri-mace of agonised determination, steamed round the outside. On the closing straight, as the chants of his name rang out from the ecstatic stands, Zatopek pulled away, crossing the line in 14min 6.6sec, almost a second ahead of Mimoun.

As he left the podium, Dana took the medal from him. "She said she wanted it for luck. A little while later, when I was in the shower, an official told me she had just broken the Olympic record with her first throw." It was enough for her to secure gold.

A yet more remarkable achievement was to come. The year before the 1952 Games Zatopek had broken the record for 20 kilometres. Realising that he could stretch his gifts over a longer distance, he entered the Helsinki marathon, despite never having raced in the Olympics' signature event.

The possibility of a Zatopek treble drew a crowd of 68,700 to the Helsinki stadium that Sunday afternoon. Since winning his 5,000m gold, he had practised running slowly and he had a simple strategy for the race: "Jim Peters of England was the favourite and I just decided to run close to him. I didn't know him at all, only that his number was 187. When we were getting ready at the start line, I introduced myself to him. I just needed to know who he was."

Peters led the race for the first 16km, Zatopek stalking him about 100m behind. Then the Czech drew level. "I asked Peters if the pace was correct and he said yes. I think he was a little annoyed by my questions, so he began to run on the other side of the road, but I thought he looked a little tired."

Zatopek cranked up the speed. In the stadium, an astonished crowd saw the scoreboard record his ever-increasing lead. A tumultuous welcome greeted him as he returned to the arena, his expression as determined as ever. When he crossed the line, he raised his arms briefly and smiled.

Zatopek trots calmly over the line to win the marathon. Not only was it his first run at the distance, like all his Olympic golds it was an Olympic record.

A charge of insubordination for his part in the Jungwirth affair was quietly dropped before Zatopek returned to Prague. Sixteen years later, however, he took another stand, signing the *Manifesto of 2,000 Words*, Alexander Dubcek's declaration of ideological independence from the Soviet Union. When the uprising was crushed a few months later, he was dismissed from the army. For almost 20 years, he was effectively a non-person, working quietly as part of a geological survey team. The collapse of communism in eastern Europe brought him back into public life, but his health was already beginning to fail and, accepting only a few invitations to overseas events, he was increasingly confined to his home.

Which is where he now sits, with the ever-attentive Dana, just an old man in a pullover. You shake his hand gently as you leave, and you look into his eyes. And for one brief moment it is not the frailty you see, but the pride.

Emil Zatopek died on November 22 2000.

Stan the Man

Riding a glorious wave of popular emotion, Stanley Matthews and Blackpool came back from the dead to snatch victory in a pulsating FA Cup final. To the world at large it was "the Matthews final". To the man himself, the credit belonged to Blackpool's Stan Mortensen, scorer of a hat-trick.

Wembley wizards: Matthews (right) and Harry Johnston are chaired off after their 4-3 win, Matthews on the shoulder of hat-trick hero Stan Mortensen (far right).

JOE LOVEJOY

It was a sublime summer, that Coronation year of 1953, when over a couple of hazy, heady months sport in Britain scaled the heights, as if to greet the new Queen. Edmund Hillary conquered Everest, England regained the Ashes after two decades and the newly knighted Gordon Richards won the Derby at his 28th and final attempt. Football's contribution? Perhaps the most celebrated FA Cup final of them all. The Matthews final.

In May 1953, Stanley Matthews, possibly the best and certainly the most feted winger of all time, was well into his 39th

year when his adopted Blackpool got to Wembley for the third time in six seasons. In those days, Stan was The Man, no doubt about it. His mesmeric dribbling skills and distributive excellence had long established him as the darling of the terraces, but for all his renown, Matthews had won nothing in a club career which brought him to Bloomfield Road via Stoke City for £11,500 in 1947. All he had to show for 17 years of coruscating pre-eminence were two losers' medals, from the 1948 and 1951 Cup finals. Nobody could foresee that Stan would play on past his 50th birthday and the 1953 final was deemed his last chance. Could the "Wizard of the Dribble" make it third time lucky?

Blackpool and their opponents, Bolton Wanderers, were sprinkled with international stardust, but they were cup rather than championship sides. Their passage to the final had scarcely been irresistible. Blackpool needed a replay to see off Southampton and owed a 2-1 win in the semi-finals to a ghastly gaffe by Alf Ramsey, the Spurs full-back. Bolton required two replays to overcome Notts County, from the wrong end of the Second Division, and had squeaked past Gateshead, of the old Third Division (North) 1-0, before pipping Everton 4-3 in the semis.

No matter, by hook or by crook these old Lancashire rivals were there. Two of the all-time greats, Nat Lofthouse and Stan Mortensen, would be in opposition at centre-forward but it was Matthews who would be the magnet for every eye.

Cleverly, or fortuitously (their manager, Joe Smith, is long dead, so we cannot be sure), Blackpool eschewed their own pitch, which was rock-hard and lively in May, to prepare on nearby Stanley Park, where the grass was luxuriant, a la Wembley. Their right-half, Ewan Fenton, recalled: "The Wembley surface was very different to what we'd been accustomed to. Off our hard ground, the ball would come very fast at you, whereas at Wembley it was cushioned, and came that bit slower.

Stanley Park was a tremendous help to us." Matthews, by contrast, believes Blackpool could have played well on cobblestones.

Meeting one's heroes can be a great disappointment, and my 1999 journey to the Potteries to interview the grand old man of English football found me wondering whether this would be another idol with feet of clay. The fears proved groundless. Sir Stanley, as he has been since 1965, was charm and charisma personified as he ushered me into his stylish home. "A drink?" he said, pushing back a jaunty England baseball cap before pouring a glass of the organic tomato juice he prepares himself.

"Well done," said the Queen as Matthews collected his medal. There has been no more popular FA Cup-winner.

Eighty-four then, he was fit and sprightly, his longevity testimony to a life of sobriety. He never touched alcohol in his life – with one notable exception. How did he remember the match that bears his name? Only after much persuasion, it must be said. He was embarrassed that it was known as the Matthews final when Mortensen had scored a hat-trick: "It was Morty's final, not mine."

It is largely forgotten that both principals might not have played. Mortensen had a cartilage operation six weeks earlier while Matthews picked up a thigh strain in training on the Tuesday, needing a pain-killing injection to pass a late fitness test.

The 1953 final was deemed Matthews's last chance. Could the "Wizard of the Dribble" make it third time lucky?

Blackpool travelled to London by train the day before the match and spent the evening at the cinema. The players who were in the team, that is. This was before substitutes, and the Blackpool reserves were to travel to Wembley – and back – on the day. Jimmy Armfield broke into the Blackpool team the following year, and went on to a club record 568 appearances. "The rest of us weren't made to feel part of it. Blackpool were a bit mean like that. When the players were given tickets for their families, they were for the terraces, not seats. Joe Smith told us, 'Nobody sits down when Blackpool are playing, we're too exciting.' When I told him my dad would like to sit, he said, 'Let him watch it on telly'."

The contrasts between then and now are legion. In 1953 there was no briefing on the opposition, no talk of tactics or game plans. "We had nothing like that," Matthews said. "The manager had good players, and he left it up to us. Mind you, we had a very good team and Harry Johnston, our captain, was a natural leader. Whenever Joe Smith did say something before a game, Harry would look at me, raise his eyebrows and mutter, 'We haven't a clue, have we?' He meant we could sort things out for ourselves, and he was right. Whatever the manager said, as soon as we got on the field everything was different."

Almost at once they were a goal down. The strains of *Abide With Me* were still dying away when Lofthouse, the "Lion of Vienna", put all his considerable beef behind a 25-yard drive which George Farm could only help, feebly, into the net. A goal behind in the second minute, it could have been even blacker for Blackpool after 20, when Lofthouse struck a post. The favourites equalised after 35 minutes, when Mortensen let fly with a left-footed shot which Harry Hassall could only divert into his own net, but Bolton were ahead again within four minutes, with Farm again at fault, when Moir beat him to Langton's lob-cum-cross.

At half-time, there was no panic in the Blackpool camp. "Just concentrate on passing – that's what you're good at," Smith told his players. "What happens if that doesn't work?" somebody enquired. "Just give it to Stan."

"No team is ever in charge for 90 minutes. Our turn would come"

Matthews himself viewed the situation with equanimity: "No team is ever in charge for 90 minutes. Our turn would come. Even when we went 3-1 down I wasn't bothered. Before they scored their third we were getting on top."

Blackpool's confidence was buttressed by the sight of Eric Bell, the Bolton left-half, limping badly and reduced to a passenger's role on the wing. Significantly, the weakness was on Matthews's flank, and he was soon

The stuff of fairytales: Bill Perry turns away after slotting home Blackpool's winner with only a minute left.

to exploit it. Before he was able to do so, however, none other than Bolton's "Hopalong Cassidy" extended their lead. With the second half 10 minutes old, Bell punished indecision by Farm and Shinwell and headed home. His team 3-1 down, the teak-tough Johnston, who would turn 35 the following month, turned to Fenton with tears in his eyes. A losing finalist in 1948 and 1951, he said: "Ewan, I can't go back again without the Cup."

Cometh the hour, cometh the Stan. Or rather the two Stans. There were 22 minutes left when their near telepathic understanding brought Blackpool back into the game, Matthews accelerating past Bell before delivering a bull's-eye centre from which Mortensen squeezed in an eye-of-the-needle goal. Now Matthews took charge, embarrassing Ralph Banks, Bolton's left-back, so badly that he never recovered, and was offloaded to Aldershot soon afterwards. The respected Frank Butler wrote in the *News of the World*: "Matthews was terrific. Never has one man played such a solo part in picking up a beaten team, mending it, nursing it and then leading it on the most exciting Cup-final turnabout seen for many a long day. The huge crowd, outside of those from Bolton, became completely biased. All they wanted was

Stanley to get his medal."

Matthews, modestly, said: "I came into it more and more because of Bell's injury. He ended up on the left wing, and couldn't chase me, and I knew I had the beating of the left-back. My confidence grew as his left him. I was in full flow." Yet for all Matthews's mesmeric brilliance, Bolton still led 3-2 with only three minutes left. "I thought it was in the bag," Lofthouse recalled. "If Eric Bell hadn't been injured, I'm sure we'd have won."

Mortensen, who died in 1991, brought the audience to fever pitch, completing his hat-trick with a thunderous free-kick from 20 yards. Taylor had urged him not to shoot: "There's no gap, Stan." "Gap or no gap, I'm having a go," Mortensen replied. The decision brought riotous vindication. Taylor supplied Matthews yet again and, the genie well and truly out of the bottle, he beat Bell on the inside, then Barrass in a slalom towards the byline before cutting the ball back for Bill Perry to fire home the winner.

Fairytale stuff, but it might easily have stayed in the realm of fantasy. "I'd shouted for the ball from Ewan Fenton near the halfway line, but he wouldn't give it to me," Matthews said. "If he had, we probably wouldn't have scored, because the others weren't in the right positions.

"Give credit to Perry, but credit, too, to Morty, who created the space for Perry to score. He was a hell of a player, Morty—so fast as well as clever. I had this understanding with him, I knew where he'd be without looking, but this time he wasn't there. I said to him afterwards, 'Where were you?' He explained that as I shaped to pass he'd taken the centre-half, Jack Higgins, away from the near post and called to Perry, 'Bill, fill the gap.' Great thinking, eh? It was his final, not mine."

At the end, there was bedlam. Portly Joe Smith, who had won twice at Wembley as a Bolton player, chugged on to the field and, enveloping Matthews in a bearhug, bellowed in his face: "Lad, you've won the Cup!" The winning captain, Johnston, and Matthews were both chaired off the field

and went up to the Royal Box together, where the Queen handed them those elusive medals.

Lofthouse, these days a vigorous club president, told me: "I felt for Morty, bloody hell I did. No disrespect to Stan Matthews, but Morty scored three goals and all the accolades went to Stan, which can't be right. Don't get

For all Matthews's mesmeric brilliance, Bolton still led 3-2 with only three minutes left

me wrong, he'd made them, just as he made a lot for me when we played for England, but I did feel sorry for Morty. He got three goals in a Cup final and a lot of people don't know it."

There was no lap of honour in those less ostentatious days and the Blackpool players retired to their dressing room, where the Cup was filled with champagne and the demon drink passed Matthews's lips for the first and last time. On the Sunday, Matthews was invited on to TV's *What's My Line?* panel show, but agreed only if the others could accompany him. On Monday they took the train back to Lancashire, Johnston flinging the trophy into the overhead luggage rack. The last leg of the journey, from

Preston to Blackpool, was on an open-topped bus, with fans lining the streets. A civic reception followed, at which the players were presented with Ronson cigarette lighters.

The £25-per-man bonus they received seems modest until it is remembered that the maximum wage was £17 a week. "I thought it were a bloody fortune," Lofthouse said. "Crikey, me dad were getting three quid a week bagging coal." Matthews, too, had no complaints: 'The wages were good at the time, and we were seeing the world for free, not working in a factory. It was a great life."

Who could have known in 1953 that another 12 years of it lay ahead? The oldest winger in town might have guessed: "I never looked upon that final as my last hurrah. I knew I was okay for a good few years yet." So much so that after three years out of the England team he was restored to the No 7 shirt in October 1953, and was still playing international football four years later, at 42. Mortensen may have scored the goals, but another man's genius made the fightback possible. In that sense, it really was "the Matthews final".

Sir Stanley Matthews died on February 23 2000.

FA Cup winner at last: Matthews in May 1953 (left). More than forty years later, the twinkle in the eyes is still unmistakable as Sir Stanley holds aloft his "magic" boots. That Matthews was still playing professional football into his fifties is one of the wonders of sport.

July 1953

Hogan the hero

Ben Hogan was the great perfectionist of golf, incontestably the greatest player of his age. In 1953, after victory in the Masters and US Open, he made what proved to be his only visit to Britain to play in the Open. In an extraordinary display of single-mindedness, he took on and tamed the wild links of Carnoustie.

NICK PITT

For once, Ben Hogan had missed the green. His approach to the fifth hole at Carnoustie in the final round of the 1953 Open championship had kicked off a slope towards a bunker guarding the left side of the green. It lay at the very edge of the sand, "held by two blades of grass", as Hogan later described it. He was faced with a most treacherous shot. He would have to stand with one foot in the bunker and another on the bank, and suspend his club above the ground before striking, for if the ball should move after he had addressed it, he would be penalised.

Many thousands were on the links that afternoon on July 10, and most of them were following Hogan, "the Wee Ice Mon" whose self-possession and mastery of the game inspired a kind of enraptured awe among the Scots. Among them was a 26-year-old local teacher, Bob Blyth. "He took an age over the shot," Blyth recalled. "He was looking and looking at it, as if he expected the ball to fall into the bunker at any moment."

At last, Hogan chipped with his nine-iron. The ball ran up a slope and sped across the green, hit the cup, leapt three inches into the air and sank into the hole. After four pars, he had made a birdie to take the lead. "We all thought, now he must smile, he must show emotion," Blyth said. "But he just touched his cap and walked to the next tee."

As Hogan stepped on to the sixth tee, and the spectators scrambled to gain a view, a shower of hail whipped across the links. But Hogan was undaunted. Three times in the championship he had taken on the shot that none other dared at the par-five Long Hole, hitting down the narrow strip of fairway between the fairway bunkers and the out of bounds – Hogan's Alley – to have a chance of getting close to the green in two shots. He took his driver and aimed left along the out-of-bounds fence. His steel-sprung swing, delivered from a stable stance with machine precision,

Smiling at last: Hogan holds the auld claret jug. His achievement in winning the Open having never played a links course before remains staggering.

fired the ball with a crack down the left side until, ever obedient, it faded and dropped to the right beside the bunker. The consummation could be taken for granted: the same swing, the same explosive but precise contact, another unerring shot just short of the green and a chip and a putt for birdie.

Blyth was not surprised. For more than a week, he had been on Hogan's tail. He had seen him on the range, firing three-irons 200 yards to his caddie, Cecil Timms, who caught them first bounce in a bag, rarely having to move. "I had only recently taken up golf," said Blyth. "I was a footballer and tennis player finding out how much harder golf is than any other game. Then I saw Hogan, or rather, I heard him. It was the sound of his shots that struck me, a kind of crack and an echo. Every shot flew to a small, chosen area. I also watched Bobby Locke, who was the defending champion, and to be honest he looked a weak player by comparison. Hogan was in a different category. He was completely in control."

Blyth followed Hogan on his practice rounds. Typically, Hogan would hit three balls from each tee: one to the centre of the fairway, one to the right and one to the left, so that he could work out the best line of approach on every hole. "When he practised on the sixth, he hit three shots from the left-hand side, Hogan's Alley. He sent Timms up near the green because he was going to hit a fade, a draw and a straight one and he wanted to know exactly how the ball would roll as each shot approached the green."

ogan, one of countless perfectionists who had found themselves drawn to a game that magnifies the uncertainties of the world, had spent most of his life in pursuit of control. The roots of his obsession were deep. As a boy of nine, brought up during the Great Depression, he had been present in the house, possibly even in the room, when his father, a blacksmith of Irish extraction, shot himself. That single trauma may have shaped his character but it was repeated, enduring hardship and pain that forged his extraordinary resilience.

By the time he arrived in Carnoustie at the age of 40 for his sole attempt to win the Open, the essentials of the Hogan story had been rendered by Hollywood in the film *Follow the Sun*, starring Glenn Ford. He had turned professional at 19 and struggled for several years. From the beginning, he was a man apart. He practised until his hands bled. He practised before playing and, most peculiarly, after playing, a habit that is now almost universal. Fellow Tour professionals dreaded being in the room next to Hogan's because the noise of his putting would keep them awake

Perfect balance, fierce concentration, and another ball is dispatched with unerring accuracy, the result of thousands of hours of practice. Opponents were duly intimidated.

through the night. He believed that striking a ball correctly was more important than scoring. "You get your fun out of golf from practice," he said.

But not a living. When he arrived at Pinehurst for the North and South Open in 1940, Benny Hogan, as he was known then, had been on and off the Tour for eight years. He had been married for nearly five years, but he was barely solvent; he had yet to win a tournament; his second-hand car had bald tyres; he was close to giving up, looking for a steady job.

Hogan won the tournament by three strokes from Sam Snead, was

offered the $1,000 prize in cash but asked for a cheque instead. "I had finished second and third so many times, I was beginning to think I was an also-ran," he said. "They've kidded me about practising so much but it finally paid off. I know it's what finally got me into the groove to win."

Hogan won the next two tournaments, the Greensboro Open and the Asheville Open, as well. In three months he won $6,438; he was the leading money-winner on the US Tour that year and recorded the lowest stroke average.

The work ethic had converted a good player into a great one. But Hogan's hardest encounter with adversity was to come. On the morning of February 2 1949, by which time he had won three Majors and was clearly the best player in the world, Hogan was driving home from the Phoenix Open with his wife, Valerie, when a Greyhound bus emerged from fog, overtaking, coming head-on towards them.

Hogan flung himself across his wife to protect her and in so doing saved himself as well. In the impact the steering wheel of his Cadillac was forced through the driver's seat. Hogan suffered a double fracture of the pelvis, a fractured collarbone, a broken ankle and broken right rib. After a month in hospital, blood clots formed in his leg. It was unlikely that he would be able to walk normally or play golf again.

Once home, he walked laps around his living room for several weeks; by the summer, he was hitting shots; by December he was able to play 18 holes, his legs wrapped in elastic bandages. That outing exhausted him and he almost despaired that he would be strong enough for tournament play. Nevertheless, he sent in his entry for the Los Angeles Open, held in mid-January, less than a year after his crash.

His legs still wrapped – he never played free from pain again – Hogan's presence at the tournament was considered a minor miracle, and his first-round 73 an effort of great courage. He followed it with three 69s, tying for first place with Snead, his old rival, who won the play-off. Hogan was not merely back, but better. Indeed, his record in Major championships over the following four years represents the greatest sequence in golf history. Of the next nine Majors that Hogan entered after 1949, he won six (three US Opens, two Masters, one Open), and finished third, fourth and seventh in the remaining three. As Herbert Warren Wind, the American golf writer and historian, put it: "He was a man who dominated his age as completely as was humanly possible and whose record would arouse a sense of awe and disbelief among future generations, who would wonder how any one man could have played so well so consistently and won so many important championships so often."

But everything paled beside Hogan's achievements in 1953. He prepared for that year's Masters according to his custom: 600 balls

before lunch, 50 with each of 12 clubs at the rate of three balls per minute, repeating the exercise after lunch and playing a round a day as well. He won by five strokes. He came first in two of his next three tournaments before winning the US Open at Oakmont by six shots.

Persuaded chiefly by two old champions, Walter Hagen and Tommy Armour, that he should enter the Open, Hogan and his wife arrived in Scotland on June 23, two weeks before the championship. He checked into

"He was a man who dominated his age as completely as was possible"

the Bruce Hotel close to the course at Carnoustie, but checked out again because there was no room available with a private bath. Hogan needed to bathe his legs in Epsom salts after every round.

Hogan briefly wanted to return to Prestwick, but he was offered the use of a house in Dundee, together with a car and chauffeur, by NCR, an American company with a factory in Dundee. As caddie, he hired Timms, an athletic, opportunistic man of 34 who offered his services when Hogan arrived. Timms talked between shots and covered his eyes with his arms when Hogan putted, his crouching style not being a pretty sight. "Timmy, shut your mouth and stand still," Hogan ordered. Timms obeyed; their conversation thereafter amounted to single-word requests by Hogan: "driver", "putter", "cigarette".

More than ever, he needed to practise. Used to the manicured stadium courses of America (alone among the game's great players, he never played at St Andrews), he did not enjoy the vagaries of links golf. The wind he could handle, for it was just as bad in Texas, but the first time he hit an iron shot, he felt the shaft of his club "twang like a banjo" as he took a big divot.

There had been a drought that year in Scotland and Hogan had to learn merely to bruise the turf with his shots, and he also had to adjust to the smaller ball used in Britain at the time. The greens he found woolly and slow, and he sarcastically offered to have his lawnmower shipped over. But the Scots could find no fault, and endless fascination, in this dour golf-machine. "We used to go down and wait for him and the crowds became enormous, even when he was just hitting shots on the practice ground," said Bob Blyth. "He went over to Barry to practise there, but word soon got round. He never showed any emotion and although the weather was bad he was always dressed immaculately: his white cap or a check cap, a pale blue or yellow polo-neck sweater and grey or khaki slacks, always with a perfect crease. He was a small man, and I had the impression that he slightly dragged his right leg, yet he hit the ball better than anyone."

Hogan had to play two qualifying rounds. When he teed off for the first, at Carnoustie's Burnside course, a huge crowd had gathered to watch him and a northbound train halted on the track to allow driver and passengers a sight of Hogan's first competitive stroke in Scotland.

On the first day of the championship, Hogan shot a 73, three strokes off the lead. He was watched by Frank Sinatra, who was singing that night in

His striking of the ball was magnificent, his play on the final day monumental

Dundee. "All America is rooting for Hogan," said Sinatra. "He's the best player in the world."

On the second day, the drought ended as Hogan, who was drenched, shot a 71, another disappointment and one which left him two shots behind, facing a fearful task. On the last day of the championship, a Friday, two rounds were to be played. With no chance to bathe his legs between rounds, Hogan knew that pain and fatigue would be his adversaries. He had also caught a cold and his temperature shot up to 103 degrees.

Before teeing off at 10.27am, Hogan had an injection of penicillin. Although he continued to putt poorly, his striking was magnificent and only a mistake on the 17th, where he was bunkered and failed to get out with his first attempt, prevented him from matching the course record. Hogan's 70 gave him a share of the lead.

His final round, in cold, windy and wet conditions, when he was unwell and in pain, was monumental. He did not hole one putt of any length, but he did not make a mistake. He hit the ball better and better to break the course record with a 68, five under par, to take the championship by four strokes. With each succeeding round, he had played better and scored lower. The most single-minded player in the world had tamed the most formidable course. Hogan had won all three Major championships he had played in 1953, and although he told the crowd he hoped to come back to defend the title, he never did. As a result, the legend of Hogan and Carnoustie endures.

The crowd around the 18th green had to wait more than 10 minutes for the presentation, for Hogan refused to attend without his jacket. Timms, the caddie, was sent to fetch it and Hogan accepted the old claret jug. As his wife, who alone, perhaps, understood him, put it: "Everyone thought he was a hard man. He wasn't. He just wanted to get it right."

Hogan drew crowds in their thousands during his brief stay in Scotland. They came to marvel at a man who was rewriting golf history and who bestrode the game like a colossus. The pity of it, perhaps, was that he never came back to Scotland, the historic home of golf.

Hungarian rhapsody

In November 1953, England faced a Hungarian side at Wembley they complacently expected to trounce. The Hungarians not only won, they played with breathtaking panache and imagination. It was a humiliating reversal for the country that still saw itself as the hub of world football. The old order was turned decisively on its head.

BRIAN GLANVILLE

On November 25 1953, on a murky afternoon at Wembley Stadium, it happened at last. Nemesis, the moment of truth, call it what you will. England's luck finally ran out. They lost at home for the first time to a team from outside the British Isles. Lost, moreover, in such emphatic, humiliating fashion, to the astonishing Hungarians, that there was no vestige of an excuse. Six-three was the score; for the Hungarians, their football memories so much longer than those in England, it was an ample revenge for the 6-2 defeat they had suffered on their last visit to London, in 1936.

To give the occasion an added, ironic twist, the Hungarian triumph was watched from the Royal Box by a little white-haired old man, the guest not of the Football Association but of the Hungarians themselves, though he was English to the core. Jimmy Hogan: interned in Budapest during the First World War, he became their revered national coach, preaching methods and techniques almost forgotten in his own country. Back home, in 1936, he was sacked as manager of Fulham while lying in a hospital bed. In Hungary, though, they never forgot.

Only six weeks earlier, England had escaped at Wembley by the skin of their teeth. A very late penalty indeed by Alf Ramsey, their senatorial right-back, had saved them from defeat by Fifa's Rest of the World XI. Four-four was the result, and the occasion cast doubt on the kind of palliative later advanced by England's manager, Walter Winterbottom: that whereas the Hungarians had played together and trained together for years, England teams were just thrown together almost at the last moment, then sent on the field to sink or swim. The Fifa team contained players from no fewer than seven European countries.

But no Hungarians. Gustav Sebes, the country's deputy minister of sport, presided over their team and was wary, perhaps, of disclosing even part of his hand at Wembley. He refused to release any of his men. Sebes was at Wembley himself, however, and while there acquired three English-made balls. Testing the famously lush pitch, he noticed that no ball, from whatever height, bounced "more than a metre". Clutching his footballs, Sebes returned to Hungary, where his team were training three times a week.

The FA had had abundant opportunity to assess the Hungarians, who had finally abandoned seasons of splendid isolation the previous year and come out from behind the Iron Curtain to compete in the Helsinki Olympics. Though they won the tournament, by rights the Hungarians should not have been in Finland at all. Though most of them were notionally in the police or in the army, the joke in Budapest was that they turned up only at the end of the week at police stations or barracks to collect their pay. Most of the team played, however reluctantly, for

Hungary's third. Puskas turns away in triumph, Wright looks on bemused. In scoring the goal he would later call "my favourite of all time", the Hungarian had left England's robust captain flat on his back, scything vainly at thin air. It was a portent of things to come.

Honved, the army side based in Budapest. Reluctantly, because they were forced to quit their original clubs.

By May 1953, when they played Italy in Rome, the Hungarians had well and truly honed their game. I saw that match, in which the Hungarians' technique was masterly, their tactics inspired. Above all, by contrast with so many Continental teams of the past, they could finish. This quality showed especially in the shape of the tubby, left-footed Puskas, nicknamed "The Galloping Major", Nandor Hidegkuti, who packed a ferocious right foot, and Sandor "Golden Head" Kocsis, who was exceptional in the air – another quality seldom associated in the past with European attacks.

Puskas and Kocsis largely stayed upfield, not bothering with defence. Jozsef Bozsik, a member of the rubber-stamp Hungarian Chamber of Deputies, was a driving right-half. The full-backs, Jeno Buzansky and Mihaily Lantos, were not quite the equal of their colleagues, but Gyula Lorant was an uncompromising stopper centre-half, well supported by the left-half, Zakarias, while Laszlo Budai and Zoltan Czibor sparkled on the wings with

their pace and control. In goal, Gyula Grosics was a thoroughly modern figure, always ready to dash out of his penalty area to operate as a virtual sweeper when his defence was breached.

So were the Hungarians irresistible? The answer, in short, was no, as was proved a few weeks before their Wembley victory by Sweden – a team managed, as it happened, by an Englishman. Little George Raynor – like Hogan a prophet without honour in his own country — carefully devised the kind of strategy England might have done well to use at Wembley, aimed at negating Hidegkuti's influence and exploiting the reluctance of Hungary's wingers to chase back for the ball. "If we win," Raynor told his team, "I'll paint the moustache on Stalin's statue red!" They didn't win, but as Raynor had forecast they forced a draw. Sebes blamed the English ball, chosen to prepare the Hungarians for Wembley. His players found it much too hard, but he ignored their pleas to change it at half-time.

A confident Billy Wright leads England on to the pitch. Puskas, his counterpart, looks tense. But assumptions of natural superiority were about to receive a rude awakening.

En route to England, the Hungarians stopped in Paris, encouraging themselves by scoring 13 goals against a Renault works team. When they flew into London they stayed not in training camp but right beside busy Marble Arch, at the Cumberland Hotel. There, Sebes would launch into a tactical briefing which seemed to go on forever, while the players looked increasingly bored and baffled. Puskas told his team to forget all about it.

Sebes's tactical influence was, in any case, a moot point. He was, after all, a political appointment, while the actual coach was a former international, Gyula Mandi, who has become something of an non-person in recent times. Mandi had interesting things to say about Hungary's modus operandi. Training, he said, was based on two

Above all, by contrast with so many Continental teams, Hungary could finish

chief principles: "technical training", which meant practice with the ball; and tactical knowledge. "A good football player," declared Mandi, "must know the best solution for a given situation. If he knows this, he can quickly size up the situation and speedily carry out the required solution, in agreement with his team-mates. No player is born with tactical knowledge: he must acquire it."

Close to the Cumberland, the Hungarians found a Czech restaurant with a Hungarian cook, and ate there regularly. The team were not allowed to train at Wembley, though they were permitted to tread the pitch. Training took place at the Queens Park Rangers ground in Shepherds Bush.

There was no euphoria among the Hungarians as their motorcoach took them to Wembley for the game, just "an indescribable tension in the air", according to right-back Buzansky, while Grosics said: "One could almost feel the fear and concern among us." Little was said.

Despite the lucky draw against Fifa, there was no general anticipation that

England's record was in peril. Frank Coles, sports editor of *The Daily Telegraph*, had written that any English championship team, struggling for points at the end of the season, would simply "run through" the Hungarian Olympic winners.

England made changes from the game against Fifa and one was forced. Tom Finney, one of the finest attackers of his generation, dropped out from the left wing and the ex-amateur George Robb was chosen in his place. This was not the decision of scholarly Walter Winterbottom, who in 1946 became England's first-ever manager, an appointment which would last 16 years. Winterbottom was always on a

"The first half was a shambles. We never knew who to mark"

hiding to nothing, since his team, ludicrously, was picked by a selection committee, then handed to him.

On the right wing was Stanley Matthews, who had inspired Blackpool to a famous FA Cup triumph six months earlier. Stan Mortensen, usually his partner at Blackpool, was lead-

ing the attack, with Jackie Sewell, whose £34,000 transfer from Notts County to Sheffield Wednesday had broken the record, at inside-left. Little Ernie Taylor, another Blackpool man, was inside-right. Billy Wright, as usual, captained the team from right-half. Centre-half Derek Ufton of Charlton, a debutant against Fifa, gave way to Harry Johnston, Blackpool's captain on that golden day in May.

Puskas looked tense as he exchanged pennants with Wright before the kick-off; his mood reflected that of the entire team. Earlier, he had tried to relax his team-mates by telling them that, in Taylor, England had a player even smaller than himself. Strangely, one of the most anxious players on the pitch was the most experienced of them all, the 38-year-old Matthews. "You must have butterflies," Matthews would say, but they seemed to plague him throughout a match in which he felt he never really took off.

"Wright went past him like a fire engine going to the wrong fire"

Less than a minute had been played when Jimmy Dickinson, England's capable left-half, put the ball out of play. With bewildering speed, it went from Bozsik to Hidegkuti, lying unmarked outside the penalty box. Two swerves and a side-step confused the English defence, giving Hidegkuti space to smash the ball past the helpless England keeper, Gil Merrick.

Sewell's equaliser after 13 minutes was a false dawn, although the inside left had no notion of this at the time. "We were going to win, there was no doubt about that because we hadn't been beat at home," he recalled 46 years on. "It was a case of just keeping fit, doing our normal things, and that was the thing in a nutshell. Nobody knew anything about them, did they? Walter Winterbottom hadn't got their team pinned down like the Austrian side [beaten by England in Vienna in 1952]. We thought, 'We'll be all right'."

They were not. Puskas, Czibor and Kocsis, with an inspired flick, enabled Hidegkuti to get his second. Then Puskas scored a coruscating third, when he pulled the ball back with the studs of his boot and, in the memorable words of Geoffrey Green of *The Times*, "Wright went past him like a fire engine going to the wrong fire". Puskas calls that goal "my favourite of all time". He saw Wright "on his way with an enormous lunging tackle, hurling himself at the ball". Had Puskas turned inside, "Wright would have taken me and the ball off the pitch and into the stands." Instead he pulled the ball back with his left, and with the same foot struck it between Merrick and the near post. Bozsik's deflected free kick made it 4-1 and, though Mortensen reduced the deficit, at half-time England were reeling.

"The first half was a shambles," Merrick remembered. "We never knew who to mark. As we walked off, Harry Johnston, said, 'I don't know what I'm

doing here, I haven't had a kick'. And he hadn't, because Hidegkuti had moved back 20 yards and left Harry marking nobody." Subsequently Johnston would claim he was never given instructions on how to deal with Hidegkuti. Now 86 and knighted, Winterbottom resents such criticism, insisting he had told Johnston exactly how Hidegkuti played and asking him if he wanted to follow his opponent or stay put. Johnston elected to stay put. "We were very subdued in the dressing room," said Sewell. "We just sat there." And Winterbottom's instructions? "He never said anything, did he? That was the problem." Winterbottom himself emphatically denies this.

In the Hungarian dressing room, words were not in such short supply. Puskas remembers they were saying: "Come on, we've got them, let's just relax and carry on playing." The first goal had given them "a fantastic feeling of confidence".

Early in the second half, after Merrick turned Czibor's header onto a post, Bozsik struck Hungary's fifth. Puskas's clever chip gave Hidegkuti his hat-trick. England did at least have the last word, if hardly the last laugh, when Robb broke through, was brought down by Grosics, and Alf Ramsey scored from the spot. Six-three, and some solace for Ramsey, who had had a most difficult game. "Their two wingers could catch pigeons," said Merrick. "Poor Alf didn't know which way to turn, because the little left winger was going by him like a train. Although we suffered, it was a privilege to play against them, to see football like that."

The Hungarians, said Puskas, reacted to their triumph with surprise and pleasure: "The match took an enormous amount out of all of us." Two days of celebration and adulation in Paris followed. The return by train through Hungary was a triumphal progress; flowers, applause and gifts at every station. Did England learn from their defeat? The following May, they played Hungary in Budapest – and lost 7-1.

Out cold: Hungarian keeper Grosics supports a groggy Stan Mortensen. It about summed up England's dire afternoon. Out-played and out-thought, they were left thoroughly dazed.

The miracle mile

On a wet and blustery afternoon in 1954, Roger Bannister, a junior doctor in London, climbed sport's Everest: he ran the world's first four-minute mile. It was a feat many thought impossible, "like trying to run through a brick wall". Bannister's achievement sent tremors through the sporting world. He had joined the immortals.

DAVID WALSH

Before we talk," he says, "I'll make coffee." And away he goes at the brisk pace of a man half his age. Though Bannister is now in his 70s, the years rest lightly. He returns with coffee, slices of chocolate sponge and again strikes the right chord: "I did write for *The Sunday Times*, you know, so we're sort of colleagues, aren't we? Of course, I still subscribe."

Venerable is the word for him nowadays. How can he make you feel more comfortable, how can he help? He was knighted for his services to sport and medicine in 1975 and it is the scholarly doctor that is now more easily recognised. Every observation comes with the precision of a trained mind; the worldly perspective is that of the esteemed neurologist and the former Master of Pembroke College. It is hard to find the runner.

By a large window there is a rocking chair. His transport to the past. What does he think when he eases back and then pushes gently forward? His beloved Moyra, their four children, 10 grandchildren, his career in neurology, the medical books through which he passed on what he had learned. But sometimes he must recall that evening of Thursday May 6 1954, when the clock stopped at 3min 59.4sec and he became Roger Bannister, the world's first four-minute miler.

The day had begun at St Mary's Hospital in London, where he was a junior houseman. But that morning, nothing mattered to Bannister except the evening's race at Oxford and his ambition to run it in less than four minutes. A year earlier Edmund Hillary and Tenzing Norgay became the first climbers to conquer Everest, and Bannister believed he could be first to overcome sport's equivalent.

After breakfast he sharpened his spikes on a grindstone at St Mary's and then rubbed graphite into them. He was like that: everything that could be done had to be done. Although the race was not due to begin until six o'clock, he walked the short distance to Paddington Station in plenty of time for the 11 o'clock train to Oxford.

Momentous events often happen in a way which suggests everything is preordained. On the platform he met Franz Stampfl, the Austrian who coached Bannister's close friend Chris Brasher and whom he had got to know the previous October. Stampfl always insisted Bannister could break four minutes and, even though each knew the other was going to Oxford that day, the meeting at Paddington was entirely accidental. Naturally the conversation turned to the evening's race.

Bannister pointed to the grey sky and rising wind; he didn't think they could do it in the conditions. He said "they" because the plan involved his friends Brasher and Chris Chataway acting as pacemakers. Stampfl said the wind would cost Bannister two seconds, no more, and as he was capable of running 3min 56sec he could still do it. "Roger," Stampfl said, "if you have the chance and don't take it, you may

The history makers: Chris Brasher leads Bannister through the first half-mile at Iffley Road, Oxford. Behind them, Chris Chataway waits to take up the pace before leaving Bannister to make the final draining push to the line.

never forgive yourself. Sure, it'll be painful but what's pain?"

"What is pain?" Bannister thought to himself. He knew Stampfl's story: interned because he was Austrian at the start of the Second World War, he went on hunger strike in prison and was eventually put on a ship to Canada. It was torpedoed and Stampfl and hundreds of others had to jump overboard. All around him he saw men praying and then giving up. Why didn't they fight? Most perished within an hour and Stampfl spent eight hours in the water before being rescued. "This man had done something," Bannister would later say, by way of acknowledging the effect of Stampfl's encouragement.

The aspiration to run the mile in under four minutes had preyed on the minds of the world's top middle-distance runners since the Swede Gundar Hägg ran 4min 1.4sec nine years earlier. They all felt it was possible. The Australian John Landy had come closest since Hägg, running 4min 2sec, but he heightened the barrier by saying that getting inside four minutes was like trying to break through a brick wall. The challenge was as much psychological as physical.

Time wasn't on Bannister's side.

Immortality attained: eyes closed, head flailing, mouth gasping, Bannister crosses the line and runs into the history books.

Favourite to win the 1500m at the Helsinki Olympics in 1952, he finished fourth. Soon afterwards he wrote to Chataway, with whom he had roomed in Helsinki, suggesting how the four-minute mile might be cracked. But it didn't happen in 1952 or 1953 and with Bannister determined to concentrate on his medical career the 1954 season was his last chance.

It has always been easy to form the wrong impression about Bannister. However mild-mannered and scholarly away from the track, he was extra-ordinarily intense on it. A team-mate said he could be heard making noises in his sleep on the night before a race, as if he was being tortured: "Then when he goes out to run, he looks like a man going to the electric chair." In many races, Bannister ran to the threshold of unconsciousness.

Through the winter of 1953–4, he trained with Chataway and Brasher, the three building themselves up through sessions of 10 440s with a two-minute interval between each. They drove each other, the indomitable Brasher believing hard work would conquer everything, Chataway more pragmatic but a fighter nevertheless. Of the three, Bannister was the one with the speed to break the four-minute barrier and because the others recognised this they agreed to be his pacemakers.

Athletes, though, cannot easily suspend their competitive instincts. Chataway and Brasher considered an ending to the mile race in Oxford that Bannister would never have foreseen. "It was absurd," said Brasher, "but the night before the race Chris and I were thinking we would do our pacemaking job and then latch on to Bannister before taking him in the straight. I mean, it was bloody ludicrous, but it tells you something about the mind of the athlete. You've got to believe it is possible."

Brasher believed the four-minute mile would happen in Oxford. Before leaving London he reserved a table for the celebration dinner at the Royal Court Theatre Club that evening, telling their three girlfriends to be ready for a late night. He travelled to Oxford with Chataway; two servants who shortened the journey with thoughts of subversion.

Bannister's fears about the weather deepened as the day progressed. "The wind was gusting, it was a dank, wet, cold and miserable day," recalled Norris McWhirter, one of the meeting's organisers. "One was very conscious that the attempt was on the edge of possibility and in the conditions it

seemed it would be unwise to try." McWhirter had encouraged the BBC to cover the meeting, all of the athletics writers were there and when Milton Marmar, an American journalist based in London, called to ask if it was worth his while, McWhirter told him to come along. Twenty minutes before the start, the attempt hung in the balance. Stampfl and Brasher thought it should go ahead, Chataway was philosophical, Bannister undecided.

After a relaxing afternoon in Oxford with his friend Charles Wenden, Bannister's mood changed as the race neared. An hour before the start, he looked out from the old

"What is pain?" Bannister had mused before the race. For an undoubted thoroughbred of the track, even at the moment of supreme success Bannister seemed to have reached beyond the limits of human endurance.

Victorian pavilion at the track to the St George's flag straining on its pole on the tower of Iffley Road church. The wind was too strong. Bannister feared an unsuccessful attempt would lessen the chances of running the first four-minute mile in the following weeks. He sensed Brasher and Chataway grow slightly impatient, though they said nothing. Then, shortly before six o'clock, it stopped raining and the skies cleared. A double rainbow appeared. Bannister looked again for the St George's flag. For the first time all afternoon, it hung limply. Bannister conferred with Brasher, Chataway and Stampfl: the record was on.

Into the home stretch his body pleaded for him to slow but his spirit impelled him to go on

Brasher's impatience caused him to make a false start but, called back by the starter, seconds later they were on their way. As planned, Brasher set the pace, Bannister in second place, Chataway third. McWhirter had got the local electrician to erect two speakers, one on either side of the track, and as the race announcer he could inform the athletes of their times for every quarter. Brasher ran the first 220 in a fraction over 27 seconds, which was quick. Bannister misheard the early announcements. "Faster, faster!" he shouted at Brasher. But the hare understood more than the hound. "Without getting on my toes and sprinting, I was going as fast as I could. It had to be right," said Brasher. At 1min 58sec for the half-mile, the pace was right.

For three intelligent men they had made an important mistake in deciding the order should be Brasher, Bannister and then Chataway. As Brasher tired, Chataway had to run round Bannister to get to the front, an unnecessary imposition for the second pacemaker. Chataway was at full stretch to take the lead but, running on guts, he took Bannister to 260 yards from the finish and left him within reach of the target.

They had offered Bannister the chance to race in the way that only he could. No matter how tough the pace, Bannister could produce a sustained sprint over the final 200 yards of a race. It was this kick which separated him from his contemporaries. He accelerated past Chataway and ran the last 240 yards on his own. Into the home stretch his body pleaded for him to slow but his spirit impelled him to go on.

The winning moment is perfectly captured in the photograph of the wasted Bannister breasting the tape. Everything he had went into the performance, the sharpened spikes as visible as the gasping mouth. Wenden, official recorder for the meeting, has his hand over his face, unable to look up.

For the record to be ratified, three of the timekeepers had to agree on the winning time. Each one stopped his watch at precisely 3min

59.4sec. Bannister fell into the arms of the Rev Nicholas Stacey and McWhirter moved like a practiced impresario to the centre of the stage. "Ladies and Gentlemen, here is the result of Event No 9, the one mile. First, No 41 R G Bannister of the AAA and formerly of Exeter and Merton colleges, with a time which is a new meeting and track record and which, subject to ratification, will be a new English native, British national and British all-comers', European, British Empire and world record. The time is three . . ." Nothing else was heard as public acclamation rolled like a tidal wave over McWhirter's final words.

Soon recovered, Bannister went to old Walter Morris, the Iffley Road groundsman, and thanked him for having the track in such fine shape. He told journalists that it had been a team effort, that without Brasher and Chataway it could not have happened. McWhirter then took Bannister to the Vincent's club on Oxford's High Street, where sport's newest legend celebrated with a glass of water sprinkled

More than four decades on Sir Roger, distinguished academic and doctor, relives the momentous day in his Oxford study.

with sugar and salt. Word filtered through to that evening's meeting of the Oxford Union and the president interrupted proceedings: "Gentlemen, Roger Bannister has run a four-minute mile, we shall adjourn for three minutes, 59.4 seconds."

Bannister's run sent tremors through the sports world. Marmar was sure glad he showed up; next day his by-lined story was on the front page of 1,600 American newspapers. Olympic historian David Wallechinsky would later describe Bannister's run as "probably the greatest day in track and field history".

On the morning after the race, 13-year-old Martin Nicholson turned up at Risley's shop in Chingford, Essex, to do his paper round. Interested in athletics, Nicholson used to worry that Landy would beat Bannister to the four-minute mile. He didn't know of Bannister's attempt the previous night and as he picked up his bundle of newspapers the front page of the *Daily Mirror* boomed: "Bannister Does It".

Nicholson's fascination for the achievement remains. At an auction, he bid for the stopwatch of Charlie Hill, one of the timekeepers that evening. Having gone to more than £7,500, he surrendered to Jeffrey Archer. Later, he wrote to Archer, saying he would love to see the watch and suggesting gently it might mean more to him than anybody else. Archer sold the watch to Nicholson for the amount of his last bid.

Bannister, Brasher and Chataway have remained good friends and meet each year with their wives on the anniversary of the Iffley Road run. They don't discuss sport like they used to but it would be a strange reunion if they didn't at least touch upon it. In May 1999, Brasher told his friends of something recently remembered about Franz Stampfl. Assessing a coach who was good but not quite the best, Stampfl said, "I do not think he has the ability to make a man go past the point at which he thinks he is going to die." Bannister and Chataway would have chewed over that – and understood.

Laker the destroyer

In an extraordinary Ashes Test at Old Trafford, Jim Laker span his way into cricket history, taking all 10 Australian wickets in the second innings and 19 in the match overall. His feat, unequalled in Test cricket, was not without controversy: jealousy of Laker in the England team and Australian suspicions of a doctored pitch.

SIMON WILDE

Shortly after 5.30pm on Tuesday July 31 1956, a crowd gathered beneath the England balcony at Old Trafford, Manchester, waiting for a glimpse of the man of the hour. For a day of history-making, it was a small gathering, but weather-wise this was a benighted summer. Inside the dressing room the champagne was being uncorked. Not for the first time that day, Jim Laker judged the situation to perfection. Passing on the champagne, he filled his glass with Lucozade, who were sponsoring him that year. Only then did he go on to the balcony to salute the public.

Laker came late to sporting immortality. He was 34 and had spent years as a downtrodden professional. Some said it sullied his character. Certainly it instilled a sense of his own worth. His fee for playing in this Test match was just £75. He would now make another £1,000 from newspaper articles and other spin-offs, while the greatest bowling performance in history would swell his benefit fund to £11,000.

The celebrations were brief, for the players had fixtures to fulfil, but one of his team-mates had changed and left in the time it took Laker to wave from the balcony, pose for photographs and return. Of the 20 Australian wickets to fall, Tony Lock had taken only one to Laker's 19. "Nobody felt more humiliated," Sir Colin Cowdrey recalled.

Laker and Lock were due in London where Surrey were to play the Australians the next day. They did not travel together.

Of all the contributory factors to Laker's feat, the failure of temperament by his spinning partner was the most significant. Ian Johnson's Australians were no vintage outfit, nor were they versed in dealing with high-class off-spin, and they rightly suspected that the pitch was tailored to beggar their chances. Lock should have capitalised.

This was no ordinary pair of spinners. Except in their fierce desire for wickets, Laker and Lock were different characters. Laker was self-effacing but self-assured, proud and highly gifted. Though Yorkshire-born, he cultivated his talents with Surrey at The Oval. He spun the ball like a top (Richie Benaud said it could be heard buzzing through

Self-possessed and supremely self-confident, Laker was Yorkshire reserve personified. Even at the moment of his greatest triumph, his celebrations consisted of nothing more demonstrative than a hitch of his trousers and a return to his bowling mark. (Right), walking off the pitch at Old Trafford.

the air), possessed wonderful control and had a cool brain.

Lock, his junior by seven years, was as rough at the edges as Laker was smooth. A country boy from Limpsfield, he was eager to make his presence felt among the sharp metropolitans. First impressions were that he would not amount to much as a bowler. It was only after remodelling his action that he did more than roll his left-armers, but there were mutterings about legitimacy and Laker, seeing his ally turn the ball even more than himself, was among the sceptics.

"He [Lock] projected himself differently from his natural self, which cut across the grain with some people," Micky Stewart, a Surrey colleague, remembered. "Lockie tried to cultivate the social niceties but didn't

Not for the first time that day, Laker judged the situation to perfection

have the ability. Jim made him ill at ease. He might have got up Lockie's nose at times."

Whatever their differences, Laker and Lock enjoyed great success together for county and country. Although Laker was not an automatic selection for England – off-spin had been out of fashion and he did not endear himself to the game's establishment – it was recognised that he posed a threat to the 1956 Australians and from the outset had smothered them with his science.

In Surrey's first match against them in May, he became the first English bowler for three-quarters of a century to take all 10 (for 88) against an Australian side and in the three preceding Tests took 20 wickets, 11 of them on a dry, dusty surface in the previous game at Leeds, where England had levelled the series.

Lock also played his part. He was displeased that a catch was deliberately dropped off him to enable Laker to take all 10, but two days before the third Test Lock emulated this rare feat against Kent. His 10 for 54 left him well placed to collect a £100 prize for the season's best figures. On a turning pitch, the Australians looked nervous and impetuous and there was a feeling that England's spinners could expose them further.

The day before the game, Bert Flack, the Old Trafford groundsman, was approached by a group including Gubby Allen, chairman of the England selectors. Rain had played havoc with his preparations and the marl was not properly bound into the surface. Things were about to get worse. For 40 years, until Allen and Laker were dead, Flack kept secret details of the conversation that followed. Allen, taking his first look at the pitch, asked for more grass to be removed. Flack was indignant: "That's stupid. The match won't last three days. The surface is not all that well-knit." But he did as requested, before hastily putting on the covers. Asked by England players why the pitch was covered, Flack curtly replied: "We're expecting rain." It was a bright afternoon.

With a subtly different account, Allen, who would have known that it was permissible only for the ground authority to involve itself in pitch preparation, always denied skuldug-

Fierce concentration and a metronomic action: Laker spins his way into cricket's pantheon. Though the pitch helped, his bowling was astonishingly reliable that day.

gery. He claimed the idea of taking off more grass came from the chairman of the grounds committee. "It wouldn't break my heart," was Allen's supposed reply, "but ask the groundsman, not me." But for the Australians there was never any doubt: he had been up to mischief.

They were thus disillusioned from the outset, especially after Peter May won the toss. England spent four sessions amassing 459, with the Rev David Sheppard making a hundred in his first Test since his ordination. The pitch, infuriatingly lifeless for Keith Miller and Ray Lindwall, turned on the first day, but Johnson, with his off-spin, and Benaud, bowling leg-breaks, failed to take advantage.

At first, Australia prospered. The roller had subdued the turf and Colin McDonald and Jimmy Burke saw off Brian Statham and Trevor Bailey with the new ball. Then, after 40 minutes, battle was engaged in earnest; Laker and Lock came on. For half an hour nothing much happened, so May switched them around, Laker taking the Stretford End from which he would claim all his wickets. Soon, he made the breach. Coming over the wicket, his flight unsettled McDonald, who feathered a catch to Lock in the leg trap. Immediately, Laker added the prize wicket of the left-handed Neil Harvey, who had led the resistance at Leeds and had had the better of him in the past.

Laker was delighted: "I managed to bowl him a beauty first ball. From around the wicket, I held it back sufficiently for the ball to drift in and around the leg and middle stumps. It turned just enough to clip his off stump." Harvey gave the pitch a withering stare. Of all his wickets, Laker treasured this most.

He felt it marked a turning point, though Lock, understandably, made special claim for removing Burke, who pushed the first ball after tea to slip. Burke had coped well but, incredibly, Australia's innings would be over within eight overs. Unfortunately for Lock, the last seven wickets all fell to Laker in 22 balls.

This sensational collapse paved the way for the historic feat. The Australians tried to hit Laker off his length, with the result that they were in thrall to him thereafter. Lock grew impatient to get in on the act. But if the Australians and Lock stopped using their brains, Laker, to his eternal glory, continued to use his.

Chillingly calm, he dropped ball after ball on the spot. Round the wicket to the right-hander, he looked to curve or float the ball, before turn-

ing it into the batsman and towards an array of close-up leg-side fielders. "We could get in close," said Alan Oakman, who held five catches, "because Jim was so accurate." What was the best response? The forward prod, bat tucked behind front pad, had yet to be invented; anyone looking to get down the pitch would be forced back as Laker quickened his pace.

Australia subsided from 48 for no wicket to 84 all out. Laker took nine for 37 in eight overs. His figures were the best in Ashes history but survived as such for four days. Before batting again, Johnson tried to persuade his side they could still save the game. Miller, momentarily detaching himself from the race form, said: "Bet you 6-4 we can't." The Australian captain did not believe it either. Asked by Flack which roller he wanted, he replied: "Please your effing self."

For the second time that afternoon, McDonald and Burke gave their side a solid start, before luck again favoured England. McDonald retired with knee trouble and Harvey drove his first ball straight to Cowdrey at short midwicket – Laker, trying too hard, had served him a full toss. Uttering a cry of despair, Harvey tossed his bat high: he had made a pair in little more than an hour. Australia closed on 53 for one.

That Friday evening, Laker was joined by his wife, Lilly. He met her at Warrington station, trailed by photog-

Chillingly calm, he dropped ball after ball on the spot

raphers. "Good Lord," she said, unaware of events at Old Trafford, "what on earth have you been up to?" She stayed until Sunday evening; both would regret she did not remain another 48 hours.

Had the Manchester weather held, Mrs Laker might have witnessed a conclusion, but that night a storm broke. Play was confined to 45 minutes on Saturday, during which Australia scored six and Burke provided Laker with his 11th wicket. The pitch, uncovered during scheduled hours, was now wet and altered in character.

The atrocious conditions threatened to deny England victory. It allowed less than an hour's play on Monday and deadened the pitch.

Laker was even taken off, and although the weather improved on the last day McDonald, fit again, and Craig battled through the first session. They had been together for four hours and England were getting desperate. Laker lunched alone in the dressing room and was reinvigorated. "As I gazed out towards the Derbyshire hills," he said, "the clouds began to disappear and the sun broke through." As the turf dried, the ball began to spin.

It was on this final afternoon that Lock was most culpable. "Some said he was bowling so well that the Australians could not get a touch," said Laker. "In fact, he wasn't bowling well; he was pushing them through too quick, tending to be a bit short." Bailey was more scathing: "Lock bowled badly and got upset. Laker was getting all the wickets. The more annoyed Lock got, the faster he bowled. It was a wicket which took spin if you did not bowl too fast." Oakman does not remember him having a catch dropped, a stumping missed – or a word to say: "He could sulk a bit."

Laker, meanwhile, had embarked on another devastating spell. In quick succession he removed the stubborn Craig, Mackay, Miller and Ron Archer in nine overs for three runs, to leave Australia 130 for six. But then Benaud stayed until tea and May was obliged to juggle his bowlers. Laker and Lock were restored to their favoured ends and, after tea, the ball turned more sharply.

With his second ball after the interval, Laker finally induced an error from McDonald, who, after five and a half hours of intense concentration, became another victim to the leg trap. The tail indulged in every time-wasting tactic in the book but, amid rising tension, Benaud, Lindwall and then, to a rousing cheer, Len Maddocks fell in turn to Laker. Johnson was the first to congratulate him.

Although England won with an hour to spare, it was a close-run thing. They were dependent on their spinners to finish the job and both were tiring. Lock sent down 69 overs in the match, Laker 68. Had there been less urgency, doubtless

The Australians looked nervous and impetuous. There was a feeling that England's spinners could expose them further

efforts would have been made to help Laker to complete Test cricket's first all-10. But contrivance was out of the question. Laker walked off, sweater flung over shoulder, showing so little emotion that the enormity of what he had achieved cannot have sunk in.

John Arlott's BBC radio commentary captured the final scene: "Now, here's the avenue forming up for Laker there as May pushes him ahead to go in first into the pavilion.

It all went horribly wrong for Tony Lock at Old Trafford. Goaded by Laker's continuing and extraordinary success, Lock lost the lot: his control, his line, his length – and his temper. Team-mates or not, Lock would not easily forgive Laker for stealing his thunder.

All the members standing, waving their score cards, standing up on the balcony, leaning down and applauding him, as he runs up the pavilion steps in through that crowd and is followed into the pavilion. And there's friends of mine who said they weren't going to come today, they thought it might rain. Well, I admit it did look as if it was going to rain. They missed a very great piece of bowling."

It was Lindwall's wicket that provided the record; previously, nobody had taken more than 17 wickets in a first-class match. Again, there was little fuss. It fell to the unfortunate Lock to complete the catch; he just folded his arms. Sydney Barnes, the previous Test record-holder, was at the ground, his usual gruff self: "No bugger ever got all 10 when I was at t'other end."

"Well bowled, Tony," May said to Lock. "Forget the scorebook. You played your part, too." But Lock found it hard to forget the scorebook. For one thing, Laker had taken 10 for 53, one run cheaper than Lock's return against Kent. On top of everything else, Laker had deprived him of £100.

Laker's name became famous overnight but, with television less pervasive, his face took longer to become familiar. Driving home, he stopped at a pub in Lichfield where, in the crowded bar, a tiny black-and-white television was showing highlights of the day's play. He went unrecognised. It was late before he got home, but waiting up for him were his family – and photographers.

After little sleep, he must have been grateful that play was washed out at The Oval. Lancashire's groundsman was also thankful for a quiet day: "Thank God Nasser has taken over the Suez Canal. Otherwise, I'd be plastered over every front page like Marilyn Monroe." In fact, Laker's bowling was so stupendous the pitch controversy was forgotten – by Englishmen, if not Australians.

Maestro of the Nurburgring

At the 1957 German Grand Prix, the peerless Argentinian driver Juan Manuel Fangio, already a four-time world champion, faced a fearsome challenge. Coming from far behind, he pushed his Maserati to the very limit, surging past the rival Ferraris on the last laps to claim his most spectacular victory.

ALASDAIR REID

In the contest to be considered the greatest racing driver of all time, only a handful of individuals make it to the start line and fewer still to the finish. Too many are disqualified by flaws of character, by their failure to stack up hard achievements, or by the fact they never produced the single, signature drive that was the ultimate demonstration of their talent. When all the criteria are taken into account, the podium belongs, unassailably, to one man.

Juan Manuel Fangio won the Formula One world championship for drivers five times between 1951 and 1957, delivering the title to four different manufacturers. He won 24 of the 51 grands prix he contested, started 28 of them in pole position and 48 from the front row of the grid, and set the fastest race lap on 23 occasions. Yet all through his career he was renowned as much for his dignity, humility and warmth as his astonishing driving ability.

All this in an era when Formula One was, quite literally, a game of death and glory. In the nine years he raced in Europe, 30 of Fangio's fellow drivers were killed in racing accidents and he was also close witness to the horror at Le Mans in 1955 when the Mercedes of Pierre Levegh crashed into the crowd and killed 80 spectators. In that context, survival was an achievement in itself. Fangio was, unquestionably, an astute and peerless tactician in the face of awesome danger.

Born in Balcarce, a country town 250 miles south of Buenos Aires, in 1911, Fangio had honed his stamina, skills and mechanical sensitivity in the marathon city-to-city races that wound for thousands of miles through South America in the 1940s. In 1949, at the age of 38, he travelled to Europe and won a clutch of non-championship races in a Maserati that, with the personal sponsorship of President Juan Peron, had been entered by the Argentine Automobile Club. He was signed by Alfa Romeo for Formula One's first world championship the following year, finishing second behind his Italian team-mate, Guiseppe Farina.

He took his first title with Alfa Romeo the next year, 1951, and four more in straight succession between 1954 and 1957, twice with Mercedes and once each with Ferrari and Maserati. He was usually the oldest man on the grid, yet always the one that other competitors feared most. His greatest talent was his sheer relentlessness, the ability to concentrate for lap after lap as he ground down rivals with the consistency of his pace and line. And when the occasion demanded, he could always find that little bit more.

Fangio's stature in the era of the heroic amateur arose from the fact he could probably be considered the sport's first true professional. He engineered his ascendancy by ensuring that he was in the best car and that his

His greatest talent was his sheer relentlessness

race strategy had been calculated to oblige others to indulge in feats of derring-do in his wake. He rarely had to play catch-up, so it is almost ironic that the race which is remembered as his finest ever should have seen him do just that.

Fangio had won the world championship for Enzo Ferrari in 1956, but the relationship between the two men was neither warm nor close. Fangio secured the title by finishing second in the last race of the season, at Monza, but he was too mature an individual to deliver the obsequious flattery that Ferrari demanded of his drivers and was more than happy to leave the Maranello team when his work was done. At the end of the year, having turned down an offer from the fast-emerging British team Vanwall, he signed for Maserati.

Fangio considered retirement, but he enjoyed a close personal friendship with Count Adolfo Orsi, the Maserati team patron. More pragmatically, Fangio also saw that the Maserati 250F, recognised now as one of the finest grand prix cars ever, was approaching the peak of a development curve which had begun four years earlier. Having been disappointed by the car Ferrari had given him the previous season, he saw the superbly engineered 250F as the vehicle most likely to secure his fourth successive drivers' title.

"They had changed the 250F model considerably since I first drove them," he was later to say. "The car was lighter, had a bit more power and had ended up very well balanced. You could do what you liked in that sort of car. It was nicely poised, responsive, fast and suited my driving style."

Fangio's judgement was vindicated by a rather fortuitous victory in the Argentinian Grand Prix, the first of the season, in January 1957. After a long break, the world championship resumed in May at Monaco, where he won again. The French Grand Prix, at Rouen, gave him an easy third victory and a healthy

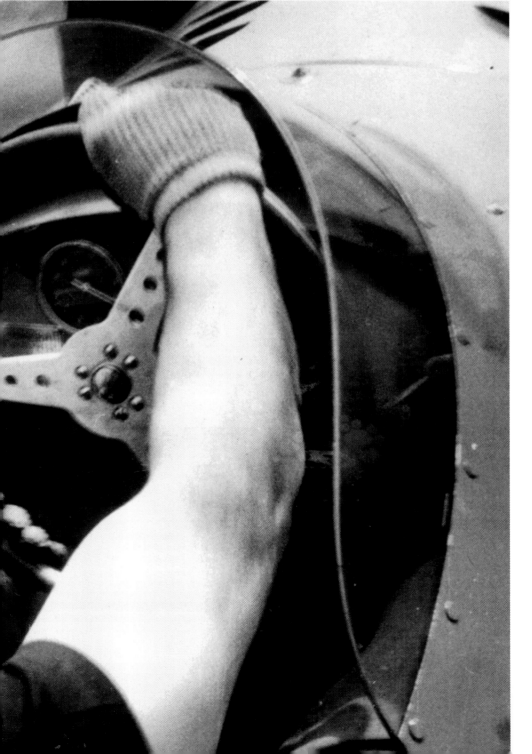

Fangio at the wheel of his Maserati 250F, one of the finest grand prix cars ever. Fangio joined the team to have chance to drive it and to win his fifth drivers' championship.

enough lead in the championship to survive his retirement from the British Grand Prix at Aintree.

But the greatest challenge in motor racing, the awesome Nurburgring, lay ahead. Fangio had won the German Grand Prix there in 1954 and 1956, and had twice finished second, but he recognised the uniquely arduous test that the circuit presented. Set in the Eifel mountains, its 14-mile length included 175 corners, vicious dips, gradients, surface-changes and blind summits. Fangio was the acknowledged master of the Ring, having set the lap record there at just over 9min 40sec the previous year, but he knew its perils and pitfalls as well.

He knew, as well, that Ferrari had been working hard to overcome the reliability problems that had beset the cars of Peter Collins and Mike Hawthorn, their two young English drivers, earlier in the season. Vanwall, who had just claimed their first-ever grand-prix victory at Aintree with a car shared by Stirling Moss and Tony Brooks, also posed a threat. The Maserati had an acknowledged handling edge, but the Nurburgring seemed better suited to the strength and raw power of the Ferraris.

Fangio set the fastest time in practice for the race, slashing 26 seconds off the pole time he had established the previous year, a mea-

sure of the speed of Formula One development through the 1950s as well as the Argentinian's skill. But his pace was almost more than his car could handle and the Maserati mechanics twice had to replace suspension components to keep it running. The

> ## "He knew he would have to drive absolutely on the limit to make up the time"

Vanwalls were well off the pace, while Ferrari, for whom Hawthorn had set a time only three seconds slower than Fangio's, seemed happiest with their efforts as practice drew to a close.

"While there are many people who know every bump and curve, every ascent and descent, and every blind throw with absolute certainty, applying this knowledge to conducting a grand prix car round the circuit at the very limit of tyre adhesion is another story". So wrote Denis Jenkinson, the renowned grand prix correspondent of *Motor Sport*, in his report of the Nurburgring race.

Guerrino Bertocchi, chief race mechanic and test driver for Maserati, recognised the problem. Bertocchi doubted whether the delicate 250F would last the distance of more than 300 miles on the Nurburgring's twisting, abrasive surface, especially in the warm and dry conditions. Boldly, he

decided that Fangio should start with a half-tank of petrol and stop for fuel and tyres at half-distance. Pit-stops were not unknown at that time, but it was a brave and unusual strategy.

The Ferraris would run non-stop from start to finish. When the race began, at 1.15pm and in front of a crowd of 200,000, Hawthorn and Collins blasted from the line and Hawthorn immediately posted a standing-start lap time of 9min 42.5sec, barely two seconds slower than Fangio's best from the year before. Fangio bided his time in third place, bedding in his tyres, before sweeping past the Ferraris at the start of lap three after lowering the lap record to 9min 34.6sec on his second circuit.

"The fantastic Fangio was in his element with so many fast corners and descents and increased his lead by seven seconds a lap from Hawthorn and Collins, who were in close formation," wrote Jenkinson. With Fangio driving at the limit of his powers, grazing the apexes and exits of the Nurburgring's unforgiving bends as he extracted every ounce of power and grip from the Maserati, the lap record was lowered five more times as he built the half-minute lead Bertocchi had calculated was required for the pit-stop tactic to work. When he pulled in at the end of lap 12, he was 28 seconds ahead of the Ferraris.

As Fangio stepped from the car to change his goggles, however, his mechanics, inexplicably, made a total mess of the refuelling and tyre change. The Maserati was stationary for 52 seconds and when he returned to the track Fangio was almost three-quarters of a minute behind the two English drivers. The race, it seemed, was over and there were celebrations in the Ferrari camp as Fangio, heavy with fuel and bedding in his tyres again, made no headway into their drivers' lead over the next three laps.

"He knew he would have to drive absolutely on the limit to make up the time," recalled Brooks, who was to win the race the following year. "It's one thing to do that with the cars and circuits we have today, but it was a totally different matter then, as cars fell apart in accidents and there were no trackside safety features whatsoever. Fangio was so far behind after his stop that, even allowing for his reputation, nobody thought he could make up the deficit."

Fangio takes the chequered flag to win the German Grand Prix at the Nurburgring. He made up a deficit of 45 seconds in just 10 laps to claim his astonishing victory.

Life in the slow lane: Juan Fangio, seen with his long-time partner Doña Andreina in February 1958. Fangio was the sport's first true professional. Yet his astute and ruthless tactical sense was combined with a rare dignity and humility.

lost only one more second on that final lap, but his defiance was fruitless. Fangio, known for his poker-faced magnanimity in victory, flew over the line with a broad grin.

Stirling Moss, who finished fifth in his troublesome Vanwall, has no doubt the 1957 German Grand Prix was the ultimate exhibition by Formula One's greatest-ever exponent: "Fangio, to my mind, was the finest driver who ever lived," said Moss. "What he did that day was a clearer demonstration of his skill than any, especially on such a difficult circuit. Fangio was in a class of his own, the only man who could produce a performance like that."

Moss doubts whether Fangio's motivation was heightened by his rancorous relationship with Ferrari, but Brooks believes it may have had a bearing. "He had certainly parted with Ferrari on less than good terms, so it would be reasonable to think that it gave him a big high to thrash their two best drivers," said Brooks. "I don't think Hawthorn and Collins could believe what had happened. They must have eased off and left it too late to get going again. They were just unable to resist Fangio that day and they were shattered by the experience."

It was a sensational win, made poignant by the fact it was also his last. Victory at the Nurburgring gave Fangio the points to secure the 1957 world championship, but he finished second to Moss in the two remaining grands prix of the season. Hawthorn went on to take the title the following year, before being killed in a traffic accident a few weeks later. By then, Collins, too, was dead, the result of an accident at the Nurburgring in 1958.

Sensing that his powers and his commitment to racing were waning, and struggling with an under-powered Maserati, Fangio retired after only two races of the 1958 season. His last race was the Italian Grand Prix, at Monza, where he could only finish fourth. Hawthorn, the victor, had a chance to lap him as they approached the finish. As a final tribute to the maestro, the Englishman backed off.

But he did. While Collins and Hawthorn eased off, confident that victory had been secured, Fangio took himself to the limit again, reducing the gap to 33 seconds by the end of lap 16. With no radio communication, the Ferrari team were unable to relay the message of Fangio's charge to their drivers until the end of the following lap, by which time another five seconds had been eaten out of their lead.

Serenity, it was once said, was the hallmark of Fangio's customary style, but he reined in the Englishmen with

icy aggression. The lap record fell and fell again, and by the end of the 18th lap, the Argentinian having lowered it to 9min 23.4sec, the gap was down to 13.5 seconds. When Hawthorn and Collins crossed the line at the end of the 20th lap, Fangio was only three seconds behind. He quickly swept past Collins and, with a lap and-a-half remaining, overtook Hawthorn at the Breidscheid, the lowest point on the course.

There was uproar in the stands and despair in the Ferrari pits as Fangio began the last lap three seconds ahead of Hawthorn. Creditably, Hawthorn

December 1960

The titanic Test

By the early Sixties, Test cricket had reached a sterile dead end. But in an explosively tense match between Australia and the West Indies at Brisbane, the game received an electric charge of excitement. A dramatic match played at full-throttle throughout came to an astonishing climax with the Test cricket's first tie.

SIMON WILDE

When Australia and West Indies met for the first of five Tests in Brisbane in December 1960, cricket was at one of its lowest ebbs, an increasingly drab game played at a snail's pace by teams whose fear of defeat conquered all. The previous Test in Brisbane, when England were the visitors, had been one of the dullest on record. But five days of see-saw cricket, and a finish that would be almost impossible to better, were about to change all that. Later claims that the captains, Richie Benaud and Frank Worrell, set out to revitalise the game have been exaggerated. As Benaud admits, his immediate reaction was bitter disappointment that Australia had had victory snatched from their grasp. And in fact the two had met only briefly – first when Worrell changed planes on arrival in Sydney and Benaud, at the Australian board's instigation, went to greet him; second, when New South Wales played the West Indians and Benaud's sense of hospitality did not stop him from leading the state to a crushing victory.

Unhesitatingly, the Australian press wrote off West Indies, who had stuck to character in the warm-ups by playing brilliantly one day, head-shakingly bad the next. To add to his problems, Worrell was under pressure as the first black man to lead West Indies abroad. Having damaged a muscle, he was also nearly unfit to play in Brisbane. So was Benaud, who had had flu.

If anyone called for a sea-change in attitudes it was Sir Donald Bradman, chairman of the Australian board. On the eve of the Test, he spoke to the Australian team. "We had no idea what he was going to say," Benaud recalled, "but it was that the selectors, Jack Ryder, Dudley Seddons and he, would be looking in kindly fashion on players who provided entertainment rather than thinking of themselves. Although he didn't say it, they would also be looking in unkindly fashion on those who didn't listen to what he had said."

Who knows whether these words made a difference? What is certain is that two exceptional leaders played throughout to win. There were times on the last, emotion-swept day when either could have opted for the draw but did not. The upshot was what Benaud describes it as "the most breathtaking cricket happening I'd ever been through".

Before approaching its dramatic climax (and unlike Test cricket's second tie – between India and Australia in Madras in 1986), the game took several twists and turns from the moment West Indies won the toss, chose to bat and set off like a runaway train. For four days the contest was at worst absorbing, at best breathtaking, while broadly giving the impression that it was moving towards an expected Australian victory.

The Australians knew West Indies would be entertaining, but the way Worrell's batsmen attacked on the first day must have taken them aback. Benaud's bowlers countered fire with

The final and decisive run out. Meckiff just fails to make his ground and is beaten by Solomon's brilliant direct hit. Pandemonium duly ensued.

To Benaud it was "the most breathtaking cricket happening I'd ever been through"

fire by attacking their strokemakers, but even though Alan Davidson, the versatile left-arm swing bowler, claimed three early wickets West Indies just kept on coming. Worrell and Gary Sobers put on 100 in 90 minutes and 174 in all. Staggeringly, 200 was on the board before half past two.

Sobers launched an astonishing assault. In the past Benaud's googly had troubled him; now he blazed his way to 132. It was hailed as one of the finest innings in memory and particu-

larly impressed Bradman, who would be instrumental in Sobers's signing for South Australia the next year. With the lower order wagging vigorously, West Indies totalled 453 at the extraordinary rate of 4.5 runs per eight-ball over.

Australia's reply was less colourful, but still brisk. Thanks chiefly to 92 from Bob Simpson and 181 from Norm O'Neill, whose slide from youthful musketeer to seasoned accumulator had been among the most depressing features of the times, they

built a lead of 52. But with several catches going begging, West Indies should have done better and when the visitors reached the fourth day's close on 259 for nine – Worrell and little Joe Solomon alone showing solidity after others had displayed suicidal tendencies – their chance seemed to have gone. It was a view reflected by a last-day crowd of just 4,100. But they were about to see expectation turned on its head several times and history made.

Wes Hall, the muscular and mesmerising fast bowler from Barbados, would be a central figure. His last-wicket stand with Alf Valentine, ended when Davidson

bowled Hall, subtly altered the equation by extending Australia's target to 233 and using up 40 minutes of playing time. Then he struck with the ball.

Hall was in his pomp as fast bowler. Arguably he was the best in the world and surely the quickest. He did not swing the ball but his height meant batsmen constantly fended good-length deliveries from their ribs – and he liked to use the bouncer. Now, he produced a lion-hearted effort, removing Simpson for nought and then Neil Harvey, Len Favell and O'Neill as he bowled a dozen overs on the trot. The game had been turned on its head. With Worrell bowling Colin McDonald and Sonny Ramadhin unearthing a beauty to account for Ken Mackay, Australia were 92 for six and facing defeat.

Benaud and Davidson took them into tea at 109 for six. Having begun needing 45 runs an hour, Australia now needed another 124 in two (there was no stipulation about overs in those days) and many thought they would opt for the draw. During the interval Bradman made his customary dressing-room visit for a cup of tea. He sat with the two batsmen. Benaud recalled: "The three of us were sitting there when he [Bradman] said to me, 'What are you going for, a win or a draw?' I told him we were going for a win of course and all I got was a rather dry, 'I'm pleased to hear it'."

There were pragmatic considerations, too. "Both of us were attacking batsmen," Benaud added. "It would have been suicide for either of us to attempt to play defensively. In any case we both reckoned we could win. I said to Alan we should try to rattle them with our running between the wickets, just to see if we could introduce a little panic. And, anything at all loose, give it a real belt."

That is just what they did, keeping up with the clock despite a pitch – straw-coloured with black patches around the crease – that was anything but easy. Davidson had begun shakily but was now in his element, negotiating Hall's second spell and getting on top of Ramadhin, who had baffled him completely with his first ball.

The West Indies fielding, once shabby, was now balletic

Always canny, always single-minded, always fair. Richie Benaud established himself as a great captain of Australia.

Clipping the spinner to the fine-leg boundary, he brought up the century stand in 95 minutes. Worrell, running out of options, belatedly asked Sobers to try his over-the-wicket tweakers, but Benaud kept the good balls at bay and swung the bad ones for four. Worrell's last hope was the second new ball, which Hall took with Australia 206 for six, needing only 27 in the last 30 minutes. Now Worrell could have closed up the match, but chose not to. Hall bowled a bouncer. The crowd, alight with excitement, jeered. Worrell told him to bowl another, just to rid his fast bowler of tension.

Hall's over cost eight runs. Davidson hooked him for four but Benaud was almost caught at square leg. Worrell brought back Sobers to bowl fast and a couple of precious minutes were occupied moving the sightscreen for the left-armer, but Benaud, white with tension, on-drove him to the boundary in an over that cost nine more. Hall, summoning all his skill and energy, then bowled eight balls for just one run. Australia needed nine in 10 minutes.

But moments later, Benaud pushed Sobers to midwicket for one scampered single too many and Solomon hit the stumps direct from 25 yards. Davidson, short of his ground by a yard, was run out for 80. But as he walked off he could reflect on a unique double of 124 runs and 11 wickets. In other circumstances, the Test would have been remembered as "Davidson's match".

So what was almost certain to be the last over began at 5.55pm – five minutes from the scheduled close – with Australia needing six runs from eight balls with three wickets left. Wally Grout, the new batsman, had the strike after taking a single in the previous over but Benaud remained confident Australia would win, though he knew Worrell's side would not give up without a fight. But the pressure was on West Indies – or rather Hall. One loose ball would virtually cede the match. Benaud said: "I sensed that Wes had been instructed,

The last, dramatic over of the match lasted nine palm-soaking minutes

almost on pain of death, not to bowl a bouncer because both Wal and I didn't mind the short ball."

Amid the Gabba's lengthening shadows, the over – perhaps the most dramatic in history – lasted nine palm-soaking minutes. Hall's first ball thumped Grout on the thigh but Benaud was alert enough to tear through for a single. Then Hall bowled what he was not supposed to bowl, a bouncer. Benaud – knowing a four would level the scores – swung with all his might. He got no more than a touch and Alexander caught it. The crowd went through the roof.

"I still can't believe that ball did not go for four or six over Alexander's head," Benaud said. "All I remember is the intense disappointment: about to level one moment, trudging back the next." Worrell reiterated to Hall: "No bouncers." Hall replied: "But I got him out." Worrell: "That's not the point."

Ian Meckiff took Benaud's place and played his first ball back to Hall. Five off five. A bye was run off the next ball, Hall missing a chance to run out Meckiff and Valentine saving his shy from going for four overthrows. The West Indies fielding, once shabby, was now balletic. When Grout skied the fifth ball to the leg side and a single was scurried fielders again converged from all directions before Hall, knocking over Kanhai, claimed the catch. But the ball bounced out of his hands. Three off three. Hall described this later as one of the worst moments of his life.

Heads dropped, but not Worrell's. Urging his men to stay relaxed, he kept his annoyance hidden, but the next ball almost finished off his hopes, Meckiff heroically thumping the ball high and deep to leg. But Hunte, refusing to give up, cut it off on the boundary and as the batsmen turned for a third, winning run threw magnificently, fast and

low, to Alexander, who swept over the stumps as the diving Grout slid in. Everyone turned to umpire Hoy, who raised his right arm high. Grout had been out by a foot.

The West Indians danced with delight. Pandemonium reigned – nowhere more than in the Australia dressing-room, where Lindsay Kline, the last man, could not find his batting gloves until someone pointed out he was sitting on them. Scores level. One off two, one wicket left. Worrell was speaking to Hall, telling him what every captain tells bowlers in such situations. "Whatever you do, don't bowl a no-ball!"

Hall did not bowl a no-ball but Kline, his panic over, calmly played the ball to square leg and Meckiff, backing up well, charged down the wicket for the winning run for the second time in two balls. But at square leg Solomon had picked up and shaped to throw. He had only the width of a stump to aim at. Miraculously, he hit direct – just as he had done to beat Davidson 11 minutes and a lifetime earlier. Everyone again

Despite the inevitable pressures facing him as West Indies first black captain, Worrell consistently exuded style and authority.

turned to Hoy. Again his finger went up. Again pandemonium. In his disappointment, Meckiff thought Australia had lost by one run. Worrell, it was said, was the only man on the field who knew the true result as the crowd streamed over the field.

Not everyone thought a tie a good thing. Benaud remembered: "Bradman came into the dressing-room to assure me that I would, in later years, believe this to be the greatest thing that could possibly have happened for the game of cricket. My reply was that I doubted it because I would always be remembering that we had thrown away a Test match by having three run outs in the last couple of overs ... he was right, but only because of the manner in which the series later panned out." In the aftermath of the game, Benaud and Worrell were quoted as saying it was the greatest game they had ever played in. It was Bradman who made the most expansive claim: "The greatest Test match of all time."

Once the enormity of what had happened sank in, the sides stayed at the ground, the celebrations muted only by exhaustion. Worrell was perhaps the most spent; Hall, who led the calypsos, the liveliest. Shamefully the party was frowned upon by the Australian board, who passed a motion dictating that teams had to leave the dressing rooms within minutes of the close. Bradman was the sole dissenter.

Remarkably, the series maintained its drama. Australia won the second Test, West Indies the third and the fourth was another cliffhanger, drawn only after Kline, again Australia's last man, survived 100 minutes. A world record crowd of 90,800 saw the second day of the decider in Melbourne, a gripping affair which Australia won by two wickets. Two days later, half a million lined the streets of Melbourne to give the West Indies a ticker-tape send-off. Yet though Australia won the series, it was West Indies that gained most. The brilliant cricket they would play in the next decade would lay the foundations for the game's worldwide revival.

Feat of Clay

When the 22-year-old Cassius Clay fought Sonny Liston for the heavyweight crown of the world, nobody gave him a chance – except the Louisville Lip himself. Liston was menacingly terrifying, Clay a no-hoper and a clown. Yet an extraordinary phenomenon was poised to emerge.

NICK PITT

After another warm, sunny day there was a rainstorm in Miami that evening in February 1964. It was pouring down outside when the first bell sounded, summoning not merely two men from opposite corners of a ring, but a turn in history, the entrance of the century's most compelling sportsman.

Let us freeze the moment. The announcer had said his piece: "The challenger, from Louisville, Kentucky, wearing white trunks with red stripes, weighing 210lb, Cassius Clay! And from Denver, Colorado, wearing white trunks with black trim, the heavyweight champion of the world, Charles 'Sonny' Liston!" The bell was ringing. Clay, 22 years old and beautifully athletic, was about to bound across the ring. Liston, the most menacing man on earth, was ready to step forward for deliberate, violent work.

Hardly a person inside the half-full Miami Beach Convention Hall, or watching the closed-circuit broadcast across America, had suspected they would witness an event of cataclysmic impact and mysterious circumstances. At ringside, the knowing ones of the boxing press were all but unanimous. It was an easy call. The mismatch odds, seven-to-one in favour of Liston, were about right.

Clay had already found some celebrity and was rapidly adding notoriety. Among those who had trooped up the wooden stairs leading to the seedy Fifth Street gym where he trained were The Beatles (Clay: "You're not as dumb as you look." Lennon: "You are.") and Malcolm X, the most gifted and feared leader of the Black Muslim (Nation of Islam) movement to which Clay was becoming attached.

But the worth of the Louisville Lip as a fighting man had yet to be recognised, especially by the experts. For them, he was a clown, a dancer, fancy and fast, but an act. In his last two outings, he had struggled against Doug Jones and been knocked temporarily senseless by Henry Cooper. No punch. No defence.

Like everybody else, the pressmen were in awe of Liston, viewing him more as monster than man. Many rated him the greatest heavyweight of all, and certainly the most intimidating. He was a brooding, unforgiving bully, a deadly puncher with huge hands and enormous reach, whose three previous fights had ended concussively in the first round. He could box, but

King of the world: Clay realises Liston has quit on his stool and is embraced by his cornermen Bundini Brown. "I am the king! King of the world! Eat your words! Eat your words!"

he hardly needed to. Most victims were beaten long before he hit them, for few could look into his eyes and those who did saw dark pools of malevolence.

And if anybody on assignment had wondered during the idle days of waiting in the Miami sunshine whether Clay might have a chance, he no longer did so on the evening of the fight. All doubts had been swept away that morning at the weigh-in.

Here at least was an angle. The weigh-in was the most chaotic ever. Clay, who had been pestering Liston for months, annoying him at gaming tables in Las Vegas, "bear-hunting" at his house in the early hours, surpassed himself. Accompanied by his chief cheerleader, Bundini Brown, Clay beat the floor with an African walking stick as he entered the weigh-in area. Brown chanted the catchphrase he had recently coined: "Float like a butterfly; sting like a bee!"

When Liston arrived, Clay and Brown yelled like competing hysterics: "I'm ready to rumble now! You're scared chump! You ain't no giant! I'm going to eat you alive!" Clay lunged at Liston as if to mix it, and was held back by Brown and five others. "Hey sucker, you're a chump," Clay screamed. "You're a bear, you're ugly, I'm going to whip you so bad!" Liston responded with a withering stare. "Don't tell everybody," he said, though quite what he meant nobody knew.

"Cassius Clay fined $2,500," announced an official of the Miami Beach Boxing

Commission after several warnings. The commission doctor examined Clay. His pulse, normally 52, had shot up to 120. His blood pressure was equally high. "Clay is acting like a man scared to death," the doctor told several journalists. "He is liable to crack up before he enters the ring."

Such behaviour at a weigh-in was unheard of. "No man could have seen Clay that morning and believed he could stay on his feet three minutes that night," wrote Murray Kempton of the *New Republic*. In the *Daily Mail*, Jim Manning went further, declaring that the fight must not be allowed to proceed because Clay was clearly insane. As evening approached, there were reports that he had been seen at the airport, buying a ticket.

What of the fighters as they heard that first bell? Nobody trusted more firmly in the Liston myth than Liston. As a former strikebreaker and convict, the current champion and symbol of the gangsters who had controlled boxing in the United States for a decade and more, there was nothing he recognised more

clearly, or could conjure more naturally, than fear in others.

And Clay, he knew, was frightened. Two rounds was Liston's estimation: a round to catch the dancer and a round to destroy him. But there was a small worm of doubt in Liston's mind. Maybe Clay really believed he could win. If he did, he was mad. And you never know what to expect from a madman.

For Clay, at last about to engage Liston with fists, the moment of truth had come. Baiting the bear had been an act, of course, but the hysteria was

It was the entrance of the century's most compelling sportsman

made convincing by genuine anxiety. Psyching-up himself was as important as psyching-out Liston. Clay was frightened of Liston, all right. But not for the last time, he was ready to confront his own fear head on.

Clang. Round one. Clay bounded forward to meet the shuffling Liston. He cantered around him, circling,

"You're scared, chump!" Clay yelled at the weigh-in. His performance there astonished the watching press, who had never seen anything like it. Clearly, the man was insane. But the extraordinary scenes there were perfectly in keeping with the extraordinary fight that evening.

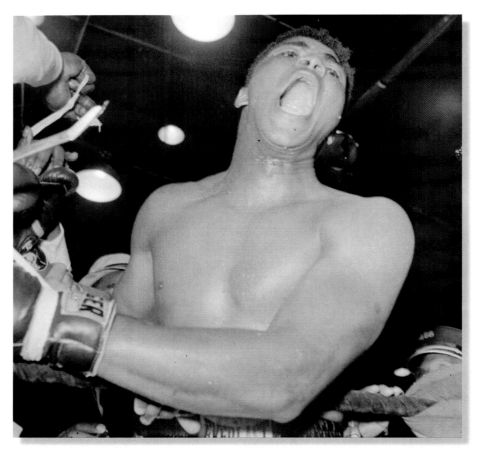

"I'm ready to rumble now! You're scared chump! You ain't no giant. I'm going to eat you alive … I'm going to whip you so bad!"

now this way, now that. Liston tried a left lead. His jab could lift men from the floor, knock them cold, but not if they were absent, and Clay was long gone. The punch, like most of Liston's that night, missed by a couple of feet.

When Clay ended his reconnoitre, he found his target immediately. Still circling, he stung Liston with single blows to the head, leading with either hand. He next produced combinations, equally effective, and, to conclude the round, eight consecutive jabs speared Liston without reply.

Joe Louis was commentating for the closed circuit broadcast. "We've just seen one of the greatest rounds we've seen from anybody in a long time," he said. "Clay completely outclassed Sonny Liston." Clay might have been crazed outside the ring. Inside it, he was in perfect control. Liston was outclassed, beaten for speed of foot, hand and brain. Early in the third, he was cut, a gash appearing high on his left cheekbone. The title was being swept away in a flood.

"We've just seen one of the greatest rounds we've seen from anybody in a long time"

But when Clay returned to his corner at the end of the fourth, his eyes were stinging. "I can't see!" he shouted. "Cut them off. Cut off the gloves! We're going home!" During the following 60 seconds, Angelo Dundee, Clay's chief cornerman as well as trainer, earned all the money his association with Clay

of Clay's eye. He rubbed his own eye and could feel it burn. He took a sponge, plunged it into the waterbucket and bathed Clay's eyes. Clay still shouted: "I can't see!"

A group of Black Muslims, heavy guys, was sitting behind the corner. They were murmuring that Dundee, whom they suspected of mafia, and therefore Liston, connections, was blinding his man. Warned by his brother, who heard the murmurs, Dundee quickly proved his innocence, plunging the sponge back in the bucket and bathing his own eyes.

If foul play there was, it was from the other corner. Joe Pollino, one of Liston's cornermen, later admitted to a reporter that he had "juiced up" Liston's gloves after the third round and then threw the container, which he took to every Liston fight just in case, under the ring apron.

Dundee pushed Clay from the stool. "Stay away from him. Run!" Clay went out, blinking, half-seeing Liston, who knew his chance had come. Instinct and speed saved Clay, who was never more magnificent. Liston hit him, but never repeatedly, never decisively. By the end of the round, Clay's eyes had cleared and he was back in command. In the sixth, Liston took a beating. Clay cut out the floating, set his feet and punched not to wing Liston but to bring him down. He was hitting an old man and he did not miss.

Liston walked slowly back to his corner and sat down. "That's it," he told his cornermen. At first, they thought Liston was telling them that he was finally going to involve himself, stop the nonsense. They treated the cut, rubbed him down, replaced his gumshield. Liston spat it out: "I said that's it!" Liston had quit on his stool.

When Clay realised, he rushed around the ring with his arms raised, shouting to the world and to the ringside experts: "I am the king! King of the world! Eat your words! Eat your words!" As Clay and his entourage whooped around the ring, disbelief was universal. "What the hell is this?" said Rocky Marciano at ringside. In the Jefferson City jail, where Liston had first learned to box, the inmates, watching on closed-circuit TV, howled in derision, convinced he had thrown the fight.

It was said that Liston had injured his left shoulder. Over the years, it was claimed that he had approached the promoter and the boxing commission, wanting a postponement. But apparently he was so certain of beating Clay that he made little fuss when they turned him down. And, so it was said, his shoulder was injured further and rendered numb during the fight.

Why, then, did Liston return to his dressing room, pick up an armchair in his left hand, throw it against the wall and scream a dreadful curse? Had the mob cashed in on the odds? Had the Black Muslims got to Liston? Most of those who might have the answer are dead. Frankie Carbo, the gangster who was Liston's ultimate boss, died in prison. Malcolm X, the most influential of the Black Muslims present in Miami, was assassinated a year later. Liston was found dead in his Las Vegas home in December 1970.

So unbelievable was the gap between what was expected and what happened, so foolish were commentators made to look, that fantastic explanations were required. Denying the evidence of Clay's brilliance, the experts in assumption before the fight became conspiracy theorists after it. Liston knew better. In less than half an hour his view of the world and his place in it had been uprooted. He quit not because of pain, but disillusion.

As an event, it was sensational and historic, but as a promotion it was a flop. A black man with links to the mob against a black guy with links to the Black Muslims, and anyway who had no chance, was hardly an attraction in Florida in the early 1960s. Only 8,297 tickets were sold for an arena holding 15,744. The promoter lost more than $300,000.

The day after the mayhem, Clay, the new heavyweight champion of the world, confirmed that he was embracing Islam. As Cassius X, briefly, and Muhammad Ali thereafter, his reign as the sporting figure of the age had begun. Half an hour's fighting in Miami Beach on a wet evening had changed his sport, changed all sport, for ever.

He was hitting an old man and he did not miss

SHOOTING FROM THE LIP: THE WIT AND WISDOM OF MUHAMMAD ALI

ON SONNY LISTON

If you want to lose your money, then bet on Sonny

I'm young, I'm handsome, I'm fast, I can't possibly be beat. I'm ready to go to war right now. If I see that bear on the street, I'll beat him before the fight. I'll beat him like I'm his daddy

I'll hit Liston with so many punches from so many angles he'll think he's surrounded. I don't just want to be champion of the world, I'm gonna be champion of the whole universe. After I whup Sonny Liston, I'm gonna whup those little green men from Jupiter and Mars. And looking at them won't scare me none because they can't be no uglier than Sonny Liston

ON BEING THE GREATEST

I must be the greatest. I showed the world. I talk to God every day. I shook up the world. I'm the king of the world! I'm pretty! I'm a bad man! I shook up the world. You must listen to me. I am the greatest! I can't be beat!

I should be a postage stamp. That's the only way I'll ever get licked.

Howard Cossell, US broadcaster: You're being extremely truculent.
Ali: Whatever truculent means, if that's good, I'm that.

Joe Frazier is too ugly to be champ. Joe Frazier is too dumb to be champ. The heavyweight champ should be smart and pretty like me

ON GEORGE FOREMAN

Listen to the people George has fought. Don Waldheim. He was a nobody. Fred Askew. He was a nobody. Sylvester Dulliare. I can't even pronounce his name. Chuck Wepner. He was a nobody. John Carroll. He was a nobody. Cookie Wallace. He was a nobody. Vernon Clay... Clay? He might be good

Float like a butterfly, sting like a bee
His hands can't hit what his eyes can't see
Now you see me, now you don't
George thinks he will, but I know he won't

You think the world was shocked when Nixon resigned? Wait till I whup George Foreman's behind

ON BLACK OPPRESSION

Everything good is supposed to be white. We look at Jesus and we see a white with blonde hair and blue eyes. We look at all the angels; we see white with blond hair and blue eyes. Now, I'm sure there's a heaven in the sky and coloured folks die and go to heaven. Where are the coloured angels?

I'm expected to go overseas to help free people in South Vietnam and at the same time my people here are being brutalised and mistreated

The white race attacks black people. They don't ask what's our religion, what's our belief? They just start whupping heads ... So we don't want to live with the white man

March 1964

Arkle the immortal

It was England against Ireland when Mill House met Arkle in the greatest race Cheltenham has ever seen. Mill House was confidently talked of as the greatest chaser of all time: no horse could live with him. But in a dramatic race, the Irish challenger sprinted away from his rival and galloped into history. It was an epic encounter.

DAVID WALSH

Friday afternoon on March 6 1964. A horse-box pulls up outside at Cheltenham racecourse and a handsome gelding is led down the ramp and into the yard before being allocated a stable for the night. Soon, word spreads that the big horse has arrived and stable lads who hadn't seen him before gather outside his box. "So this," they say, "is Mill House, the champion with the potential to be horse of the century."

Johnny Lumley is swept along by the current. Lumley is in Cheltenham because, as stable lad to the Irish trainer Tom Dreaper, he looks after the horse considered Mill House's only rival, Arkle by name. Curious about this English favourite, Lumley wants to see for himself. With a distinguished white star on his forehead and his long, broad back, Mill House looks magnificent. Lumley says as much to the English lads he meets.

Innocently, he expects that they in turn will want to see his charge and is disappointed that they do not. Do they consider Arkle just another horse? Lumley takes it personally.

Later, in the canteen, they are sitting over cups of tea when someone opens the racing page of the *Gloucestershire Echo* and ignites a debate about the Gold Cup. As happens in Cheltenham arguments, men quickly remember where they're from and opinions are simply expressions of patriotism. Especially among the Irish. This evening they make the case

for Arkle. He has more speed than Mill House, they say. He's still improving and he's in great form. But they are trying to convince themselves as much as their adversaries. The Lambourn lads aren't buying the Irish bravado. Mill House will slaughter their horse, they say.

"He will not," says Joe Carey, determined to speak up for his country. The

The Lambourn lads aren't buying the Irish bravado. Mill House will slaughter their horse, they say

Tipperary man, in his mid-50s, drives horses for the Curragh trainer, Aubrey Brabazon. He has travelled to the Festival with a horse called Portail Rouge. Joe is a portly man with a build well suited to lorry-driving. He might be 15 or 16 stones. "You know what?" says one of the Lambourn lads, pointing to Joe, "Mill House would win tomorrow with you riding him." To this there is no answer and, as quickly as the bantering has begun, it ends.

It might have continued had Pat Taaffe been seated at the table. But top-rank jockeys didn't stay at the lads' lodgings and Arkle's pilot had a room at the Carlton Hotel on Cheltenham's Parabola Road. An affable and softly spoken man, Taaffe passionately believed Arkle would beat Mill House, but though many listened, few took his word for it. Hadn't Mill House won the previous year's Gold

Cup as a novice, hadn't he given Arkle five pounds and a thrashing in the Hennessy Gold Cup at Newbury? Didn't Fulke Walwyn, his trainer, say Mill House might be better than the great Golden Miller?

Taaffe blamed himself for the Newbury defeat: "I was three parts of a length behind Mill House going to the third last. It was precisely the position I should not have been in. Forced to reach for the fence, Arkle stumbled on landing and the race was lost. I told the duchess [Anne, Duchess of Westminster, Arkle's owner] that our horse would win the next time they met."

How ironic that this race should have become an international match. Mill House for England, Arkle for Ireland. Mill House, after all, was bred in Ireland and taught to jump by Taaffe himself at his home in County Kildare. Once the horse had shown he could handle obstacles, Taaffe hunted him with the Naas Harriers, the South County Dublin Harriers and the Kildare Hunt. Then, when Mill House first raced, Taaffe rode him to runaway victory in a maiden hurdle at Naas. He immediately judged him one of the best young horses he had ridden.

Pat's father, Tom, trained the horse for the Lawlors of Naas and the families had long been friends. Because of their friendship, old Tom Taaffe was quick to tell the Lawlors when he thought they were overstocked with horses. Mill House arrived at such a time and, after a couple of races in Ireland, he was sold to an Englishman, Bill Gollings. After spending a short time with Syd Dale, the

horse soon moved to the Lambourn trainer, Fulke Walwyn. The Irish jockey Willie Robinson would ride him.

Robinson and Taaffe had long been friends. They were what Irish people call "Jesuit boys"; Taaffe had been educated at Belvedere, Robinson at its sister college, Clongowes Wood. Soon after Mill House moved to Walwyn, Taaffe wrote to his friend and told him he would be riding "the best horse in Britain, probably the best in the world". It took Mill House a couple of months to settle in Lambourn, but once he did Robinson realised Taaffe had not been exaggerating.

"When I rode him," said Robinson, "I thought to myself he was the horse they had been trying to breed for years. One that was big enough to carry weight, one that would eat up his fences, gallop for ever and had any amount of class. I had never ridden anything like him." A six-year-old novice, Mill House won the 1963 Gold Cup by 12 lengths. It was a breathtaking display of jumping and galloping.

At the time Taaffe had come to the conclusion that Arkle was better. Although the same age as Mill House, Arkle had been patiently trained by

When Arkle jumped the last a length in front of the seemingly invincible Mill House, it was clear something very special was unfolding. Though Mill House, gallant to the last, challenged again in the final run-in, he had no answer to the Irish horse, who simply surged away to the winning post.

Tom Dreaper and allowed the time that young National Hunt horses need. But once Arkle showed his true potential, Taaffe knew he had stumbled across a special horse. "When horses come under pressure they slow; when Arkle came under pressure he found a new gear," said Taaffe. "I have always believed he sensed the end of a race, he knew where the winning post was and he was excited by it. No matter how easy you rode him, or how easy you were winning, he always wanted to go as fast as he could at the end of a race."

Two days before Mill House won his Gold Cup in 1963, Arkle sprinted away with the Broadway Chase for novices. Afterwards Dreaper said the 1964 Gold Cup would be the target, but the hint of great things to come was lost in the excitement that followed Mill House's Gold Cup performance. English people saw no danger to their champion and it was strange that this strapping horse should have changed the character of a nation.

Gone was England's innate reservation, forgotten was the time-honoured tendency to understate and keep emotions on a tight rein.

Englishmen were loud and lavish in their praise of Mill House. Such was the cacophony, they never heard the clamour of approaching hooves. "You must remember," says the commentator Sir Peter O'Sullevan, "that Mill House was England's Arkle before the real Arkle came along, if you see what I mean."

Pat Taaffe tried to warn his friend Robinson but, now in lodgings at Saxon House in Lambourn, his old pal was more committed to Mill House than the English themselves. Before their first meeting, in the Hennessy Gold Cup at Newbury on November 30 1963, the jockeys discussed the race and each professed sympathy for the fate which awaited the other. As compensation, they agreed the winner would buy a gift for the loser.

Standing in the parade ring before the race, Robinson took a long look at Arkle. "Compared to our horse . . . well, he did not compare. Mill House was a manlier, stronger, better-looking horse. I found it hard to believe there could be a better horse than Mill House." The

"When Arkle came under pressure, he found another gear"

race appeared to vindicate the belief in Mill House, who jumped quite beautifully and galloped relentlessly. Arkle's mistake, three fences from home, cost him his chance but that hardly mattered – the champion had put the challenger in his place.

"I sent Pat to my tailor, W J Kelly of Grafton Street, and told him to have a fine suit made for himself," said Robinson. And a fine suit it was; in subsequent years Taaffe remarked on how well it had worn. The horses would next meet at Cheltenham for the Gold Cup, a rendezvous destined to be remembered as the greatest steeplechase of all time.

Unbeknown to the wider racing world, Arkle improved considerably between the two races. Paddy Woods, a very capable jockey in his own right and Arkle's work rider, could see it: "He improved by leaps and bounds. I could feel it on the gallops and everyone in the yard knew from his behaviour. After morning exercise he would go back to his box and have a good roll. He'd be standing, then he would roll. After about 20 seconds he'd be back on his feet, then down again for another roll. As he got fitter and in better form, he rolled more and more. The boss [Dreaper] would ask, 'How many times this morning?' and Paddy Murray would say 'Six, boss, six'. Next morning it would be seven or eight. By the time we were going to Cheltenham it was up to 12. We knew Arkle was something else."

On the morning of the Gold Cup, Taaffe exercised Arkle on the infield at Cheltenham. It gave him an appetite for breakfast, which he ate heartily. A good breakfast, he used to say, would take him through the day. As was his custom, he liked to walk from the Carlton Hotel to the course. People stopped and offered him lifts but, preferring to be on his own, Taaffe refused. Willie Robinson breakfasted at Lambourn and he, too, travelled alone to the racecourse.

In the weighing room, English jockey Dave Dick suggested to Taaffe that he hold Arkle back and not make his challenge until the very end. He could then make the most of Arkle's

Pat Taaffe (left), Arkle's jockey, and (above) Willie Robinson, who rode the beaten Mill House. Robinson, though Irish, was convinced his English-trained horse was easily superior to the Irish challenger, Arkle.

All smiles in the paddock after Arkle's sensational win. Tom Dreaper (left), National Hunt trainer supreme, and (right) Arkle's owner, Anne, Duchess of Westminster. Dreaper's record in the Gold Cup both as jockey and, later, trainer was unrivalled.

superior acceleration. Taaffe had already decided he would ride Arkle that way, but he still appreciated hearing it from Dick.

Whatever the jockey's anxieties, they were nothing compared to Jim Dreaper's. Twelve years old, the trainer's son was at boarding school in Headfort, County Meath. Even though it was Saturday, the headmaster was not a racing man and did not consider Cheltenham a necessary element in the boy's education. But in every school there will be one teacher with an understanding of what matters. Jack Sweetman interceded on young Dreaper's behalf and one needless injustice was avoided. It was a battle the boy would never forget.

Four horses went to post: Mill House, Arkle, Pas Seul and King's Nephew. Just two mattered. As the horses paraded, a sudden snowstorm blew up. A Cheltenham official spoke with Tom Dreaper and wondered if they would be able to run the race. Dreaper was too far gone for turning back. "The way I felt," he said later, " I wanted to tell him to let them go right away – storm, snow or anything else." But as quickly as the blizzard came, it went and, as often happens, the light after the storm was

crystal clear. Nobody could miss what was about to happen.

Mill House tried to draw the sting from his rival by setting a strong pace and attacking every fence. Arkle raced comfortably, three or four lengths behind. As they moved downhill to the third last, Arkle tried to close right up to his rival but Taaffe restrained him. Robinson asked his horse for a big leap at the third last and Mill House responded gallantly. Two lengths in front going into the fence, they were three lengths ahead as they surged away from it.

Taaffe, however, was just biding his time, waiting for the right moment before pouncing. Racing to the second last, he moved closer to Mill House and, rounding the home turn,

"This is the champion! This is the best we've seen for a long time"

they were alongside. O'Sullevan quickly saw the changing picture. "It's going to be Arkle if he jumps it!" he called.

Arkle cleared the last a length in front and even though Robinson had lost his whip brave Mill House rallied. His courage counted for nothing against his rival's class, for as he

climbed the last half-furlong to the post, Arkle lengthened his stride and stretched clear. It was an extraordinary performance by the new champion and an admirable run by the old one. From the next parish, Pas Seul and King's Nephew arrived to take third and fourth places.

As they turned to head back to the unsaddling enclosure, Taaffe stretched out a hand to his friend. To compensate Robinson, Taaffe paid for the airfare when Willie and his new bride, Susan, honeymooned in Paris and Sardinia shortly afterwards.

However euphoric the Irish, their emotion was no greater than the devastation in the Mill House camp. Fulke Walwyn told a friend he could "hardly believe that any horse breathing could have done to Mill House what Arkle did". Bill Gollings, the disappointed owner, raised his bowler hat in symbolic salute as Arkle was led triumphantly away from the winner's enclosure.

Darkie Deacon, Darkie Leatham and Henry Forrester travelled home in the horse-box with Mill House. Deacon says they were disappointed but philosophical. Maybe Forrester mourned more than his pals. He looked after Mill House, and when the horse won Gollings looked after him. Two days later Deacon went up to the Downs at Lambourn with Fulke Walwyn, who was still recovering from the shock. "The guvnor talked about how confident Arkle's people had been and how, on the Hennessy form, they had no right to be. 'I think they were just bloody hoping,' he said."

At Cheltenham on the evening of that fateful Saturday, Johnny Lumley had come to the conclusion that he now looked after the greatest steeple-chaser of all time. Arkle had sprinted away from the great Mill House and that evening at the stables in Cheltenham a number of lads from Lambourn had come and asked to see Arkle: "We went to see their horse before the race, they came to see our fellow after the race. That's the way it happened."

England's finest hour

England's World Cup win in 1966 remains the single most important victory by any British team in any sport. The purists may have been offended by England's preference for muscular virtue over inspiration. But for the young Geoff Hurst, who was to score a hat-trick in the final, vindication was sweet.

IAN HAWKEY

Ahead of England's 11th meeting with West Germany, at Wembley Stadium in 1966, some weighty speculation filled the sports pages. Some wondered about the rate of Jimmy Greaves's return to fitness. *The Times* thought the very direction of the sport would hang on the match, and under the headline "Free-thinking and English football" its elegant essay looked forward to "signposts to the future" in a "fixture of paramount importance". Praise be, England won and their manager, Alf Ramsey, saluted the industry of his players. Outside, the jeers from 75,000 disgusted spectators faded into the night.

It was February, and the country had not yet learned to trust Ramsey the prophet. Two and a half years earlier, he had told a reporter England would win the World Cup on home ground in 1966. Now, after this dull 1-0 friendly victory against a weakened German XI, Ramsey told his players something else. Geoff Hurst, who had made his international debut while Greaves recovered from illness, remembers the words: "It was Alf who said that night that if we beat West Germany by a goal in the World Cup final in July the fans would be very happy indeed."

So they would – and happier still when the margin extended to two. What the late Sir Alf would not know was just how high his debutant striker would soar or with what drama England would secure the country's most celebrated success in a team sport.

If Ramsey was something of a Cassandra, Hurst was a mere cadet. For the 24-year-old West Ham striker, a call-up to an England squad, at the tail-end of 1965, had been "a huge shock". Despite his record as the leading goalscorer in English football, the queue ahead, led by Greaves, seemed long. "I wasn't fashionable," Hurst reflects. "I wasn't recognised as an out-and-out striker. I'd never dreamed I'd be called up for England." This despite Ramsey's willingness to search high and low. Since 1963, he had sized up almost 50 players in an England shirt. Once in, Hurst found enough familiar touchstones to feel he could belong: "It was quite daunting, but there were no cliques, no hierarchy, no stars, no prima donnas, no loners. Alf and his assistants, Harold Shepherdson and Les Cocker, had this knack. They were able to pick hard-nosed professionals who had a good attitude individually."

What did Ramsey value in Hurst, whom he admonished for being too reticent at his first England training

The teams line up before the final. Even at this stage, there were many who doubted that England could win the trophy. If Ramsey's decision to play without wingers caused controversy, his preference for the robust Roger Hunt and Geoff Hurst over the quicksilver Jimmy Greaves worried many. England were thought to be too predictable and too one-dimensional. Hurst, knighted in 1998, would prove them spectacularly wrong.

ENGLAND 3 GERMANY W. 2

session? "If I had to analyse myself, I'd say I was very dedicated, very professional. And I desperately wanted to play. I never asked Sir Alf what he saw in me and, sadly, I can't now. Mind you," Hurst smiles, "Jack Charlton asked him once and the answer peed Jack off a bit. Alf said, 'Jack, I don't always pick the best players'."

Nonetheless, Ramsey's team contained five or six men of the highest class and, by July, they were into a good run of form. Hurst was not. Ordinary performances in the last two friendlies before the World Cup had made Greaves and Roger Hunt the preferred striking partnership in Ramsey's then unorthodox 4-3-3. Two wins, against Mexico and France, and a draw in the opening match with Uruguay put England through to the second round, although they had seldom inspired. Sitting the stand, Hurst saw at first-hand the frustrations of supporters, arguing with one vociferous critic towards the end of the match against France. Then, returning to the team hotel, Hurst saw the extent of Greaves's shin injury. He couldn't help but wonder.

Two changes, then, for the quarter-final against Argentina: Hurst for Greaves, and Alan Ball in place of a traditional winger. Ramsey had tried three in three first-round games and now jettisoned them all. According to Hurst: "Too much is made of the Wingless Wonders. It became a press headline. Alf felt that he could get more out of Martin Peters and Alan Ball because they could do a lot more work defensively, and still do the job when they got to the byline." Moreover, in Ray Wilson Ramsey had one of the most accomplished left-backs in the game, while George Cohen, on the right, had helped patent the overlapping full-back.

It was a Peters centre, met by Hurst, which would settle the Argentina tie, although what the match needed was not so much a crosser as a priest. Hurst stood in the tunnel before his World Cup debut watching the opposing captain, Antonio Rattin, talk to his team with "sneering arrogance". Rattin was booked early for a foul on Bobby Charlton. Shortly

Apotheosis: in the last seconds of extra time, Hurst burst past the spent German defence and lashed the ball high into the net for his hat-trick. If there had been doubt about his second goal, no one could question his third.

afterwards, Hurst made his first close acquaintance with the man, when he was bustled over out on the left. Rattin then debated the free kick against him with referee Rudolf Kreitlein.

After 36 minutes, and a longer, stronger dispute, Kreitlein sent Rattin off. It took eight minutes for play to resume, in the course of which the Argentinian team had looked likely to walk off in sympathy with their captain. Between episodes of spitting, kicking and diving, England squeezed into the semi-finals, Hurst exploiting the space vacated by Rattin to score. "They were skilful, which some people forget," he notes, "and expected to win it. When

"I don't always pick the best players," said Alf Ramsey to Jack Charlton

you consider that they lost a man early on and still kept the ball for so long, that shows you how good they were."

Ramsey's opinion? When the BBC's Kenneth Wolstenholme thrust the microphone at him, the England manager replied: "We have still to produce our best football. It will come against a team which comes out to play football and not act as animals." The "animals" part caused immediate controversy. "The trouble," recalls Wolstenholme mischievously, "was that the television cameras were feeding the interview straight into the press box."

If England's football had not charmed so far, the semi-final against Portugal would celebrate the best of the European game, with its echoes of Manchester United–Benfica clashes past and to come. United's Nobby Stiles shadowed Eusebio; Bobby Charlton scored twice in a 2-1 win. England, originally 10-1 with the bookies, had reached the final.

Hurst, meanwhile, gathered that Greaves was regaining fitness. England were four days from the climax against West Germany. The squad players not used in the knock-out stages had a practice match against an Arsenal XI in which doubts surfaced over Greaves's recovery. Still speculation mounted that one striker, Hunt or Hurst, would give way.

Some 26 hours before the kick-off, Hunt learned that he would play. So did Hurst, although he did not sleep well on the night of Friday July 29, and woke at 6am. There were no particular nerves, he remembers, partly because cup finals had become an annual event for Hurst, Peters and their captain, Bobby Moore, the West Ham contingent having won the FA Cup in 1964 and the European Cup Winners' Cup a year later. All manner of hat-tricks were in prospect.

Across London in the German camp, Horst Höttges woke with some anxiety. He had missed the semi-final against Russia with tendon trouble. "I was probably not fully fit," recalls the full-back. "If I had had that sort of injury later in my career, I would not have played. But I was 23,

young enough to be determined to make the final." Helmut Schoen, the German manager, gave Höttges the go-ahead and, seeing the England teamsheet, assigned him to shadow England's No 10.

"Geoff Hurst had a lot of luck in that game," Höttges says now. To an extent, Hurst agrees: "I was fortunate. Roger and I knew we'd be picked up man for man, plus their sweeper, Schulz, and I knew they'd have a problem. With us playing two up front, one of their full-backs, normally wide players, would have to mark Roger or me. Once we started, Wolfgang Weber, the central defender, wandered towards Roger and I felt, as soon as Höttges picked me up, I would do all right. I'd be taking him into positions he wasn't familiar with and he wouldn't be particularly good in the air, which was my forte. I had a lot of joy, not just in the goals. I caused a few problems, and I battered the goalkeeper early on."

Tilkowski, in the German goal, needed treatment after that Hurst challenge as a dramatic final opened with England in command. "They were the favourites and we were a bit nervous," says Höttges. Yet an error by Wilson, quite out of character for

"You've beaten them once, now you've got to go and beat them again"

England's defence, allowed Haller to put West Germany ahead after 13 minutes. Hurst's equaliser came quickly, a header from Moore's pinpoint free kick. Before half-time, Tilkowski pushed another Hurst header past the post, and Hurst set up a fine chance for Hunt. "Tactically," says Hurst, "it wasn't good from a German point of view. Neither Weber nor Höttges were good in the air."

The second half was tighter, and as Brian Glanville's vivid match report for *The Sunday Times* recorded, England's "chief weapon continued to be the glorious leap, the skilled aerial deflections of Hurst". Hurst and Höttges would be at the heart of England's second goal, too. Hurst picked up a corner from Ball, worked his way to the box, but his shot found Höttges comfortably positioned to clear. Left-footed, Höttges miscued. "I made a mistake," the German recalls, "but I wasn't 100 per cent fit." Peters struck the loose ball past Tilkowski: 2-1.

Ramsey had reminded England before the game that no German side were beaten until the final whistle. When Weber slid in their second with 90 minutes already on the clock, via an arguable free-kick and a ricochet off Schnellinger's back, a hat-trick of misfortunes crowded in on England. "Bobby Charlton was very disappointed," remembers Hurst. "But not for a minute did we drop our heads. After the full-time whistle, Alf came on with his famous words, 'You've beaten them once, now you've got to go and beat them again'."

Ten minutes into extra time, England did just that. Ball chased down the right and centred to Hurst, who, cheeks puffed out, thumped the ball onto the underside of Tilkowski's crossbar. It bounced powerfully down and back into play. The rest is history ... and geometry, and computer sci-

Horst Höttges in 1966. The young German defender was given a torrid time by Hurst in the final. And he still claims that England's third should have been disallowed.

ence and several branches of applied physics. Hurst has grown weary of the analyses over whether the goal should have stood: "I believed it was in." After consultation with his linesman, Tofik Bharamov, of Russia, the Swiss referee Gottfried Dienst decided England's third would count. "It wasn't a goal," says Höttges. "After the match Bobby Charlton talked to us and he said it wasn't a goal."

In the TV gantry 25 minutes later, still at 3-2, Wolstenholme spotted some spectators advancing towards the pitch. "I was worried about hooligans," he recalls. His commentary which followed became a national catchphrase after the BBC's repeated broadcast of the game two months later: "Some people are on the pitch. They think it's all over. It is now!"

England's fourth goal, Hurst likes to tell his after-dinner audiences, had been hit with all the power of his left foot so that it might clear the crossbar and use up precious seconds. With less

The world in their hands: an image Englishmen can't forget. Held aloft by Hurst (left) and Ray Wilson (right), a triumphant Bobby Moore holds the World Cup.

poetic licence, he adds: "I wasn't sure that last one counted because the referee had almost blown up." Hurst checked with the scoreboard afterwards. He had scored the first – and still the only – hat-trick in a World Cup final. "It's a nice statistic to have," smiled Sir Geoff.

The Lisbon Lions

Moulded by the subtle determination of Jock Stein, Celtic in 1967 took on and beat the best that Europe could offer. They played with intelligence and a panache that has rarely been matched – and they became the first British team to win the European Cup. Their swaggering victory over Internazionale was indeed a kind of miracle.

HUGH McILVANNEY

Many pub teams have been drawn from a wider catchment area than the group of footballers Jock Stein sent out to make Celtic the first British winners of the European Cup in May 1967. Ten of the men who created history by totally outplaying Internazionale of Milan under a hot sun in the tree-fringed amphitheatre of the National Stadium in Lisbon were born within a dozen miles of Celtic Park. The eleventh, the flying winger Bobby Lennox, was from the Ayrshire coastal town of Saltcoats, barely 30 miles southwest of Glasgow. As a story of local boys making good, the achievement of the team that became known as the Lisbon Lions defies all efforts to find a comparison in world football. It was a fairytale told in a West of Scotland accent.

If the narrowness of their geographical origins made Celtic a wonder even before they took the field on that far-off Thursday evening in Portugal, scarcely less remarkable were the verve and rampant self-belief with which they reduced the vaunted sophistication of Inter to tatters. Never has the old line about a one-goal slaughter been more justified than it was by that 2-1 result.

A penalty after seven minutes for a mistimed tackle by the Scots' right-back, Jim Craig, gave the Italian champions a perfect opportunity to profit from the mastery of the *catenaccio* version of the sweeper system that had made their Argentinian coach, Helenio Herrera, a symbol of negativity throughout the game. Two years previously, Inter had won the European Cup at their own San Siro stadium by gaining the lead luckily and then shamelessly concentrating on smothering defence against a Benfica team who had only nine fit men. In Lisbon, the penalty encouraged a similar attempt to back-pedal towards their idea of glory. But they had fatally under-estimated the opposition. Covering up on the ropes is bad policy against a whirlwind puncher who is picking his shots, and Celtic's aggression had just such an unlikely mixture of urgency and calculation.

Giuliano Sarti in the Inter goal refuted Stein's suspicions that he would be an Italian weakness, but neither his inspired form nor the good fortune which brought the posts and crossbar to his rescue could prevent justice. The Celtic assaults were too constant and too penetrative and the only surprise was that the equalising goal came not as the climax of yet another concerted surge but from a shot unleashed suddenly and with brutal power out on the edge of Inter's box. But even that stunningly violent strike was, like so much of Celtic's attacking, produced by a fusion of spontaneity and premeditation.

At half-time, with his team's blatant supremacy still obscured by the 1-0 scoreline, Stein was full of praise for

History-makers: (back row, left to right) Craig, Gemmell, Simpson, McNeill, Murdoch, Clark; (front row) Wallace, Chalmers, Johnstone, Lennox, Auld. (Right) The greatest manager in the history of the game? The dominating figure of Jock Stein, the Big Man.

their first-half efforts but asked for one important adjustment. Repeated thrusting along the flanks was basic to his strategy and he was pleased with the way the marauding runs he had demanded of his full-backs, Craig and Tommy Gemmell, were reinforcing the threat of his exceptional wingers, the direct and electric Lennox and the jinking, mesmerising little redhead Jimmy Johnstone. But he felt that the massed ranks of expert defenders were coping too readily with balls crossed or passed into the Inter penalty area from

Never has the old line about a one-goal slaughter been more justified

advanced wide positions. The orthodox cut-back from the byline was obviously part of the solution but Stein, as he told me later, was certain that damage could be inflicted if those breaking along the wings released the ball earlier, rolling passes across the front of the retreating Inter defence.

About 17 minutes into the second half, a confident run on the right by Craig culminated in a measured cross-field delivery to Gemmell as he closed on his opponents' 18-yard line. Normally, Gemmell would have been expected to wheel round behind his central defenders and provide additional cover when Craig was going forward, but the fact that Inter had only one man upfield had persuaded him to give rein to his aggressive instincts and now he was presented with an invitation he could not refuse. By blasting in one of the most memorable goals Europe's supreme club competition has seen, he destroyed the opposition's last hope of contriving an exercise in larceny.

It was extraordinary that the match was not settled until six minutes from the end, when a shot driven low and venomously towards Sarti's goal by Bobby Murdoch – whose rich and authoritative skills had combined with the hard-edged cunning of Bertie Auld to grant Celtic an overwhelming dominance in midfield – was briskly turned in by the alert Stevie Chalmers. Every Celtic player had been a hero

and a four- or five-goal victory would not have been flattering. But none of us in the National Stadium on that sweltering evening could fail to recognise the swaggering comprehensiveness of the success, or how much it meant as a triumph of positive spirit over the barren pragmatism that had been spreading a blight across the bright traditions established for the European Cup by the vibrant football of Real Madrid and Benfica.

Neutrals had no doubt about what they had seen. *Mundo Desportivo* of Lisbon spoke for many: "It was inevitable. Sooner or later the Inter of Herrera, the Inter of *catenaccio*, of negative football, of marginal victories, had to pay for their refusal to play entertaining football." That the payment was extorted by a team that could be described as a Glasgow and District Eleven added to the romance of an unforgettable occasion. Amid the delirious clamour of the Celtic dressing room, Stein's large miner's face beamed as an elderly Portuguese official poured out lyrical tributes to the fearless sense of adventure that had characterised everything Celtic did on the park. "This attacking play, this is the real meaning of football," he said. Slapping his Latin admirer on the shoulder, the Big Man from Lanarkshire laughingly urged him to continue: "Go on, I could listen to you all night."

Being in the company of Bill Shankly, another product of the West of Scotland pits who was in those days building Liverpool towards greatness, had helped me to battle my way past the security guards into that ecstatic throng, where players were bellowing supporters' songs in the showers and inviting each other to "have a bevvy" of champagne from the huge trophy. As we approached Stein, Shankly's love of resonant utterance surfaced on cue. Reaching out a hand to his friend, and summoning that coal-cutter voice, he said: "John, you're immortal."

To the extent that football can bestow such status, the statement was reasonable. Stein's statistical record marks him out as one of the most successful managers the game has known but the list of prizes collected is an inadequate representation of his talents and his impact. His high intelligence, the imaginative scope of his

"This attacking play, this is the real meaning of football"

thinking and his long exposure to harsh realities in the wider world beyond football (he worked underground until he was 27) equipped him with a strength of personality and deep perceptiveness that would have been outstanding in any field of endeavour. What struck him as common sense was identified by the rest of us as wisdom.

As I found myself writing after he died at 62 in 1985, when all Stein's technical assets had been assessed – the vast technical awareness that owed

It should have been scripted. When Inter went ahead from a penalty after 10 minutes after this foul by Craig, they prepared to sit cynically on their lead to full-time. But for all their experience, they had no answer to Celtic's counter-punching bravado.

nothing to coaching courses, the precise judgment of his own and opposing players, the encyclopedic retention of detail, the emphasis on the positive while eradicating the foolhardy – the essence of his gifts as a manager was seen to reside in something more basic and subtle: in his capacity to make men do more for him than they would have been able to do for themselves.

Willie Wallace, a shrewd and productive forward, was the only member of the winning team in Portugal recruited by Stein. But Billy McNeill, the centre-half whose towering, imperious presence justified the nickname Caesar, and made him the pillar around which the great manager constructed the Lisbon Lions, scoffs at any suggestion that possessing a bunch of talented footballers would have guaranteed success for Celtic if Stein had not come among them. As an example of how differently the resources might have been used, the former captain points out that Celtic at one stage were ready to transfer Lennox to Falkirk. Under Stein, Lennox was given the proper context for the murderous pace and sure striking with either foot that bracketed him with the deadliest predators in Europe.

McNeill insists that his mentor was "a genius" who transformed the players he inherited into a collective force of a potency inconceivable before his arrival. He believes that the period Stein had spent as a coach at Celtic Park as prelude to moving into management, first with Dunfermline and then at Hibernian, had left such a powerful residue of influence around the place that it prepared the ground in his absence for the revolution his return would launch. Unquestionably, those who observed him at close quarters appreciated the scale of his abilities long before the European Cup campaign brought him to the notice of an entire continent. Bob Kelly, the Celtic chairman who lifted Stein as a player from the obscurity of non-League football in Wales to make him captain at Parkhead, was a purist who saw that the moderately gifted but highly thoughtful centre-half might mature into someone who could coax others to the heights of excellence that were never within his own range on the pitch.

Stein was always grateful to Celtic for sending him and other members of his team to watch the Hungarians at Wembley in 1953 and to study tactics and techniques at the World Cup of 1954. "We saw the great things that were happening in the game and we talked about them and I think we understood them," he told me. It was Kelly's theory that Stein, as a player of only modest natural ability, was obliged to learn the game almost in an academic sense. "When you assimilate things that way, they stick," the chairman said. When I talked with Kelly shortly before Lisbon, his respect and affection for his manager were unmistakable but he expressed reservations about the Big Man's emotionalism, his temper, his fits of stubbornness and his insistence on getting his own way even if that required Machiavellian manipulation of directors. Then, quite casually, Kelly added: "Oh yes, I think he'll finish up the greatest manager in the history of the game." The opinion was unlikely to be modified after Thursday, May 25 1967.

Everybody who witnessed the glorious performance in Lisbon agrees that images of all the dazzling football played are liable to fade before the profound impression created by the integrated determination of the Celtic team, the massive will they brought to a task that the bookmakers and just about every other outsider regarded as beyond them. "They've all got Stein's heart," a Glaswegian colleague said to me at the time. "There's a bit of the Big Man in all of them."

That unbreakable morale had gelled on a five-and-a-half-week tour of North America in the summer of 1966. "If any football club proposed being away for so long nowadays, they would be ridiculed," said McNeill. "But it was the first time most of us had been to America and sharing the great adventure cemented relationships to an amazing degree. We did not all love one another but we developed the closeness of a big family. Like a family, we might have our little wars internally but to the rest of the world we offered a genuinely united front. Each of us had immense respect for the others' strengths, for what they could bring to the team. We were the usual cross-section of personalities and temperaments you expect in a group of football players but that tour impressed on us how much we depended on one another and how much more effective we could be if loyalty and trust were real. When we meet up now, there is still a fantastic bond, tremendous warmth.

"Jock had the name of being a severe disciplinarian and it is true that he could be frightening when his temper went. But he understood how people's natures worked and he could be easy-going when he thought it was appropriate. In America he was pretty lenient even when he knew we weren't holding back about enjoying ourselves. Mind you, I think he was probably standing back and taking a good look at all of us, assessing us for the future. I believe, in the main, he saw what he had hoped to see." In Lisbon, many of us saw more than we could ever have reasonably hoped to see from a Scottish football team. It was in truth a kind of miracle, and all who were there can still feel the glow of it.

"They've all got Stein's heart. There's a bit of the Big Man in all of them"

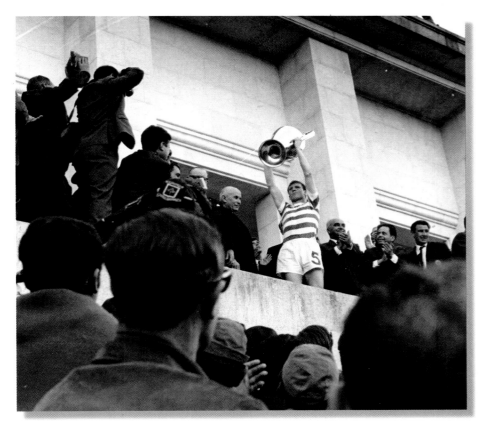

The European Cup, hoisted overhead by Billy McNeill in time-honoured fashion. Remarkably, it was Celtic's fifth trophy of the year. They had already won the Scottish League Cup, FA Cup, League Championship and the Glasgow Cup, an unprecedented haul.

Simpson's lethal ambition

As a sporting moment, Tom Simpson's fateful climb up Mont Ventoux in the 1967 Tour de France is memorable for all the wrong reasons. Yet Simpson's tragedy tells us much about the forces that still drive big-time sport long after his death. The Englishman wanted glory so badly that it killed him.

DAVID WALSH

If it hadn't been for the long coach journey from London to St Quentin in northern France in 1992, when he fell into conversation with an American, Colin Lewis's story might never have been told. "Gurney," said the American, "the name's Dan Gurney, editor of *The Trader*." Each month the magazine came to Lewis's cycle shop in Devon, and there was something about Gurney that dissolved Lewis's natural reticence. They were on their way to Peugeot's cycle plant in St Quentin and talked about the magazine and how tough things were in the bike business. Damned electronic games, they agreed. Then Gurney asked the question: "Did you ever ride the bike?"

"Yeah," said Lewis, "I was pro for nine years, twice British champion and one of 17 British guys to finish the Tour de France." "You don't say! Where'd you finish?" "Seventy-eighth. Might not be great in your book, but when I'm on my death-bed and they ask me about the best ride of my career, that'll be it. It was the Tour of 1967. I shared a room with a guy called Tom Simpson. He died." Lewis then recalled his memories from that Tour. Spellbound, Gurney listened. "This is something else," he said. "Get yourself away for three or four days, sit down, think back, then put it on tape."

After he returned from St Quentin, Lewis went to the Greek island of Kos. He took his bike, a backpack and a tape recorder, and did

what Gurney had told him. When he finished, Lewis had 12 hours of tape. On his return, he wrote to Gurney: "I have it on tape, what should I do now?". Weeks passed before the reply came. Gurney was no longer editor of *The Trader* and had returned to America. Lewis put the tapes into a box and let the memories lie. In 1997, a tabloid offered him £2,000 to talk about Simpson and that Tour, but what he remembered wasn't for sale. Until now, his memories of Simpson's final two weeks have been his secret.

At first Lewis was to share with Vin Denson, another member of the Great Britain team on the 1967 Tour and Simpson's best friend. But on the evening of the prologue at Angers, some Italian riders whom Denson knew came into the room,

Simpson had never come across a rival to whom he felt inferior

made a commotion and Alec Taylor, the team manager, decided he was getting Lewis out of there: "You're a young pro, you're in your first Tour and I'm going to put you in with somebody you will learn from, the best there is." What struck him was the neatness of the room, how, every evening, Simpson laid out his kit for the following morning. As room-mates they gelled immediately. For Lewis there was the thrill of being close to the greatest rider Britain had produced, "the complete professional". Simpson warmed to the neophyte's enthusiasm.

Maybe the novice's readiness to do

his leader's bidding also impressed Simpson. On the second stage, Lewis's loyalty was put to the test. Riding alongside his *équipier*, Simpson said: "Give us your hat." Lewis was reluctant; with its red-and-blue stripes and "Great Britain" emblazoned on the peak, he liked the hat. "You have your own," he said. "Yeah, but I want to s***." "Sorry?" "I want to wipe my arse with your hat." "Oh, okay."

"And that's what happened. There was a lorry by the side of the road, Tom took my hat, went behind it, did what he had to do and then cleaned himself with my hat. This, I thought, is life as a *domestique*. I'm going to enjoy this."

In the evenings, Simpson talked to Lewis about the future and why he needed to do well in the Tour. He had bought land in Corsica and planned to develop it, either with a hotel or apartments. He needed £22,000 and gave himself two years to raise it. With success in the Tour he could easily achieve that target. And he planned to be successful. Before lights out, they would look at the next day's route and Simpson would identify the stages where he could gain time. He talked about his rivals and their strengths before concluding that he could beat them. Poulidor hadn't got it any more; Aimar was good but not a pure climber; he had the legs on Pingeon.

Simpson had never come across a rival to whom he felt inferior. "He was the most competitive person I have ever met," said Lewis.

In extremis: Simpson on Mont Ventoux, pushing and pushing again. A haunting image of the man who didn't know when to stop.

"Throughout the Tour he talked about the Ventoux stage. 'By the time we finish the Ventoux, we will know who is going to win the Tour', he said."

"It was obvious Tom was getting into difficulty. He started to ride erratically, zig-zagging from side to side"

They didn't often talk about drugs, but the subject hung in the air. There was no testing on the race, no drug laws governing its riders. But having spent a season as an amateur in Brittany, Lewis knew drugs were widely used: "I used to see amateurs injecting themselves before races and thought, 'Well, that's what they do over here'." Although proud of his Englishness, Simpson embraced the Continental way. He spoke their languages, loved the food and had settled in the Flemish town of Ghent. When questioned, Simpson was straightforward: he was not prepared to be beaten by doped rivals if, by taking the same substances, he could beat them.

One evening, Lewis was on the bed when Simpson walked in and emptied the back pocket of his jersey. Wrapped in silver foil were six tablets. Simpson laid them on the table but didn't notice one fall on the floor. After showering, he returned to the table and saw only five tablets: "Why did you take one without asking? If you want one I can sell it to you, but don't take it." Eventually the missing pill was found and things settled down. A first-year British-based professional, Lewis did not take drugs.

Another incident has remained vivid. The team was in a hotel near Grenoble when there was a knock on the door. "It must have been a short stage because it was around 6.30pm and we were in our rooms and showered when the Italians came. Two of them. Tom's Italian was passable and, even though I didn't understand, I could tell they were arguing. It got heated, but then it cooled down, they shook hands and the Italians left. They gave Tom a box. 'What was that all about?', I asked. 'That's my year's supply of Mickey Finns. That lot has cost me £800,' he said."

Simpson had not ridden well on the Col du Galibier in the Alps and on the evening the race rolled into Marseilles he was 8min 20sec behind in seventh place. But he refused to accept he was too far off the pace, reminded everybody in the team of how important the climb to Mont Ventoux was, and inspired others with his confidence.

Lewis was convinced Simpson would do well on the Ventoux: "Tom was so confident; when he said he would do well, you believed him. He had done it at the world championships two years earlier, he had proved himself in the one-day classics. He had class and extraordinary will-power."

The first indication of trouble came in an off-the-cuff remark by Simpson about two-thirds of the way between Marseilles and the climb to the Ventoux. "The heat was awesome," said Lewis, "100 degrees plus and there was still some way to the next official feed. Passing through a village,

Colin Lewis in 1999, Simpson's room-mate on the 1967 Tour. The two rarely spoke about drugs, but the subject hung in the air.

a number of *domestiques* pulled in to do a 'café raid' – to walk into a bar and take whatever drinks they could for their team-mates. It was scorching and I followed them.

"I didn't really know what I was doing. There was this big bar, other riders were grabbing bottles, the proprietor was chasing one of them, although the customers were on our side. Coca-Cola was one of the prize possessions and, seeing a bottle on top of this fridge, I got that into my back pocket and then grabbed four other bottles, not knowing what they were. I stuffed three of them into my back pocket and the other down the back of my neck.

"Back on the bike, I worked my way through the convoy and got back to the *peloton*. Tom was my major concern and I gave him the Coke, which he was really pleased about. He took a long drink and handed it to the next guy. 'What else have you got?' he said. I fished in my pocket and pulled out a half-bottle of brandy which was just a quarter full. 'Bloody hell,' he said, 'my guts are queer today, I'll have a drop of that'. He drank some and then threw the bottle into a sunflower field."

Lewis remembers the sign for Bedouin, the last village before the climb of the Ventoux, and the nervousness which spread through the *peloton* as they got nearer. He still thought Simpson would be okay, but when the first attack went, he missed it. Having a good day himself, Lewis was near enough for glimpses of the race at the front. Simpson was chasing two leaders, he seemed okay. Getting towards Chalet-Reynard and the end of the first part of the Ventoux, an English voice came off the side of the road: "Tom's been dropped."

After Chalet-Reynard, the pines disappear and the terrain becomes bare and inhospitable. On a day as searingly hot as this, the Ventoux is the last place

The consummate professional. A week into the Tour and Simpson refuels.

his bike. We laid him by the road. We had an old tea-towel which we wet and mopped his forehead. Dr Dumas, the Tour doctor, came with a nurse and the nurse and I gave him mouth-to-mouth resuscitation.

"After about five minutes we had to leave him. The helicopter was coming. Dr Dumas was with him. I was thinking maybe they could bring him back, but I feared the worst. Tom was dead. He had lost consciousness while riding and he never regained it. He had gone beyond his capabilities." Lewis saw Simpson lying on the road, but Taylor, the team manager, told him to keep riding. At the Ventoux summit, Lewis had a long look down the mountain. There was no sign of his room-mate. That evening, Simpson's *soigneur*, Gus Naessens, knocked on his door. "Tom is dead," he said.

An hour later, another knock on the door. This time it was a rider telling him there was a police search and the riders were dumping their stuff in a nearby canal. Lewis had nothing to dump. Though he had a room to himself for the first time, he couldn't sleep. He kept thinking that if Tom had hit a wall or been in an accident with a car, his death would have been easier to accept.

Next morning, Jean Stablinski approached Vin Denson and said it was the *peloton*'s decision that Denson should win that day's stage. Then, a strange thing, Stablinski lifted his jersey and showed Denson where he hid his stimulants. Lewis couldn't make out the conversation. Was Stablinski's act a response to pills being found in Simpson's jersey? His admission that it wasn't just Tom Simpson who used drugs, but most riders in the *peloton*.

The post mortem showed cognac and stimulants in Simpson's system. "I am the one responsible for the cognac," said Lewis, "but neither of them killed Tom Simpson. The guy could have done exactly the same after drinking a glass of water. Basically, his ambition outstripped his body, and his spirit was just too much."

"The stimulant that killed Tom Simpson," said Hall, "was Tom Simpson."

you want to be, but driven by an iron will Simpson couldn't surrender. From the British team car directly behind, the mechanic Harry Hall watched as the life drained out of Simpson on that torturous climb: "I had a cine-camera on the race and was filming Tom on the Ventoux. Then it was obvious Tom was getting into difficulty. He started to ride erratically, zig-zagging from side to side. There is quite a drop on the left side and he went towards that. There was a bit of a panic, but he corrected himself and went back to the right side. He tried to straighten up, but got stuck in the stones and fell off into them.

"I jumped out of the car, undid his straps and said, 'the Tour is over for you', but he was very insistent. 'Go on, must go on', he said. We pulled him back on to his bike, because if he said he was going on, that was it. Tom was the boss. I knew he was compos mentis because he said, 'Harry, Harry, me straps, me straps'. I knew I had undone them and, of course, he couldn't tighten them. I ran along-side him, tightened his straps and he kept going.

"He rode straight for a couple of hundred yards but then it started again, the zig-zagging. I jumped out of the car but before I got to him he had fallen over on the middle of the road. He was strapped to the bike. Ken Ryall, the driver, was also there. Ken peeled Tom's fingers off the bar, I got under his chest and literally had to separate him from

"He lost consciousness while riding and never regained it"

August 1968

Six of the best

In an everyday county game in Swansea, Garry Sobers, calypso cricketing genius supreme, achieved perfection. Facing left-armer Malcolm Nash, he hit every ball of the over for six. It was a feat no one had achieved before, one which has been matched since only once. Sobers had made history in the most emphatic and dramatic way.

SIMON WILDE

Garry Sobers is, in the opinion of many, the greatest cricketer who ever lived. His achievements with bat and ball for West Indies were breathtaking and unrivalled, yet if there is one thing for which he is remembered it is something he did in a county match on a dull bank holiday Saturday on August 31 1968.

Batting for Nottinghamshire against Glamorgan at St Helen's, Swansea, he struck every ball of an over from Malcolm Nash for six. Nobody had ever done that before, and only one man, Ravi Shastri, has done it since.

"Wherever I go, everybody talks about the six sixes," said Sobers, more than three decades on. "Nobody talks about anything else. At times I have to say, 'You know, it seems as though the only thing I have ever done in cricket is hit six sixes'. It is shown in England so often," – a BBC Wales film crew chanced to capture the over for posterity – "that people are reminded about it all the time. It has stuck in their memories."

Yet records mean nothing to Sobers. It was completely unplanned and the participants, having little inkling of what was happening until the last ball was about to be bowled, have only hazy recollections of what took place. Not that that has stopped some of them dining out well on the tale. If Nash was the first casualty of this story, the facts have come a good second.

There is something compelling about the feat. A six for all six balls has an attractive symmetry. It also cannot be improved upon – and if there is one thing people like more than a record broken it is a record incapable of being bettered. Sobers achieved perfection and few in sport have ever done that.

It might not have happened had not Sobers been feeling annoyed and Nash perverse. Both teams could still finish high in the championship and on the first day Nottinghamshire, led by Sobers, were not scoring as quickly as he wanted. When he went out to bat at 308 for five, shortly before tea, he was intent on quick runs and a declaration. It was the first season of overseas players in county cricket and Sobers had set himself to revitalise a languishing team.

"I was trying to get as many runs as possible and the easiest way to get them then was to hit the ball over the top," Sobers remembers. "Losing my wicket was not a problem. Some of them were not bad deliveries, it was just the mood I was in. If I was playing a more serious innings and we had been in trouble it might not have happened. There was a short boundary on the leg side and there was no risk if you really connected." Generally speaking, Sobers was not a man to hit the ball in the air.

Whether he actually witnessed the slow scoring is another matter. Brian Bolus, who opened the batting for Notts and scored 140, believes his captain briefly left the ground during the afternoon: "He popped out to have a bet on a few horses, which was his wont, and I believe he won."

The Glamorgan players knew a declaration was coming. One of them, Peter Walker, bowling at the other end from Nash, recalled: "We were bowling and trying but not particularly worried about getting people out."

This was the cue for Nash, a curly-haired 23-year-old in his third season, who had a bit about him, to suggest he try his arm at left-arm spin. His usual style was left-arm seam and swing – and highly effective it proved during a distinguished career – and Walker reckons that Nash had only ever bowled spin before in the nets. "He was trying something he had not practised seriously," he said. Another team-mate remembers him as a "cocky bugger" who fancied himself to get anybody out any way.

An over or two before the six-in-six, Tony Lewis, the Glamorgan captain, let Nash have his way. He would bowl fastish left-arm spin from round the wicket in the style of Derek Underwood.

"He was always fiddling with cutters and having a chortle and saying 'I can do an Underwood'," Lewis said. "It seemed a safe time for him to experiment." Four days earlier, Underwood had bowled England to a dramatic victory over Australia at the Oval. Little did he know it, but Nash was about to make history himself.

By the time the over began, Sobers had moved to 40 in under half an hour and a large crowd was revelling in the

Sobers achieved perfection, and few in sport have ever done that

entertainment. But it was clearly not going to last. Nottinghamshire were 358 for five and, surely, almost had enough runs.

Sobers's partner knew his captain was about to call a halt. John Parkin, who made few first-team appearances for his county and was only playing because a senior batsman withdrew the previous day, is now a bricklayer in Nottingham. "Before the over started he said to me, 'Park, I think we'll have another 10 minutes'. But we didn't have 10 minutes and I didn't get on strike again. I was thinking of trying to run and he was not bothered at all. I had just hit Nash over extra cover for four and he must have thought, 'If he can do it then I can go a bit better'."

Nash, at the Pavilion End, checked his man on the long-off boundary was positioned for the straight drive like an old pro. And his first ball was good, on a length around off stump, but the left-handed Sobers was on to it like a flash, pulling it high over mid-on, past a floodlight pylon and out into Gorse Lane in the direction of The Cricketers, a nearby pub. After a short delay, the ball was thrown back by a passer-by. With a rueful smile, Nash walked back to his mark. Sobers smiled too. It was his second six of the innings.

The second ball was of full length on leg stump and Sobers almost whipped himself off his feet in attempting to get power into his shot. He did not get hold

The best all-rounder the game has ever seen? There can be little doubt. Sobers was grace, power, brutality and delicacy in one, an electrifying and sumptuously talented player who wore his triumphs lightly.

of it as well as he might, for it skimmed over midwicket, not far from a man on the boundary, before apparently hitting the concrete terracing and flying into Gorse Lane again, where it struck the upstairs of a house. Again, the ball was returned. "Glamorgan could do with a few fielders stuck on the top of that wall over there," said Wilf Wooller, the BBC Wales commentator. "Some seven-footers."

Sobers had reached his fifty in 29 minutes but Nash was not discouraged by the last ball. He threw up his next on middle stump but Sobers effortlessly drove it off the back foot high over mid-off, so high that Nash's man for the shot, Roger Davis, became a mere spectator. The ball bounced down the terracing of the members' enclosure and Davis threw it back to Nash.

Lewis says that it was at this point that he proffered some words of advice. "Look," he said to Nash, "if you want to look after yourself, get back over the wicket, bowl seam up and whack it in the block

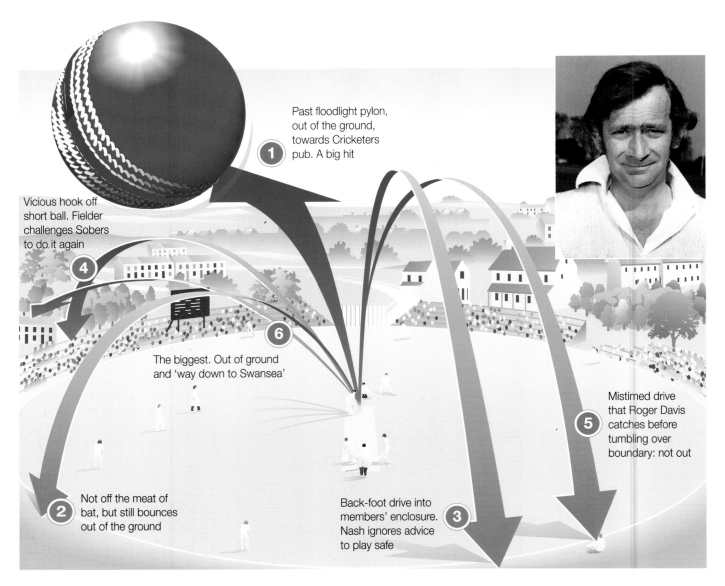

Past floodlight pylon, out of the ground, towards Cricketers pub. A big hit **1**

Vicious hook off short ball. Fielder challenges Sobers to do it again **4**

The biggest. Out of ground and 'way down to Swansea' **6**

Mistimed drive that Roger Davis catches before tumbling over boundary: not out **5**

Not off the meat of bat, but still bounces out of the ground **2**

Back-foot drive into members' enclosure. Nash ignores advice to play safe **3**

hole, like you normally do." Nash replied: "Don't worry skipper, I'll be fine."

But he was not fine. He dropped his next ball short on the leg side. It was a free hit and Sobers pounced on it hungrily, swivel-pulling it flattishly over backward square leg. It was a terrific blow. Eifion Jones, the Glamorgan wicketkeeper, jokingly told Sobers: "You didn't quite middle that one, did you?" Walker, fielding at slip, said: "I bet you can't hit the next one for six." Sobers, grinning broadly, replied: "Ah, that's a challenge."

Wooller was getting excited. "Four sixes in four balls … I wonder where Nash is going to bowl this one?" Nash was wondering the same thing. Parkin recalls him trudging back to his mark saying to himself: "Where the bloody hell do you bowl the next one?" Parkin

"And he's done it, he's done it! … And my goodness, it's gone all the way down to Swansea"

added: "He was truly trying to bowl yorkers … Get it up there so you could not hit it in the air." Some time late in the over Don Shepherd, Glamorgan's senior bowler, also offered some advice: "Look, if you pitch it right up, he can't hit it for six."

Nash's fifth ball was straighter and fuller, and Sobers accepts he did not hit it cleanly: "I got on to it a little too much." Had he middled it, it would have sailed into the pavilion; instead, the ball went high to Davis at long-off. Davis thought Sobers had been trying to hit it over mid-on and got a thick edge. The ball hung in the air. Was it going to clear the boundary, or would it be caught? Davis, inches inside the boundary line, took the ball cleanly with both hands in front of his face and at first it looked as though Nash had got a classic left-arm spinner's dismissal.

But the impact sent Davis tumbling backwards, over the boundary

line. A year earlier, the catch would have been good, but an experimental law was introduced in 1968 stating that a fieldsman "must have no part of his body grounded outside the playing area in the act of making the catch and afterwards".

Confusion reigned. Not everyone knew about the experimental law. Initially, Davis thought his catch good. "I was pretty sure my feet were inside the boundary and thought that if I caught it inside and then fell [over the line] it did not matter. But Ossie Wheatley was off the field injured and shouted to me from the pavilion, 'That's not out'. That put doubt in my mind. The crowd wanted a six, too."

Eddie Phillipson, the umpire at the bowler's end, went over to speak to Davis and, on seeing this, Sobers, who had begun to walk off, stopped. There followed a lot of discussion and walking about and it was not until Phillipson consulted his colleague John Langridge that, to cheers from the crowd, he raised his arms to signal a fifth six.

"I don't think Eddie knew the rule had changed," said Davis, "and I think that John did know and everybody was convinced that he knew what he was talking about and went with it." The debate continued long after play finished but there is no doubt the correct decision was made.

It was only then that Sobers thought of the record. "It really and truly never crossed my mind," he said, "and it was only after the fifth ball that I decided, well, no one had ever done it, there was nothing to lose, and to really give it a go."

Poor Nash was in panic. He had had enough of spin and reverted to seam for the last ball. But he probably made a mistake in continuing to bowl over the wicket, which he would not normally have done as a seamer. It was the worst delivery of the over.

"As I expected, Malcolm dropped the ball short," Sobers said. "In a situation like that a bowler obviously is going to try and change his action and bowl a quicker one. That is exactly what Malcolm did, but he dropped it halfway down the wicket, which made it a lot easier. Once it was pitched there it was all over because I was just going to swing across the line. That was the shot to play and I got it right in the middle. As soon as I hit it I knew that I had hit the six sixes."

For the third time in the over the ball sailed out of the ground – this time across Gorse Lane and into St Helen's Avenue. Sobers was not the only one who realised the record was his the moment he hit the ball. "And he's done it, he's done it!" an exultant Wooller cried in the commentary box. " ... And my goodness, it's gone way down to Swansea." Way down to Swansea, and right around the world.

After looking away in the direction of the ball, as though curious to know where it had gone, Sobers gave a modest raise of the bat. Parkin, the greenhorn, stood at the other end thinking to himself, "What on earth has gone off here?" There was a lot of cheering. A few people in the crowd stood up, but most remained seated.

Then Sobers walked off, innings declared closed, much to the relief of Walker, who was about to resume bowling at the Sea End and had already warned Parkin against taking a single first ball. Nottinghamshire 394 for five, Sobers 76, Parkin 15.

At close of play, the BBC Wales crew, who had been stood down but continued their coverage on a whim, called batsman and bowler for interview. "Malcolm was walking next to me and I was smiling," Sobers recalled. "He said to me, 'Just remember, you could not have done it without me. You might be in the record books, but I am there with you'."

Sobers, cornered in the club bar that evening, swiftly suggested to his players that they retire to the team hotel for a drink. Nash, who now coaches in North American schools, has taken his lot in good part: "Apart from that last ball, it wasn't a bad over. He was the greatest man who has ever played the game and he showed why. I was a bit shell-shocked, but it did me no harm. If people remember me for that day, that's fine."

He and Sobers see each other now and then. Tony Lewis once came across them playing golf together at Sandy Lane, Barbados. One hopes there were not many sixes on Nash's card.

A clean swing of the bat and another ball flies over square-leg. It was an essential mark of Sobers's great talent that his batting was orthodox in the extreme.

September 1968

The D'Oliveira Affair

The selection of Basil D'Oliveira for the England tour to South Africa in 1968-69 sparked a political storm that lasted 25 years. D'Oliveira was a Cape Coloured, barred from first-class cricket in South Africa. In England, natural talent took him to the top. What should have been his finest hour became a battle with international repercussions.

IAN HAWKEY

Fred Trueman broke the news. Spotting Basil D'Oliveira's car at traffic lights in Worcester, Trueman's deep voice interrupted the driver's anxious chain of thoughts. "What the 'ell you doing 'ere, Bas?" Trueman boomed. "You should be at t'Oval, old son. You've been named in't England side. They've just said so on t' wireless." At first, D'Oliveira would not believe him; Trueman liked a practical joke. Besides, D'Oliveira had much on his mind, notably his telephone conversation earlier that day with Tiene Oosthuizen, a mysterious businessman who had offered him £40,000 a year for the next decade for winter coaching in South Africa on condition he made himself unavailable for England's forthcoming tour. In late August 1968, £40,000 was an awful lot of money.

What Trueman told D'Oliveira would alter the landscape dramatically. "Roger Prideaux's pulled out of the team," Trueman insisted, "you're in." They dashed into a pub to confirm the news. It was true. The landlord had just heard it on the radio: Prideaux, a batsman, had suspected pleurisy. "Dolly", an all-rounder closer to 40 than he let on, had been called up.

The implications would dominate debate in pubs, pavilions and two parliaments for the next month and redraw the sporting map for 25 years. By naming D'Oliveira in the team to face the Australians in the fifth Test, English cricket had done rather more than look for runs in the middle-order. A week after the Test, MCC's touring party would be named for the winter series in South Africa. If D'Oliveira, a so-called "Cape Coloured" born into the indignities of apartheid, was picked, he would be taking guard against white privilege, cheered on from the cheap seats with every stroke by his own people.

In the team at last and conferring with Colin Cowdrey, the England captain. The next day, MCC confirmed the tour was off.

From that moment on Tuesday, August 20 1968, D'Oliveira recalls "a sense of destiny". Oosthuizen never called, as promised, the next morning, and he set off for London. England were 238 for four when D'Oliveira, playing his 16th Test for his adopted country, strode out at the Oval "to a terrific ovation. I felt like a million dollars. I had a date with a century."

It was not a chanceless innings, but D'Oliveira's 158 was emphatic, setting up a tense victory and presenting an apparently unarguable case for his winter ticket. What he had achieved with the innings, D'Oliveira reflected, "I was doing for the non-whites in South Africa. I was on my way back to them with an enhanced reputation." On the Saturday the chairman of selectors, Doug Insole, asked D'Oliveira about his availability for the tour. Colin Cowdrey, the England captain, checked his colleague's feelings about playing at Newlands, in his home patch, Cape Town.

At Newlands, E L McKay, the president of the Western Province Cricket Union, considered the grass banks on either side of ground and pondered the practicalities. D'Oliveira playing for England would be "a big draw" for the Coloured spectators in Province's segregated stadium. He would look at ways of increasing their ticket allocation. He might have to remove one or two of the "Whites Only" signs.

Newlands is six miles from where D'Oliveira had grown up, the area known as the Bo-Kaap, where a sing-song dialect of Afrikaans is the most common tongue and the evenings are punctuated by the call to prayer at local mosques. "In the 1950s, before the forced removals, it was really cosmopolitan," remembers Frank Brache, D'Oliveira's neighbour, teammate and later brother-in-law, "and we were into sports. As kids we would play cricket in narrow streets where you

The headline-maker: D'Oliveira ponders the news that he will not be going to South Africa. When he first heard, D'Oliveira broke down and cried.

had to bowl the ball up steps to get a good length." As a boy, Basil was always a cut above the rest – a cut, a hook or a pull, sometimes a straight-driven six back over the telegraph poles.

His talent was exceptional but unfulfilled. D'Oliveira had just reached voting age when the National Party came to power in 1948 and introduced apartheid. His community would not be voting for many years, their opportunities in every walk of life curtailed. Among much else, legislation such as the Group Areas Act and the Separate Amenities Act

As a young player in South Africa, D'Oliveira had walk 10 miles to play in the non-white leagues

turned a proud history of organised cricket in the black community into a cul-de-sac. To play in the non-white leagues, as he had to, D'Oliveira would walk the 10 miles early on a matchday morning to roll the mud surface on Greenpoint Common, pull the coir matting from a shed and nail it down. The outfield was rough sierra, good for the reflexes, not so good for raising standards. "There was glass and stones everywhere," remembers Brache. "The facilities were totally poor. Cricket was for white people."

Apart from the small, Coloured section of the grass banks, Newlands was out of bounds, too. "I remember sneaking in with Basil to watch Neil Harvey batting for

Australia," says Brache. Naturally they supported the Australians. Even so, Brache and D'Oliveira were careful not to be seen at the ground of the enemy, "in case we got spotted by the more militant people". Brache's home would later be petrol-bombed three times by those who called him "a sell-out" for engaging with the white establishment.

D'Oliveira simply wanted to play, to know how good he could be. His achievements on the margins of the South African game had been spectacular – 80 centuries in nine years of "non-European" cricket – but unable to compete against privileged contemporaries, he dreamed of going abroad. So D'Oliveira wrote to the friendliest

113

voice he had heard, John Arlott, the English broadcaster and journalist, who persuaded the Lancashire league club, Middleton, to take a chance. The Cape cricket community, white and black, rallied round to raise the fare to England. Once adjusted to turf wickets and the English game, "Dolly" soared.

Every innings and every over for Middleton drew close scrutiny back home. Returning to Cape Town in September 1960, he was shuttled via a motorcade to reception with the mayor. "If I had any wry reflections about my changed status with the white men who were now cheering me, I kept them to myself," he recalled. It hurt, though, when D'Oliveira, giving press interviews at the docks on his arrival, saw his wife Naomi, then seven months pregnant, refused access to a whites-only washroom by the police.

England welcomed him with warmth. In 1964, Worcestershire stepped in to sign him ahead of

Lancashire and D'Oliveira's county career was launched, officially at the age of 29, but, he now admits, actually rather older. A dynamic all-rounder, powerful off front and back foot and a canny medium-pacer and sometime off-spinner, D'Oliveira would become hugely popular, not just for the parable of his achievement but for his immense gifts and gregarious spirit. Worcestershire won the championship in 1965, Dolly scoring 1,691 runs. He became a British citizen, and made his England debut against the West Indies in 1966. After his first 10 Tests, he was averaging well over 50.

By 1967, South Africa was climbing up the political agenda. A new prime minister, John Vorster, in whom optimists could see hope for reform, was in office and the anti-apartheid movement had in-creased pressure on sports bodies to extend sanctions. Mindful of the

Genial to the last, D'Oliveira surveys Newlands in January 1996. In his younger days he wasn't even allowed into most of the ground as a spectator, let alone as a player.

England tour scheduled for 1968–9, soundings were taken. Foreign Office correspondence released in 1999 records that "Vorster wants to change the pattern of apartheid in sport ... to overcome the sort of difficulties that have arisen over tours." The optimism was misplaced.

D'Oliveira saw little sign of reform. What was impressed upon him, though, was that "most of the non-white community desperately wanted me tour South Africa with England. Others thought I was in danger of becoming an Uncle Tom. I felt pulled

"I remember thinking, you just can't beat the white South Africans"

and tugged to bits." The uncertainties lingered into England's 1967–8 tour of the West Indies. D'Oliveira's form was erratic, his focus blurred: "There was no let-up in the hassle. I became aware that many black people expected me to take sides."

Dropped after the first Ashes Test in the summer of 1968, D'Oliveira's story now seemed more and more drawn from the pages of Ian Fleming. Word reached him that Lord Cobham, a former MCC president, had been told by Vorster that an England side with D'Oliveira would not be accepted. Weeks earlier, Sir Alec Douglas-Home, following a meeting with Vorster, briefed D'Oliveira to the opposite effect. Then there was the mysterious Oosthuizen, an executive of an international tobacco company "with good political contacts". Oosthuizen met D'Oliveira in Oxford and made his offer of the coaching job, stipulating that the player must make himself unavailable for England's tour of South Africa. D'Oliveira turned the persistent Oosthuizen down.

Not that he had expected his recall until he bumped into Trueman in Worcester. Having provided the platform for victory at the Oval, D'Oliveira then took the sixth Australian wicket as the visitors scrapped in vain for the draw which would save the Ashes. England had won the Test with moments to spare.

D'Oliveira left London buoyant. The selectors, meanwhile, sat down to discussion of the winter party, which would keep them busy until two o'clock the next morning. As they ran through their options, D'Oliveira, on the road back to Worcester, was turning over the same names, wondering about his touring companions. With him was Peter Smith, a journalist with the Hayters agency, who had D'Oliveira under exclusive contract. "The whole of the next six weeks was traumatic," recalled Smith, "there was pain and passion. Bas is an emotional man."

On the Wednesday, Worcestershire were playing Sussex. The MCC team was to be announced that evening. Smith recorded how "every time Bas touched his teacup at breakfast, the saucer rattled". The same adrenaline took him to an authoritative 128 before he gave his wicket away so he could listen to the first announcement of the squad on the radio at 6.30.

D'Oliveira reached the dressing room just in time to hear the names: "Cowdrey, Brown, Cartwright, Dexter, Edrich ... ". By the time "Graveney" had been read out, in alphabetical order, D'Oliveira knew he had been left out. Tom Graveney was with him. "Bastards," spat the Worcestershire captain. "I never thought they'd do it to you, Bas." Graveney led D'Oliveira into the physiotherapist's room where he broke down and cried. "I was like a zombie. The stomach had been kicked out of me. I remember thinking, 'You just can't beat the white South Africans'." Later, D'Oliveira could not help but smile when he turned on his television and dancing across it was a minstrel entertainer. "I could even see the funny side of things," he said. "A white guy dressed up as a black man, singing Al Jolson songs."

MCC now faced the music. D'Oliveira's century against the Australians had pushed him close to selection, it explained, but Tom Cartwright offered more as a bowler. The selectors had picked the team purely on cricketing criteria, they insisted. It later transpired that, although MCC had taken on board Cobham's information that a team including D'Oliveira would not be allowed to tour South Africa, it had kept his warning from four of the six selectors so as not to prejudice them.

Lord's was under siege. An opinion poll recorded two-thirds of Britons saying "Dolly" should have been picked. His post-bag contained 2,000 letters in the next four days, only one of them (from a white South African) not supporting him. "It is difficult," wrote Arlott, "to think of any step taken by the cricket establishment more likely to mar the image of the game." Several MCC members resigned and the Reverend David Sheppard, who had refused to play against the Springboks, demanded a special general meeting of the club.

By the time the meeting was held, the drama had vaulted through two further twists. First, to the irritation of Vorster, the *News of the World* engaged D'Oliveira to cover the tour. The effect was to concentrate public awareness on the absurdities of petty apartheid:

Vorster denounced the touring party as the "team of the anti-apartheid movement and pink ideals"

to join his white colleagues in the press box, D'Oliveira would have to apply for a permit for each venue. Club pavilions would be out of bounds without "special dispensation".

A week later, Cartwright withdrew from the tour because of injury. MCC's selectors, having insisted D'Oliveira was originally considered only as a batsman, now chose him in Cartwright's place. England's reborn all-rounder was in Plymouth when Smith contacted him with the news. The cricket dinner he was at turned into something more like a birthday party. "The goal was again in sight," wrote D'Oliveira in his memoirs, "and the well-wishers were again slapping me on the back.

"That marvellous feeling lasted about 24 hours," he added. Over in the redneck Orange Free State, Vorster was telling Afrikaaner loyalists he would not accept a "team thrust upon us. It is not an MCC team. It is the team of the anti-apartheid movement and pink ideals." The tour was off.

"Was I sorry for myself?" asks D'Oliveira. "Of course, but not as desperately as during those terrible heart-rending few hours after the team had originally been selected and I wasn't in it. I felt simply sadness, never hatred." Those around him remember above all D'Oliveira's repeated apologies. He even considered making himself unavailable. Cowdrey immediately dissuaded him.

MCC told Vorster they would not change the squad. The Committee survived a vote of no-confidence over their handling of the affair, though their reputation had been damaged. The minutes of the special general meeting record the arguments which defined the successful, and eventually sports-wide, boycott of South Africa. Also minuted are the comments of the club president, Ronnie Aird, who spoke of "the great dignity which Basil D'Oliveira had maintained throughout the whole business". On that alone, there was no dissent.

October 1968

The legendary leap

Bob Beamon's long-jump world record at the Mexico Olympics in 1968 was the most startling athletic feat of the century. To the disbelief of his fellow competitors, Beamon didn't just break the record, he destroyed it utterly. But as important for Beamon, it was also a victory over his childhood, one scarred by violence and despair.

NICK PITT

It was calculated that at the apex of his world-shattering jump Bob Beamon reached a height of six feet above the pit. He sprinted for 19 strides, hit the board and launched himself into space, where he seemed to hang, his legs splayed, his eyes and mouth wide open in astonishment.

In that tiny portion of a second, Tony Duffy, crouching at the front of the crowd and looking through the viewfinder of his Nikkormat camera, pressed the shutter. As Beamon hit the sand, so obviously prodigious was the leap that a kind of gasping roar arose within the Olympic Stadium. The jumper was back on earth, but the image, the evidence of his victory against gravity, remained, engraved on a single frame of film.

That photograph stimulated the wonder of the world, giving visual form to a statistic that was almost beyond comprehension. It also changed the life of the man who took it. This, though, is Beamon's story. Struggle and triumph, alienation and

Bewilderment and violence marked Beamon's childhood

redemption are its counterpoints, for the record of Beamon's early life is so pitiable that it calls to mind the wretchedness of poverty in early Victorian London, material for Dickens rather than post-War urban life in the United States. Indeed, Beamon today reckons that his most notable achievement was not the jump, which is often cited as the greatest single feat in athletics history, but "pulling through" his childhood.

Beamon's mother, Naomi, had two children. The first, Andrew, was born deformed and brain-damaged, the result of her husband repeatedly kicking her in the abdomen when she was seven months pregnant. The second, Bob, was conceived while her husband was serving a three-year sentence in Sing-Sing prison for attempted robbery. Bob's natural father was a doctor who moved to Los Angeles before his son was born.

When Bob was born, in New York in August 1946, Naomi Beamon was a lonely, desperate woman. The baby had been disowned before birth, the mother had tuberculosis. The birth was premature and painful. When she left hospital, she left the baby behind. In time, Naomi begged her husband's mother to look after her sons, and they were at first brought up by their grandmother. Naomi died at 25, a month before Bob's first birthday.

Bewilderment and violence marked Beamon's childhood. At kindergarten, a teacher encouraged children to bring items from home to show to the class. Beamon brought a knife, a gun and a handful of bullets. When, later, he went to live with his mother's husband and his new wife, he saw the wife regularly beaten by the husband, and was beaten himself by the wife. Running close to the gangs, he was present when a boy was stabbed to death with an ice-pick.

Slim and long-legged, always a natural runner and jumper, Beamon's first training in athletics took place at reform school. In 1962, when he was near his 16th birthday, he saw an advertisement for the Junior Olympics, in New York. He entered, borrowed a pair of shoes from another competitor and won the long jump with 24ft 1in. "That gold medal was as important to me as the one in Mexico City," Beamon said. "It was a turning point. It proved to me that I might come through with something worthwhile in my life." It symbolised the beginnings of self-esteem and provided the map for escape.

The idea that sport could remain isolated from politics, from the rest of life, was demolished forever by the 1968 Olympics. Before the Games opened, Mexican soldiers had fired on protesting students, killing 260 and injuring more than a thousand. That summer, in the United States, Martin Luther King and Robert Kennedy had been assassinated. Blacks could run and jump for the United States in the Olympics, or fight and die in Vietnam, but they remained second-class citizens. A boycott of the Games by blacks in the American team was mooted, but instead a more symbolic and effective gesture was made. At the medal-ceremony for the 200m, Tommie Smith and John Carlos bowed their heads and raised black-gloved fists as the *Star-spangled Banner* was played. As a placard held by a man in the crowd put it: "Why be a

A moment immortalised: Tony Duffy's photograph of Bob Beamon suspended in mid-air and about to create a long-jump record that would endure for 23 years.

"Instinct took over and lifted me from the white board. All I heard was the pumping of my heart"

hero in Mexico and a slave at home?" Beamon was a sympathiser rather than an activist. When he arrived in Mexico City, his priority was to "stay focused, no matter what" and he was glad to stay at a private villa rather than the political hothouse of the Olympic village. Winning the gold medal would be his personal salvation, he thought, and he was favourite.

The great long-jumpers of the two previous Olympiads were reckoned to be past their best. Ralph Boston, the American veteran, had won the gold in 1960 in Rome and had finally beaten the world record set by Jesse Owens in 1935. It now stood at 27ft 4⅜in, jointly held by Boston and Igor Ter-Ovanesyan, the Soviet long-jumper who had won bronze in Rome and Tokyo and who remained a threat. The third great Olympian was Lynn Davies, the first Welshman to win an Olympic gold medal when he won in 1964 in Tokyo, an inch and a half ahead of Boston. Davies had never jumped 27 feet, and never would, but he remained a great competitor, a man for the big occasion.

At 22, Beamon was the young gun. He had won 22 of his 23 long jump competitions that year, including the American Olympic trials. No one quite knew what his potential might be, but he appeared capable of breaking the world record. At altitude, perhaps he could even break the 28ft barrier. Boston knew better than anyone what Beamon might or might not do. Since being beaten by him in the trials, Boston had been training with him, helping with his mental approach, watching as he worked to add speed on the runway to the spring in his legs that also made him a first-class triple-jumper and high-jumper. Beamon's talent was raw and relatively untutored, his approach often moody, his performances erratic, despite his recent record.

One afternoon before the event, Boston encountered Davies. "Don't get Bob Beamon riled," Boston warned Davies. "He's likely to f***ing jump out of the pit." He was also likely

Lynn Davies said that Beamon's jump was "in the realms of fantasy". It was perhaps a dream that Beamon found as hard to understand as everyone else.

to blow out. Beamon did not use check marks on the runway and often overstepped the mark. In qualifying, he overstepped his first jump by almost a foot and fouled again on his second. One jump remained. Boston suggested he measure his run-up from a mark well behind the take-off board. Beamon did so, and qualified.

On the afternoon of the final, October 18 1968, Duffy, a part-time photographer with no accreditation, worked his way to the front of the crowd so that he had a head-on view of the long-

jump pit. Duffy was an Englishman who dreamed of being a professional sports photographer. In reality, he was a 31-year-old accountant in the City of London. To get to the Olympics, he bought a package from a travel agency: flights, hotel, tickets. He took one camera, his Nikkormat, and a big 300-millimetre lens. It made him look more professional.

Beamon's preparations for the final were also unorthodox. In the villa, the night before, he made passionate love to his girlfriend, Gloria. "I had committed the cardinal sin in sports," he wrote in his autobiography. "All I could think of were words that started with D – deplete, drain, dissipate, distract, da da da dum! 'You have just left your gold medal on the sheets', I told myself."

The final began at 3.40pm. It was humid, with rain threatening, when the first of the 17 competitors jumped. He fouled, and so did the next two men. Beamon was drawn to jump fourth. Boston called out to him: "Come on, make it a good one." For 20 seconds, Beamon stood at the end of the runway. He felt "very peaceful and calm," he recalled 31 years later. "My body was never more relaxed. There was no sound. I felt alone. I could not feel my legs under me; I was floating. I shook my arms and hands to loosen up. I took the first step on the runway. After that, it was all automatic; instinct took over and lifted me from the white board. All I heard was the pumping of my heart. I landed with such impact that I continued to jump like a kangaroo hopping out of the sandpit."

Beamon's first thought was that he had "messed up, lost at least a foot by landing on my butt". But Boston knew the jump was huge. "That's over 28 feet," he said. "With his first jump? No, it can't be," said Davies. For the first time at the Olympics, an optical measuring device was used. An official slid it along the rail towards the marks made by Beamon's landing. It fell off the end of the rail. The official sent for a steel tape.

It took 20 minutes before the result was flashed up: 8.90m. Beamon was unfamiliar with metric measurements. He ran up to Boston. "What does it mean?" he asked. "It means you jumped 29 feet," said Boston. Beamon succumbed to tears and nausea, collapsing in what was later described as a cataleptic seizure. "I was jubilant," he recalled. "I didn't want to wake up and find it was a dream."

As Boston helped him to his feet, it began to rain. Beamon's rivals, who had yet to jump, felt impotent, drained by a sense of futility. "Compared to this jump, we are as children," said Ter-Ovanesyan. "I can't go on. What's the point?" said Davies. "He's destroyed the event." In the preceeding 33 years, the world record set by Jesse Owens in 1935 had advanced by 8½ inches. Beamon had added a further 21 inches. The 28-foot barrier had been bypassed. In fact, the first 28-foot jump would not be made until the 1980 Olympics.

Touchdown. It was fully 20 minutes before Beamon knew what he had just done. He never jumped over 27ft again.

Beamon had one more jump. He wore black socks as a nod towards the comrades and recorded 26ft 4⅛in. Boston gathered himself sufficiently to win bronze. Davies finished ninth.

Duffy had no idea that he had taken a picture of value. He kept the film in his pocket for a couple of days before taking it to a one-hour photo shop in Mexico City. When it had been developed, there were two pictures of American jumpers, one in focus, one blurred. He checked the numbers on their vests: his picture of Boston was blurred, that of Beamon pin-sharp.

Only four photographers managed to take Beamon's record leap, and only Duffy caught it at the apex. When he started to market his picture, Duffy at last realised he was on to something. The picture quickly made money; it also gave Duffy the confidence to turn professional. He subsequently founded Allsport, the biggest agency for sports pictures in the world, and became a multi-millionaire.

For Beamon, the benefits of the jump were slower to materialise. Indeed, he remembers an extraordinary exchange when he was presented to President Johnson some months afterwards. '"Nice job," said Johnson. "I need a job," said Beamon. He still had a long way to go. By 1993, Beamon had four failed marriages and a lifetime of disillusionment behind him. But he was on the threshold of the most rewarding years of his life. Today he is happily married and content.

A dinner was held in Miami to mark the 25th anniversary of the jump. Lynn Davies was present, and so was Tony Duffy, who became friends with Beamon and serves on the board of Beamon's youth foundation. Afterwards, a film of the great jump was shown. Most of the guests had seen it again and again. But its power to astonish was undiminished. He ran, took off and seemed to hang in the air forever. Around the room, a gasp went up. As one, every guest stood up to clap and cheer.

"I can't go on. What's the point?" said Lynn Davies. "He's destroyed the event"

When they were kings

Brazil in the 1970 World Cup gave the world a masterclass in football. To the flair that was their birthright and to the luminous talents of such as Pele and Gerson, they added a masterful tactical awareness and an indomitable spirit. With their emergence as world champions for an unprecedented third time, this, beyond question, was the greatest team of all.

HUGH McILVANNEY

Those of us who were there needed no great sense of history to appreciate that over the first three weeks of a Mexican June in 1970 the most popular ball game ever devised might be reaching its aesthetic zenith. Football has grown bigger and richer since then but there is no case for believing that the qualities which make it irresistible to countless millions will ever again be paraded as compellingly as they were by Brazil in those World Cup finals.

Long before they played their first match against Czechoslovakia at the Jalisco stadium in Guadalajara on June 3, there was clear evidence that winning a third championship was not the limit of the Brazilians' ambitions. They had come to Mexico to make a statement, to remind the world that their triumphs in Sweden in 1958 and in Chile in 1962 represented the truth about their status in the game and to show that the humiliating first-round exit in England four years earlier had been no more than an ugly aberration.

Having prepared with an intensity that was unprecedented, and which is plainly unrepeatable now that their best players are scattered across the globe in a money-driven diaspora, they were ready to gain maximum benefit from a squad laden with footballers who were not only brilliant but blessedly complementary. Pele, whose incomparable gifts formed the golden thread linking 1958 and 1970, once told me that he thought the men he

joined as a 17-year-old phenomenon in Sweden were more talented individually but that the 1970 crop produced a better team.

The players who were to perform with such electrifying effect in Mexico were brought together by one of the most remarkable figures ever to coach at international level, the frail-looking but often warlike Joao Saldanha. There has been a tendency during the past three decades to belittle Saldanha (who died in 1990) as a wild eccentric whose appointment was a regrettable hiccup on the way to glory. He had never played at a high standard and was earning his living as a broadcaster and columnist when abruptly called in

to take charge of the national team. Many suggested that the main advantage of his recruitment for the CBD, the governing body of Brazilian football, was some respite from his merciless criticisms in print and on the airwaves. But it is nonsense to talk of Saldanha as just a jumped-up journalist. He had known success as a coach with Botafogo, one of Rio's leading clubs, skilfully handling two of his country's greatest-ever players, Garrincha and Didi.

In addition to selecting a squad that swept imperiously through a South American qualifying group, and barely changed after he was ousted, he

A team fit to enter the realms of fable. From the left, Carlos Alberto, Brito, Gerson, Piazza, Everaldo, Tostão, Clodoaldo, Rivelino, Pele, Jairzinho, Felix.

had the inspiration to create the partnership between Pele and Tostão which was one of the key elements of Brazil's deadliness in the finals. Yet even as somebody who cherished Saldanha as a friend, and had deep respect for his worldly intelligence and the wise concepts that buttressed his romantic view of football, I could not quarrel with the decision that he should be replaced only weeks before the Brazilians implemented his plan for an early arrival in Mexico that would allow them an extended period of acclimatisation. It is true that his removal had the unpleasant flavour of a political coup, since he had fallen foul of the military president of the country, General Emilio Garrastazu Medici. Saldanha's sympathies were left-wing but that may have hurt him less than his refusal to heed the general's opinions about team selection.

Equally damaging, presumably, was the hostility that had developed between the coach and the nation's other, unofficial, president, Pele. What is undeniable is that Saldanha's personality was sufficient in itself to put his regime in jeopardy. He could be dangerously volatile – when a dispute became heated, he was not averse

to drawing his pistol – and the mind reeled at the explosive possibilities implicit in asking him to cope with the burden of Brazilian expectations in a World Cup. Dumping him to make way for Mario Zagallo was harsh but not irrational. If Saldanha had been left in charge of the talents he had shrewdly assembled, would Brazil still have been capable of lifting the Jules Rimet trophy? One man who thinks so is Gerson, the balding midfielder who so combined combativeness, tactical cunning and the endlessly varied exploitation of a glorious left foot that he was as important as any Brazilian in 1970, not excluding Pele.

But Zagallo, who as a player had contributed vitally, if unspectacularly, to the winning of the World Cup in 1958 and 1962, made a difference in Mexico that went far beyond bringing a steadier hand to the controls. Admittedly, the one major change of personnel he instigated was the recalling of Felix, a veteran goalkeeper who had been discarded by Saldanha, and Felix's erratic form hardly

Pele, incomparably the greatest player of them all, spins away in triumph after scoring Brazil's third against a demoralised Italy in the final. The coronation was complete.

defined that as a stroke of genius. Zagallo, however, tightened and clarified the tactics of the team, emphasising the dual appreciation of defensive and offensive responsibilities that was the basis of his own effectiveness in his playing days. Crucially, he jettisoned the idea of using an orthodox left-winger, such as Edu, and asked Rivelino to operate as a midfielder with freedom to attack along that flank. This was another echo of Zagallo's past, but whereas he had justified the nickname *Formiginha*, Little Ant, by pumping tirelessly up and down the left side of a 4-3-3 formation, Rivelino's interpretation of the role embraced more creativity and the application of the team's second devastating left foot.

They were not only brilliant, they were blessedly complementary

It is the clinical assessment of Dr Eduardo Gonçalvez that what Zagallo did with the Brazil team in Mexico amounted to a notable advance in tactics, something that largely anticipated Holland's total football of the mid-1970s. And the doctor was well placed to make a close study of the case. Before he took his medical degree, he had another incarnation as Tostão. Speaking from his home in Belo Horizonte nearly three decades on, the man who was the focal point of Zagallo's attack, and an infinitely resourceful amalgam of linkman and striker, said of the coach: "He has not been given proper credit for his achievement. In our team there was a perfect integration of defence, midfield and attack. Under Saldanha we were entertaining but the team

England went into the 1970 World Cup as champions and with a team arguably superior to that of 1966. Though the only side in the competition to run Brazil close, they, too, succumbed to the Brazilians' pragmatic magic. Here England captain Bobby Moore and Pele embrace and swap shirts after the game.

"Zagallo was a master of tactical organisation. He was the first to let the world see truly modern football"

did not have a sound structure. Accommodating Gerson and Rivelino together, so that they complemented each other, showed that Zagallo was a master of tactical organisation. He was the first to let the world see truly modern football."

That tribute is made all the more impressive by the fact that Zagallo took a long time to acknowledge that Tostão and Pele could function together. He found difficulty in accepting that each would not duplicate the other's functions. The soul-searching he did over that issue underlines the naivety of those on this side of the Atlantic who have imagined that the potency of Brazil's football in 1970 was mainly a matter of spontaneous improvisation. The improvisation was there in abundance but it all occurred within a framework of careful planning and discipline.

Even Zagallo's tactics were scarcely more important in the run-up to the World Cup than the appeal his experience and professionalism held for Pele. Entering the finals for the fourth time, the supreme player was, at 29, in the best condition he had ever brought to the tournament. Injury had curtailed his involvement in both the triumphant story of Chile and the debacle in England, but for Mexico he was sound, vigorous and determined to be a factor in every minute of Brazil's participation. When interviewed at Suites Caribe, the hacienda-style motel in the suburbs of Guadalajara that had been taken over as squad headquarters and transformed into a fortified camp, he made no secret of his resolve to have an unforgettable impact on what he assumed would be his last World Cup.

He already dominated the mythology of football as no man before him had, but he remained happily dissatisfied, intent on confirming his right to sport's version of immortality with one last, inimitable flourish on the biggest stage his game could offer. There would be no self-indulgence, for Pele never exhibited his virtuosity at the expense of the team. If the team's best interests were served by rolling a simple pass over a few yards of turf, that was what he did. Of course, if they needed a miracle, he was the man for the job. But nothing was done for show. The most extravagant trickery had a predatory motive. However, since the scope of his imagination as a player was matched by the joy he took in accomplishing wonders, even an arena as serious as the World Cup finals could not discourage him from attempting the outrageous.

Pele proved as much in that first match against Czechoslovakia. Near the interval, he gathered the ball in his own half of the field and moved forward. While still inside the Brazilian segment of the centre-circle, he raised his right leg in a prodigious backlift and swung it through with the flowing, effortless precision of a perfect golf shot. As Pele had noted with a surreptitious glance, Viktor, the Czech goalkeeper, had come some yards out from his posts and now the poor man was scrambling back under the venomous loop of the ball. Viktor was left in an agony of helplessness as Pele's extraordinary strike swooped less than a yard outside an upright. The moment is still vivid in the memory long after most of the details of Brazil's 4-1 victory have faded.

Next came an epic collision with England that was unquestionably the contest of World Cup 70 and as enthralling a football match as this reporter has witnessed. Though some of its most lasting images are of English defending, of Gordon Banks's miraculous save from Pele's header and a string of inspired interventions by Bobby Moore, England were perhaps marginally the more threatening of the two sides and certainly deserved the draw they would have taken if Jeff Astle had not perpetrated the miss of

The scintillating Jairzinho, here seen against Italy, scored in every match in the 1970 finals. He remains the only player in World Cup history to achieve this feat.

his career. Ultimately, the supernatural alertness of Pele was decisive. Presented with Tostão's centre from the left, most players would have felt that an effort at scoring was obligatory. But, in the fraction of a second available to him, Pele sensed that Brian Labone and Terry Cooper were closing to block his route to goal. So, letting himself fall away to the left, he stroked the ball to his right and in front of Jairzinho, who rammed it high into the net.

After Romania had been rather laboriously dealt with in another group match, and Peru had been crushed in a quarter-final, the Brazilians faced opponents they were always inclined to dread. In 1950, Brazil staged the World Cup, creating the largest stadium ever built as a suitable setting for celebration. But the Uruguayans thwarted their dream and since that nightmare in Rio the footballers from the tiny neighbour to the south had been able to induce neurosis in the masters of the game. Now they loomed again in a semi-final. If the 1970 final against Italy at the Aztec Stadium was to dazzle a global audience with the verve and grandeur Brazil brought to a sweeping 4-1 victory – and leave every watcher with a hundred glittering, indelible recollections of their greatness – nothing they did in those June days long ago was more dramatic or more revealing of the humanity at the core of their brilliance than the events of that semi-final in the Jalisco Stadium.

By the 18th minute of the action, their darkest fears had been realised as a combination of errors by Brito and, more palpably, Felix granted Uruguay a grotesquely soft goal. Instantly several of the Brazilians were on the verge of despair, none more blatantly than Gerson. That hard man held his head as if to staunch a wound. It was then that Pele emerged as a true leader as well as a talisman. He ran calmly through the shattered ranks of the

Brazil's verve and grandeur in the final were nothing less than dazzling

team and collected the ball to bring it back for the kick-off. All the way to the centre circle he was talking soothingly to those around him.

A piece of tactical calculation, as bold as it was simple, produced an equaliser in injury time at the end of the first half. Gerson withdrew into a deep position, taking his obsessively negative marker with him and releasing Brazil's marvellous defensive midfielder, Clodoaldo, to exploit the hole

created and score. But a feeling of crisis persisted and Tostão remembers astonishing scenes in the dressing room: "Zagallo, who had a reputation for calmness, was behaving like a man possessed. He was calling everybody names, condemning the team for not fighting bravely enough, for having no soul. He did not say a word about football. All he talked about was the *camisa amarela*, the yellow shirt of Brazil, and what it meant to wear it."

It was worn with pride in the second half and Uruguay were beaten 3-1. Twice Pele went close to fulfiling his declared ambition to score a goal that would be unique, that nobody could emulate: Pele's goal. First he almost did it by inflicting the dummy to end all dummies on Mazurkiewicz, the Uruguayan goalkeeper, and then he returned a mishit goal-kick with such an incredible volley that only a frantic save denied him. What mattered was that Brazil's belief in their own magic was restored.

I travelled with them in the plane to Mexico City for the final. They were sure they were on their way to a coronation. How else could we describe what happened there?

June – August 1971

Pride of the Lions

The British Lions had always known how to play with style – and lose. But the 1971 party was different. The traditional brilliance of the back play was supplemented by forwards who would not be intimidated. New Zealand's All Blacks, who had made something of a cult of violent rugby, were about to meet their match.

STEPHEN JONES

Dr Doug Smith, an engaging, craggy Scot who won eight caps for his country on the wing from 1949, was chosen as manager of the British Lions party for the 1971 tour of New Zealand. In Brisbane on the eve of the team's first match, against Queensland on a short warm-up leg in Australia, he made two predictions.

The first was that the Lions would lose against Queensland next day because of circadian dysrhythmia. Smith enlightened the bewildered journalists. "Jet lag," he explained. They duly lost. The second was that the Lions would win the four-Test series in New Zealand by two matches to one, with one drawn.

These days, the status of Lions tours remains largely and blissfully untouched by the march of time. In 1971, their magic and mystique were even greater. With matches televised only in black and white snatches, if at all, the tours were a cross between a Sunday School outing and a crusade: the sense that they were taking place almost unseen was uniquely powerful. The traditional means of following them was with a radio under the blankets in the early hours, with doyens such as Winston McCarthy or Alun Williams cracklingly calling the plays.

Another tradition was that the Lions always lost. They had never won a Test series in New Zealand. They always had the perennial British back-line brilliance and yet were traditionally poor in the forwards. It was thought vaguely un-British, even "professional" for a Lions team to do much in the way of preparation. Vastly entertaining and yet losers. What more could a Kiwi rugby follower want? So Doug Smith's Brisbane prediction came across as a mixture of jibing good humour and rampaging over-optimism.

On to another press conference. It was given 13 weeks later, after the fourth Test, which the Lions drew to take the series by two to one, with one drawn. Colin Meads, the legendary lock and New Zealand's captain in the series, looked across at Dr Smith. "He must be the greatest bloody predictor of all-time," he growled. The Lions had turned rugby history on its head.

Alongside the old back-line brilliance, the Lions had a new hardness

If it was the forwards who provided the platform for the ultimate victory, it was the backs who finished it off. (Right), JPR Williams in full flow. (Above) Gareth Edwards and Chico Hopkins after the fourth Test.

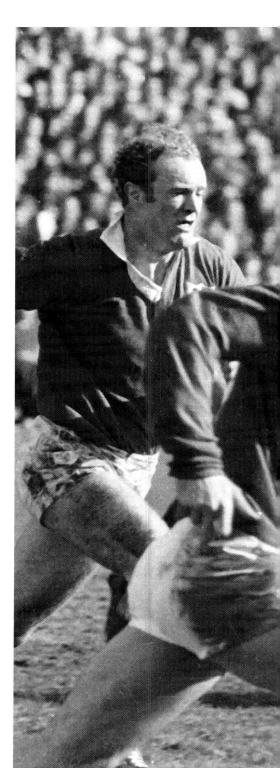

and edge in the forwards. It gave rugby in Britain and Ireland bounding self-confidence. It gave public and players a taste for Lions glory which they have yet to lose – of the last eight tours, the Lions have won four, after failing in every one before 1971. It galvanised the sport here. It was the finest hour for rugby in the British Isles. Gloriously, the question at the end was different from the normal. It was: "What went right?"

The foundations were laid well before the party left. On most tours the management teams had been time-servers, happiest on the cocktail circuit. In 1971, the men in charge dove-tailed perfectly. Smith, revered by his players, took care of touring protocol and admin to allow the others to concentrate on the business. The coach was Carwyn James, a quiet, emotional, chain-smoking, lapsed Welsh nationalist genius from Llanelli with a vision of rugby in sweeping style. On the evidence of that one tour alone, he is regarded as probably the greatest coach European rugby has seen. His untimely death in 1986, after a life unfulfilled, only added to his legend.

The captain was John Dawes, skipper of London Welsh and Wales.

Alongside the old back-line brilliance, the Lions had a new hardness and edge in the forwards

Though not a centre of dazzling skill, he was a splendid technician and leader with a rugby intellect to match that of James. More, Dawes was the springboard behind the golden era of the London Welsh club, which at the end of the 1960s had revolutionised the game. The sweep and attacking zip of that side, with the great JPR Williams

The King: Barry John, a sublime will o' the wisp, possessed of quicksilver talents and immense self-confidence. The All Blacks had never seen his like.

eral recognition of him as probably the greatest rugby player in history. John was something else. To this day, New Zealanders who followed the tour hardly know what to make of him. "They thought of John as a being from another planet," wrote John Reason, the journalist. Kiwis have always revered players of power and thump. John was sinewy and slight, almost ethereal. But his pace-kicking was brilliant, his generalship immaculate, his tactical kicking of such majesty that in the first Test he ended the career of the dangerous Fergie McCormick at fullback, torturing him with diagonal kicks which had the poor man scrambling and fumbling.

Yet it was John's self-confidence that enraptured his colleagues, who called him, simply, The King. Mervyn Davies recalls: "He played rugby on a different plane to anyone else. We'd all be in the dressing room thumping the wall and he'd be there in such a relaxed state that you'd think he was going out for a stroll. He'd say: 'Don't worry boys. It's only a game. Just give me the ball and I'll win it for you. It's only the All Blacks.' He confidence was tremendously influential."

Tours are strange affairs, detached from real life. Small personal enmities can flare, players outside the Test team can become bitter and sap morale violently. Dawes recalled: "It was a united group. Our three main humorists were Bob Hiller [England full-back], Chico Hopkins [Welsh scrum-half] and John Spencer [England centre]. None of them played in the Test matches. But their contribution was as great as those who did." The midweek team won all their matches, a priceless boost to morale.

But there was more to the Lions. There had to be, because happy teams of brilliant back skills had gone to New Zealand before and been crushed. James knew that his pack had to take on the home forwards head on. New Zealand in the Meads era was an intimidating place to play. "They were bastards at that time, the New Zealanders," said Doug Smith.

re-writing the role of full-back so that he became a prime attacker, was reproduced in the Welsh national team. With Dawes in charge, Wales won a reverberating, thrilling Grand Slam in 1971. Thirteen of the 30-strong original Lions party were Welsh, and six were London Welshmen, including Williams at full-back, Gerald Davies, the sublime wing, and Mervyn Davies, the gangling No 8 later singled out by Meads as one of the sharpest thorns in his side. Together, they gave the Lions a hard core of proven winners.

If the management was world-class, the material they were working with was of similar quality. The Lions could call on Williams at full-back; they had three outstanding wings in Davies, David Duckham, the Rolls-Royce Englishman, and John Bevan, who scored 16 tries on tour with blasting power. Alongside Dawes in the centre, Mike Gibson played the rugby of his life, anchoring an extravagant back division with a mixture of hard-headed defence and tactical nous. And at half-back, there were Gareth Edwards and Barry John.

Edwards was rapidly finding his feet in a career which would end with gen-

"They were bastards at the time, the New Zealanders"

For technical excellence in his forwards, where he was no specialist, James relied on Ray McLoughlin, the Irish prop. McLoughlin played only four games before being invalided home, but he left a profound mark. "Carwyn learned more from Ray about forward play in the short time Ray was there than from anything that happened after," said Dawes.

But it was not enough to know what to do. The Lions need the guts to carry it out. James came out with a famous exhortation that the Lions "must get their retaliation in first". James was a mild-mannered man, who disliked thuggery. But he knew the home packs had to be faced down. It made for some gory viewing, the angry undercurrent reaching its height in the epoch-making near-riot when the Lions met Canterbury early in the tour.

Canterbury had a well-earned reputation for thuggery and the match brought a succession of appalling incidents. The Lions prop, Sandy Carmichael, who was repeatedly punched, had his cheekbones broken and had to leave the tour. Canterbury were a disgrace. John Reason suggested they play in a mental ward. But the Lions slugged it out and won. New Zealand's hard men took note. "The New Zealand teams made the mistake of trying to smash us to pieces," Smith said in 1998. "They got their comeuppance by us hitting them back. That was what riled them the most." In another landmark match of a different kind, powerful Wellington were massacred by a dazzling Lions display.

So to the Tests, with a New Zealand team suddenly on its guard. Dawes and James knew that the momentum had to be maintained. In the first Test, at Dunedin, the Lions' backline brilliance never had a chance to surface. They were battered all across the pitch. It was their tackling and their courage which surfaced. They won 9-3, against the run of play, and the difference was made when Ian McLauchlan, the diminutive prop known as Mighty Mouse, scored a try from a charged-down kick. "We had to win by hook or by crook," Dawes remembered. "Nobody was more surprised than the Lions. We hardly saw the ball."

The Lions were ahead, and the waves of momentum and hope now washed up 12,000 miles away. Vivian Jenkins wrote in *The Sunday Times*: "Hallelujah! Sound the trumpets, bang the drums, crash the cymbals, make any old noise you like. The Lions did it, they beat the All Blacks."

The second Test brought the backlash. Inspired by half-backs Sid Going and Bob Burgess, New Zealand pulled clear. "When I realised that the game had gone, I said to the boys that we needed to build for the next game, there and then," Dawes said. "We came back strongly, Gerald scored two late

Thanks to the 1971 Lions, rugby would never be the same again

tries, and when I came off the field I told Carwyn we could win the whole thing if we started the third Test as we'd ended the second."

They did. In Wellington, the Lions produced one of the most devastating opening passages in history. The pack, now led by Willie John McBride, again gained that key parity. The backs responded. They scored 13 points in the first 13 minutes, with Davies squeezing over in the corner before a burst from Edwards, with a hand-off that lifted Burgess off his feet, gave a try on a plate to John. They Lions never scored again, but won 13-3. At the very least, the series was shared.

History day came in Auckland and the fourth Test, The tension affected both teams, and the Lions were dog-tired. "I don't know how we did it," Dawes said. "I suppose we turned on the remote control." The All Blacks led 8-0, but a try by Peter Dixon, the flanker, and a 48-yard penalty by John gave the Lions a three-point led early in the second half. After the All Blacks had equalised again, JPR Williams, not noted as a kicker, dropped a mighty goal and ran back with long hair billowing, waving to the stands. A final All Black penalty only drew the match, fulfilled the prophecy of Dr Smith and gave the Lions the series.

Previous parties had been greeted at Heathrow by two officials of the Home Unions committee. This one returned to an airport overrun by well-wishers. Rugby would never be the same again. Southern hemisphere domination was bruised, not broken. But anyone involved in subsequent Lions tours, and anyone with British Isles rugby in their hearts, will always be in the debt of Dawes and his men.

Dog-tired but a history-maker. Skipper John Dawes addresses the crowd after the drawn fourth Test in Auckland has clinched the series win. Behind him, Lions manager Doug Smith looks on.

The longest three seconds

When the US, hot favourites for gold, finally took the lead in the 1972 Olympic basketball final, there were only three seconds left to play. What happened next was pure chaos and at the end of it the Soviet team were the ones with the gold medals and the Americans were left crying foul. It remains a bitter memory for some.

DAVE HANNIGAN

The 12 silver medals have never been presented. They remain in a Swiss vault, the unwanted tokens of perceived injustice. Over the years, intermittent attempts to persuade their owners to take possession of them have come to nothing. In Munich on September 10 1972, the 12 members of the US basketball squad who lost the most bizarre Olympic final of all voted unanimously not to accept silver. To renege now would diminish their stance. As they watched the medal ceremony on television and their opponents, the USSR, fingered their gold discs triumphantly, the empty second-place spot on the podium bore witness to their dissatisfaction.

"If you win gold, you are there in the record book for the rest of eternity," says Mike Bantom, one of the recalcitrant dozen. He is in his office at the National Basketball Association's marketing operation in New Jersey, remembering the days when he sported an afro, contemplating what might have been. "It hurt a lot but the passing of time has made me realise that having a medal is not the most important thing in my life. The things that made me work hard and earn that medal are the things that have made me what I am today. I'm not going to achieve anything by getting that medal. Just like to me the Russians didn't prove they were the best team by holding their gold medals either." A couple of Bantom's team-mates have put a clause in their wills stating that their descendants must never accept silver on their behalf. That is how much it still means.

With 10 seconds on the clock, and his team nursing a one-point lead, the USSR's Alexsander Belov threw a poor pass that was intercepted by America's 6ft 6in guard, Doug Collins. Driving the length of the court, Collins was on his way to making an easy basket when he was upended and knocked unconscious. As he came to, he heard coach Hank Iba dismissing his assistant John Bach's suggestion that someone else take the free throws. "If Doug can walk," said Iba boldly, "he'll shoot."

Collins was invigorated by the 66-year-old coach's gung-ho attitude. Though still groggy, he knew what was at stake. Since basketball became an Olympic sport in 1936, the US had never lost a match at this level. On this Saturday night in Munich, having trailed the USSR all evening, they literally had two shots at redemption. If Collins could sink them, the founders of the game would have to hold their 50-49 lead for a mere three seconds.

"I can't even remember feeling any pressure," recalls Collins, now an analyst with NBC. "Three dribbles, spin the ball, toss it in, same as in my backyard. I hit 'em both and we've got the lead. I didn't know what I was made of until then."

On the Soviet bench, Vladimir Kondrashin couldn't believe what was happening. Bossing the game from the tip-off, his team had held an eight-point lead with six minutes remaining. And now it had come to this. As the medics had fussed over Collins on the court, Kondrashin tried to call a time-out, intending to use it after the first of the free throws to unveil his last-ditch plan to his players. But the German officials at the scoring table didn't inform the Bulgarian and Brazilian referees on the court of Kondrashin's request immediately. Instead, as Collins's second throw arced through the air towards the basket, the time-out horn sounded belatedly.

American elation – but it wouldn't last long. The officials are just about to order the game restarted and dash the US team's hopes.

Belov leaps to score the winning basket. The Americans are still convinced he fouled two defenders – and that the time-out should never have been played anyway.

No time-out was allowed. Sergei Bashkin, the Soviet assistant coach, protested but was over-ruled. The USSR were ordered to restart the game. Ivan Edeshko's attempted pass was deflected to safety, the American bench streamed onto the court and for the first time that night the Olympic final was over. But the longest three seconds in the history of sport were only beginning.

As if the quasi-political clash of the superpowers in the final had been anticipated, the Americans had spent their training camp at Schofield Army Barracks in Pearl Harbour, Hawaii. They slept 12 to a dormitory, worked out three times a day in basketball's version of boot camp, and, when their concentration waned, John Bach would tell his charges that those crimson stains on the walls were blood, the last remnants of the Japanese attack in 1941.

With an average age of 20, this was the youngest US basketball team at any Olympics. They were all students coming off campuses wracked by the protest culture of the day and representing a country whose reputation was being impugned daily by Vietnam. In a time of social change at home, and assaults on the world order abroad, they were playing the only major American sport with a genuine international dimension. When it was all over, the circumstances of their defeat would confirm a lot of people's prejudices about communism.

"For the most part, none of us had been out of the country before," says Bantom. "We were Americans and all, but some of us were black Americans and there is a difference there in terms of how you feel about your place in society. Once we got there, we saw all the different nations, all the different people, and how it was representing your country. It made you more conscious of nationalism, and I would have felt proud to win a gold medal for my country, to be up on the podium when the anthem was playing."

The Soviets, too, were products of their environment, their Olympic ambitions inevitably subject to the decision-makers at the Kremlin. Only

This time it really was all over – and entirely against the odds the Soviets had won the gold by the narrowest of margins. It was the underdogs' day.

20 years after entering their first team in the competition, they did not realistically think they could beat the best American amateurs. Reaching the final was the summit of their achievement. Before the game, the players had prepared a banquet. They would celebrate their second place because that was what they were there to win.

"Even our chiefs in Moscow planned for us to take second place," said Edeshko in a 1992 interview. "Everything in our country was

The Soviets never expected to win. Their goal was no more than to reach the final

planned at that time, including international sports. Having secured the desired second place in reaching the final, we were able to play an unrestrained game. We didn't care much if we lost; we had done what we were told to do by Moscow."

Before East could collide with West, another of the world's conflicts would intrude. Five days before the final, Black September terrorists stormed the building where the Israeli team was staying, setting in motion a train of events which culminated in the massacre of nine athletes and two coaches. Just one week before, the American team had been moved by what they saw on a visit to the concentration camps at Dachau. Now they thought these Games were over.

"The incident with the Israelis happened just across the courtyard from us," says

Bantom. "So at that point, we were saying, 'We want to go home, we don't want to finish these games'." Like all those athletes who expressed such sentiments, the Americans were told the Olympics were bigger than everything. The show had to go on.

It was the Bulgarian official, Artenik Arabadjan, who decided there were people on the court when Edeshko had tried to find a team-mate. Arabadjan ordered the three seconds replayed. Again, Edeshko couldn't complete the pass. Tom McMillen did the job of guarding him, the ball never reached a Soviet player. Once more the court filled with the jubilant American bench. Fans spilled out of the stands in a frenzy of yelling and hollering, all the more pronounced because of the fright they had just received. Once more, the joy was shortlived. As the Soviets argued, pandemonium ensued. R William Jones,

them. I'm sitting there on the bench because I had fouled out and it happened right there in front of me."

Belov tipped the ball into the basket as the clock ran out: 51-50. "And this time, it is over," said Frank Gifford, commentating for ABC. His counterpart on Soviet television, Nina Eremina, a former star of the women's national team, couldn't even manage that much. She just burst into tears.

On appeal, the decision was allowed to stand, the FIBA jury of five countries dividing along predictable geo-political lines. Hungary, Poland and Cuba sided with the USSR, Italy and Puerto Rico with the USA. Uncertain how the vote would go, the Soviet players went without their victory banquet until Vladimir Kondrashin returned to their camp with news of the vote. "Well guys," said the coach, with a straight face. "There is going to be a replay ... in 1976 in Montreal." Their party began.

"We sat in our rooms watching the medal ceremony and at that point, we realised, they were going to screw us over like this," says Bantom. "There was nothing left to do but go out and let our hair down at the disco. We were 19- and 20-year old kids and we had dedicated our summer to doing this. We were really disillusioned because at that point in all our lives, we all still felt that right triumphs."

"We had two guys on Belov. He blatantly pushed them in the back"

his involvement in a smuggling ring. In his honour, a prestigious basketball tournament was named after him, and Kondrashin turned his office into a shrine for his favourite player. For years after his death, the coach would drive around his home town of St. Petersburg with a photograph of Belov in his car, a reminder of their finest three seconds together.

Mike Bantom has his keepsakes, too. Through the years, several people have sent him videos of the game, and in his New Jersey office he has a picture of himself in the red, white and blue uniform of his country. "It was a great learning experience and it helped us become the people that we are today," he says. "We would all love to be able to tell our kids we have an Olympic gold medal. The fact that we don't, well, if this is the worst thing that happens to any of us, we are all going to have very blessed lives." He dissolves into the sort of cheery laugh that sounds like it has been decades coming.

Mike Bantom in 1999, the afro long since gone. He may be philosophical about what happened in Munich but he hasn't forgotten.

the British secretary of FIBA, the International Basketball Federation, then entered the scene.

Jones decreed the USSR be allowed their time-out and have their three seconds given back. That intervening in the officiating of a game was way beyond his remit was just one more grotesque facet of the affair. In the brouhaha, Iba had his pocket picked and the Americans did not have time to formulate a proper defensive strategy. Their disorganisation was compounded when McMillen was ordered to back off Edeshko, crucially allowing him a better view of the floor. Even then, Edeshko committed a foul by stepping inbounds before hurling the ball 94 feet to Belov under the American basket.

"We had two guys on Belov," says Bantom. "When they threw that pass, he blatantly pushed them in the back. It wasn't like he used guile to move them with his body, he f***ing pushed

On returning home, there were recriminations in the American press. Some pundits reckoned it was Iba's old-fashioned, ultra-cautious style of play which had got the team into this mess in the first place, conveniently ignoring the fact that the same coach's methods had been good enough to take gold in 1964 and 1968. Each player received a letter from President Nixon telling them "You're still champs in my eyes", and life went on to treat most of them better than the 1972 Olympics. Nine of the 12 made it to the NBA, Tom McMillen ended up a congressman for Maryland, and all seemed to have prospered professionally.

Alexsander Belov was dead within six years of making the basket which turned him and his team-mates into folk heroes all over the Soviet Union. The official cause of death was a form of heart disease but rumours abound that Belov died violently as a result of

The try of the century

For sheer sporting exhilaration, few moments match the try scored by Gareth Edwards for the Barbarians against the All Blacks in January 1973. The background was a match of fearsome intensity, the try itself the product of the kind of sublime skill many would count themselves lucky to see once in a lifetime.

STEPHEN JONES

It starts in staccato rhythm, with the zip-zip-zip of Phil Bennett's side-steps, which freeze him for frantic instants as he plants his right foot wide, to push off in the other direction. But the marvel then of rugby's most famous try is the effervescent fluidity of it all. It is all done in one sweeping phase of play, with no pause for rucks or mauls.

It is also done on pure rugby instinct – nobody involved, with the exception of John Dawes with his faint suggestion of a dummy and a jink (and the only man in the move to pass to his right), appears to lift his head and size up the situation. The others do what comes naturally, whether it be John Pullin, the hooker, shipping the ball on to someone – anyone – as quickly as possible, or Tom David, then a marvellous buccaneering flanker, injecting power and pace. It is David's burst which transforms the move from brave counter-attack to possible try. But from wherever it came, on a dull day at Cardiff Arms Park on January 27 1973 rugby was enormously enriched.

It is the most famous rugby movement of all time; many people know every zip and every sweep of it. It has been a draw card for those who knew rugby not, 25 seconds of perfect PR. For those who loved the sport already, it is something which never seems hackneyed or stale, as if after a thousand replays you are still anxious that Alastair Scown, the All Black flanker, might cut down the jagging Phil or that Joe Karam might just get across to

ankle-tap the flying Gareth Edwards.

Or even that the referee will stop it all dead with a blast from the whistle. It is part of rugby's folklore that the final pass, one-handed from Derek Quinnell, intended for John Bevan but intercepted by Edwards, was forward.

The referee that day was Georges Domercq, a dapper, beaming Frenchman. Domercq had a reputation for *laissez-faire* refereeing which could enrapture crowds and infuriate coaches. One week before the match, he had taken charge of a Wales-England match and the official assessor had taken him aside. "He told me that I must be more strict," Domercq remembers. "Thankfully, I didn't take any notice."

Or was he so infected by the glory of the moment that he could not bring himself to stop play? Not a bit of it. "I

could have whistled twice in the move, both times for high tackles by the New Zealanders. But I think the spirit of rugby's beauty was flowing through my mind. I was only a few yards from the final pass, and it was not forward. There was never any question in my mind. I have seen the replays, of course, and I believe it is a trick of the camera angles that it seems forward. If I had blown, we would have missed a *jolie epoque.*"

Domercq travelled back to Tarbes airport next day and the All Black party were also on board, bound for the French leg of their tour. "There were 1,000 people at the airport," Domercq says. "But the All Blacks were almost ignored. They all approached me instead. It seemed that everyone wanted to see someone who had played some part in such an amazing

Phil Bennett is under pressure after fielding a long New Zealand kick. But rather then kick for touch, he unleashes a sidestep that wrong-foots Ian Hurst (12)

With the second slashing sidestep, Bennett leaves Peter Whiting (5) staring into space as the wrong-footed Hurst sprawls to the ground in Bennett's wake

More All Blacks appear. But Alastair Scown (7) has over-committed himself, and is easy prey. He is picked off by the third and final sidestep, and Bennett scents open spaces

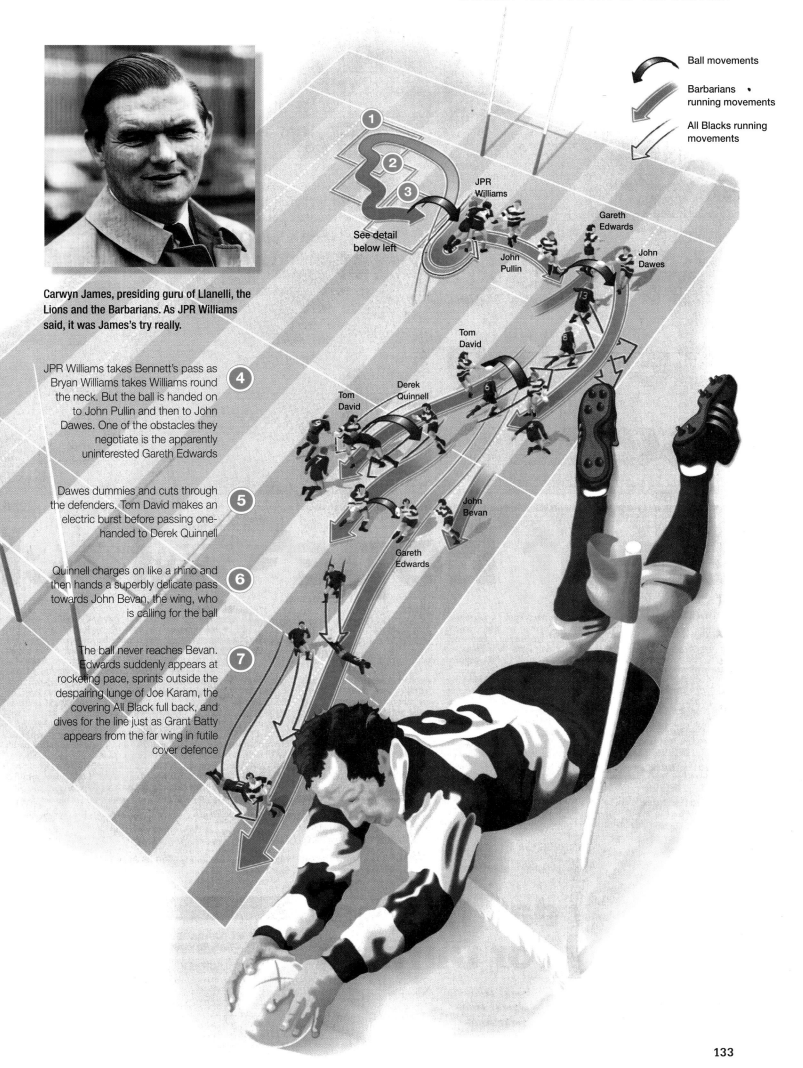

Carwyn James, presiding guru of Llanelli, the Lions and the Barbarians. As JPR Williams said, it was James's try really.

JPR Williams takes Bennett's pass as Bryan Williams takes Williams round the neck. But the ball is handed on to John Pullin and then to John Dawes. One of the obstacles they negotiate is the apparently uninterested Gareth Edwards

Dawes dummies and cuts through the defenders. Tom David makes an electric burst before passing one-handed to Derek Quinnell

Quinnell charges on like a rhino and then hands a superbly delicate pass towards John Bevan, the wing, who is calling for the ball

The ball never reaches Bevan. Edwards suddenly appears at rocketing pace, sprints outside the despairing lunge of Joe Karam, the covering All Black full back, and dives for the line just as Grant Batty appears from the far wing in futile cover defence

Ball movements

Barbarians running movements

All Blacks running movements

See detail below left

JPR Williams

Gareth Edwards

John Pullin

John Dawes

Tom David

Derek Quinnell

Tom David

John Bevan

Gareth Edwards

thing." So the try, after all these years of doubt, is officially validated.

And it should also be fiercely protected against claims that it was a frippery in a festival match, just a giant candy-floss striped in the black-and-white of the Barbarians. Consider the context. Eighteen months before the match, the British Lions had won their first-ever Test series in New Zealand (*see page 124*), an achievement which turned rugby's world on its axis. Lions only play away, and this was the nearest that home crowds could ever come to seeing their heroes in the flesh and dreaming of a repeat of the majestic style of play which the Lions produced.

By now, Barry John and Gerald Davies were gone while Mervyn Davies withdrew from the match in the morning and, stubbornly, the Barbarians stuck to their tradition of choosing an uncapped player in their major matches. Instead of a Lions lock, they chose Bob Wilkinson, a lanky young trier from Cambridge University. But the growl of the Lions was on the Cardiff wind that day. Huge pride was at stake on both sides.

And frankly, the stakes were high because people wanted to see that New Zealand team beaten, and if the "Lions" could achieve it in style then so much the better.

The All Black party was the least popular ever to visit. Their rugby was painfully dull, their behaviour and public relations dreadful. Keith Murdoch, the thuggish prop, had been sent home for punching a security guard in a Cardiff hotel; the team had a forbidding inner cabal who wore black hats and were content to play up to a boorish image rather than, as do modern New Zealand teams, polish hard their outward appearance. There was derision directed at the All Blacks even during the try. On the commentary soundtrack you can hear loud boos at Bryan Williams's high tackle on JPR Williams, and there was further trouble later when Grant Batty, the peppery wing, clashed with the massive David. The crowd were in ecstasy when David tousled Batty's hair as if he had been a recalcitrant schoolboy.

Gareth Edwards remembers that, far from breathing the air of a festival,

The growl of the Lions was on the Cardiff wind that day. Huge pride was at stake

it was all suffocating with pressure. JPR Williams recalls "a lot of needle" before the match.

"People expected us to beat them, but also in a certain style," said Edwards. "I have never felt so weak at the kick-off, because of the pressure." It is easy to be speculative, to be as bold as Bennett's sidesteps, when there is nothing riding on the outcome. The greatness of the try which Edwards was to score lay in its psychological backdrop. It was a true Test try.

The tension, of course, makes the boldness of Bennett even more praiseworthy. When he picked up the long kick from Bryan Williams he really should have delivered one of his long spirals into touch. Consider also Bennett's position at the time. He was trying to fill the boots of the wondrous, departed Barry John and, although he had always played with brilliance for Llanelli, his confidence could be ephemeral.

But in the dressing room at the Arms Park, he had just the man to boost it for him. Carwyn James, the

Gareth Edwards personified a whole generation of dominating Welsh rugby. He was hardly less effective with the Lions – or the Barbarians.

brilliant coach and conductor of the 1971 Lions, was Bennett's club coach at Llanelli. The Barbarians stubbornly clung to the tradition that preparations should be cursory – a stance which seems ludicrous today and, to be honest, seemed hardly less so in 1973. But they did ask James to talk to the players on the morning of the match. He invoked the spirit of the Lions, and also the spirit of Bennett's genius. "I remained convinced," JPR Williams said, "that the whole thing really was Carwyn's try. He soothed us, told us to enjoy it. And I'll never forget his last words – to insist to Phil, who was full of trepidation, to go out and play just like he did for Llanelli." Bennett was told by James that he could "sidestep this lot off the park".

Bennett himself knew it: "I always felt that it was easier to sidestep the New Zealand-style flankers because they always ran hard straight at you, then didn't hold off as others did to shepherd you." Alastair Scown charged straight at Bennett, found himself crash-tackling thin air, and Bennett and the Barbarians were away and gone. The noise of the crowd as the move rumbled on must have been diminished simply because Bennett's sidesteps had taken the breath away. Possibly, these were rugby's most dazzling microseconds. This was the lighting of the blue touch paper.

And now, to the strike, the devastating surge by Edwards. Bennett had conjured, Williams had scraped a pass away as Bryan Williams hit him high; Pullin had moved the ball fluently; Dawes had produced his canny invention and his cut; David had made his boisterous surge; Quinnell had handled the ball delicately, on his fingertips, and handed it on towards John Bevan on the left wing.

More dazzling microseconds as Bevan shaped to catch the ball, still with the defence in reasonable shape; and suddenly, Edwards came to the scene from nowhere, at a pace so blistering that he added another gear entirely to a movement that was already at high speed.

Pace, power, panache: the Barbarians on the attack as Gareth Edwards shapes to ship the ball on to a team-mate.

early play. "We are going to have the thrill of our lives this afternoon," he said. The thrill of our lives duly arrived, only seconds later.

The least-known player on the field certainly regards it as such. Wilkinson went on to six England caps but still regards the game as his career highlight: "The thing that sticks in my memory was the atmosphere that day. I'm a bit of an atmosphere freak, and there are not many Englishmen who have played at the Arms Park and been cheered like that. It was a wall of sound."

He has memories of the pre-match ("although I was the gatecrasher I was made welcome"), but fewer of the post-match celebrations: "As the baby of the party I collared the champagne and took it round. Fatal, because you always end up filling your own glass. But very special memories."

But where had he been? Why so late at the party? "Even though the game was only a few minutes old I was feeling weak with the pressure. I was running round like I had no legs and never really feeling part of it. When Phil fielded the ball I was 50 yards away in the other corner, running back towards our line." Indeed, the first contribution which Edwards made to the move lay in avoiding his own onrushing colleagues. At one stage, as he turned to back them up, he was probably as much as 25 yards behind the ball: "I was still asking myself why didn't someone kick the ball out, so that I could get my second breath."

But instincts were quickly aroused. "John Dawes got the ball, and like the poacher I was, I thought that if I chased then there could be something on." There was. Edwards spotted a running line down the left wing and the ball gradually moved back towards that flank of the field.

Edwards is the greatest rugby player I have seen in my life. He was also one of the fastest, a marvellous athlete and sprinter. Bennett and the others have conjured marvellously. But the final ingredient, which takes the try from possible to certain, is raw pace. Suddenly, it is as if all the rest

Edwards appeared at a pace so blistering he added another gear entirely to the move

had been treading in treacle after all. Edwards snatches the ball from the outstretched fingers of Bevan and covers the final 33 yards at searing speed. "I was 20 yards back initially but when I caught up I was in full stride. I know John Bevan was screaming for it and maybe he was earmarked by some of the defence. But it doesn't matter who Derek was trying to pass to. I was in full sprint stride when I caught it. By the time I got round Joe Karam, the only thing I thought about was hamstrings. Never before had I felt I had run so fast." The Edwards hamstrings were notoriously twangable, but this time they held up. Gareth dived. Gareth scored

Many people are word-perfect on Cliff Morgan's electrified commentary. "Brilliant. Oh, that's brilliant," he says as Bennett begins the move. "This is Gareth Edwards!" he almost bawls at the dramatic entry of the great man. "A dramatic start...What a score!" Not so many remember the radio commentary of Bob Irvine, a New Zealander, but it was just as evocative. Immediately before the movement started leading to the try, Irvine was already enraptured by the dazzling nature of the

The delights and the debates still live on. Was it the greatest try ever scored, or has the legend surrounding it prevented greater tries being given their due? How odd that none of Mike Gibson, David Duckham, Fergus Slattery and Bevan took part in the try, because that quartet was at the very heart of the Barbarians 23-11 victory that day. Was it truly a great game? Perhaps the perspective of the years judges harshly, because the video now reveals a good deal of dire ball-retention and aimless kicking – admittedly as mere punctuation marks between some sumptuous rugby. The try by JPR in the second half passed through more pairs of hands and had more twists and turns than even the Great Try itself.

But if the try and the match are legendary, then they deserve to be. Many of us know where we were when it was scored. Prosaically, I was in a college common room, staring at celebrating college mates and finding the wonder in my eyes reflected. I also know where I was when I saw it most recently. It is nearly 30 years since Phil zip-zipped and Gareth sprinted. But in June 1999, British Airways long-haul flights had the match on their in-flight entertainment programme. And 26 years on and 37,000 feet up, you could hear the roars from 1973 above the thunder of the engines; and the hairs on the back of your neck still prickled with the sheer sporting joy of it all.

March 1973

Galloping into history

Red Rum and Crisp in 1973 served up a Grand National that was a leap into exhilaration – the great-hearted Crisp against the horse destined to become an Aintree legend. Crisp had established a huge lead until, tiring dramatically, he was reeled in by the pursuing Red Rum. If his defeat was anguishing, Red Rum's victory was the stuff of myth.

DAVID WALSH

Richard Pitman sits in the press room at Ascot, a stage hand where once he had been a player. These days he commentates for the BBC and The Racing Channel, writes racing novels in his spare time and rides through middle-age with the enthusiasm of old. The same zest that once illuminated a spring afternoon at Aintree; Pitman, his enormous steed Crisp and the most magnificent defeat in the Grand National. Devon Loch and Dick Francis without the accident.

Life in the saddle was hard. So many knocks and so much concussion; most of the memories were lost in the subsequent fog. Not Crisp. Certain experiences are destined never to be forgotten: "He was a gentle giant, a lovely, lovely horse, with a face you would die for. The core of his being was wanting to go at something, to see the biggest fence and think, 'Yes, let's take that'. Around Aintree he gave me an experience money could not buy."

Pitman won the Champion Hurdle at Cheltenham, the King George at Kempton and the Hennessy at Newbury but is most often remembered as the jockey who rode Crisp against Red Rum in 1973. The race is burned into his soul, every jump a leap into exhilaration until the poor horse had nothing left to give. Even then a sudden and quick end would have been easier, but it was slow and crushing. From the post-mortem, Pitman came to one conclusion. It was his fault. The gallant horse lost because on the long run from the last fence to the winning post his jockey let him down.

Even more remarkably, the despair came and went quickly. He remembers the journey from Aintree that March evening. He travelled with his then wife, Jenny Pitman. She cried all the way; he couldn't suppress his euphoria. It took Jenny six months to get over the disappointment; he has never been able to shake off the elation. "I rode a lot of winners, had some great times, but the pinnacle of my career was that experience with Crisp. Feelings you just can't explain. Got to have been there to know."

It is evening and Brian Fletcher sits on an armchair in a small room at his home in Drefach. Even racing people don't know he now lives in west Wales, where he breeds and deals in Welsh cobs. Neither do many realise that no post-War jockey has a better record in the Grand National. They will, of course, remember that it was Fletcher who rode Red Rum to beat Crisp on that famous afternoon in 1973. It was the second of his three victories in the race.

Fletcher's National trophies have been donated to the museum at Aintree, even the lucky saddle he used when winning on Red Rum. The experiences are in his memory; the joy and the sadness still evident in his eyes. After winning two Grand Nationals on the horse, he lost the ride on Red Rum and then, one evening driving home from Uttoxeter races, it all ended.

"For years I had been suffering the after-effects of fracturing my skull in a fall at Teeside Park. Concussion, blackouts, severe headaches and my memory became hit or miss. I would repeat something two or three times and not realise I had done it. I cried when I lost the ride on Red Rum

Red Rum (left) overhauls the despairing Richard Pitman on the gallant but exhausted Crisp just feet from the line. It was the only time in the whole race that Red Rum had led.

National heroes: Red Rum with the ecstatic Brian Fletcher on board is led into the winner's enclosure by head lad Jackie Grainger (left) and stable lad Billy Eillson.

because part of my life was taken away. That horse meant so much to me. With my broken skull and head trouble, it made things a lot worse. I said to myself, 'I can't face the world, I can't face National Hunt racing, I can't face the National without my partner'. And Red Rum was *my* partner. Words fail to express how I felt. Then one day I had

"He was a gentle giant, a lovely, lovely horse, with a face you would die for"

a fall at Uttoxeter, blacked out on the motorway going home and nearly killed myself. 'I can't do it anymore,' I said. They told me my next fall could be my last one, but I had no desire to continue. I gave up the sport I loved."

Like Pitman, there is a lot he can't remember, but that day at Aintree he shall not forget. "Crisp was a class horse, mine was a National horse, it was all go from the word 'go' and there could only be one winner. Thank God it was me. I said to Richard in the weighing room after-

wards, 'I'm sorry to have snatched it from you. It was not only my race, it was your race too'."

Jackie Grainger drove the old Bedford that brought Red Rum to his first Grand National. Billy Ellison filled the passenger's seat and even though he usually played his mouth organ on the way to the races, he couldn't on this morning. He had

137

to concentrate on keeping his breakfast down. They left Ginger McCain's stables in Southport at around 10.30. It was March 31 1973; the trip to Aintree would take no more than 25 minutes.

Grainger sometimes called the horse Cassius, after the fighter. Some kid, new to the yard, would ask, "Why that name?" "You watch them feet move, son," Grainger would reply. That nimbleness allowed Red Rum to sidestep fallen horses, one of the keys to survival in the National. As Grainger steered the old Bedford into Aintree, he felt he had the winner in the back.

"One minute he was still pulling, the next he was empty"

McCain was similarly up-beat. In the previous day's *Liverpool Echo* he said he believed Devon Loch's collapse in 1956 had been due to a premature ovation and he feared his horse could suffer the same fall.

"Red Rum is a Liverpool horse," he said. "Half of Liverpool and half of Southport will be on it. For God's sake keep quiet until he's past the post." Before going to Aintree, McCain ordered a couple of crates of champagne for the house party he would host after the race. The trainer allowed Brian Fletcher to ride the horse as he saw fit and the jockey's plan was straightforward: "I wanted to hunt round for the first circuit, getting the horse to enjoy the race. At the beginning of the second circuit I would concentrate on riding a race. I knew Red Rum would not over-exert himself and when it came to the end he would still have something left."

That morning at Aintree the stable lads who had not seen the giant Crisp before could hardly believe their eyes. So big and powerful, he towered over every other horse. But there were doubts about his stamina. Richard Pitman and Fred Winter, Crisp's trainer, had talked about how their horse might be best ridden. "We decided to allow him to make the pace," said Pitman, "and, like Lester Piggott used to do on the Flat, to slow it

down and wait in front. But our plan fell apart the moment Crisp jumped the first. As soon as he landed he could see the second and he was off again. He was loving it. The theory of slowing him down in front couldn't work. After he jumped two, I said, 'This is the ride of a lifetime'."

Brian Fletcher couldn't believe the early pace. "I thought, 'Hell, we can't keep this up'. We had four and a half miles in front of us, not six furlongs. But it never settled down and my plan of gradually riding my race on the second circuit went out the window. It became a ding-dong battle with Crisp."

At first Crisp and Grey Sombrero shared the pace, Crisp on the inside, Grey Sombrero on the outer. Thrilled by his horse's jumping, Pitman shouted across at Bill Shoemark as they approached Becher's Brook first time round. "This is it, Willie!" Pitman had never known a horse to jump Becher's like Crisp did. "When you jump Becher's you always experience a nod as you land. You slip the rein through and lean back to prevent the horse's backside from coming up. With Crisp, you didn't feel like you'd jumped Becher's. He was so fluent, there was none of this up and down."

At the end of the first circuit, Crisp led Grey Sombrero by six lengths and the rest of the field by 20. Grey Sombrero then fell at The Chair and suddenly Crisp was on his own. Pitman sensed his isolation. "Jumping the

water, going away past the start, I found it eerie because we were so totally on our own. Normally in a race there is a lot of noise, jockeys shouting, horses brushing through fences, the sound of horses' hooves and panting, but now there wasn't a sound. The silence was something I'd never experienced."

Under the strain of Crisp's pace, the pursuit fragmented. Only Red Rum could chase. Fletcher saw the danger. "Crossing the water jump at the end of the first circuit, I was third or fourth when normally I would have been mid-division. I thought, 'I have to keep Crisp in sight, I can't let him get too far in front'. Going to the big ditch the second time, I hit the front of the following pack and kept niggling my fellow because I knew he would stay."

Going down to Becher's second time, Pitman tried to cajole Crisp into not giving everything: "I didn't look round because I was sitting and holding, my fingers were aching, all I wanted to do was let go of his head but I knew I had to hold him. My arms actually started to quiver from holding him. But I listened for the course commentary because there's a public address loudspeaker at Becher's and if you listen you can hear it. It was Michael O'Hehir's voice: 'And it's Crisp 25 lengths clear and going strong and coming out of the pack is Red Rum, but he's being kicked along by Brian Fletcher'. I thought, 'Wow, that'll do me, that'll do me'."

Exhilarated by the experience, Pitman's senses may never have been sharper. "As we landed over Becher's, David Nicholson was at the side on Highland Seal – they had refused on the first circuit. He sat there like an Indian chief in a John Wayne movie. 'Richard,' he shouted, 'you are 33 lengths clear. Kick on and you'll win'."

Aware that the race was slipping away, Fletcher kicked Red Rum into Becher's and they flew it. At the Canal Turn, two fences later, they were still 25 to 30 lengths behind but Fletcher thought they had a chance: "If I had once said to myself, 'I am going to be

Though he lost – and blamed himself – Richard Pitman was never depressed. Crisp's performance had provided a breath-taking, once-in-a-lifetime experience.

At the Elbow he was stone cold and I thought, 'If I can keep Red Rum from ducking in behind Crisp, I'll win'." Two strides from the line, Red Rum got his head in front of the gallant Crisp; it was the only time in the race he headed him. As the protagonists wearily made their way back to the enclosure, emotions swirled and collided. However much one admired Red Rum's performance, the sympathy for Crisp was greater.

They had broken Golden Miller's record time by 20 seconds, but Crisp had done this under a 12st burden and had carried 23lb more than Red Rum. As well as that, his had probably been the greatest display of jumping the race had seen. But more than anything else, there was the horse's extraordinary bravery. Drained of strength, he could barely keep going, yet as Red Rum passed him, the big horse somehow found the will to fight back.

"I felt him tense up," said Pitman. "The poor old fellow, he felt Red Rum bearing down on him and he thought, 'I've got to go faster'. He had given everything but his life." It is easier now to understand why Pitman was elated. He had been the one lucky enough to have been on Crisp that afternoon.

With Fletcher again in the saddle, Red Rum carried 12st the following year and won easily. He was second in 1975 and 1976 before winning his third National in 1977. No horse loved Aintree more or performed there with such consistency. Red Rum spent the last years of his life opening supermarkets and making other public appearances. Appropriately, he is buried beside the winning post at Aintree.

Crisp injured himself when beating Red Rum in a steeplechase at Doncaster the following season and Fred Winter, who loved the horse, would not allow him to be operated on. Instead he was retired and hunted for eight happy years at John Trotter's estate in Yorkshire before he collapsed and died while galloping one morning. Trotter buried Crisp under a cherry blossom, but the big horse was as strong in death as in life, fertilising the ground so well the cherry tree died from the nourishment. Instead, Trotter picked out the biggest horse chestnut tree on his farm and, alongside it, he reburied his old friend.

second here', I would have been second. I was pushing a horse that was still going. Then after crossing the Melling Road with two fences to jump, I got my first real encouragement. Crisp's tail swished and I thought, 'He's given everything. If the post doesn't come too soon I'll win'."

After jumping the second last, Pitman felt Crisp wither beneath him: "One minute he was still pulling, the next he was empty. And suddenly the second-last to the winning post seemed a long, long way. I thought, 'Keep hold of his head, nurse him, nurse him'. We were still a long way clear. We scrambled over the last because by now his strength was gone

Red Rum won again in 1974 and 1977. Less than brilliant away from Aintree, the horse came alive at the National. His record has never been bettered.

and then, on the run-in, I made the mistake that cost us the race. A basic error that a boy wouldn't have made.

"I thought, 'I have to wake this old boy up' and I picked up the stick in my right hand to give him a couple of cracks. But we had to go right-handed to get round the elbow. As I gave him a crack on the right-hand side, he dived off left and I now have to put the stick down and correct his leftwards drift and go in the opposite direction. I lose three lengths while this is happening and I end up losing the race by three parts of a length."

"Going to the last fence," said Fletcher, "I knew I was catching him. He was a drunken horse.

Crisp's had probably been the greatest display of jumping the race had seen

October 1974

Rumble in the jungle

The case for Muhammad Ali as sportsman of the century is surely confirmed by his 1974 defeat of George Foreman in Zaire. Foreman was a genuine monster of the ring, Ali clearly past his magnificent prime. Yet in a fight of unrelenting drama, Ali first out-thought and then out-boxed his opponent.

HUGH McILVANNEY

The glorious improbability of what Muhammad Ali did to George Foreman in Kinshasa, Zaire, shortly before dawn on Wednesday, October 30 1974, is best appreciated in the context of some briefer, more one-sided violence that occurred in Caracas, Venezuela, seven months earlier. It was at the Poliedro Arena in the South American city that Foreman conducted his last rehearsal for the confrontation in Africa, and his swift destruction of Ken Norton was enough to make the most ardent admirers of Ali shudder with dread. That was the eighth contest in a row that the 25-year-old heavyweight champion of the world had terminated within two rounds. But much more impressive than the harsh statistic was the fact that he had added Norton's name to that of Joe Frazier on the list of abruptly dispatched victims.

Norton had two close battles with Ali in 1973, winning the first on points (his opponent incredibly endured 11 rounds with a broken jaw) and losing the rematch to a vehemently disputed decision. At that point of Ali's career, after 14 years and 46 fights as a professional, Norton and Frazier were the only two men who had beaten him. Foreman had won the world title by battering Frazier to the canvas six times and forcing the referee to stop the slaughter halfway through the second round. By completing an

Confused and dazed, Foreman struggles to beat the count. Ali, his supreme talent gloriously vindicated, is champion again.

effortless double over Ali's conquerors, he established a form line for the Kinshasa showdown that made nightmare reading for those of us who already regarded the 32-year-old challenger as the 20th century's nonpareil sporting hero.

There could be few with more faith than I had in Ali's magical capacity to will the triumphal extravagances of his imagination into dazzling actuality in the ring. But I feared that the nocturnal drama in the Twentieth of May Stadium would be a dream too far. A tiny minority of tipsters did side with Ali but their arguments were unconvincing and they could hardly claim credit afterwards without blushing,

since their forecasts of how the fight would unfold bore no resemblance to what actually happened. They believed that Ali would invalidate the champion's power with movement, but instead the objective was to be achieved by the miraculous combination of nerve and defensive resourcefulness that enabled Ali to remain stationary on the ropes and let Foreman swing and pound his own strength away.

The popular notion that the so-called rope-a-dope tactic was a premeditated and finely honed method of unhinging Foreman is absolute myth. It was a magnificent, spontaneous improvisation and the need to

produce it was a measure of the problems presented by Foreman. The giant Texan had all the credentials of a genuine ogre of the ring, from the chilling air of malevolence to the wrecking-ball punches that so rapidly pulverised Frazier, as resolute a warrior as the heavyweight division has seen and Ali's most respected adversary. But, though he could appear to be the embodiment of brawling crudity, it is a mistake to imagine that Foreman's assaults were as undisciplined as an avalanche.

Whereas Sonny Liston, the first ogre tamed by Ali, co-operated by maintaining a haphazard pursuit of his young, dancing tormentor, Foreman was a master at shrinking the

ring. Against Norton in Caracas, there was a deadly geometry in his footwork, which employed a perfectly timed sideways step to shut off escape routes and leave his man trapped under the bombardment of his huge arms.

Ali's true prime had ended early in 1967 when he refused to be inducted into the US Army at the height of the Vietnamese war (seeking exemption as a minister of the Nation of Islam), was stripped of the world title and exiled from boxing for three and a half years. He had been champion for three years and – applying his 15st physique with the grace and speed of the finest welterweights, while exhibiting a bewildering range of imaginative, often breathtakingly unorthodox techniques – he had developed into such a wonder that his definition of himself as The Greatest readily withstood comparisons with the best heavyweights in history. However, when he returned to action in the autumn of 1970, the leg speed had been drastically reduced, his body had suffered an overall loss of elasticity and his flourishes of skill were interspersed with more ponderous activity that frequently included holding and an alarming reliance on his freakish ability to shrug off the heaviest blows to the head.

He was to win the heavyweight championship twice more after his comeback but would never again approach the standards that were the norm for him until 1967. By 1974, even moderate opponents had little trouble reaching him with big punches. The thought of what would ensue when the punches were thrown by Foreman, whose unblemished record showed all but three of his 40 victories had been won inside the distance, sent many of us to Africa in a doomladen state of mind.

I struggled to share the optimism fed to me by Angelo Dundee, Ali's trainer. It was one of Dundee's many appealing characteristics that he could always make a case for a client but this one had a particularly simplistic ring: "Sure Foreman is a killer if you

If Foreman intended to convey an air of brooding menace, he succeeded

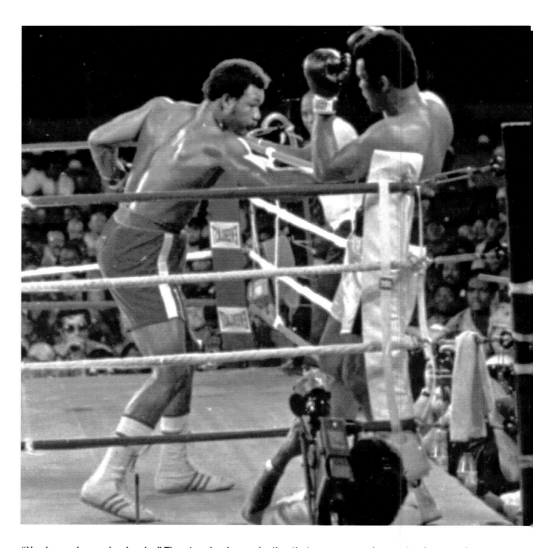

"Harder sucker, swing harder." The stunning improvisation that was rope-a-dope not only sapped Foreman's strength, it broke his spirit, too. It also caused Ali's supporters excruciating anxiety.

stand still and let him beat you to death … He can't live with my guy's movement. Foreman is a walker. No walker can beat my guy. He's made for Ali."

The first significant bit of walking Foreman did in Zaire was into the elbow of an obscure sparring partner, causing a cut near the champion's right eye that necessitated postponement of the fight from its original September 25 date until the penultimate day of October. Perhaps the most obvious beneficiaries of the delay were the Zairese charged with attending to the organisation of a promotion that made financial bedfellows of their despotic ruler, President Mobutu, and Don King, whose outrageous career as an international entrepreneur of the fight business was being launched by the Rumble in the Jungle. Those local functionaries were initially overwhelmed by their obligations, especially in relation to the

media circus that descended on Kinshasa, but when the big top went up for the second time they were just about ready to cope.

Whether Ali would react as positively to the postponement seemed debatable. With his best undeniably behind him, and a mayhem machine seven years his junior to be faced, he had recognised that he must bring inspired precision to the timing of his physical and mental preparation. Even veteran students of his genius for channelling every vestige of vigour and spirit towards a single, transcendent surge of competitiveness had to marvel at his rejuvenation. Then the cut intervened and we suspected that his psychological clock might stutter and lose track of the crescendo he had been managing so carefully.

We should have known better. Ali made light of the extension of his assignment. At the training sessions that gave focus to the hot and humid days at N'Sele, a government complex 40 miles from Kinshasa, he relentlessly indulged his love of performance, gleefully punctuating serious work with rhyming and play-acting. In the quiet of his private quarters, in a villa looking out on the vast, grassy sweep of the Zaire River, he admitted to being homesick for America but there was no falsity about the ebullience he sustained in public. His fantasising reveries about his imminent coronation did not have to be understood to be enjoyed by the Zairese of all ages who clamoured to thrust themselves within his aura. He was palpably cheered and nourished by the affection that poured in on him. In the former Congo, he suggested provocatively, Foreman was as unpopular "as a Belgium". That assessment was endorsed by the chant that accompanied the challenger wherever he went: "Ali, bomaye!" It meant: "Ali, kill him!"

In contrast with the older man's accessibility, Foreman favoured seclusion, apparently preferring the company of his Alsatian to that of most humans. He went to the gym solely to train, not to entertain. If he intended to convey an impression of brooding menace, he succeeded. But the effect was blurred occasionally by glimpses of the agreeable personality which would, 20 years on, inhabit a more rotund version of that large body. He was less self-consciously threatening to interviewers in Zaire than he had been in Venezuela. Wearing studded denim dungarees that exposed immense cliffs of shoulder, he answered questions politely and declined to respond to Ali's insults (christening Foreman "The Mummy" was typical). "He's a fine man in many ways and I like him a lot," Foreman said of Ali. "I don't mind all his talk. Talkin' is fun, a lot more fun than what we'll be doin' Wednesday."

Wednesday had barely begun when they set about that less frivolous exercise. There was more than a 4am starting time to impart a surreal quality to the fight, not least the sight of an attractive young black woman breast-feeding her baby in the third row ringside. But at the centre of all the exotic happenings, Ali and Foreman confronted the familiar basics of their business: the violence and the danger and the terrible questions put to pride and nerve. We knew the interrogation would not break Ali

as it had broken Norton, who had first cowered and then crumbled before the frightening mass of Foreman's aggression. It was, however, easy to imagine that bravery would be Ali's biggest liability, especially after he fulfilled a promise made privately that at the first bell he would go out "and hit Foreman upside his head, so he'll know he's in a fight".

Apart from that initial audacity, Ali boxed largely as expected in round one, working at long range, using mobility to keep clear of serious trouble and answering his opponent's swings with sharper punches of his own. But anybody who had charted the decline of his physical capacities knew that he did not have the reserves to remain elusive for long. Dancing was a short-term option. What shocked Foreman and everybody else was that Ali did not wait for his legs to slow but suddenly decided, just half a minute into the second round, that he would retreat to the ropes and stay there. The move that was to shape the outcome was so unorthodox, so fraught with hazard against the most feared puncher in boxing, that many of the reactions to it were bound to be fevered. George Plimpton, one of a clutch of celebrity writers on hand to chronicle the event, turned to another, Norman Mailer, and shouted: "It's a fix!" Plimpton's response suggested he was more attuned to the ways of Hollywood than the realities of the ring.

Those realities were vividly evoked a few hours after the fight in the shadowy quiet of Ali's villa (the curtains were drawn against the brutal glare of the midday sun) as he rambled happily for more than two hours through a muted assessment of his performance and its implications. Being there – with my friend and colleague Ken Jones, Ali's bodyguard and a couple of members of the household staff as the only other listeners – was the supreme privilege of my time in sports writing. Of all the abiding impressions left by an extraordinary monologue, the strongest was the reminder that greatness, for those who are capable of it, is always a practical matter. What seems impossibly bold and unconventional to the rest of us, strikes them as the only rational course. When Ali leaned far back over the ropes, stretching his

Ali refused to be flustered. His composure and self-belief were unbreakable

head away from murderous blows, covering the vital areas of his body with his arms and disdainfully absorbing the vicious punches that did land, we were sure he was acting outrageously and courting disaster. According to his criteria, he was merely being sensible.

"Truth is I could have killed myself dancin' against him," Ali said in the villa. "He's too big for me to keep moving round him. I was a bit winded after doin' it in the first round, so I said to myself, 'Let me go to the ropes while I'm fresh, while I can handle him there without gettin' hurt. Let him burn himself out. Let him blast his ass off and pray he keeps throwin' ... ' There he was swingin' away and all the time I was talkin' to him, sayin', 'Hit harder, George. That the best you got? They told me you had body punches but that don't hurt even a little bit. Harder, sucker, swing harder. You the champion and you gettin' nowhere. Now I'm gonna jab you.' Then pop! I'd stick him with a jab…I'd jab, then give him a right cross, then finish with a jab. Nobody expects you to finish a combination with a jab. Those punches took the heart away from George."

They did, but not before he had created moments of excruciating anxiety for the substantial percentage of the world's population rooting for Ali. In the fifth round particularly, survival appeared unlikely as Foreman drove sledgehammer right hands into the challenger's body. But, miraculously, Ali refused to be flustered. His composure and his self-belief were unbreakable. Foreman's were not, and in the sixth and seventh rounds, his energy spent, he wilted rapidly into a condition of confused vulnerability. At the beginning of the eighth, Ali told him: "Now it's my turn." So it was. A two-handed flurry left Foreman a helpless target and a final, dismissive right pitched him head-first towards the floor. He was still struggling to rise when counted out.

That fight was by no means Muhammad Ali's greatest demonstration of his talents, but it was his ultimate achievement. Zaire was his zenith.

Little Miss Perfect

At the Montreal Olympics of 1976 a 14-year-old girl held the world spellbound. Her name was Nadia Comaneci and she was a gymnast. Seven times she did the impossible and scored a perfect 10. Her technique and concentration were flawless in ways no one had thought possible. Not even the scoreboard could cope.

DAVID WALSH

At a restaurant in the Biltmore hotel near Miami, Bob Beamon, Mike Eruzione, Bart Conner and his wife sat down to eat. Beamon was *the* long jumper, Eruzione skippered the US icehockey team to success at the 1980 Olympics and Conner, a gymnast, won two gold medals at the 1984 Games in Los Angeles. That afternoon they had played in a charity golf tournament but the waiter, who spoke English with a foreign accent, did not recognise any of them.

Twenty years in Florida, the waiter still considered himself French. And being French, he handed the attractive Mrs Conner the wine list. "Would Madame care to choose the wine?"

in a white leotard, she performed feats of athleticism that adult gymnasts could barely conceive. Unable to figure out how one so young could be so good, the world sat back, mesmerised.

"She's Perfect", said the cover of *Time.* A man from the organising committee sought her out in the athletes' village and presented her with a going-away present. "This is the torch that lit the Olympic flame in Montreal – you should have it. You have been the success of these Games."

"She makes that beam look like a sidewalk," eulogised the commentator for the American network ABC. Indifferent to the subtleties, the public were transfixed by the young girl's virtuosity. In this they were at one with the people who knew, the official judges. Comaneci, said the markers, deserved

on the uneven bars, even less time for the four judges to acknowledge that what they had seen was perfection. They passed on their scores to the chief judge who, after eliminating the highest and lowest, was still left with two 10s. It was easy to work out the average; he gave the nod and the electronic scoreboard flashed 1.00.

"That is actually a 10, a perfect 10," corrected the arena announcer. Guided by 80 years of Olympic history, the electronic scoreboard had been programmed to show just three digits.

She performed feats of athleticism that adult gymnasts could barely conceive

The lady said she thought a Bordeaux would suit the occasion. As she studied the options, he remarked that French wine was the best.

"*Oui, bien sûr,*" she replied. "You speak French," he said enthusiastically. "Yes, I do." "But your accent, you're not French?" "No, I am Romanian." "Ah, Romania. Do you remember that girl, the little one who was called Nadia?" "I am Nadia," she said, stretching out her hand.

At the Montreal Olympics 23 years before, Nadia Comaneci had announced herself with similar panache. Then a pig-tailed 14-year-old

10 out of 10. "The perfect 10" it was called. She scored seven 10s in Montreal. Before her, no Olympic gymnast had received one.

Jackie Fie, an American, sat on the judging panel. "Giving Nadia 10 was an enormous leap because it had never happened at the Olympics," she said. "We didn't have a choice. The others had been good but then little Nadia came to the bars and was so superior, we had nowhere to go. You wanted to give her 10.2 out of 10. That would have better reflected the difference between her and the rest."

It took 19 seconds for Comaneci to complete her opening performance

We meet at her office in Norman, Oklahoma. Outside the door hangs the torch that ignited the flame for the Montreal Olympics. Inside, the lady who illuminated those Games. Now in her late 30s, the girl is long gone and the woman who has taken her place betrays only flashes of the innocence that beguiled us. That vanished in the dark days before the fall in 1989 of the Ceausescu regime in Romania. The stories are legion: it has been claimed Comaneci once tried to commit suicide, that she had a relationship with Ceausescu's son Nicu and that she married a footballer. All untrue, she says. Her defection in 1989 was arranged by a Florida-based Romanian, Constantin Panait, with whom she had a brief and unhappy relationship.

The storms calmed after she married Bart Conner, with whom Comaneci now runs a gymnastics academy and a promotions company. She works out every day, chides Bart when he doesn't and has long made her peace with Romania. Whatever the truths of the troubled years, the search hurt her rep-

Not even Olga Korbut, the darling of the Munich Games four years before, could match Nadia for precision, athleticism and grace.

utation and temporarily spoiled the memory of her phenomenal athleticism. That was wrong because it obscured the truth about Nadia, the gymnast. A truth that may be immortal, for how can perfection be bettered?

The story began in Onesti, a town in eastern Romania, and a casual remark by a little girl who lived down the road from the Comanecis. She told how at the end of her gymnastics class, the coach threw chocolates into the air that everyone could catch. Nadia Comaneci was sold. Five-years-old, she had taken the first step. As introductions go it could hardly

have been more gentle, but Nadia and her friends did learn to cartwheel. Some months later, the husband-and-wife coaching team of Bela and Martha Karolyi moved to Onesti and things for the town would never be the same

Romania's first communist president had come from Onesti and it was a favoured town. The Karolyis were asked by the government to set up an elite gymnastics school in Onesti and recruited from local kindergartens. The Karolyis now live in Texas and coach US gymnasts. They have many critics: Bela has been accused of exercising a kind of dictatorship over his charges – but their most illustrious pupil has never complained.

"I went to this school and the kids were out playing," said Bela Karolyi.

"You know if you want to find the most athletic it is better to watch them playing unsupervised than to bring them into a gym and give them trials. Looking out a window there were three girls throwing cartwheels in the yard and they were so obviously gifted.

"Just then, the bell went and it was like someone dropped a stick onto the ant mound – all the ants disappeared. I was in a panic, I couldn't recognise the three, so I had to go to all the classrooms. 'Okay, who can do a cartwheel?' This little girl lifted her head – it was Nadia. She was like a squirrel. 'I can,' she said. 'And where are your two friends?' 'They are in the other class,' she said. I got the three girls and their parents to come down to our centre and that's where it started."

At six, Comaneci began practising under Karolyi: "People said my wife and I were two crazy people, the kids would end up crooked, crippled and they would all die prematurely. I could see they loved it and it came to them so easily. We wanted to do something exceptional with the kids. For us, this was a chance to break out of the communist system."

Bela pushed the girls to their limits and often beyond. Comaneci was different: "She was the one I never had to force, she did everything freely. Even to this day, she is the only one who was like this." Karolyi couldn't break Comaneci: "When he asked me to do five repetitions, I would do seven or eight. I wanted him to know I could always do more than he asked."

Comaneci's ambition was fed by her talent: because she mastered new skills quickly, the repetitions were easier for her. Her relationship with Karolyi worked for both of them. She was the gymnast who would make his name, he was the teacher for her. Compliments were followed by taunts. "That was good but you must do it better, Nadia. Wait until you come up against the Russian girls," he teased. But she was above that: "I didn't want to be like anybody else, I wanted to be greater than everybody." Comaneci found ways of surviving the tough moments. When a drill seemed difficult, she thought of Gheorghe, her dad, walking six miles to work at the chemical refinery every day and then six miles home. What could be tougher?

At the age of 12, Karolyi decided his best girls should live in the sports club where they practised. "People say it must have been tough but we loved it," recalled Comaneci. "The girls were such good friends, we didn't miss home. The quality of everything was first-class. Bela insisted that we were given beef with our main meal each day, something no Romanian family could afford. At the weekend, I was given a supply of beef to take home with me but I gave it to my parents and brother. 'You take it, I get enough during the week'."

Boarding at the sports centre, everything changed for Nadia. Teachers came and provided private tuition and the training intensified; each morning the girls practised for two and a half hours, then for four hours in the afternoon. It was a demanding schedule for 12- and 13-year-olds: "The authorities made us lie about the amount of training we did. We were told to say we trained for three hours each day. Girls from other countries would say, 'We train for three hours a day but we get nowhere near your standard'."

Bela and Martha Karolyi grew to love Comaneci. "Training those girls was the sunshine of my life," said Bela. "It's a first love, it stays with you. Nadia was closer to my heart than any other gymnast. We loved her for how hard she worked and of course she was also gifted. But we did not know how good she would be until 1975, the year before the Olympics."

Twelve months before the 1976 Games, Grete Treiber went to Montreal to judge the pre-Olympic tournament in gymnastics. A Hungarian, Treiber now lives in Indiana and remembers that trip as the most exhilarating experience of her life. She had been a judge for 30 years and had never before given a 10: "Philosophically, I was opposed to giving a 10. It is perfection and perfection exists only in nature, or so I thought."

Seemingly unaware of what she has done Nadia stands in front of a scoreboard showing a perfect 10 – or at any rate a 1. The board could only show three digits. No one had thought it would need to show more.

Poetry in motion. Comaneci, now married to Bart Conner, has found new contentment in America. That she remains extraordinarily athletic goes almost without saying.

The first event Treiber judged was the balance beam: "The way we mark in gymnastics is that every gymnast starts with 10 and as they make mistakes we make deductions from the 10. I sat and watched this young girl from Romania on the beam, so deep in concentration that she seemed almost hypnotised but doing things that nobody had ever attempted. She had such continuity of movement, such fluency, control, dynamism, daring and so beautiful to watch.

"As it was happening, I could see my problem and I began to hope she would make a mistake so that I wouldn't have to give her a 10. But there wasn't the slightest error. When it was over I looked at my notepad: the page was completely blank and I felt such a fool. 'Have you been out to lunch while this was happening?' I crushed my own belief and flashed the first 10 in my whole life."

At breakfast next morning Treiber was approached by a distraught Bela Karolyi: "Grete, what am I going to do? Nadia is in her room, she has started bleeding and she doesn't know what is happening. She thinks she is going to die. What can I do?"

"I told Bela to go back to the room, tell Nadia it was a natural thing, give her a couple of aspirins, a cup of hot milk and she would be fine in a few hours." Overnight, the young girl of gymnastics had become a young woman.

And yet she was just 14 when she held the world spellbound in Montreal a year later. From uneven bars to balance beam to vault and then to the floor, she had to perform 16 times in her first Olympics. Protected by her inno-

cence, Comaneci also drew on her mental strength to block out every distracting thought and to reach the point of complete and utter concentration.

The actor Robin Williams once said that "sometimes being in a character is like being possessed". Those who watched Comaneci will appreciate the truth of that: she locked herself into a performance that seemed almost hypnotic. Afterwards they asked why she didn't smile more. The question astonished her: "I smiled and laughed a lot, but only when the job was done. You don't smile on the balance beam."

Comaneci had travelled to the Montreal Olympics with the lightest suitcase and no baggage: "In my mind I had just moved my training from Onesti to Montreal." She loved her first taste of the Games: "I had never been anywhere where everything was free. The food in the restaurant, the movies in the evening, the drinks from the machines. We would go to the movies even though they were in English; we didn't understand but that didn't stop us laughing."

All around the village she saw athletes she recognised. Cuban heavyweight boxer Teofilo Stevenson was the one she wished to meet and, suppressing natural shyness, she

approached him. "I know who you are," he said. As they spoke, Stevenson turned the balloon in his hand into the shape of a dog. "This is for you, a little gift," he said. She treasured it until, a few hours later, the poor dog expired.

At the press conference, after her third gold, one journalist asked her what thought went through her mind as she stood on the podium and the Romanian national anthem was played. "I was just hoping my mom was watching her television back in Onesti," she replied. Then another journalist asked what was her greatest wish. She said: "I want to go home." Teodora Ungureanu, her best friend and fellow Romanian gymnast, would have understood that. She slept in the bunk below Comaneci and before going to sleep they talked about the presents they would take back to their parents and their families.

Nadia slept with her medals, three gold, one silver and one bronze. Sometimes she would dream of winning the gold medal and then wake suddenly, wondering what was real. She would slip her hand under the pillow, feel those Olympic jewellery boxes and go back to sleep.

It is now five o'clock in the evening in Nadia's office. A long afternoon is nearing its end when Bart walks in. There is a tornado heading towards Oklahoma. "We should be getting home – and quick," he says. Outside, dark clouds gather, hail crashes against windscreen glass and an afternoon spent with one force of nature will be followed by an evening in the company of another.

"Nadia was closer to my heart than any other gymnast"

July 1976

The most cheated athlete

Shirley Babashoff went to the 1976 Olympics determined to prove herself the best female swimmer in the world. But her principal rivals were the products of an East German regime that systematically drugged its athletes. Afterwards, she was dismissed as nothing more than a bad loser. Disillusioned, Babashoff turned her back on the world.

DAVID WALSH

At Fountain Valley in southern California, she and Michelle Pfeiffer are remembered as the most famous women to have passed through the school. Beyond that, not many remember Shirley Babashoff. Trawl through sport's history and occasionally her name surfaces; the eight Olympic medals, the world records but not the details. Not the cynical and damning story of how a great swimmer was cheated by drugged rivals. When she dared to complain, they ridiculed her: "Cry Baby", "Surly Shirley". Sport destroyed her innocence before disillusioning her.

Babashoff is one of countless athletes whose career was diminished by others' use of banned drugs, but her story has a brutality and a poignancy that sets it apart. From the Olympic arena she left with two gold and six silver medals and the feeling of having lost. Nor was Babashoff alone in thinking of herself as a failed athlete; a small army of commentators was ready to portray her as a loser.

Twenty-five years have passed since the then 19-year-old walked away from the sport. Enough time for wounds to mend. In a sense they have, but there is no stoic acceptance of the old injustice. Asked if she had spoken to her

East German rivals in 1976, she replied: "What was I going to say, 'Congratulations – you took the most steroids'?" She would sell the Olympic medals at the right price. Adam, her teenage son, says she should advertise them on the Internet. But who can say what Olympic medals are worth? We might think them priceless. She knows different. Life moves on and these days Pfeiffer waits in Hollywood for scripts to come through her door while Babashoff, a little further south, delivers the mail to 600 residents in Huntington Beach. She's not complaining; a job is a job and it pays

Adam's school fees. Most of the time her life is fine. Okay, once on her rounds she was shot at and another time a man exposed himself, but you get those kinds of days.

There is that one torpedo, though, forever capable of upsetting her. So Babashoff refuses to return to the subject of her swimming. Requests for interviews are turned down. Her phone is constantly on answer machine. "I swam for fun," she said, "nobody told me this would go on forever." Her disenchantment has its source not in the colour of her medals but in the futility of her sporting life.

All the training, all the sacrifice, all the dreams shattered by chemically enhanced rivals. You spend all your life preparing for a swordfight but your opponent shows up with a shot-gun. Those who said she was a bad loser understood nothing. A few years ago she was asked if she still swam: "If I fell into a pool," she said, "I would swim to the side."

Jack Babashoff worked in a steel plant at Vernon, California, and took other jobs to boost the family income. At home his wife Vera put away the money needed to send their four children to swim practice. Shirley showed exceptional ability and swam competitively from the age of eight. Once she reached the highest level, she trained eight hours a day, seven days a week. Everyone told her she would be a champion.

At Munich in 1972, she won gold and two silvers. She was 15

Kornelia Ender, scourge of Babashoff and prime product of the East German doping machine. She won four golds and two silvers at Montreal.

Plunging into despair: it was the knowledge that talent and hard work were irrelevant in the face of deliberate cheating that Babashoff couldn't accept.

then, highly talented but a few years short of her best. As a person she was straight up and didn't hide her determination to be the best swimmer of her generation. Neither was she discreet about her East German rivals. Unable to win a gold medal in Munich, the East German girls were unrecognisable a year later at the world championships

"They were beating us by yards," Babashoff said of the East Germans. "They looked like men"

in Belgrade, where they won 10 out of 14 events. "They were beating us by yards," Babashoff said. "They looked like men. One breaststroker, I swear she was a guy. I didn't feel comfortable in the changing room with, uh, people that big, that hairy, that baritone."

Three years later, in Montreal, Babashoff shared a room with fellow-Californian Nicole Kramer and otherwise kept to herself. Those US team members who didn't get to know her, and they were the majority, considered her aloof and arrogant. Still, they recognised her as the team's star, the American woman who would not be cowed. The world-record-holder in the 800m freestyle and 100m butterfly, Babashoff had no reason to fear anyone. "Shirley was a very hard worker," recalled Jack

Nelson, the US women's coach in Montreal, "a positively stubborn woman who didn't believe there was anyone under the sun who could beat her. At the time we suspected but didn't know exactly what the GDR was doing."

The East Germans were creating the most evil empire sport has known. At the highest governmental levels, approval was given for the systematic doping of the country's elite athletes. Swimming champion Karen Konig would later describe how each athlete was given a cocktail of drugs each morning. "It was," she said, "a ritual activity, like brushing your teeth." Athletes as young as 12 and 13 were doped and, particularly in the case of women receiving male hormones, the drugs produced astonishing improvement. Their size, musculature and deep voices distin-

guished them, but nothing prepared rivals for that first encounter with the East Germans.

Wendy Boglioli made the US team for the 1976 Games. "We were conscious of what they looked like," she said, "we'd seen their photographs in *Swimming World* and we had our suspicions. In Montreal they were staying in a boat in the harbour while most of the other teams were in the athletes' village. We didn't see them until the first day at practice. It was Jack Nelson who pointed us towards the changing room. 'In there,' he said. We went in and there were some swimmers standing on the other side of a partition, [with] deep male voices that we mistook for men. We turned and walked out." Nelson remembers their exit: "Kathy Heddy, the little distance swimmer, was first out. 'Coach Nelson – you sent us to the wrong room. They're the men.' I said 'No sweetheart – they're the East German women and you better get used to what they look like."

Sport's greatest nightmare began to unfold. Babashoff anchored the US medley relay team that was massacred by the East Germans, who broke the record by almost six seconds. The dice had been rolled and they would keep turning up East German numbers. "I watched that race from the stands," said Boglioli. "It was shocking, sobering and demoralising."

At least that relay prepared the American team for what they would experience throughout the week. Babashoff swam four individual freestyle events at 100m, 200m, 400m and 800m. She thought she could win the three longer races. Kornelia Ender beat her in the 200m; Petra Thumer beat her in the 400 and 800. Losing to Thumer in her specialist events crushed Babashoff. Petra who? Before Montreal Barbara Krause was the GDR's great distance swimmer but she cried off at the eleventh hour. No panic, East German officials dipped into their bag of medical

A smaller splash: Babashoff in 1998, delivering the mail in Huntington Beach, California – and still refusing to talk about Montreal and the East Germans.

tricks and came up with Thumer. Babashoff beat the old world records in both the 400 and 800, Thumer beat them by more.

After the 400m, Babashoff refused to shake Thumer's hand. "I watched Shirley finish those races – she was in tears," said Nelson. "In her mind she was in a war against the Germans. Have you ever heard of anybody finishing second in a war and being happy about it? You couldn't expect her to behave like a choirgirl. That wasn't her game. They robbed her – how could she feel any other way?"

Babashoff's disenchantment deepened as she realised that, for confessing to scepticism about the GDR team, she was portrayed as a bad loser. Journalists sweetly asked how she felt about another second place and later reported that her answers tasted like sour grapes. Jerry Kirshenbaum covered the swimming events for *Sports Illustrated*: "I felt badly for Shirley but I don't feel she conducted herself all

"Swimming was her life. She was supposed to win in Montreal. She didn't have another plan"

that well. From my point of view, you couldn't pretend to know things that you didn't know. A number of journalists had visited the GDR before the Olympics. We had been to their sports institute in Leipzig and the first question was always about steroids. I recall a doctor in a white frock looking us in the eye and saying they would never consider doing anything like that. They weren't just gold-medal swimmers, they were gold-medal liars."

The day after the 400m loss Babashoff met her mother in a nearby hotel, collapsed on her shoulder and sobbed. "The thing about Shirley," said Boglioli, "is that swimming was her life. She was supposed to win in Montreal. She didn't have another plan.'"

The 400m freestyle relay was the final swimming event at Montreal. Outside of the US team and coach Nelson, nobody considered the possibility of the GDR squad being beaten. America qualified third for the final, behind the GDR and Canada. Nelson looked at the times of his swimmers, compared them to the East Germans' and thought there was a chance. At the submission of team lists for the final, Nelson offered a Canadian official a much-coveted US team pin. "There," he said. "Now, who's leading off for the Germans?" "Ender,'"replied the official.

The coach went back to his team. "Kim," he said to Peyton, "you're leading off against Ender. You're going to finish within one length of her, right?" "That's okay coach," replied Peyton, who had a quiet authority much admired within the group. "Wendy," he said to Boglioli, "you're a horse. You're going to catch the second East German so that Jill [Sterkel] begins the third leg level. That's all you've got to do. Jill, you will start level and finish in front. You will enable Shirley to start in front and we all know no one is going to catch Shirley."

According to Nelson, the team prayed together before that final and achieved togetherness he had never previously seen in a relay group. "Before the final," recalled Boglioli, "we were in a glass, sound-proofed room with all of the other teams and we were goofing around, giggling, laughing, making jokes and the East Germans saw us and thought we had given up. That was what we wanted them to think."

The final worked out precisely as Nelson anticipated. After touching the wall, Babashoff took off her goggles and squinted at the flashing time on the scoreboard. "We've broken the world record!" she roared. "It was the only time we heard the national anthem for the US women," said Boglioli. "We stood up there together, holding hands and all crying. I thought I had died and woken up in heaven."

John Leonard, a member of the US management team, watched the race from the stands. "From the beginning you could tell something special was happening," he remembered. "I cried all the way. So did many others. To beat the East Germans in those circumstances was the greatest moment I have had in a lifetime in this sport." "I put that victory," said Nelson, "against any victory in the history of sport. And I am talking any sport."

"They weren't just gold-medal swimmers, they were gold-medal liars"

It may have been the greatest of all victories but it didn't change the perception that Babashoff had been a loser. And a bad loser. Letter-writers to *The New York Times* complained about Babashoff and other American team members: "Our swimmers should look beyond the count of their medals to the ideal of the spirit of competition and friendship that these Games are to espouse." Lofty notions that refused to consider the possibility of GDR cheating. One journalist in Montreal dared to ask about the strange, manly voices of the triumphant women. "We are here to swim, not sing," replied the East German coach, Rolf Glaser.

Twenty-two years later, Glaser would be one of the coaches prosecuted for his part in the doping of GDR athletes. And life in East Germany didn't just move on in the late Eighties. It changed. The Berlin Wall came down, Stasi papers were found documenting details of the doping programme and Shirley Babashoff was just not interested. Tell her something she didn't know. In 1998 the US swimming association tried to have athletes like Babashoff upgraded to gold medals but she wanted no part of the campaign. "Nothing is going to happen," she said. "It's like flogging a dead horse."

The IOC refused the request. Doped East German swimmers still fill the pages of sport's imperfect history and, officially, Babashoff is a loser. Jack Nelson refuses to give up. "It's like this," he said. "It wasn't right that they killed Jesus Christ, but for 2,000 years they have been using that to make people better. We must look back at what happened in 1976 and use it to make people better. We have our coaches' annual dinner coming up. We want Shirley to be our guest of honour. We can never give her back the moments she lost in Montreal, but we intend to officially acknowledge just how great she was."

They contacted Babashoff about the dinner. She said sorry, she wasn't interested.

The victorious members of the 400m freestyle relay, Babashoff on the right. But the solitary gold was scant consolation.

July 1978

Meltdown on Centre Court

The 1978 Wimbledon ladies' final saw the first act in what became one of the most compelling rivalries in world tennis: Chris Evert, the relentless baseliner from America, against the hugely talented but mercurial Czech-born Martina Navratilova. Navratilova's victory set her on the way to a remarkable nine Wimbledon titles.

NICK PITT

For Chris Evert, the eve of the final of the women's singles at Wimbledon in 1978, her fourth, was almost perfect. During the day, she practised and relaxed. In the evening, she dined with John Lloyd and, on returning to the Inn on the Park, she joined him for a romantic midnight stroll in Hyde Park. The golden girl was falling in love.

For Martina Navratilova, the eve of the 1978 final, her first, was less wonderful. She, too, was staying at the Inn on the Park; staying in bed all day with cramps, having her period. "That was my preparation for the final," Martina said as she wound back her memory. "I didn't practise at all. I was doubled over and just miserable. It was in the days before Ibuprofen, which is what women take now. Thank God the final wasn't that day."

Somehow, it was never supposed to be easy for Martina. She could not even share her pride and opportunity with those for whom it meant the most and who meant the most to her. For nearly three years, since her defection to the United States from Czechoslovakia, she had been separated from her country and her family.

Her stepfather had given her the dream when she was a spindly girl hitting double-handed backhands with an old wooden racket: "One day you will win Wimbledon." For her parents, that was always the ultimate. Titles around the world, fortunes beyond imagination, becoming No 1 in the world, that was all very well. But nothing compared with Wimbledon.

Emotions rule: Navratilova (right) was overcome by her win. Her temperament could sometimes be harder to beat than her opponents. (Above) winner and loser embrace – but their rivalry never lost its edge.

Her parents would know she was in the final, but she could not talk to them. To telephone Czechoslovakia in 1978, you had to order a call and you might be put through two hours later. But her parents were not at home. She had spoken to them before the tournament and her stepfather had told her that if she did well they would visit friends near the western border. Czech television didn't broadcast Wimble-don but near the border they could pick up German television.

For those watching on television in Britain, kindly Dan Maskell would use the warm-up to intro-duce the players. Chris Evert is the world's No 1, the No 1 seed, right-handed from Florida, twice the Wimbledon champion, aged 23. In the semi-final she beat Virginia Wade, the defending champion. Her opponent, Martina Navratilova, from Czechoslovakia but now living in the United States, left-handed, ranked No 2, seeded two, aged 21. She beat Evonne Cawley in the semi-finals,

although of course Evonne was so unfortunately injured during the final set. Miss Evert and Miss Navratilova have met 26 times, with Miss Evert winning 21 and Miss Navratilova five. They have played one another once at Wimbledon, two years ago, when Miss Evert won 6-3 6-0. But in their last match, two weeks ago in Eastbourne, Miss Navratilova won a thrilling three-setter, 9-7 in the final set after Miss Evert had held a match point.

But, of course, the monumental rivalry between Evert and Navratilova, even in its infancy, was much richer than biographical record. Their 15-year confrontation, which stretched

Navratilova was brave and fragile, tempestuous and brilliant. She never lost the thrill of play

from 1973 to 1988, presented not merely opposite styles of tennis but different approaches to life.

Evert ruled from the baseline, where she spun perfect measured groundstrokes. Her coolness was cruel, her flawlessness inhuman. The only mercy she allowed her opponents was the choice of how they would be beaten. If they stayed at the back of the court and rallied, they would be out-manoeuvred and worn down. If they came in to volley, at least the execution was brief: cut down by a single, unerring passing shot.

For Peter Bodo, an American tennis writer, she was "a neurological miracle whose consistency was the product of extraordinary but not necessarily athletic gifts. The signal sent from Evert's eye to her hand was almost never interrupted by its passage through her mind, where anxiety or fear or overeagerness so often blur the message. Even when she was exhausted, Evert's strokes remained silken, perfectly timed, and, above all, purposeful."

Evert learned the game in Fort Lauderdale at the tennis facility where her father, Jimmy, coached. She announced herself to the world in 1972 when, at 18, she beat Billie Jean King, who that year won three Grand Slam singles titles and didn't compete

in the fourth, 6-1 6-0. Ever since, she had been imperious, poised and in control.

The fire that came to fight the ice was Navratilova. From the age of nine, when she watched King win the Wimbledon crown on television, she had been a net-rusher, a serve-and-volleyer, a risk-taker. She was brave and fragile, tempestuous and brilliant, and never lost the thrill of play.

For the late Ted Tinling, who knew all the great players since Suzanne Lenglen, "she has that dramatic Slav temperament that requires the stimulus of a crisis. She is always going to have the storm; she is always going to underassess her opponent and underassess her own ability to handle it when the storm breaks. I have always said that she goes from arrogance to panic with nothing in between."

A killer she was not. Instinctively generous, and with a sense of justice which she admits "borders on the ridiculous", she felt sorry for opponents and would sometimes throw away points when favoured by a bad line call. She was more comfortable with the comradeship of doubles and team play than the nakedness of singles. And if you could not beat her, she might beat herself.

Soft, then, as a matchplayer in comparison to Evert, Navratilova was also the innocent in the mental game. "Chris did not tell me until she retired, but she used to read me like a book," Navratilova said. "She could tell before a match whether I was good-nervous or bad-nervous. She could tell from whether or not I was talkative, how I spoke, what I said. I had no idea. I didn't even know how I felt, let alone how she felt. She was just a great mind-reader. If I had known, I would have behaved very differently."

With precision and no fuss, Evert took the first set of the 1978 Wimbledon final 6-2. Navratilova thought her nerves (which were to become alarmingly visible later in her career) had settled during the knock-up, but her legs were not moving, caught in the web.

Early in the second set, frustration was joined by plain public embarrassment, twice. First, like a beginner who has forgotten to keep her eye on the

ball, Navratilova completely missed – "whiffed" – a straightforward smash. In the same game, she played a drop shot and advanced on the net. Evert moved forward smartly, and arrived early enough to drive the ball. Navratilova anticipated to the backhand side and moved to the right as Evert went the other way, and the ball struck Navratilova flush on the temple.

"You don't get hit very often, and certainly not in singles," Navratilova said. "But it woke me up. It was as if a light went on and it set me on my way. From that moment I was much better." She took the second set 6-4 but trailed in the third, by 2-4 and then 4-5. Here was the issue, and surely Evert would be better equipped to seize and turn it.

Fire and ice: where Evert (above) was coolness personified, her play metronomic in its regularity, Navratilova (right), a natural risk-taker, blew hot and cold. But at her best she could be irresistible.

To explain what happened, we must briefly go back to the eve of battle, when Evert strolled with handsome John Lloyd in Hyde Park and Navratilova lay wretchedly on her bed with cramps. Navratilova was not alone. She was supported by her girlfriend, Sandra Haynie, a professional golfer. Haynie had been helping Navratilova with her mental approach, teaching her to tame her on-court emotions, not to remove her passion but to harness it, to be herself when it really mattered. On that day, before the final, she also told Navratilova not to worry about the cramps, that it was all right not to practise.

Evert had been smitten and distracted: "In the last four games, all I could think about was going out with

From 4-5 down in the final set, it was Navratilova who found her game, winning 12 of the last 13 points

John. Something fresh and wonderful was happening to me. I should have beaten Martina. If I had been hungry, the match was mine." From 4-5 down, it was Navratilova who found her game. "I played like I can," she recalled. Attacking, but without desperation, she won 12 of the last 13 points, and when she had done it she put her right hand to her forehead. "I can't believe it," she said, and kept repeating it.

Evert in defeat was warm, putting her arm around Navratilova and smiling so that if you hadn't seen the match you would not have known who had won. That generosity was to be a two-way feature of their rivalry as its epic quality developed, but the suggestion that Evert was hamstrung by Cupid in 1978 is given little credence by Navratilova. "When I started falling in love, I always played my best tennis because it gave me such freedom," she said. "You know, there were very few times when Chris came out and actually said I beat her. There was always something that happened, some other reason for it."

There is still a competitive edge, and no wonder. After the 1978 Wimbledon final, it took Navratilova six years to draw level in their head-to-head series. When she won Wimbledon in 1984, they had won 30 matches each. By the end, after 80 encounters, 60 of which were in finals, Navratilova led 43-37. Both won 18 Grand Slam singles titles.

"It's a love-hate relationship," said Navratilova. "We're good friends but things get a little touchy on both sides when we talk about our accomplishments. We know that if only one of us had been there, we would have won more but we would not have become as good a player.

"I remember in 1981 Chris was still going on about her great rivalry with Evonne Cawley and I thought, 'Wait a minute, what about me?' I was inching in by then, but Chris was still in the way. She was No 1. She was my goal. She was what was driving me to achieve. That meant getting in better shape, getting proper coaching and really learning about the game. I reached a level where I knew that at my best I could beat anybody and that took the pressure off. I could beat Chris on my average day, but if she played unbelievably well, I needed to raise my game. My best was better than hers.

"No matter how catty we get with each other in private or public, I still have a closeness with her that I will never have with another human being because of what we went through together, on and off court."

The Iceman and the Superbrat

By 1981, Bjorn Borg had won Wimbledon five times in a row, grinding opponents into submission with relentless baseline tennis. He seemed unbeatable. Against him in the final that year was the anarchic John McEnroe, foul-mouthed and volatile but with a game touched with undeniable genius.

NICK PITT

Even before the entry of the gladiators, the Centre Court was stoked with dramatic tension. The scoreboards were empty of points, games and sets, but what names they held, what a collision they foretold: B Borg, JP McEnroe.

A year before, in 1980, those scoreboards, with the same names attached, had recorded a match of tumultuous emotion. The fourth-set tie-break had been won by McEnroe, 18-16, but the fifth set went to Borg, 8-6. The 1981 final could hardly be as exciting, but it was to prove more significant and conclusive.

The umpire, Bob Jenkins, waited nervously beside his chair. "Don't stand any nonsense, Bob," he had been told by the tournament referee, Fred Hoyles.

The McEnroe family occupied the back row of the box reserved for friends and relations of the competitors. Their head, John P McEnroe Snr, a New York lawyer whose Wimbledon trademark was a floppy white hat, was anxious. "John's first final with Bjorn was pretty harrowing," he recalled, 18 years on. "Then in 1981 there was so much controversy surrounding John that I didn't know how he was going to deal with all the external pressure."

In the row in front of the McEnroes sat Borg's coach and mentor, Lennart Bergelin. For five years running he

had watched Borg win, and for more than five years a single adjective had been attached to him: inscrutable. But he, too, was worried. "It was something in the air," he said. "A feeling that maybe Bjorn was no longer the best. He knew he could lose."

Up in the Royal Box, sitting behind the Duke of Kent, Lady Diana Spencer, blushing in her innocence, chatted to a friend. In four weeks, she would be getting married. At last, and to wild cheering, Borg and McEnroe entered, heads high and serious as the diminutive senior dressing-room attendant, Leo Turner, struggled with their unwieldy bags. McEnroe's long unkempt hair sprouted upwards; Borg's was sleek to his shoulders. Both wore headbands.

Borg was generally dismissed as the man with the one-dimensional personality. But underneath the blank Nordic exterior he was crucially driven by a desire to succeed. He lost something more than a tennis match in 1981. Perhaps tennis had taken too much.

Banners had been outlawed by the All England Club, but you didn't need to hold a notice to bait the Superbrat. "They were very noisy in the warm-up, and I was more worried about the crowd than I was about McEnroe," said Jenkins, the umpire. "They were very partisan, like a football crowd, and some of them were trying to needle John."

In winning his five Wimbledon titles, Borg had established a run of 41 consecutive winning matches. Just turned 25, he had recently won his sixth French Open title. McEnroe was

"It was something in the air ... Bjorn knew he could lose"

22 and had twice won the US Open title. They had met 12 times, with Borg ahead seven-five.

Such statistics were impressive, indeed Borg's were monumental, but the essence of their rivalry was symbolic, a struggle for supremacy between two players who were not merely among the greatest of all, but the most individually distinctive and opposite. Borg and McEnroe were ice and fire, iron and mercury, order and anarchy.

Borg's progress that year had been smooth until he met Jimmy Connors in the semi-final and lost the first set to love and the second 6-3. But knowing Borg, everyone knew, and Connors knew best of all, that if Connors lost the third set, Borg, inexorably, would grind him down. He did.

McEnroe's progress had been incendiary, even by his standards. On the opening day of the championships, he tangled with Edward James, umpire and dentist. McEnroe stood on his racket and broke it. He called James "an incompetent fool" and described umpires as "the pits of the world".

"What did I say?" demanded McEnroe when James awarded a penalty point against him for obscenity. James refused to repeat the phrase. On his match card he had written: McEnroe said "umpires are the piss of the world".

McEnroe called for the referee, swore at him and was docked another penalty point, and fined $1,500. A few days later, he earned another fine,

McEnroe seemed incapable of playing an ugly shot. His talent was extraordinarily instinctive, whether conjuring passing shots or volleys. Yet this delicacy and invention was entirely belied by his personality. Like a child, McEnroe seemed at the mercy of his emotions.

$2,500, for accusing a linesman who wore a turban of bias during a doubles match against the Amritraj brothers.

"I hate umpires," McEnroe yelled during his singles semi-final. "I get screwed by them in this place." Then, after missing a volley, McEnroe shouted: "You are a disgrace to mankind." McEnroe later claimed he had been talking to himself. The umpire, Wing Commander George Grime, another dentist, thought otherwise and deducted a point.

For John McEnroe Snr, the blame lay as much with the All England Club as with his son. "At the start of the tournament, I went to see Chris Gorringe, the club secretary, and asked for a meeting with the chairman, Sir Brian Burnett," he said. "I wanted access to the dressing room so that I could help John and try to calm things down.

"I couldn't see any difference between me and Lennart Bergelin, who had complete access to Borg, but Gorringe said, 'There is a difference, Bjorn is a member of the club.' 'What difference does that make?' I asked. 'Well,' he said, 'people around here think it makes a great deal of difference.' Then he said, 'Excuse me, I shouldn't have said that.' Anyway, I couldn't see Sir Brian because he was too busy entertaining royalty."

What McEnroe Snr did not know as he watched the players knocking up with wooden rackets (the last time both men's finalists used them) was that the All England Club had already decided that even if McEnroe won he would not be granted honorary membership of the club, as every previous champion had been. It had also been agreed to recommend a fine of $10,000 and to bring a charge of aggravated behaviour against him.

McEnroe had won the toss and chose to serve. Play. From the start, his sideways-on, slowly wound, left-handed slingshot service action was in venomous order. Four first serves in, four points won, first game to love.

Borg's service was a classic version of the arched back and high throwing action.

Every variety and trick was his, the racket his wand and dagger

But it lacked the disguise and devil of McEnroe's delivery, and, with a notably inferior second service, Borg knew his percentage of first serves must remain high.

Borg also held his first service game with ease, but by the third game rallies were developing, and with them the contest. There was no surprise at the qualities on display, but, as always with Borg and McEnroe, there was wonder. Borg was superbly built, impossibly fast in the chase and inexhaustible. Top-spin was his trade, always hit hard and with flourish, double-handed on the backhand. On either wing, he could pass left, right or over the top. And he was monolithic. Emotionally, he gave nothing.

While Borg was forged by Borg and Bergelin, labouring five hours a day for several years, McEnroe was so blessed with gifts that Maestro Salieri might have wondered at the Almighty's choice of recipient. Every variety and trick was his, power or touch, top-spin and slice, early or late, the racket his wand and dagger. Emotionally, he was an open book.

In the fifth game, two searing cross-court returns gave Borg the first break of service. He held his own to lead 4-2 as the crowd, sensing the first significant thrust, became more animated. "Quiet please, ladies and gentlemen, in the interests of both competitors," ordered Jenkins, who hitherto had announced nothing but the score. The stress on the word "both" suggested that even the villain, McEnroe, should be accorded fair play. The crowd laughed. McEnroe looked to the sky.

Although McEnroe threatened Borg's serve repeatedly during the first set, he could not break it. Borg faced four break points as he served for the set, saved them all and closed it out 6-4. For Borg, it was business as usual.

McEnroe pressed again, holding further break points early in the second set, when at last the first line-call controversy, the first test of McEnroe's brittle temperament, arrived. Break point against Borg – he passed McEnroe cross-court. It looked out but was given in. All eyes on McEnroe. He stood still and bit his lip, before walking back to receive. The crowd applauded; McEnroe held up his arms in triumph. He had a sense of humour.

McEnroe had told himself before the match that whatever happened he must not lose his temper. "I'm sure he did," said his father. "But then he'd told himself the same thing time and again before other matches and hadn't managed it. I used to say to John, 'These incidents don't help you.' He'd put his arms round my shoulder and say, 'Dad, you're absolutely right, it's not going to happen again.' Two days later it did."

McEnroe's frustration increased. Every marginal line-call seemed to go against him; every time he fashioned a chance, Borg came up with an escape. But the tie-break was a different matter. McEnroe produced a stream of winners and won it seven points to one as the sun briefly came out.

When Borg broke to lead 3-1 in the third, they had been playing for two hours and McEnroe had yet to break serve. But up in the stands, Bergelin, Borg's guru, seemed to be frowning. "Yes, I was worried," he said. "He was ahead but I had a feeling that he did not have real confidence in the match. He was unsure. He had lost a little fighting spirit, and he had been finding it tough to get up and practise four or five hours a day. He no longer had real happiness in his tennis."

End of an era. McEnroe and Wimbledon may have seemed worlds apart but there could be no denying what victory meant to the inspirational American.

McEnroe finally broke the Borg service thanks to a bad bounce. But he was soon back in trouble. Serving from the Royal Box end, McEnroe stood 4-5 and 15-30 down after Borg had produced the shot of the match, a cross-court backhand pass from a ball that seemed irretrievable. McEnroe served, Borg returned, McEnroe volleyed, the ball, somewhat mishit, landed with a puff – chalk? dust? – around the baseline. Borg made a half-hearted attempt to shovel it back.

The critical point, the turning point, the test, had arrived. The linesman placed his hands together to signal that the ball was in. Umpire Jenkins overruled. "The ball was out," he called.

With half the crowd shouting "In!" and the other half "Out!", McEnroe, on his way back to serve, had not heard. Jenkins repeated himself: "The ball was out. 15-40." That meant two set points to Borg. "I thought, it's now or never," Jenkins recalled. "He's either going to blow his top now, or we'll be all right."

"I remember it so clearly," said McEnroe Snr. "The umpire should never have overruled because it was not a clear error. It was too close. John sort of bent down and then squatted on his haunches, saying to himself that he musn't let it upset him." "What?" he said, after standing up.

"He called it good and I called it out," said Jenkins. "He called it good and you called it out?" "Yes."

McEnroe stood still for several seconds, collecting himself. Then he proved that, along with the rest of his mental baggage, he had courage. He saved both set points, and saved two more as the game went back and forth to deuce until he finally held serve.

Indeed, it had been the turning point, for the rest was straightforward. McEnroe won another tie-break and took the fourth set 6-4. He had won his first Wimbledon singles title on American Independence Day and proved himself the best in the world.

At 25, Borg retired. To this day, he has not returned to Wimbledon

THE TERRIBLE TANTRUMS OF MAC THE MOUTH

"You cannot be serious man! That ball was on the line! Chalk flew up!"
To a Wimbledon umpire in 1981, the complaint that has since been mimicked millions of times on courts throughout the world

"I am not having points taken off me by an incompetent old fool. You're the pits of the world!"
McEnroe after breaking his racket

"Is it switched on?"
Questioning the efficiency of Cyclops, the electronic eye, after another dubious line-call

"When I said, 'You're a disgrace to mankind', I was talking to myself, not you"
Trying in vain to convince yet another maligned official that he had been misunderstood

"You must arrest him. He is the worst umpire I have ever seen!"
To a policeman at Wimbledon

"I am so disgusting that you musn't watch. Everybody leave!"
Fans get their marching orders

Borg at last was vanquished. Two months later, he lost to McEnroe again, in the final of the US Open. "That hurt him hard, I tell you," said Bergelin. Soon afterwards, at 25, Borg retired. To this day, he has not returned to Wimbledon.

"I won Wimbledon," said McEnroe. "That's all there is to it." But the All England Club had other ideas. They had already decided not to give him the tie to welcome him as an honorary member, and his invitation to the champions' dinner at the Savoy was withdrawn when McEnroe Snr said his son didn't want to attend for the duration but would turn up "somewhere around the dessert". The club also recommended a fine of $10,000 for their new champion and a charge of aggravated behaviour, which could lead to a further fine or even a ban from playing. A letter to the governing body of men's professional tennis had been prepared and under the rules it had to be served on McEnroe.

Hoyles, the tournament referee, and Gorringe, the club secretary, heard that McEnroe was on his way out of the ground and set off for the gate to intercept him.

"Mr McEnroe, we have an envelope for you to receive before you leave the ground," said Hoyles. He reached into his blazer pocket and handed McEnroe an envelope. "I think that's the wrong one," said Gorringe. It was. Hoyles snatched back the envelope, took another from his pocket and gave that to McEnroe.

What a shame that Gorringe noticed the wrong envelope. If he hadn't, McEnroe would have sat in the back of the courtesy car with mixed feelings: he was Wimbledon champion, but he'd been refused membership to the club; he'd ended the Borg era, but he wasn't going to the dinner; then he would have opened the envelope and concluded that those All England guys were even weirder than he thought. They'd given him two tickets for Cats.

Phoenix from the Ashes

Ian Botham was an all-rounder of prodigious talent who blazed across the cricket world. Yet by 1981 it had all gone wrong. His form had deserted him and he had resigned the England captaincy. It was at this lowest ebb that all his old brilliance exploded again into glorious life. Almost single-handedly he took on and routed Australia.

SIMON WILDE

It was an eventful summer, 1981. Thatcherism was biting. There were inner-city riots. Britain appeared to be fragmenting. There was also a royal wedding that brought the nation together. This confusion of highs and lows was mirrored by the Test series between England and Australia – particularly the third, fourth and fifth games, three incredible Tests won by England after the same man strode centre stage when disaster loomed.

Ian Botham went through his own highs and lows that summer. In early July, he gave up the England captaincy and was struggling for form; by late August, he had scaled peaks of achievement and acclaim savoured by few.

Botham denies those heady weeks gave him intimations of immortality. "It was simply a case of being in the right place at the right time, and being in a side that believed it could win," he said two decades on. "It happens once in your life. It didn't affect me." But for many that summer, the notion of Botham as immortal match-winner was real. They took it hard that Botham never repeated such heroics; take it hard that no England all-rounder has been able to do anything remotely similar since.

But the story could easily have been different. Botham was nearly sacked as captain before the second Test at Lord's – where he made a pair and gave up the captaincy in protest at the lack of selectorial support – and was nearly dropped as a player afterwards. No sooner had Botham quit than Alec Bedser, chairman of selectors, said he would have been removed anyway.

Mike Brearley, who had successfully led England against Australia a few years earlier, had been sounded out about taking over while the side was slipping to defeat in the first Test. Now, Bedser stopped off on his way home from Lord's to offer him the job; halting at a pub, and unable to get coins into the payphone, he asked Brearley to accept the charges. Brearley, unsure of his own form, agreed to take over for three games.

When Brearley met his players on the afternoon before the third Test, at Headingley, morale was low. The team had not won in 12 matches under Botham; there was anger at Botham's press treatment. Brearley's first words of consolation were that Botham would probably make up for his demotion by scoring a hundred and taking 12 wickets.

For three days, the game was a disaster for England. On an unreliable pitch, Australia ground out 401, a score Kim Hughes, their captain, thought worth 1,000. They then dismissed England for 174. Following on, England lost Graham Gooch for nought before bad light cut short the third day. England, and the Ashes, looked gone. The only solace was Botham's form. On the first day he had dropped two catches and been jeered by the crowd. After tea on the second he suddenly rediscovered his bowling rhythm and took six wickets. And, by opting for all-out aggression with the bat, he had profited to the tune of a brisk 50.

With Sunday a rest day, Botham held his usual Saturday night barbecue at his Humberside house. "It ended with both sides having rucking sessions on the lawn," he recalled. When the England players left their hotel on Monday, most checked out.

In the swing again: Botham bowling in Australia's first innings at Headingley. The old zip was beginning to come back.

They tried grafting, but it did not work. The pitch was too untrustworthy and by three o'clock England were 135 for seven, still 92 in arrears. By now Botham had been joined by Graham Dilley, the first of the tailenders. Botham encouraged Dilley to play naturally. "I told him not to scratch around. 'You're a good striker of the ball. Let's be aggressive and enjoy ourselves.' If we'd hung around we'd have got out."

Before tea, Dilley was the more aggressive. At the interval England were still 16 runs behind, with Botham having moved quietly to 39. It was then that Ladbrokes put odds on an England win at 500-1. Lillee, on a whim, sent his team's bus driver to put money on for himself and Rod Marsh. It was a mission that would later cause both players embarrassment.

After tea, Botham hit even harder than Dilley. In 70 minutes, he struck one six, 14 fours and two singles to move to his century off 87 balls. He was using one of Gooch's bats: "He hadn't used it much during the match, and I thought there were a few runs left in it." Many strokes were outrageous, shots aimed at midwicket flying over the slips or behind square leg for four. One miscue off Alderman, sailing over long on, was immortalised by Richie Benaud's television commentary: "And there's no need to chase that one. It's gone into the confectionery stall – and out again."

England took the lead but when Dilley was out for 56, after a stand worth 117 in 80 minutes, the score was effectively 25 for eight. But Australia's three seamers were exhausted and frustrated. England's mood changed. Chris Old was sent out with orders to keep in line. He added 67 with Botham while Bob Willis, whom Botham shielded well, helped put on 31. At stumps Botham was 145 not out and England, 351 for nine, led by 124.

Brearley, thinking England needed another 60 to have a genuine chance, breezed into the Australian dressing room. "Perhaps I went too soon," he wrote later, "for in the few seconds that I stood there I sensed thunderous silence, like the moment of Doom, everyone frozen in postures of dejection."

Botham in full flow at Headingley, smashing his way imperiously to 149. Suddenly, it was Australia who were on the back foot.

Botham left the ground with a towel in his mouth, a signal to waiting reporters whom he knew would link his success with jettisoning the captaincy. After fish and chips the England players checked back into their hotel, where Brearley offered to buy Botham a glass of his favourite brandy, then asked him to guess its age. It was the hotel's worst cooking brandy. "Twenty years," said Botham.

England added only five the next morning before Willis was out, leaving Australia 130 to win. Brearley urged aggression: "The Australians will be nervous." He threw the ball to Botham, reminding him that he owed his side six wickets.

Though the first wicket went to Botham, it was Willis who created the miracle. He blew Australia aside. Supported by superb catching, he took six wickets in as many overs as Australia slumped from 56 for one to 75 for eight. Lillee and Bright hit 35 in four overs before Willis claimed the last two wickets to finish with eight for 43. England had won by 18 runs. They were only the second Test team in history to win after following on. At 1-1, they were back in the series.

For three and a half days of the next Test, at Edgbaston, Botham played only a minor part. Again England made life difficult for themselves. They batted badly on a lifeless pitch for 189, with Botham, playing defensively, bowled for 26. They then bowled indifferently to allow Australia a lead of 69 (Botham taking one, fortuitous, wicket) which they reduced to 20 for the loss of Brearley by the end of the second day. That evening, at a garden party hosted by Bernard Thomas, the England physio, Hughes confided: "I only hope we don't have 130 to get again." That looked unlikely when England slid to 116 for six. There were no heroics from Botham. Wafting at a wide ball from Lillee, he was caught for three. Instead, Mike Gatting and Old added 38 and John Embury and Bob Taylor put on 50. Hughes's fears were realised. Australia needed 151 to win and, nerves clattering, closed on nine for one.

In his prime, irresistible– certainly the greatest all-rounder in the world. His talent was outrageous, his luck sometimes equally so. Yet his spirit was never less than immense.

Brearley privately thought England's hopes slim, as did the press, one correspondent pointing out that miracles, like lightning, do not strike twice. But the public were optimistic and on a sunny Sunday 10,000 turned up. Australia lost two early wickets but Allan Border and Graham Yallop took root. England's seamers looked ordinary and it needed Emburey to effect a change, taking the wickets of both Yallop and Border. Australia were 105 for five. Moments earlier, Brearley had been uncertain who to bowl with Emburey. "Botham was strangely diffident," he wrote. "He wondered how he would get anyone out." But once Border was gone, Brearley knew he should bowl. "Keep it tight for Embers," he told him.

He did. In 28 balls, he conceded one run. He also took the last five wickets. Botham's first ball almost yorked Marsh; his second was faster and uprooted middle stump. Bright, surprised by sheer pace, was plumb leg-before first ball and Lillee almost edged the hat-trick ball.

The crowd was baying Botham on as at each wicket he displayed un-inhibited joy, arms stretched high, chest filled. Lillee stayed two overs before being caught swinging at a wide ball. Martin Kent was bowled off his pads; three balls later, Alderman was bowled. England had won by 29 runs. There had been another miracle.

Botham's confidence was sky-high. Walking out to bat in the fifth Test at Old Trafford 11 days later, he made his most regal entrance, loosening his shoulders with circular swings of his bat. It counted for nothing. Off Lillee's first ball he was caught by Bright in the gully. This time, he was not out of the game for long. When Australia responded to England's inadequate 231, he claimed three wickets and three feline catches to give England a lead of 101. But in the face of disciplined Australian cricket, England surrendered the initiative, creeping to 104 for five in 69 overs of their second innings.

At that point, just before half past two on Saturday, in front of a crowd of 20,000, Botham strode out again, to join Chris Tavaré to play what John Woodcock suggested in *The Times* two days later may have been the greatest

innings ever played. "Leading by only 205, we thought we were way light," Botham remembered. "I had to play carefully. There were a few men round the bat, the light was not brilliant and I had to get myself in. If we'd lost two quick wickets, there was not much left in the hutch."

"I refuse to believe that a cricket ball has ever been hit with greater power and rarer splendour"

It was an ominously lengthy reconnaisance. Off his first 32 balls, he scored just five; off 53 he scored 28. Then Alderman and Lillee took the new ball. "I just went for it. Any batsman who fancies himself against the quicks and is 'in', the time to attack is with the new ball. Sometimes you are lucky and it happens that way."

Almost immediately, Botham struck a high swirling mishit off Alderman that nearly fell to Mike Whitney in the deep. Three times in two overs he hooked sixes off Lillee, who directed his bouncers with pinpoint accuracy at his helmetless head, Botham twice ducking but going through with the stroke anyway. He believes that had he thought about it he might never have attempted such shots. "No brains, no sense, no feeling," he mused.

"He kept hooking me, taking his eye off the ball," Lillee said. "I was sure I would get him with the bouncer, but the more I fed him with it, the further the ball disappeared." Most of Botham's strokes, as he reaped 66 from eight overs, were measured and orthodox. His only other chance was on 91, when a square cut was almost caught on the boundary. With the pitch playing reliably, there was little need for heaves and slices. Woodcock wrote: "I refuse to believe that a cricket ball has ever been hit with greater power and rarer splendour."

The contrast with Tavaré was comic. While Botham swept from five to 118 in 70 balls, Tavaré just kept defending. After playing out another maiden, he tendered an apology. "Sorry, Beefy. I hope I wasn't too boring." He was actually the perfect foil. They added 149, Tavaré's share 28 to Botham's 118, and Australia were left a mammoth 506 to win. In keeping with the freakish nature of the cricket, they made a good fist of it, but victory gave England the series and the Ashes.

During a drinks break, it was announced that Brearley would lead England in the last Test. Brearley believed Botham wanted the job back but Botham denied it: "I was totally disillusioned with the way the selectors worked. I didn't want anything to do with it." And in 11 more years as a Test cricketer, he never did.

The sweet taste of success: the England players on the balcony at Edgbaston after Botham, man of the match again, has just blasted away the last five Australian wickets for one run. Bob Willis holds the champagne bottle for Botham. Mike Brearley (left), England's Svengali, watches.

The White Shark

By 1983, the Americans had been disdainfully holding off challenges for the America's Cup for 132 years in sport's longest-ever winning run. Yet that year they came up against an Australian crew which matched them for professionalism and had a seemingly miraculous boat with a mysterious winged keel. The unthinkable was at hand.

KEITH WHEATLEY

Aboard the slim white yacht off Newport, Rhode Island, a dozen normally ebullient Aussie sailors were silent, staring at the deck, avoiding eye-contact. The greatest prize in yachting was slipping through their fingers. For millions of Australians watching on television or listening on radio, a win seemed one miracle too many. Over the previous week, their yacht had come from 3-1 down and entered the final race of the America's Cup series tied at 3-3. But now things looked grim.

They knew they were underdogs, competing against the greatest sailors from the most powerful nation on earth. Yet even the supposedly magical

It was a pivotal event, one that would change the social balance of America for ever

powers of their secret winged-keel and the ebullience of tycoon owner Alan Bond could not lift the spirits of the millions of armchair yachtsmen in Melbourne and Meekatharra. As Australia II, nicknamed the White Shark for its habit of eating opponents alive, rounded the Brenton Reef buoy off Rhode Island 49 seconds behind maestro Dennis Conner at the helm of his scarlet 12-metre yacht Liberty, Aussie hearts sank. With just two legs remaining it seemed impossible to pass the Americans.

"I just cannot believe this, I cannot believe this," groaned Australia II navigator Hugh Treharne, as a freshening breeze carried Liberty down the course on a perfectly set spinnaker. His skipper, John Bertrand – highly strung at the best of times – was an impenetrable mask. Aboard the Australian launch Black Swan, the mercurial genius that was the late Ben Lexcen, designer of the winged-keel, lay on a bunk and turned his face to the wall. Alan Bond chewed his fingernails and talked nineteen-to-the-dozen.

Tom Whidden, Conner's tactician, recalled the silence aboard Liberty: "Dennis always liked a quiet ship. He picked the best guys for the jobs and then expected them to do it, not shoot the breeze." Conner was easily the most impressive sailor of his generation. When he strove to be chosen as the defender of the Cup for the 1980 series, Conner practiced for 340 days out of the preceding year. Not for nothing did Conner title his autobiography *No Excuse to Lose*. "When we were 3-3, Bertrand said something about it being a scenario Hollywood couldn't match," Conner said disdainfully. "Where he saw it as a big drama, to me it was just another boat race."

Born into a blue-collar San Diego family, the teenage sailor broke into spiffy yacht club circles on talent alone. Once he started to climb the

Afterwards, the Americans griped the Australians won only because they had a boat that couldn't lose. Not surprisingly, the Australians disagreed, asserting that tactics and commitment were the key.

ladder of success, Conner realised he had one huge advantage over his middle-class rivals. He took sailing totally seriously. Preparation was his key. Conner never wanted to start any race without feeling he was the favourite. The routine sailing philosophy – "give us an equal boat and we'll sail it faster" – held no appeal to this obsessive, insecure man. Yet over that Newport summer Conner had followed the challenger elimination series and knew that Australia II was a very special boat. The exact details of the winged keel were a still a mystery, but it gave the Aussies something the opposition lacked. "The winged keel made Australia II more manoeuver-

able than Liberty plus much faster downwind in light winds, very equal from 8-13 knots and we never sailed much above that," recalled Bertrand. So not an overwhelming advantage, but enough to give Conner the jitters even if he was 3-1 up and need just a single race to retain the Cup. He knew the NYYC's jibe about replacing the trophy with the head of the losing helmsman.

Psychology is crucial to match-racing. Though often described as boat-on-boat, it might be more accurately summed up as skipper-against-skipper. If one of the contestants is able to obtain a dominant

position over the other in the vital 10 minutes of close-quarters manoeuvring prior to the star, 99 per cent of the time they will win the race. Some helmsmen refuse to look at their rival during this jockeying, especially against Conner. They fear eye contact with a sailor whose blank, deadly gaze said I Am the Man. Australia II's skipper had his own way of dealing with it. "I never allowed anyone aboard to refer to him by name. No Dennis, no Conner, not even DC," said Bertrand. "I tried to dehumanise them. Liberty was always spoken of simply as the red boat."

As they chased Conner downwind, Bertrand reminded his crew that the rule was Eyes in the Boat. "Think about

your job, about the sail trim, about helping one another," he urged. Only Colin Beashel, now an Olympic gold medallist in the Star class, was to look down the course. Beashel, trimming the vast mainsail on the 12-metre, was recognised as the finest natural sailor in the boat, with an uncanny ability to spot vital windshifts minutes before they reached the yacht. "I knew we were fast but I really wasn't sure we could catch Liberty," he remembered. "There was a big gap to make up." Conner himself was less sanguine: "We knew that the Aussie boat was up to a minute quicker than us on every downwind leg. I thought we were in deep ca-ca and wasn't at all certain we were going to win."

None of this was known to the thousands out on the Atlantic that afternoon. Overhead, helicopters clattered through a hazy sky. Nearly 2,000 spectator boats were out on the course, kept away from the racing yachts by coastguards but following every move through powerful binoculars. The media presence was huge. *The New York Times*, not normally big on sport, had four reporters cov-

ering this one race. Of course, the America's Cup was never just a yacht race. Its appeal lay in the mythology, the 132-year unbroken winning streak since the New Yorkers came to Cowes in 1851 with a radical new schooner, the *America*, and trounced the finest yachts the grandees of the Royal Yacht Squadron could put on the water.

Her owner, John C Stevens of Brooklyn, offered a $50,000 wager for any vessel willing to take her on. It was probably around $5m in today's money and Britain's sailors were intimidated. In the end the Yanks had to settle for participation in a routine RYS race around the Isle of Wight. Yet everyone knew what was at stake. Even Queen Victoria and Prince Albert tootled down to the Needles on the royal yacht to watch the final leg. *America* passed HMQ 21 minutes ahead of her nearest rival.

The inquest filled the letters page of *The Times* and the clubs of St James's for weeks, the subsequent attempts at

revenge for over a century. Lord Dunraven, Sir Thomas Lipton, Tommy Sopwith – these were just a few of the tycoons and sailing enthusiasts who expended blood and treasure travelling to the New World to wrest back the wretched Cup. By 1983 there

Bertrand and his crew were in tears, overwhelmed by the enormity of their victory

had been 25 challenges, and since the 1960s these had begun to involve nations other than Britain and Canada, the traditional participants. Yet despite the best efforts of France, Australia, Italy and Sweden, the technology, wealth and self-confidence of the Americans had stopped any challenger taking more than two races off the defenders in a best-of-seven final.

What drew journalists and commentators with no interest in sailing to Newport that hot, foggy summer was the sense that this was possibly a defining moment for the American establishment, a pivotal event when the social balance of the country might change in subtle but important ways.

Almost no organisation in the USA is more self-important than the New York Yacht Club. Membership is largely hereditary and, while the railroad barons and real estate speculators who founded it in the mid-19th century might have been more than a touch raw, by 1983 their descendants had become the starchy embodiment of old money. Yet here the NYYC were, staging a drama in which they were unthinkably the underdogs and their gladiator was a not a preppy scion of the Social Register but an unsophisticated draper from southern California. Pitted against him was an Australian team whose superior technology and commitment had looked like winning them the Cup. Desperate, the NYYC succumbed to the temptation to manipulate the rules. These revolved around a clandestine attempt

Bond hoists the Cup aloft watched by the genial genius Ben Lexcen, designer of the feted keel. John Bertrand is on the left, hand stretching to touch the cup. They formed the heart of the Australian effort.

Revealed at last: Australia's wonder weapon, the winged keel. Lexcen's innovation sparked a revolution in yacht design – as well as charges of espionage as the NYYC made frantic efforts to discover its secrets.

to obtain proof that that the famous winged keel had been designed not by Lexcen but by a Dutch scientist named Peter van Oosanaen, who had done some tank testing for the Australians.

The first bid came when a NYYC member (travelling incognito) went to Holland to ask Van Oosanaen to sign a document, presented as simply a research paper, saying that he had designed Australia II's keel — a direct contravention of nationality rule which would have seen Bond's team thrown out of the regatta. "I would have to have been drunk or out of my mind to sign such a document, which even had the word affadavit at the top, clumsily crossed out in biro but still visible," commented the Dutchman.

When the news of this crude ploy leaked out the NYYC sank even further in the eyes of all challengers, not just the Aussies. "The New Yacht Club membership are the kind of people who start wars," said a furious Lexcen. The NYYC's final, humiliating throw was to telex van Oosanaen to ask him to sell them confidential details of the Australian keel. The Dutchman promptly passed the message to Bond, who gleefully released it to the world's press. If the Americans wanted to keep their Cup, they would have to do it in the water.

What the spectators saw next definitely qualified as a fair dinkum miracle. The breeze went light off to the left side of the course where Liberty had chosen to race. Australia II kept more pressure in her spinnaker and powered on down the course. When the two yachts converged just short of the leeward mark, it was the Aussies who crossed ahead of their rivals. The cheers from the Australian spectators could be heard in Sydney.

Three upwind miles left to the finish and Conner vowed to grind the

Aussies down in a tacking duel of unprecedented ferocity. If his crew seldom spoke, on that clammy afternoon it was impossible for them. "Okay guys, this is the big one. Keep it focused," murmured Whidden. Conner was impassive at the wheel, trademark white zinc cream around his lips. The crew's hands and arms were a blur on the giant coffee-grinder winches. Liberty tacked 47 times in 40 minutes. Fit, muscular young men thought they were going to pass out with fatigue. Australia II matched them tack-for-tack. By now it was dawn in Sydney but the Harbour Bridge was empty of commuter traffic. An entire nation was transfixed. What made it so heartfelt – a bit like cricket's Bodyline Test series in the 1930s – was the feeling that the opposition were cheats.

Two final tacks to the line. Over the thousands of miles of crackling ionosphere came the result. "Stand up Australia – you've won the America's Cup!" bawled Bruce Stannard, a semi-distraught radio commentator who had been broadcasting for seven hours. Prime minister Bob Hawke spontaneously awarded the Australian nation a public holiday. It was party time from the suburbs to the outback.

The winning margin was 41 seconds. In the white boat, Bertrand and his crew were in tears, overwhelmed by the enormity of their victory. Was it the secret keel that gave them such an amazing win or was it the sheer never-say-die guts, seen in so many different competitions, of Australian sportsmen? "The boat gave us the foundation to believe that we could do it," reflected Beashel. "Because of that strength we were able to come back after being 3-1 down. And that took a lot of confidence and the ability to stay focused when things were going the wrong way."

To the last the NYYC were ungracious. TV cameras and photographers were banned from the low-key handover of the ornate silver ewer on the terrace of Marble House, the extravagant Newport mansion built by railroad tycoon William K Vanderbilt. Halsey Herreshoff, navigator on Liberty and a member of another American dynasty (this time in yachting), tersely summed up the mood at the brief ceremony. "The unthinkable has happened," sulked Herreshoff as Bond carried the trophy away to its new home in Perth, western Australia.

Black magic

Humiliation beckoned for Dennis Taylor in the final of the world snooker championship. Eight-nil down to defending champion Steve Davis, his annihilation seemed assured. But in a wildly improbable fightback, Taylor gradually reeled in his opponent. At 17-all, the match hinged on the final frame ... and final black.

DENIS WALSH

For 15 days Trevor East had tracked every ball of Dennis Taylor's journey to the 1985 world snooker final at Sheffield's Crucible Theatre. When his quarter-final against Cliff Thorburn slipped into the early hours and ambivalent souls deserted the arena, East sat in vigil. As executive producer of ITV's snooker coverage, East was a citizen of the circuit and what began as a friendship with Taylor developed into a bond. On Taylor's journey he was more than a fellow-traveller, he was a crutch, a sympathetic ear, a propulsive force.

But when the final began on the last Saturday of April, East forsook the Crucible Theatre for the Baseball Ground and his beloved Derby County. It was only the first session, he thought. How much could happen? Getting into his car shortly after five, he sought reassurance on the sports news. He was met with calamity. The first session had been a whitewash: 7-0 to Steve Davis.

East drove the 30 miles to Sheffield with the pedal to the floor. He knew better than most the doubts that had stalked Taylor and undermined his career. Good judges said he would be world champion before he was 30, but one final and three semi-finals later he had confounded the prediction. Taylor had turned 36, unfulfilled.

"I knew I had to see him before he went out for the evening session," said East. "I could see he was devastated. He needed a major pick-up so I gave him a bollocking. 'We've not come all this way, I've not sat through every one of your matches, for you to throw it away like this.' We agreed that if he could win the next four frames he'd be back in it." Davis won the first frame of the evening: 8-0.

The most compulsive final in the history of snooker had barely reached its first watershed.

Taylor pots, Davis watches. As the game wore on, the tension became almost unbearable. In the end, it was the imperious, unbeatable Davis who cracked.

Taylor arrived at the world championship on the swell of his best-ever season. Three tournament victories included the Rothmans Grand Prix, his first Major, and at the Crucible that form swept him through a tough draw. Tony Knowles, fresh from conquering Jimmy White, was his semi-final opponent but Taylor dismissed him 16-5 with a session to spare.

Davis was in his worst run for four years. Like Taylor he had won three titles that season, but for the master of snooker's universe such a modest haul was unbecoming; the season before the bounty had been nine. The world championship, though, was different. Davis was the defending champion, seeking his third title in a row, and for months his preparation had been calibrated for the Crucible.

At Sheffield, Davis cocooned himself from the world. Five weeks before the championship, his old minder, Ron Radley, was persuaded to return. Radley slept in the next room and screened all Davis's phone calls. He was a buffer from fans and the press; driver, secretary, confidante. For the world champion, laboratory conditions.

Davis's snooker in the first session was imperious. Taylor was allowed a 50 break in the opening frame, but for the rest of the afternoon he was incarcerated in his chair. Davis's safety play was immaculate, his potting dead-eye. As the afternoon progressed,

Taylor's head sank deeper into his shirt collar, his idle mind tormented.

"I was so embarrassed," he recalled. "You're thinking of the BBC and the sponsors, Embassy. They must be thinking this will be the worst final in the history of the game. You're thinking of all the people that you know are there. But then, on the positive side, I was thinking, 'I haven't done much wrong here'."

Taylor concentrated on buttressing himself from the mental onslaught:

"We've not come all this way ... for you to throw it away like this"

"Steve had such a domineering demeanour around the table and some players used to get annoyed by that. When he was at the table, it was his arena and that upset some players. That afternoon I pretended I was looking at the table, but a lot of the time I wasn't, I was looking underneath it. I wasn't watching what he was doing."

Taylor joked a little with the gallery; gallows humour. In one frame Davis rolled the white ball tight to the yellow instead of taking on a pot. "I've got him worried," said Taylor as he got up to play. The crowd laughed with Taylor, as they always did. The ordeal dragged on.

It was 8.15pm before Taylor won his first

The world in his hands: Taylor at his moment of ecstatic triumph. When he potted the final black, it was the first time he had led in the entire match.

frame, more than six hours after play had begun. Davis only needed the green to go 9-0 in front and when he attempted a risky pot along the cushion the ball wobbled in the jaws of the pocket and stayed out. Taylor cleared up the remaining colours and the crowd rose to his liberation.

In the psychological landscape of the match, Davis's miss was mountainous. He had crushed Taylor 9-0 in the final of the Jameson Open four years earlier and, as the evening session began, the resonance of that scoreline occurred to them both. "I had been

37

used to Dennis falling apart," said Davis, "and I think a lot of people had. But he had improved his standards immensely in the period leading up to the world championship. I presented him with a frame at 8-0, instead of him having to win it, and the change in Dennis was amazing. Then, all of a sudden, I was looking over my shoulder. There is a difficulty when you have a big lead in a match. When you're so

far in front, you lose your direction. You have nothing to fire at because the finishing line is too far away. That frame was a turning point."

Davis took the next, but confidence surged through Taylor's game in a floodtide and he mopped up the remaining six frames of the evening to trail by just 9-7 as Saturday's play came to a close. Heading back to the St George Hotel, Taylor's head was buzzing and adrenaline coursed through him like a narcotic. He knew that sleep was a hopeless aspiration, so he shared a bottle of champagne with his wife Trish and East: "I was on such a high, I felt like I'd virtually won the world championship."

Three of Taylor's sisters and their husbands travelled from his home-place of Coalisland in County Tyrone on Sunday morning. His

There have been few more popular winners than Taylor. Whatever the sympathy for Davis, it was impossible not be moved by the resilience and skill of the genial Irishman with goggles for glasses.

"It was a frantic scramble, just a scramble for the line"

father, Tommy, stayed at home. He had been at the Crucible six years earlier when Taylor collapsed on the last day and Terry Griffiths won nine of the 10 frames played to win 24-16. Tommy thought it might bring a change of luck to stay away. At home he made a tin-foil cup in the shape of the world championship trophy and put it on the television.

Taylor's mother, Annie, had died suddenly the previous October. They had been close and the loss wounded Taylor deeply: "On the Sunday morning I went for a wander around the small lake at the hotel and all kinds of thoughts were going through my head. I thought a lot about my mum. What had happened to her was still fresh in my mind. That weekend I felt like she was there with me, potting every ball."

Davis's play in the final session on Saturday night encouraged Taylor. The missed green seemed to play on the champion's mind and his shot selection became more conservative. Whenever Davis's potting lost its fluency, his safety play was usually enough to strangle opponents, but Taylor was one of the few players whose tactical nous was comparable with Davis's. All day Sunday they were bound in a clench. "It was a frantic scramble," said Davis, "just a scramble for the line." At different times the tension paralysed them both. In one frame, Davis missed a straight brown only to be reprieved when Taylor missed a black off its spot from no more than a foot.

Taylor levelled the match at 11-11, Davis pulled two clear again. Taylor came back to 13-13, Davis accelerated to 15-13. Taylor made it 15-15, the champion surged to 17-15.

Davis left the arena for a break and Taylor left, too, indicating to East, sitting on the press benches, to join him: "His uncomplicated belief in me was what I needed." At that moment, more than ever. "Your soul is out there for everybody to see," Davis said once of playing at the Crucible. By Sunday evening both men were stripped bare.

The next frame was a tangle of anxious incompetence. Miss followed miss until Taylor finally saved himself on the pink. The second-last frame was scrappy, too, but Taylor dominated it and Davis failed to pot a ball: 17-17. The endgame was upon them.

Long before then the match had seduced and entrapped an audience far beyond the Crucible. BBC2 reported a viewership of 18.5m, but that omitted the Republic of Ireland and did not include pubs and clubs. In Coalisland, John Joe Girvan's sports club, where Taylor learned his snooker, was the only venue licensed to sell alcohol on a Sunday night and 400 people were packed in. A band was booked, but they soon realised that three small televisions were upstaging them and they laid their instruments down.

The final frame lurched and trembled, moved one moment by weakness, the next by courage. Taylor took an early lead, but Davis led going into the colours. He fluked the green to go 18 points ahead with 22 left; Taylor needed the rest of the balls to win. They both missed the brown twice before Taylor surrendered himself to reckless daring. It was the winning of the match. The brown was near the side cushion at the other end of the table, the white close to the top cushion. He took on the shot and made it.

Blue and pink followed but, when it came to the black, the only option was a double across the table. He went for it: "I was striking across so I couldn't see, but it looked like it was going in, the crowd were cheering and then it hit the knuckle of the pocket."

The ball ran safe, Davis played a brilliant safety shot and Taylor countered with an outrageous double, the length of the table. He was on the high wire, without a net: "I had my mind made up, I wasn't going to lose playing a safety shot."

Davis played a poor shot and left Taylor with a chance; he fluffed it and left Davis in. "I walked back to my seat,"

Victor and vanquished: Davis congratulates Taylor. For Davis, the turmoil of defeat was almost more than he could bear; for Taylor, winning was sheer heaven.

said Taylor, "pushed my glasses up and thought, 'That's it, it's gone'. But, when I turned round, the black wasn't as close to the pocket as I had thought."

The world's greatest player, the master of his universe, rose from his seat. "When I got up," Davis recalled, "my legs were like jelly." The angle was such that the pocket was outside Davis's line of vision when he looked at the object ball. In those situations the tendency is to under-cut the shot. Davis knew that: "The coward's way out is to under-cut it. But I over-cut it by quite a way and, because I over-cut it, the white ball didn't stay at the bottom of the table. I knew I'd lost it."

Under pressure, Taylor's tendency was to snatch at his shots, but in the maelstrom he composed himself one last time. The stroke was smooth and true. At 23 minutes past midnight, an hour and eight minutes after the final frame had begun, the black ball disappeared. The houselights went up, the camera bulbs flashed, Taylor thrust the cue above his head like a weightlifter and Malachy Duffin ran from the back of the auditorium to hug his brother-in-law, the new champion of the world.

John Williams, the referee, went to shake Taylor's hand, but Taylor sought out his opponent first. All colour had drained from Davis's face. David Vine, of the BBC, approached Davis as he sat in his chair, broken. "Can you believe what just happened out there?" asked Vine. "You've just seen it," said Davis, "in black and white." When the cameras stopped rolling, Davis sought the sanctuary of his dressing room and wept. In the delirium of his disappointment he spoke of going on "a two-day bender", but by morning his fever had cooled. Davis came back to win three more world titles but that night will never leave him: "When I look back on my career, one day that'll probably be the only thing I'll remember from snooker."

A week after he beat Davis, Taylor was approached by a man in Dublin. Taylor could sense his shyness but, compelled by something he needed to say, the stranger pressed on. "Do you know," he said, "that you've given my wife more pleasure than I ever have." How could any of us forget?

The final frame lurched and trembled, moved one moment by weakness, the next by courage

Charge of the Golden Bear

Jack Nicklaus may have been the greatest golfer of them all but by 1986 his career was surely in terminal decline. Nicklaus, however, saw things differently. He was never a player content just to make up the numbers and at the 1986 Masters he turned the clock back in spectacular style. It was a day when the gods of golf smiled.

NICK PITT

Nobody really believed that at the age of 46 Jack Nicklaus would win the 1986 US Masters except Jack Nicklaus. The public didn't. They had grown used to granting Nicklaus an ovation for past services to the game as he walked waving up the 18th, before they settled down to wait for the contenders. The press didn't. Bolder than most, but expressing the consensus, Tom McCollister of the *Atlanta Journal* recommended retirement. Thanks for the memories, Jack, don't hang around to embarrass yourself, good luck with designing golf courses.

Even Nicklaus's friends, such as John Montgomery, who was a houseguest for the week in Augusta, looked forward to watching him with hope rather than belief. In an attempt to rouse the old Golden Bear to growl once more, Montgomery stuck a copy of McCollister's column on the refrigerator. But that wasn't so much psychology as a wind-up, for Montgomery was a master of the practical joke. He had once dumped two tons of cow manure, topped by a little flag reading Happy Birthday, on Nicklaus's drive.

This bear needed rousing. It was six years since his last win in a Major. He had a bad back and his form was awful. He had played seven US Tour events in 1986 and had missed the cut in four. His best finish had been 39th. In the money-list he was in 160th place.

Nicklaus had asked his eldest son, Jackie, to caddie for him. It was an honour as much as anything. Jackie carried the bag and worked out the

If the coat fits: former champion Bernhard Langer helps Nicklaus don the famous green jacket. It was his sixth Masters.

yardage for each shot (but only as a double-check: Nicklaus made his own measurements). "Dad let me help him read the putts," Jackie recalled. "But I think that was to make me feel part of the show."

For Jackie, the thrilling realisation that his father might win was a gradual and accelerating process. "He struck the ball wonderfully well over the first three days, but he wasn't making the putts," he said. "Even the first day, when he shot 74, he was playing well. And his third-round 69, which

put him on the fringe of contention, could have been five or six shots better. By then, it was getting exciting."

And when did Nicklaus himself take seriously the possibility of accomplishing a feat that almost everyone else dismissed out of hand? This is the key to it. He always did. "There wasn't a time when he didn't think it could happen," said Jackie. "From his first shot on the practice ground to the final putt, he was certain about it."

Of course. That's what had made him the best there ever was, the winner of five Masters titles, four US Opens, three Opens, five USPGAs and two US Amateurs. It wasn't so much the power or the ball-striking but the golfing brain and the will. And they were still intact. Indeed, although Nicklaus always acknowledged the warm applause for being Nicklaus, the idea of being part of the ceremony rather than the battle filled him with contempt. He came to win and when he couldn't, he wouldn't come.

"What will it take?" asked Jackie in the car as they made their way to the grounds of the Augusta National Club on the morning of the final round. "Sixty-six to tie, sixty-five to win," said Nicklaus. He had done his calculations. Greg Norman held the lead at six under par, four strokes ahead of Nicklaus. But more important for Nicklaus, only eight players lay ahead of him.

This bear needed rousing. It was six years since his last win in a Major

That morning, Nicklaus had also made a significant personal gesture. His mother-in-law had recently died, and her funeral service had been conducted by a family friend, the Rev William Smith. Two years earlier, Smith's son Craig had died from cancer at 13. He had always wanted Nicklaus, his idol, to wear yellow shirts for luck. One day, Nicklaus's wife Barbara had told him, he must wear yellow at the Masters, for Craig Smith. This, Nicklaus decided, was that day.

In keeping with the adage that the tournament does not begin until the final nine holes of the final round, Nicklaus made little progress before the turn. He was level par for the day as he addressed a downhill putt on the ninth green, when a huge cheer went up from the hole behind. "That's either Seve Ballesteros or Tom Kite making eagle," Nicklaus said to himself as he backed off the putt. When he returned to his putt, another roar came up. "That's the other one making eagle." In fact, they had both pitched in from off the green. "I think it's time we made a little noise ourselves," Nicklaus told the crowd. He made the putt, and the crowd obliged.

So it began and so extraordinary was the conjunction of players and events over the following two hours, and so grand the theatre, that it was as if the gods of golf, no doubt with Bobby Jones among them, had decided on a little sport to settle an argument. Perhaps the dispute concerned Nicklaus's place in history, and to test him they threw him in with the best of the succeeding generation. In the shake-up, Nicklaus had to contend with Ballesteros, Kite, Tom Watson, Norman and Nick Price.

Nicklaus birdied the 10th by holing a 25-footer. "Nice putt," said Jackie. "Now let's go and make another one." Nicklaus birdied the 11th as well, but then he faltered. At the short, treacherous 12th, where selecting the right club is so vital yet so difficult, he went over the back, and left a pitch-and-run five feet short. His putt for par hit a spike-mark and jumped two inches to the left.

High and mighty: Nicklaus birdies the 17th and takes the lead for the first time after Ballesteros bogeys the 15th. The bear was roused now.

It was a blow not many could have shaken off. "That bogey was a real downer," said Jackie Nicklaus. "But I've seen him come back so often after being kicked in the shins. I remember at the 1984 Memorial Tournament, he blocked his drive out of bounds on the 71st hole, and I was sure he'd blown it. Then he holed a 30ft putt on the last to go into a play-off and won it."

With four holes left, Nicklaus trailed Ballesteros by four strokes. On the fairway of the par-five 15th, he was left with 205 yards to the pin, downhill and over water. "Boy, a three would go a long way right here," Nicklaus said, meaning an eagle three. He took his four-iron and hit his trademark shot, high and soft, fading to the target and settling 14ft to the left of the hole. "He made the putt and I jumped as high as I ever did in my life," said Jackie. "We moved on towards the

16th tee and the crowd was going nuts. It was warm and sunny and everything was a mass of colours, like a kaleido-scope. I tried not to show emotion, but inside I was going berserk."

On the 16th, par three over water, Nicklaus usually hit a six-iron. With a breeze against, and the pin tucked in on the left close to the drink, he chose the five-iron. It needed to be a few

"I tried not to show any emotion but inside I was going berserk"

yards to the right of the pin and per-fect in length. "As soon as he hit it, I knew the direction was perfect," said Jackie. "So I murmured, 'Be the right club' and although the ball was only 50 yards from him, hardly off the end

The roar of the gallery: Nicklaus salutes the crowd as he leaves the 18th green – and the crowd hails Nicklaus.

of the tee, he looked at me and winked. He knew it was the right club. Sometimes his concentration and confidence is so extraordinary that he knows he's going to hit the shot before he hits it." The ball pitched 10ft to the right of the flag and rolled down the hill, missing the hole by half an inch and coming to rest two and a half feet past. When the putt fell, Nicklaus was six under for the day, eight under for the tourna-ment, firmly in contention.

The roped-off corridor between the bowl of the 16th green and the raised tee of the 17th is very narrow. "My ears were ringing," said Jackie. "I've never heard noise like I heard on our walk through, not at any other sporting

event or even at a rock concert. All I was doing was saying, 'Keep your head still' before he putted and 'Nice putt, let's go and make another one' after he had putted."

As Nicklaus marched to 17, the one man whose belief burned as strongly stood on the 15th fairway. It was Ballesteros. His recent form, too, had been poor, mostly because he had had a harrowing year. His father, Baldomero, who had been the mainstay in his life, had died from cancer the previous month. Ballesteros was also at war with the US Tour, which had banned him for failing to play the required number of events.

The Spaniard's response was typical. He would show the Americans by winning the Masters for a third time, and he would dedicate his victory to his father. It was *destino*. And so it seemed, for he had been high on the leaderboard throughout and now stood alone, two strokes clear.

Faced with a very similar shot to the one that Nicklaus had played majestically to set up an eagle a few minutes earlier, Ballesteros selected the same club, the four-iron. He could have hit a five-iron flat out, but reasoned that as long as he cleared the water, he ought to win the tournament. Sub-consciously, Ballesteros must have known he had too much club. He stopped on the shot and watched horror-struck as his ball plunged into the water.

Nicklaus was on the 17th tee, preparing to drive. He heard the noise. "It was a strange sound: loud but somehow more like a moan than the roar Masters galleries let loose when a contender does something dramatic," he recalled. Profoundly shaken, Ballesteros made a six. He subsequently three-putted the 17th and finished fourth. Although he would win one further Open title, and contend again in the Masters, the sense of optimism, certainty, *destino*, that had shone so brightly in him had been extinguished with a single shot.

Carried on a flood-tide of support that was beginning to assume the miracle, the most difficult problem for Nicklaus was composing himself and regrouping as he reached each green. Unlike Ballesteros, he would never play by inspiration alone. On the 17th, he had a 10ft downhill putt. Jackie reckoned it would swing to the right. "No, this one I know," his father said. "It'll hold its line." It did, for another birdie and the outright lead. The television announcer turned to Tom Weiskopf: "Tom, tell us what he's thinking here as he makes his way up the 18th." "If I knew what he was thinking, I would have won a lot more tournaments," said Weiskopf.

A three-wood from the tee avoiding the bunkers on the left; a five-iron well struck but knocked down by the wind; a 40ft putt to within a few inches and a tap-in for a back nine of 30, a round of 65, precisely what he had forecast he would need, and a total of 279.

Nicklaus and son embraced on the 18th green, but it wasn't over. Ballesteros and Watson were out of it, but Kite could force a play-off with a birdie at the last and Norman, the

"Nothing less than the most important accomplishment in golf since Bobby Jones's Grand Slam in 1930"

overnight leader who had stumbled over the front nine, was charging up the leaderboard with a succession of birdies from the 14th.

Kite first. He had a 12ft putt for the birdie he needed and struck it well. At the last moment, it moved left and came to rest on the lip of the hole. Nicklaus and son were in the Jones Cabin, watching on television. "He had been very much in control on the course," said Jackie. "But watching TV, he could not keep still. He was pacing up and down."

"That's it. It's all over," somebody in the cabin said when Kite's putt stayed above ground. "No it isn't," said Nicklaus. "There's still Norman." Indeed, Norman had made his fourth consecutive birdie on the 17th. He needed a par to tie, a birdie to win. Nicklaus, who had stiffened up, began to stretch his back, ready for a play-off.

But in the final examination set by the gods, Norman, like Ballesteros, made a fatal error. For safety, he struck a three-wood from the tee, leaving an uphill shot from the centre of the fairway with – once again – a four-iron. But for the circumstances, the shot was so straightforward for a professional as to be automatic. But Norman's swing was ugly and unbalanced, and his shot was blocked way right into the crowd. Norman made a brave attempt to redeem himself. He played a pitch-and-run to 15ft but missed the putt, finishing tied for second place with Kite. Nicklaus emerged from the cabin to a mighty cheer.

For Herbert Warren Wind, the golf historian and writer, Nicklaus's victory was "nothing less than the most important accomplishment in golf since Bobby Jones's Grand Slam in 1930". For Nicklaus himself, it was "by far the most fulfiling achievement of my career". For the rest of us, most bitterly for Ballesteros and Norman, it was a drama with an unmistakable message: that of all the champions who have taken club to ball, the most resourceful and formidable was Jack Nicklaus.

July 1986

Knocked out by the Hand of God

When England met Argentina in the quarter-finals of the 1986 World Cup, the two countries were still technically at war: Argentinian bitterness over the Falklands defeat was palpable. And then there was Maradona, the most gifted player of his era yet a deeply flawed character.

JOE LOVEJOY

Football is replete with allegory – David and Goliath, hero and villain – but no match in the history of the World Cup has been more symbolic than England v Argentina in 1986, when two goals in the space of five minutes exemplified the flawed genius that was Diego Maradona. The first was a blatant fraud, the second a treasured masterpiece, an unmatched pair representing the personality of a virtuoso who ought to have been an inspirational example to a generation, but instead became the antithesis of sportsmanship, a bloated, debauched degenerate who was kicked out of the 1994 World Cup when he failed a drugs test.

So much of what we have learned of one of the world's truly great players has been a sad disappointment. Even that famous euphemism used to describe the infamous goal he punched in – the Hand of God – was not his. It was spoon-fed to him by an Argentinian journalist after the game.

Maradona apart, England v Argentina in Mexico City was always going to be what Bobby Robson, England's manager, described as the "spiciest" match of the 1986 World Cup. There had been little love between the teams since 1966, when a bruising battle at Wembley saw the Argentina captain, Antonio Rattin, sent off and had Alf Ramsey describing Rattin and his team as "animals".

Now, 20 years on, the incendiary baggage of the Falklands war had everybody fearing the worst. The conflict had ended four years earlier but, technically at least, the two countries were still at war.

England's hooligan following was even worse in those days and, 12 months on from the Heysel tragedy, there was a real fear that the national team would be ostracised, too, at the first hint of trouble in Mexico. The Argentinian fans were no angels either, and when the *barras bravas*, as they styled themselves, were pictured burning British flags as they boarded flights to Mexico City, the Mexican army was put on stand-by. *The Sun*, sensitive as ever, headed its front page: "It's War, Señor!" Its Argentinian equivalent, *Cronica*, chipped in with "We're Coming To Get You, Pirates".

Carlos Bilardo, Argentina's manager, was happy to play the diplomat: "I told the players, 'Señores, this is a World Cup, this is football. You just talk about football.' The Malvinas war was still fresh in people's minds, but I wasn't seeking revenge." Nevertheless, despite the managerial instructions, the Argentina goalkeeper, Nery Pumpido, was quoted as saying: "To beat the English would represent a double satisfaction for everything that happened in the Malvinas." Robson was clearly aware of the implications, but decided it was a case of least said, soonest mended, and his warning was brief enough for the players to have forgotten that the Falklands were ever an issue.

Argentina had scraped through to the finals, a team of whom much was expected failing to gel. There were debilitating personality clashes dating back to the 1982 World Cup, when the

A downcast Glenn Hoddle with Bobby Robson. There was never much consolation for England. Though they were cheated by the first goal, no one could deny the brilliance of the second.

captain, Daniel Passarella, worked hard to maintain morale in the face of disappointing results, only for discipline to disintegrate, with Maradona the worst culprit. Now, to Passarella's chagrin, Maradona was captain.

From the outset, Bilardo conferred "special status" on the player who was going to rescue his sinking managerial reputation. He was allowed his own personal trainer and masseur, and kept whatever hours he chose, often going to bed at 2am or 3am, long after the rest of the squad. "I realised from an early stage," Bilardo explained, "that he had to have a different regime from the others. I said to myself, 'There is Maradona and there is the rest of the team'."

By the time the first match came around, against Portugal, England were well prepared and, the talismanic Bryan Robson having declared himself fit, bristling with confidence. The behaviour of the supporters was impeccable, their team anything but in losing 1-0. Three days later a goalless draw with Morocco conjured the grim prospect of early elimination.

England now had to beat Poland to stay in the tournament. Bryan Robson, whose shoulder had "gone" again, and Ray Wilkins, sent off against Morocco, were unavailable, Chris Waddle was sacrificed for an extra midfielder (shades of 1966) and Mark Hateley was dropped in favour of Peter Beardsley. Bingo. Gary Lineker, revelling in Beardsley's clever support, rattled home a hat-trick in a 3-0 win which saw England transformed. In the second round they were impressive again, seeing off Paraguay by another 3-0 margin with Lineker scoring two and Beardsley the other. Argentina, meanwhile, were beating their neighbours, Uruguay, 1-0, with Maradona man of the match.

El Mano de Dios, captured for all time. It was more than 10 years after the game before Maradona finally admitted that he had handled the ball. But for many Argentinians the goal remained a moment of glory. The pirates had been beaten at their own game.

As Robson put it, the tournament proper was about to start. On the eve of the fateful quarter-final, he told the press: "I've got 24 hours to devise a way of stopping Maradona. It won't be easy. Without Maradona, Argentina would have no chance of winning the World Cup. That's how great he is."

With 114,000 in the Azteca stadium the noise was as oppressive as the midday heat. The Mexicans were on England's side, chorusing "Inglaterra" and *The Times* reported that "horns blared like the humming of a thousand bees". Insults were exchanged on the terraces, mainly through banners of dubious taste. One proclaimed Argentina's right to the Malvinas, another hailed "Exocet Lineker" but, in a conciliatory gesture, the Argentinians presented each England player with a gift before the kick-off.

Once it had been noted that England had opted not to man-mark Maradona, there was precious little else to report in an unremarkable first

"And the ball, with a little sigh of apology, just bounces into the English net"

half, in which Argentina had the edge. The blue touchpaper was eventually lit seven minutes into the second half.

At 13 Brisbane Road, Port Stanley, on the Falklands, Patrick Watts and his mates on the local football team settled down for the second half. Watts, born in the Falklands, was 41 and the oldest member of the team. Four years before, on the same patch of land on which his new home was built, Argentinian anti-aircraft guns had fired at British jets. No television pictures of the game were available, but the men warmed up for the contest they so desperately wanted England to win by watching a tape of Argentina's defeat of Bulgaria 12 days before. "Our lot will have their hands full against Maradona," someone said. Even for a Falkland Islander, Maradona's genius was undeniable.

Thanks to the British Forces broadcasting service in London, England fans on the islands at least had a satellite feed of the BBC radio commentary. In the 52nd minute, Maradona picked up the ball 30 yards

Maradona gives thanks. The English fans in the crowd behind him are less than impressed. The goal, however, stood.

from England's goal, and immediately raised the tempo of Bryon Butler's commentary.

"Maradona on the ball, always danger, lays it outside him, finds Valdano, he can't turn, Maradona's there, rises above Shilton ... And is that goal going to be allowed? Shilton came out, Maradona challenged him, Peter Shilton is claiming he was fouled."

Unable to judge with their own eyes, the members of Stanley FC waited for Butler to confirm their worst fears. After seeing a replay, the commentator was in no doubt. "And it was a handball! No question about that! That was the only reason that Maradona was able to rise above an incensed Peter Shilton. He got his left hand to the ball, he stretched, he turned it past Shilton. Shilton could not believe it. And the ball, with a little sigh of apology, just bounces into the English net."

The story has been told often enough by outraged English participants. Let's hear it from the Argentinian perspective for a change. Sergio Batista, their midfield schemer, remembers: "The first goal surprised everybody. The ball was in their half and Valdano tried to play it in – one of those centres that shouldn't cause trouble because they had their defenders back and we had only Diego and Burruchaga up. The ball was hooked back towards Shilton by Hodge and suddenly, in a flash, there was Diego. We had no idea he guided the ball in with his hand. It never occurred to us until after the game. Shilton and Fenwick began arguing with the referee, but we couldn't understand why – not until we saw the replay."

How had the referee, Ali Bennaceur, from Tunisia, and his Costa Rican linesman, missed the infringement? Glenn Hoddle was apoplectic: "I've seen that done in Sunday morning matches on the local park and they don't get away with it there." Shilton, later criticised by Kevin Keegan and Mark Hateley for not "taking Maradona out", was even angrier: "If the referee wasn't in a good position to see it, the linesman certainly was. I looked straight across that way, and the linesman looked at me and then ran off up the pitch. I started running after the referee, but you learn over the years that's it not going to do any good. It was a sickly feeling.

"A lot of people said to me, 'Why didn't you go and crunch him?' but it wasn't like that. He actually played the ball into the box and started running for a one-two. I think he would have been offside, but I think it came off one of our players [Hodge]. He was running into the box at full pelt. I sud-denly realised what was happening and I felt that I could go and get it. And I think I would have got a fist to it. And that's why he handled it. He knew I was going to beat him to it."

The first goal was crucial. England were still reeling from a psychological blow exacerbated by its unfairness when, four minutes later, Maradona fashioned a second of breathtaking excellence. Terry Butcher, the England centre-half, had the closest view of it. His memory is still painfully sharp:

"When Maradona got the ball, just inside his own half, he came to me and I showed him inside, thinking Peter Reid was there. But poor Peter was struggling, and he went past him quickly. Then I tracked him all the way back. He went at Terry Fenwick, who had already been booked, and knew that if he upended Maradona, who was now in full flight, he'd be off, so he had to hope for help from someone else. So Maradona went past him and then Shilts came out. I'm still tracking him, still alongside, and when he went past Shilts I thought, 'I've got a chance to nick it off him here.' I stretched out my left leg, but I just couldn't get there. The next thing I knew the ball was in the back of the net with me on my backside." England rallied well enough for Lineker to pull one back after 81 minutes, but it was too late. The skill and skulduggery of Maradona had done for them.

In Argentina the illegal goal was regarded as no big deal. The Argentinians have a word for such things, *Inveza*, a quality of sly craftiness that is much admired. Fito Paez, a rock star, was by no means atypical when he said: "The first goal was the greatest in Argentinian history – even more so than the second because Diego hoodwinked the pirates."

Carlos Polimeni, a journalist who covered the match for the news agency Noticas Argentina, said a reporter had asked Maradona, "Was the first goal put in by the Hand of God?" The hero of the hour paused for a moment, looked his questioner in the eye and replied: "Yeah, I like that," and the legend was born. More than a decade later, Maradona finally owned up: "When I saw the ball go towards Peter Shilton, it was like being a kid again. I was having a laugh. I had good fortune that God allowed the goal to stand. It should have been disallowed."

After the game, there was anger in the England dressing room. Butcher remembers: "I was chosen for the dope testing, along with Kenny Sansom and Gary Stevens, and we were sitting there gutted. There were tears and it was all very emotional because it was the biggest game we'd ever played for England. Then the Argentinians came in, and Maradona was one of their three. We were all dehydrated, but they wouldn't allow us any beer, which would have made it easier to urinate, so we were there for quite a while. I asked Maradona, using sign language, whether he had punched the ball in and he indicated that he had headed it. 'No hands.' He was a lying toad." Wandering hands or not, he was also some player.

"I had the good fortune that God allowed the goal to stand. It should have been disallowed"

The incontrovertible proof of Maradona's cheating came with the publication of the famous picture taken by Alejandro Ojeda, the only photographer to catch Maradona in the act. Ojeda's newspaper sold the picture to an English agency and he made practically nothing from it.

Ben's big lie

Uncertain and inarticulate, Ben Johnson had one sure passport to fame: his phenomenal sprinting. When he powered to 100 metres gold at the Seoul Olympics in a world-record time, his fame seemed assured. Yet within hours he was exposed as a cheat: his wonder-run had been fuelled by a drug meant for horses.

DAVID WALSH

Jack, the young Iranian who owns the Venice gym in Toronto, takes more interest when told you have come to see Ben. "Use my office," he says. "Want some water?" Johnson is finishing his workout. It is a long time since Seoul, since the Friday evening in September 1988 when, at the Seoul Olympics, he won the 100 metres and simultaneously became the world's fastest human being. A couple of hours later he peed stanozolol and became sport's most notorious cheat.

Johnson lost his gold medal, his right to compete and his dignity. Everything except the enthusiasm that first attracted him to sprinting. These days he goes to his old training ground at Toronto's York University and in the afternoons to the Venice gym. Morris Chrobotek, his manager and publicist, badgers the IAAF to commute the life ban and talks about getting his man back into competition. Time is now his greatest rival. "I'll be 38 in December," says Johnson, leaning back into Jack's plush chair. "If I could come back and run a decent time, I'd be very happy."

He remembers Seoul reluctantly; the recollections come with resentment and, remarkably, touches of humour. It bugs him that he took the rap for everyone in sport: "Why did they pick on me?" He doesn't want you to answer this. His view is that it was down to those around him: the doctor, the coach, the agents. "At the time they were making decisions for me, I was just a racehorse." Maybe even more than he realised: injectable stanozolol,

the team's drug of choice, was manufactured for horses, not humans.

He looks fit and healthy, his once bloodshot and jaundiced eyes are clear and there is an acceptance of the way things turned out. Getting out of Seoul was tough: "I had my mother with me and I just wanted to get her out of there safely. Going through New York, there were about 200 media. The sheriff and the FBI were there to help me through. The flight to Toronto was full and the airline people said they couldn't get me out. Eventually I was taken to the aeroplane on the same route as the pilot and the flight staff. I didn't have to clear customs and because they didn't have a seat, they

Waldemar Matuszewski poses with a signed photograph of Johnson. Even today, the Pole always has time to help Johnson in his struggles to recapture past glories. But time has all but run out for the sprinter.

put me in the cockpit with the pilot. The FBI treated me good – I felt as if I was the president."

A different reception awaited at Toronto airport. Three hundred people all wanting to know. Why Ben? Why did it end like this? They wanted an explanation, he wanted his lawyer. These days the lies have been told so often that, in his mind, they become indistinguishable from the truth. He tells a story that helps him live with the memory.

"I had just finished my interview with CBC [Canadian television]. People from the local organising committee were pushing me towards the doping control room. I went in one door, Carl Lewis went in another, but I could see through to where he was. Lewis's friend Andre Jackson was with him. Some African guy wanted to have his photo taken with me and then Jackson came through to where we were.

'What are you doing here?' I said. 'Are you not supposed to be on the American side?' 'No, no, I just want to chit-chat,' he said. 'Fine,' I said. I was concerned because Carl had sent him in there. I'm laying down on the bench, he's sitting on the floor alongside, people are talking to me. I'm drinking a beer, he has a beer in his hand, I leave mine down. He could have slipped something into my drink."

In a quiet suburban neighbourhood in Ottawa, Waldemar Matuszewski, a Polish immigrant, sits on the veranda overlooking his back garden. Squirrels play in the trees and beyond there is the stillness of early summer. This was how Waldemar and Christine envisaged Canada when, in 1984, they decided to come. But the journey almost destroyed him. A physiotherapist and sports trainer, Matuszewski once travelled with Ben Johnson.

Shortly after he returned from Seoul, the telephone rang like an alarm. "Polish bastard, what did you do to Ben?"

He shows the ring on his right hand, pointing to the Matuszewski crest: "In Poland we are a high-class family, I can trace the generations back to 1630." Unable to cope with abusive calls, he told Christine he had to get away. A friend offered his remote log cabin by White Lake in Ontario and for six months he lived on his own: "The whole experience affected me badly. I didn't want to see people and at my friend's cottage I chopped wood for 10 to 12 hours every day. I cut down so many trees my friend said, 'I don't need this much wood', but I needed to clear my head. I pushed myself hard; chop, chop, chop."

Matuszewski didn't know if he would ever work again, but at 42 he couldn't afford to retire. Anxious about the future, he would chop more vigorously, wasting himself so that at night tiredness overwhelmed him. Towards the end he was laid low with

"At the time they were making decisions for me, I was just a racehorse"

Victory for Johnson (far left) didn't mean just riches: it meant humiliation for the poised, articulate Carl Lewis (far right). It was Johnson's sweetest moment. That it lasted only hours made the subsequent disgrace all more painful.

shingles, a last blast of anguish that covered one side of his face – like the outward expression of how he was inside.

Friendships that once were as close as family have dissolved. He has lost touch with the athletes he helped to prepare for the Seoul Olympics; all except for Ben. Two days earlier Johnson had telephoned, wanting to know if he could come and stay for a week – his training was getting more intense. Could Waldemar help rejuvenate his ageing body? To any other athlete, he would have said no. To Ben, he could never say no.

Charlie Francis had always been driven. At one time the fifth-ranked sprinter in the world, coaching then became his vocation. In the early 80s, he brought together a formidable team of sprinters who trained at the high-performance centre at York University. He lived for the athletes, bringing them home to stay with him when they were down, selling his beloved Aston Martin to fund their warm-weather training and all the time convincing them they could be the best.

Good on the technical aspects of sprinting, Francis didn't fully understand recuperation. He also didn't know enough about performance-enhancing drugs. His athletes, he believed, had to have the best of both. In 1982 he asked an old friend, Jamie Astaphan, to become the team's physician. From the Caribbean island of St Kitts, Astaphan had a practice in Toronto and didn't demur when Francis suggested his athletes should be on steroids.

One evening in 1985 Francis heard a Polish massage therapist give a semi-nar on recovery and regeneration in sport. The guy could barely speak English but Francis liked what he heard. Matuszewski thought working with Canada's top sprinters would lead to bigger opportunities and he accepted Francis's offer. The Canadian Track and Field Association agreed to pay the therapist $16,000 a year and for that he moved from his home in Ottawa, lived out of a suitcase in a basement flat in Toronto and was constantly available to Francis's sprinters.

Soon after joining the team Matuszewski sensed they were using steroids. The therapist can feel it in tight muscles, although Matuszewski says he wasn't 100 per cent certain. The athletes never spoke about it to him. Mostly, he said nothing. "In Japan, before the Olympics, I felt Angella Issajenko wasn't right. She had suddenly got very big. 'Angie,' I said, 'you are growing like a bamboo shoot' I spoke with Charlie. 'Something is wrong, you have to talk with Jamie'."

Unstoppable: Johnson surged to victory in his semi-final. Just how good would he have been without drugs? It's a question no one will ever be able to answer.

Astaphan didn't like Matuszewski raising questions: "He called me something very bad. That was the end of it. I didn't say any more." With Francis's encouragement, and consent from the athletes, Astaphan had master-minded the team's drug programme. He bought large quantities of injectable stanozolol from a drug company in Ontario, removed labels that said "for veterinary use only" and told the athletes they were taking an ana-bolic steroid called estragol.

Astaphan referred to the group as "belonging to the brotherhood of the needle" and, fearful that he would be blamed if any one failed a drug test, he taped telephone conversations with Francis and Johnson that showed they both knew about the steroid pro-gramme. Outwardly Astaphan could be persuasive and charming. "He was a fantastic talker," says Matuszewski. "He would buy you and sell you and then buy you back a lot cheaper. I tried to warn Ben, but he said, 'Waldemar, Jamie is like my father'."

Rome in 1987 was the beginning of the end. Johnson won the world championship 100m title in a record 9.83sec and became a major figure in world sport. In Monte Carlo, Prince Albert of Monaco picked him up at his hotel and drove him to a luxury car show. In Milan he was invited to the Ferrari factory where Enzo Ferrari waited to welcome him personally. In Rome his hectic schedule meant he was unable to make an audience with the Pope.

Modest by nature, Johnson couldn't handle such attention. Influenced by Astaphan, the athlete began to believe in his own invincibility. In February of Olympic year he damaged a hamstring racing in Germany but

"My love for track and field will never die ... Hopefully I can come back"

didn't report to Matuszewski for therapy as he would have done in the past. "At the time Jamie and Ben were going to nightclubs, staying out late," says Matuszewski. "Jamie wanted to break up the group. He and Ben were planning to split with Charlie and they wanted me to go with them."

On his return to competition at a Tokyo meet in mid-May, Johnson again injured his hamstring. Francis said he should travel with the rest of the team on a five-week tour to Europe and get daily treatment from Matuszewski. Johnson opted to go to St Kitts, where he would work with Astaphan. There he tried to speed up his recovery through growth hormones.

Six weeks before the Seoul Olympics, Johnson returned to competition with a wind-assisted 9.90sec in the Canadian championships. Subsequent races in Europe were less satisfactory; Johnson finished third to Carl Lewis in Zurich and then third to Calvin Smith in Cologne. Four weeks before the Games, Johnson's form suggested he couldn't win in Seoul. The thought panicked Astaphan and Francis.

On August 24, Francis gave Johnson a stanozolol injection at his apartment in Toronto. Astaphan twice administered the same drug to the sprinter over the following four days. It takes 28 days for stanozolol to be flushed through the human body; Francis and Johnson knew they were cutting things fine but the racehorse had to be ready for his greatest race.

While the rest of the team stayed at the Olympic village, Johnson and Astaphan checked into the Hilton hotel in Seoul, eating in the same dining room as Arnold Schwarzenegger. It may have seemed like the finest hotel, but Astaphan and Johnson were now at their last chance saloon.

It is late afternoon on the veranda at Matuszewskis' and Waldemar's story has reached Seoul and its final chapter. He recalls the journeys from the Olympic Village through Seoul's notoriously heavy traffic to the Hilton. Ben and Jamie wanted him at the Hilton; the other athletes said he should attending them in the village. He worked 16-hour days and when he complained, Astaphan promised him a house and a Ferrari Testarossa from the money Ben would make in endorsements. Because he worked like a dog, Matuszewski believed he was entitled to his share.

On that Friday evening in the Olympic Stadium, Matuszewski sat between Astaphan and Ben's mother, Gloria. Johnson's scintillating performance made all three jump: "I kissed Gloria, I even kissed Jamie, who was saying Ben would now make $18m. 'I'm glad,' I said, 'and I'll get my Ferrari, a house and money.' Then Jamie said, 'Have you a contract?'

"I said, 'No, but you said it would be for everybody'. 'Not for you,' he said. Two minutes after the race I went from being up here to down here. Jamie had poured ice-cold water on my head. I don't often cry, but I cried at that moment. They used me to the maximum and then they did this to me."

Matuszewski brought Johnson to doping control and signed the forms saying everything had been done properly: "When I heard of the positive test, I had two thoughts. I was sorry for Ben but glad Jamie had not got away with it. I thought, 'Jamie, I didn't

make any money out of this, but neither did you'."

At a subsequent hearing with the IOC medical commission in Seoul, Johnson and the Canadian delegation argued that the athlete had not taken drugs but that his sample had been sabotaged – the Andre Jackson theory. The late Professor Manfred Donike dismissed this suggestion, pointing out that the steroid profile of the sample indicated long-term use.

At Jack's office in the Venice gym, Johnson is trying to sum up how he feels and how it has all ended. Most of all he wants to compete again: "My love for track and field will never die. The sport is bigger than me. Without it I could not have shown my talent. I had good times and bad times, but that's life. Hopefully I can come back."

The old team has long disbanded. "They are married, some have kids. Sometimes I see Charlie [Francis] at the track. We talk a little bit but not too much. I keep in touch with Waldemar. He's the best therapist in the world and as long as I'm running I want to work with him. But basically I am the only guy who is still here, who is still doing it." With that thought comes the realisation that he has been speaking for too long. "Got to get back to work," he says, smiling shyly.

The man with the needle. Jamie Astaphan testifies before a 1989 Canadian federal inquiry into drug use in athletics. He made no secret of his knowledge.

Anfield agony and ecstasy

Liverpool were the undisputed masters of English football in the Eighties. Arsenal, by contrast, were struggling to regain past glories. When the teams met at Anfield in May 1989 for the championship decider, Arsenal had to win by two goals. How they did it still leaves the Anfield faithful lost for words.

JOE LOVEJOY

It was the tightest title finish of all time and impossible to overstate the drama. Arsenal snatched the championship from Liverpool's grasp in the second minute of stoppage time on one of those rare occasions when reality not only lived up to but surmounted all hype.

For a full appreciation of the magnitude of Arsenal's achievement that balmy, barmy night, it is essential to remember the awe in which Liverpool were then held. They had won the League six times in the Eighties, the European Cup four times since 1977 and were chasing a second Double in four seasons, having just beaten Everton in the FA Cup final. Arsenal had not won at Anfield for 15 years. Unbeaten in 24 matches, Liverpool had conceded just two goals at home in 1989, and had not lost by two at Anfield for more than three years. It was against this background that Arsenal had to win by a two-goal margin. Nobody gave them a prayer.

It had not been a normal season. When Liverpool played Nottingham Forest in the semi-final of the FA Cup, 96 of their fans were killed in an horrific crush. Kenny Dalglish and his players were submerged in the sea of grief, attending up to four funerals a day. When they started playing again, they were men on a mission. They had to win everything, in memory of the Hillsborough dead. Arsenal were up against a floodtide of emotion.

Fortunately for them, nothing fazes George Graham. The high priest of the work ethic favoured the long ball and a pressing, high-energy game, a grinding format very different to Liverpool's composed, passing method. If nothing else, D-Day would provide a classic contrast in styles.

Arsenal had lead the League since Boxing Day. By mid-February, they were 18 points clear of Liverpool. Then it was Liverpool's turn to charge, nine straight wins hoisting them from fifth to second by the middle of April, when they ran slap-bang into a tombstone bearing the legend "Hillsborough". The Liverpool v Arsenal match, scheduled for April 22, was postponed until May 26. Arsenal made the most of an unexpected two-week break, and returned, refreshed, to thrash Norwich 5-0.

After a 1-1 draw at Old Trafford, Arsenal then won four on the bounce without conceding a goal. Liverpool, meanwhile, came back with a goalless draw at Everton. It speaks volumes for their character that they quickly reasserted themselves, winning the next four League games and then the Cup final.

Now it was Arsenal who were staggering. Expected to clinch the title at home to Derby, they lost 2-1. When they stumbled again in their last match at Highbury, held 2-2 by Wimbledon, it seemed their chance had gone, a point underlined when Liverpool scored five to relegate West Ham and move three points clear. Arsenal now had to win by two goals that fateful Friday.

Mickey Thomas (right) turns away after scoring the decisive goal. Liverpool stare into the abyss. For Arsenal, there was only the astonishment that they had won when everyone had written them off.

Liverpool had conceded just two goals at home all year. Nobody gave Arsenal a prayer

Graham gave his players a couple of days off and on returning to work they found the manager in resolutely upbeat mood. "We've averaged two goals away from home all season," he told his players. "We just have to maintain that. Nobody fancies us, but we are the highest scorers in the League. We've played well all season, and our best form has been away from Highbury." Arsenal would win 3-0. Alan Smith, the team's principal scorer that year, remembers sceptical looks all round: "At the start of the week we were at the training ground, a bit glum, and Bob Wilson [Arsenal's goalkeeping coach] said: 'Cheer up. This is the week we're going to win the championship.' Everybody looked at each other, as if to say 'What's Bob on?', but as we started preparing for the match the mood changed. The closer it got, the more we grew in confidence."

Graham used the newspapers, in which Arsenal's chances were written off, as motivation. Two articles in *The Sun*, one headed "Men Against Boys" and the other "For the sake of British soccer, LOSE George" were pinned on the training-ground noticeboard.

Mickey Thomas remembers the team coach nosing out of Arsenal's training ground just after 8am on match day. "We got to the Atlantic Tower Hotel in Liverpool by about midday, and went straight to bed. I slept like a log for five hours, and when I got up for the team meeting I felt great." At the meeting, the players were in tracksuits, Graham immacu-

late in club blazer and flannels. Tony Adams recalled the manager's orders: "Keep it tight, keep it very tight. Don't let them settle, don't let them play because if you do, you know they can pass it and hurt you. Pressure, pressure. Pressure all over the field."

The bookmakers were offering 7-1 against Arsenal and refusing to accept bets on Liverpool, whose players were brimming with confidence. "The two-goal cushion doesn't mean we will defend; we can't play that way," said John Barnes before the game. "We will attack in the knowledge that scoring even one goal would finish them off." But behind the bravado lay a dilemma articulated by John Aldridge: "Probably the worst thing that could have happened was beating West Ham 5-1. It meant we could afford to lose 1-0 to Arsenal. I think if we'd gone out knowing we had to win, we would have done, but we didn't know whether to defend or attack and, subconsciously, that was very bad for us."

And so to Anfield. In the hubbub of the dressing room, Graham spoke to his team: "I stressed we must not concede a goal in the first half. I feared that would kill us off. I told them I didn't mind a half-time score of 0-0, because if we could take the lead soon after the result we wanted would be within our grasp. Nobody outside our dressing room gave us a chance, but I assure you that inside there was no sign of nerves."

Adams is not so sure. "Deep down," he said, "I have to admit that there was doubt as to whether we could do it."

Sensational denouement apart, the match was no classic. Nerves got the better of both teams in a sterile first half, for a large part of which the main talking point was a lovely gesture by Arsenal, whose players presented bouquets of red roses to Liverpool fans before the kick-off. Even more welcome was the £30,000 Arsenal's travelling supporters donated to the Hillsborough Disaster Appeal.

At half-time, Graham was happy. Thomas and Kevin Richardson were winning the midfield battle against the two Steves, Nicol and McMahon, Aldridge and Ian Rush had got no change out of Steve Bould and Adams, and Barnes, a potential matchwinner, had been well held by Lee Dixon. "George encouraged us to push forward a bit more," Smith said. "He thought we weren't being adventurous enough."

Seven minutes after the restart, Nicol conceded a free kick on the left side of Liverpool's penalty area. Nigel Winterburn curled the ball to the far post and Smith ghosted in to nod his 25th goal of the season. The referee, David Hutchinson, pointed towards the centre circle. But wait. McMahon, Alan Hansen and Ronnie Whelan all badgered him into consulting his

At 1-0 it was game on. Arsenal had two enemies: Liverpool and the clock

linesman, claiming variously that the free kick had been indirect and nobody had made contact with it, that Smith had been offside, and that David O'Leary had committed a foul in the goalmouth. There was an agonising wait before Hutchinson confirmed the goal.

"There were a few hearts in mouths," Smith said. "At Anfield, the fans and the players used to intimidate the ref a bit, and there was a real possibility that he would disallow it. I knew I wasn't offside and I knew I'd touched the ball. We didn't really know what the Liverpool lads were complaining about. I've spoken to Steve Nicol since, and he said they were complaining just for the sake of it, trying to get the goal disallowed for any reason."

At 1-0 it was game on. Arsenal had two enemies: Liverpool and the clock. With time ebbing away, Graham threw on fresh legs, substituting Martin Hayes for Paul Merson and Perry Groves for Bould. By now, Liverpool had settled for a 1-0 defeat. With 14 minutes left Thomas, clean through, scuffed a shot straight at Bruce Grobbelaar. Arsenal feared the worst.

As the home crowd whistled manically, Richardson went down with cramp and McMahon signalled to his anxious team-mates that there was one minute left. Barnes and Aldridge grinned and

Even Graham, Arsenal's fearsome manager, had to smile when it was all over. As he said: "Tonight was a fairytale."

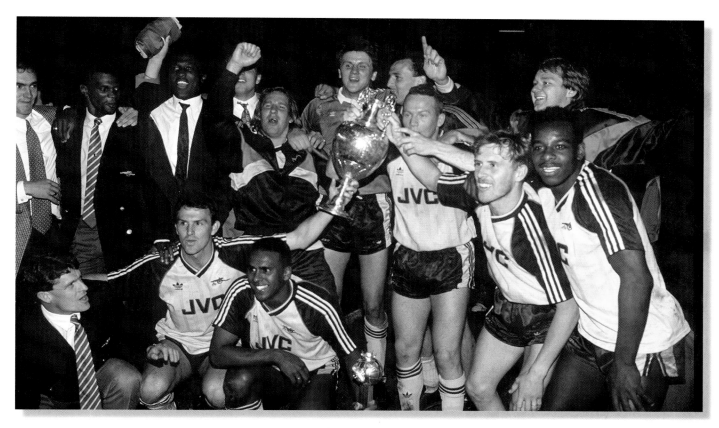

did a celebratory "high five", believing it was all over bar the presentations.

Wrong. Richardson got up, and although hobbling managed to dispossess Barnes and knock the ball back to John Lukic. By now, Arsenal were close to panic. "I yelled at him [Lukic] to hoof it upfield," Adams remembered, "but he threw the ball out to Lee Dixon." Dixon passed to Smith, who takes up the story: "I flicked it into Mickey Thomas's path, and I was running 10 or 15 yards behind him. I could see the Liverpool players converging on him. Ray Houghton and Steve Nicol were closing in, and I was thinking, 'Go on Mickey, hurry up'. From where I was, it looked like they were going to get a saving tackle in, but then he just lifted it over Grobbelaar and everyone went mad."

As Thomas cartwheeled in celebration, Barnes collapsed full length and Aldridge sank slowly to his knees. Dalglish, standing on the touchline, looked on horrified, his hands clutching his head. Graham, meanwhile, had more pressing matters on his mind. It wasn't over until it was over, and there was that precious 2-0 lead to protect. He told the hero of the hour, Thomas, to move back from midfield to augment the defence.

Smith said: "When we got back to the middle for the restart, I was thinking, 'How long to go now? They could still score". The ball did go into our box and came down at Mickey's feet. We were all willing him to boot it into row Z, but that wasn't his style. He brought it down in the midst of a scrum of players and passed it casually back to the goalkeeper. Now John had it and I was thinking, 'If I can just get

The Liverpool players slumped in abject misery, glassy-eyed and hollow-cheeked

my head to this and flick it on, the whistle is sure to go', which is what happened. I put every last effort into getting a flick on, the ball went into the corner, Perry Groves chased it and the whistle went."

Pandemonium. Graham, however, stayed characteristically cool. "When I ran to embrace George," Adams said, "there was only the most formal of hugs." Smith remembers Graham telling everybody not to jump on him. "It was a case of 'Watch the jacket' and all that. Seriously, I think he had Hillsborough in mind and wanted us to show a bit of dignity and respect, which was fair enough. He did come

on the pitch and hug everybody, which was a first for George."

After Adams had received the trophy, the Arsenal players took it over to the Kop, to be greeted with resounding applause, a salute that was the embodiment of sportsmanship. "The Liverpool people were superb," Smith said. "The stewards and the police all said 'Well played lads', which really meant a lot. In the players' lounge, normally there's no way in if you haven't got a ticket. My wife was up for the game with some friends, and the steward just let them all in, without a ticket between them."

The scenes in the dressing rooms were sport's vicissitudes incarnate, reflecting the all-or-nothing nature of the occasion. While Arsenal's unbridled revelry made a terrible mess of the ceiling, the Liverpool players slumped in abject misery, glassy-eyed and hollow-cheeked. Nobody spoke; there was nothing left to say. Graham had said it all: "Tonight was a fairytale. Who the hell thought we would come here and win 2-0?" "Nobody" was the only possible answer.

March 1990

Murrayfield mayhem

England were the class act and runaway favourites when they met Scotland in Edinburgh in the match which would decide the 1990 Grand Slam. But fired by rampant anti-Englishness and a passion rare in any sport, Scotland tore up the form book and left a bemused England team to lick their wounds. For some, the hurt has never left.

STEPHEN JONES

The intensity was murderous. In the old Murrayfield, the press seats were at the back of the main stand. As *Flower of Scotland* was roared out, the wall behind me vibrated with a thunderous echo, as if the stadium itself was coming to life. It made the neck hairs prickle as if electrified. Nobody bawled the song. Nobody became histrionic, either in the stands or among the Scotland team lined up on the field. It was the focused togetherness which was so striking. Everyone came in on the first note, everyone stayed with the band conductor. Everyone finished together.

Scotland's rugby community is more studiedly middle-class than that of any other country, but here were genteel Morningsiders wrapped in tartan rugs – and working men and women from the Borders wrapped in a cause. Everyone sang as if they had been brooding on historical slights, political slights and sporting slights. And many had. "I have never," says David Sole, Scotland's captain on that day, "experienced a crowd like it. Any time, any sport."

Was it Thatcher's match? Did she drive Scotland to their greatest triumph? This was 1990 and England's rugby team came to Murrayfield in search of the Grand Slam, the ultimate prize in European rugby. It was also within Scotland's grasp: they, too, had

Special delivery: both packs are sprawled on the ground as Scotland scrum-half Gary Armstrong gets the ball away. Scotland disrupted England for the whole game.

won three matches from three. But even though England were rampaging favourites, it was not a good era for them to visit Scotland. It was less than two years since the Conservative government had imposed the poll tax on Scotland as a pilot scheme before they levied it on England. In a *Spitting Image* sketch, somebody asked Mrs Thatcher a question about Scotland. "Scotland?" she replied, venomously. "Oh – you mean *the testing ground*." The Thatcher puppet scraped a set of claws over a map of Scotland.

It wasn't just the Conservative government that was ferociously unpopular. England was unpopular. It is undeniably true, as saner Scots assert,

that among the middle-classes this left-wing stance lasted 80 minutes, a mask donned for the rugby match.

"I'd never voted Tory. I always voted Labour," says Brian Moore, England's hooker and one of the least popular English players. "And I'd never paid the poll tax. But here they all were shouting about the Tory English." Anti-Englishness was powerful in the Scottish media. There may have been some rational rugby analysis, but not in the papers I read. The effect was to fire and bind 70,000 people.

England that season had advanced with regal stride, Scotland had scrambled scruffily along

But as a rugby match, it was not the miffed Scots against the put-upon English. Far from it. The truth is that England were vastly superior to Scotland. They had advanced towards their Grand Slam with regal stride and the two best consecutive performances that England teams have ever produced. Scotland had scrambled scruffily along.

Under Will Carling, then unchallenged as a *Boy's Own* hero, and with a mighty pack driven on by Wade Dooley and Paul Ackford – arguably the greatest lock pairing the Five Nations has seen – England had set out to banish the memory of decades of underachievement. They had also torn up supposed national playing characteristics and played with a wonderful, expansive sweep.

They hammered the Irish at Twickenham and then gloriously thrashed the French on a wild day in Paris. Two weeks later, they destroyed Wales by 34-6 at Twickenham. Scotland had won in Dublin in a dire match, beaten the abject French at Murrayfield and then been lucky against a Welsh team with a pitiful pack. The difference between the two sides was vast.

There was a reason to be jealous of England even if, like the magnificent Sole, you had no taste for the basic blind patriotism of the whole affair. Sole was one of the most fervent players in the history of his nation's rugby, but his intensity was a sporting intensity, not a small-minded bicker.

"There was an awful lot of the anti-English thing around; far more than there ought to have been, because some people wrongly try to bring all that into the sporting arena," he said nine years on. His objection lay inside that sporting arena: "What cheesed me off was that all we ever heard in the press was about how well England were playing. On that day, we were both going for the same prize but in the English media it was as if it wasn't even a contest."

Three days before the match, England's Rolls-Royce squad rolled into their HQ in the genteel surroundings of Peebles, a pretty Border town. Moore believes this was their first mistake: "It was a nice hotel in a nice town, and people were nice to us. We didn't get to Edinburgh until Saturday and then all the atmosphere and hostility came as a shock to the system to some of them."

Sole and his men checked into their city-centre hotel on the Wednesday, tension rising steadily: "The critical thing was trying to keep the lid on everything. If we'd played on the Wednesday we would have won then, too, there was so much high emotion. But if you let that run free from midweek, then you are emotionally drained by kick-off. It was important to keep it all in and let it run again on Saturday morning."

The senior players decided that the light relief of a fiendish wind-up was in order. They went to a pub on the Wednesday evening. Suddenly, a blonde barged in, strode up to Finlay Calder and said: "Finlay – the test is positive. We've got to talk." She stalked out of the pub, followed by an apparently devastated Calder. The Scots players looked at each other, apparently in shock and wonder. Only in John Jeffrey – the victim and therefore the only man not in on the wind-up – were the emotions genuine.

They headed to the hotel, to be met by a well-primed Craig Chalmers, who reported that Calder had stormed in and gone straight to bed. Sole told his players the scandal could ruin their preparation if the press got hold of it. When another primed player came up to Jeffrey and inquired what on earth was wrong with Calder, Jeffrey loyally quashed all speculation: "Nothing wrong, nothing wrong."

Next day on the bus to training, when letters of support were traditionally handed out, the players were told that a letter had arrived, addressed in a woman's handwriting, for Calder. Sean Lineen, the centre, grabbed it and began to open it. "JJ literally climbed over the coach seats

Sole still had one masterstroke to pull. He walked the walk

to try to grab the letter," Sole remembers. But Lineen kept hold as Jeffrey, trying to prevent a scandal, dived at it. He read out a heart-rending tale of a newly pregnant, wronged woman. Could Calder not do the decent thing and leave his family? The apparently shocked silence was broken by Lineen reading the postscript. "JJ – you've been had." Sole remembers a palpable drop in tension as laughter exploded round the head of the shell-shocked Jeffrey. He recalls the session that day going superbly as a close-knit bunch of players hugged even tighter.

Sole still had one masterstroke to pull. He walked the walk. International teams always charged on to the field in a gallop of adrenaline. England duly sprinted on to the pitch. Then, as 70,000 pairs of eyes focused on the tunnel to greet the Scots, Sole appeared. Walking. He stepped out of the tunnel, his men behind him; slowly, deliberately, focused and menacing. The gesture has been copied many times but at the time it was wonderfully arresting.

"We'd been thinking about something different for a couple of weeks," Sole says. "We needed to make some sort of statement, to tell England that if they wanted the Grand Slam they had to get past us first." Scotland were up

Jeffrey breaks from the base of the scrum to begin the move that led to Scotland's try and imperishable glory. The underdogs can surely never have laughed longer or louder.

for it in a mighty way. "The walk was the hardest thing to do," Sole says. "The tunnel used to slope towards the pitch. If you started trotting at the top you would be sprinting as you took the field. All my inclinations were to break into a run, so I set a target of the five-yard line and was determined to be still walking when I crossed it. The crowd sensed the idea of a challenge being laid down." And became even more thunderous.

So did the Scottish tackling. The match, in large part, was a mayhem of driving Scottish aggression, which wrecked any English notion of sweeping majestically to victory. Jeffrey, Calder and Derek White in the Scottish back row, and Scott Hastings and Lineen in the centre, performed heroically. Yet England were playing against a strong wind and as half-time approached they trailed only by two penalties from Craig Chalmers.

Then they scored a try which at the time appeared crucial, Guscott dummying his way over after good work by the back row. Chalmers did kick another penalty, but England turned to play with the elements trailing only by 9-4. Manageable.

The match-turning, world-turning moment came at the start of the second half. Scotland made a mess of their kick-off, gave England a scrum at halfway. "If we'd just won that ball and belted it down there, we could have put on the pressure and things would have been different," Moore says. Instead, England called a back-row move and Mike Teague, at No 8, knocked the ball on. Scotland won a scrum, Gary Armstrong attacked the blind side, Gavin Hastings chipped ahead and Tony Stanger, the right wing, plucked the ball out of the air and touched down for the most famous try ever scored by a Scot: 13-7. Despite desperate England attack and explosive Scotland defence, it was the final score.

Until that try, Will Carling had been strangely quiet. He had puzzled England supporters by opting to run penalties which seemed within kickable range. Robin Marlar in *The Sunday Times* compared these decisions with the blunders made by generals in the First World War. Simon Hodgkinson, England's full-back, was on tremendous kicking form that season. During the rest of the match, Carling's profile shrank even further, just when you felt he should be taking charge. Carling's reputation never recovered. He gave no tactical lead or switch; he appeared not to take responsibility; it often seemed to be Moore who was calling the shots.

England battled on, but without rhythm, without conviction, without leadership. Every England mistake was riotously received; every time Scotland were awarded a scrum, it was as if they had won the World Cup.

The final whistle bought scenes of almost dangerous mayhem. In one corner of the field, almost unnoticed as the fans streamed on to the field to greet their heroes, a distraught Moore crouched. Calder, a colleague on the previous Lions tour, generously trotted over and consoled him. Perhaps it was a sign that the essential, forgiving balance of a Five Nations match was not completely forgotten during the tumult. But England's players were utterly devastated.

Where did England go wrong? How long have you got? Moore flatly rejects the idea that they were over-confident, and expected to turn up and lord it over the Scots. "Don't forget we had people like Wade Dooley and Paul Ackford and Mike Teague and Peter Winterbottom in that side. They were simply not the type of people to swan around in their own glory. Don't forget that none of us had ever won anything with England, no championships, no Grand Slams. We may have

England battled on but without rhythm, without conviction, without leadership

prepared badly in that we concentrated on our own game, and were not quite prepared enough for the onslaughts of the Scots. But to say we were over-confident is rubbish." Moore denies that he was calling the shots, denies that England's leadership fell apart. Sole disagrees: "I could feel them going. They denied it but I felt they made some bad decisions, decisions I would not have made."

Carling's aura evaporated. Moore lost the pack leadership of England soon afterwards. Sole remembers no legacy of bitterness: "I felt sorry for them, because some were my friends and I knew how much it meant." On the other hand, relations between the two countries on and off the field took time to return to normal: there were flashes of confrontation between the England and Scotland contingents on the 1993 Lions tour three years later.

England lost more than a Grand Slam: they lost the 1991 World Cup as well. They had played a wide game all season and come up short. The senior players decided that they would win something for England no matter what. So the team drew in their horns and played a grinding and narrow game over the next 18 months, drawing opprobrium but winning matches. When they came to the World Cup final and needed a more varied game, they had forgotten how to play it.

They never lost to Scotland again in the 1990s, though in few of the English who played that day is the hurt erased. "I've never seen a single second of the match on video and I never intend to change that," Moore says. He took his medicine on the painful day after the defeat. He had agreed, before the match, to attend a reception on the Sunday at the Watsonians clubhouse: "I felt it was churlish not to go; but it was not pleasant." The more reflective Scots applauded Moore for having the bottle to front up; others merely continued the barbed anti-Englishness of the whole weekend. It was a passion which even the fervent history of the Five Nations had never seen. It was rugby set in a wider landscape, and wonderfully compelling for that.

Captain courageous: David Sole led Scotland with a rare mixture of passion and intelligence. The contrast with Carling, his opposite number, was painful to see.

October 1990

Return of the Long Fella

When Lester Piggott retired from race-riding in 1985, his place in the sporting pantheon had long since been secure. But five years later, Piggott was restless and took little persuading when asked to return. The offer came from his old trainer, Vincent O'Brien, and within weeks the world would hear a glorious echo of their pomp.

DENIS WALSH

By the middle of 1990 it was clear to those closest to Lester Piggott that retirement wasn't working out. He had walked away five years earlier, hailed so often as the greatest Flat jockey racing had seen that it had become a platitude. Thirty-seven seasons had produced nine winning rides in the Derby and a record which included more than 50 European classics. But pots and prizes were a crude measure of his genius. His instinct to race was so powerful that he was never sated or diminished by success, only driven by it. The thrill of the race had been inseparable from his being. Without it, the pulse of his existence slowed.

After riding, Piggott took up training but in October 1987 he was convicted of tax fraud and sent to prison. He was released a year later, but by then the future of his yard had been undermined and there weren't enough horses to occupy him. He rode out in the mornings, watched racing on a cable channel in the afternoons and the *ennui* was a dead weight on his heart. The ground was tilled for a comeback. All it lacked was seed.

The comeback began with fragments of conversations. In July that year Vincent O'Brien was accompa-

nied to the Keeneland Sales by his son-in-law, John Magnier, co-owner of Coolmore Stud. Magnier had sat next to Piggott at a Turf Club dinner and as they chatted he could sense the despair. On the plane journey Magnier told O'Brien he should suggest a comeback to the Long Fella.

Piggott would listen to O'Brien of all people. Their careers had coalesced while each was at the summit of his powers and the union had left both peerless. Piggott first rode for O'Brien in 1958 and over the following two decades they shared 15 Classic triumphs in England and Ireland. Piggott ceased to be his stable jockey in 1980, but their friendship remained: "To see the two together," said Piggott's daughter Tracey, "was always strange, as they seemed to say nothing and yet you could see there was an intimacy between them."

In full flow: (left) Piggott makes his last-minute charge for the line, driving Royal Academy up the outside of the field. (Right), just past the post and Piggott has already looked across at the beaten Itsallgreektome.

His instinct to race was so powerful that he was never sated or diminished by success

When O'Brien returned to Ireland he rang Piggott. Piggott didn't commit himself and O'Brien didn't press him. A few weeks later O'Brien rang again and invited Piggott to lunch in Dublin. For privacy he booked a room in the Berkely Court Hotel and there they discussed the future. O'Brien said that for the 1991 season Piggott could have the pick of his horses. Piggott's resistance would have fallen with gentle leverage but O'Brien's offer was a controlled explosion. "The ineluctable truth," said Peter O'Sullevan at the time, "is that Lester cannot do without his horses."

On Tuesday October 9, the Jockey Club's chief medical advisor, Dr Michael Allen, examined Piggott in his Newmarket home and passed him fit. Dr Allen told the 54-year-old that he had the heartbeat of a 21-year-old. Two days later Piggott was granted his riding licence and on the following

Monday, five years after he had quit the saddle, he made his comeback, at Leicester. Instinct guided him inexorably. His first mount was a green filly making her debut on the track but he drove her to the line only to be pipped by a short head in a photo finish. A throng of reporters stood in the rain afterwards, feeding on the mean rations of his every word, re-tuning their ears to the faint waveband of his voice. Had he altered his riding technique, he was asked. "Nah," said the master. "Same as before. One leg either side."

By the beginning of 1990, Classic Thoroughbreds was foundering. It had been set up as a public company by O'Brien and Robert Sangster to compete with the Arabs in the sales rings of the world and to build on the momentum of the great Sangster horses, El Gran Senor, Golden Fleece and Sadler's Wells. There were other big players in the enterprise, too, as well as thousands of small shareholders. But business had not been good. Losses in the first half of 1989 were

"You need a very specific type of horse for that race," said Charles O'Brien, Vincent's son and assistant trainer at the time, "and he was the ideal horse. You need a sprinter miler, a horse whose maximum trip is a mile, rather than one whose minimum trip is a mile, because the whole American ethos is based on speed. If you haven't got that speed you're not going to be able to lie up in the early part of the race and you just won't run well."

John Reid was O'Brien's stable jockey and Royal Academy's regular partner, but three weeks before the Breeders' Cup he broke his collarbone at Longchamp. The colt had no shortage of new suitors. Steve Cauthen and Willie Carson rang from England, Pat Day and Angel Cordero from America. In the background lurked Piggott. Mike Dillon, director of public relations for Ladbrokes and a friend of O'Brien's, suggested to Magnier that Piggott was perfect for the ride. O'Brien agreed.

"He was tailor-made for that horse for that day," recalled Dillon. "They had a six-furlong horse that they were trying to make into a miler and given that they go so fast over there the horse had to be settled and dropped out with a view to him getting the trip. They needed somebody with nerves of steel to wait long enough. The one man who would wait and not worry about arriving too late – and have ice in his veins – was the Long Fella."

The choice of Piggott caused a stir but O'Brien had no doubts. Five days before the Breeders' Cup he put Piggott up on four horses at the Curragh and all four won. It was a glorious echo of their pomp. Soon the world would hear the echo, too. Royal Academy was flown to America three days before the race; Piggott followed after racing at Newbury on Thursday. A bout of flu confined O'Brien to Ballydoyle, but his wife, Jacqueline, made the journey with Charles. Piggott sat on Royal Academy for the first time on Friday morning.

As Piggott entered the Belmont Park training complex, he waved to the waiting reporters but didn't pause to chat. The British press were used to Piggott's reticence but it was alien to the American reporters. Piggott's relationship with them was strained in any case. He had been slaugh-

$8.3m and from a high of 41p the share price had plunged to 11p by the end of the year. O'Brien faced other pressures, too. For some years, he had been in decline and by the end of 1989 he was no longer ranked as one of the top dozen trainers in England.

Royal Academy was the only light in a stormy sky. O'Brien had paid $3.5m for the colt as a yearling at the Keeneland Sales, a million more than his budget. He was a son of Nijinsky, one of the greatest horses O'Brien had ever trained and Piggott had ever ridden. At home Royal Academy had displayed some of his sire's class, but as a two-year-old he flopped in the Dewhurst Stakes at Newmarket.

The pressure to produce victories with Royal Academy in 1990 was huge.

You could tell how much the win meant to Piggott. He couldn't stop smiling. Could this elated figure really be the dour, taciturn Piggott of legend? It was a special moment.

First signs were promising when the horse came in a good second in the Irish 2,000 Guineas. But then he refused to go into the stalls before the St James's Palace Stakes at Royal Ascot and, as with other Nijinsky horses, questions began to be asked about his temperament. He responded with a blistering victory in the July Cup at Newmarket and the doubts evaporated. Thoughts turned to the Breeders' Cup Mile.

Breeders' Cup day is always special. But that day was unique

tered for his riding of Sir Ivor in the 1968 Washington International and again for his performance on Dahlia in the same race six years later. Piggott had neither forgiven nor forgotten.

"I never used to get very elated, but for once I felt truly on a high"

Breeders' Cup day is always special, but that day was unique. "A lot of people felt that that Breeders' Cup was the best day's racing of all time," said Dillon. "It was just one of those days that was quite an emotional roller coaster and in the middle of it all, up popped the grandad."

In the face of it all, Piggott showed no emotion. It was a $1m race which might yield multiples of that sum in stud income to the owners of the winner. To Classic Thoroughbreds, the stakes were even higher. Its shares had hit a new low of 6½p. Fortunes rested on a Royal Academy victory. Piggott was oblivious to everything but the race.

Royal Academy bucked on his way to the stalls, hurling Piggott into the air before he fell back into the saddle. Drawn number one, he was first into the stalls and waiting for the others he relaxed. It was a terrible draw for a horse which needed to be switched off in the first part of the race, but luckily he was dozing when the gates were opened. The horse drawn two flew out of the stalls, met interference and was bundled into the hedge. Royal Academy broke so badly that Piggott had time to steer him clear.

As they ran down the back straight Royal Academy was fourth-last of the 13 runners. Up ahead the pace was suicidal. Expensive Decision led them into the home turn but he began to falter and Itsallgreektome was getting to him. Piggott and Royal Academy had their own worries.

"Going into the final bend I moved him up towards a challenging position," said Piggott, "and as we started to straighten up I was beginning to think I'd win when all of a sudden he lost his action completely. He didn't stumble but he seemed to miss a stride and in doing so lost his place. It transformed what we had to do. I had to get after him with a vengeance, but he really stuck his head out and showed his heart."

They had six lengths to find. Piggott switched him to the outside and inside the three-sixteenth pole he went for the whip. "And Lester Piggott is flailing away at Royal Academy," roared the on-course commentator, " ... and Royal Academy is thundering down the centre of the track!"

The crowd went wild. Television cameras picked up Charles O'Brien swinging his arms manically in time with Piggott's whip. "It was a typical Lester rat-a-tat finish," O'Brien remembered, "none of this hitting them

between strides and waiting for them to respond."

With the line in sight Piggott crouched low and drove his mount home. "The amazing thing," said Dillon, "was that before he put the horse's head in front he looked across at the other horse on the fence, Itsallgreektome. He actually looked over to check where the line was and just put Royal Academy's head in front on the line." Jacqueline O'Brien led in the winner. The ring was in a chaos of rapture. Piggott smiled.

"He never expressed the thrill to me," Dillon said. "He'd barely even express it to his wife or family. You could just tell in his body language because the whole place was going wild. He was pleased that everyone was pleased. I got Lester to Brough [Scott, of Channel 4] to be interviewed. They wanted him for the presentation and he just said, 'I can't do that because Brough wants to speak to me', and he walked over to Brough. That showed me how thrilled he was because he was well known for his reluctance to speak to the media. Inwardly I know he got tremendous satisfaction out of it." In time Piggott admitted as much: "I never used to get very elated," he said, "but for once I felt truly on a high."

The best ride of his life had seen the essence of his brilliance. Age had meant nothing: his genius was timeless. "Very few jockeys," said Charles O'Brien, "would have had the balls on the 5-2 favourite in a million-dollar race to drop him out at the back for the first half-mile of a mile race. Royal Academy needed to be ridden with that kind of confidence and God knows confident rides was what that man was good at."

Perspective is safer at this remove, but first impressions have remained remarkably true. As Dillon said: "After his retirement and prison, to come back to the biggest pressure cooker that there is in racing, with 12 days of match practice, and produce a ride like that was amazing. Amazing."

Nine days later Piggott turned 55. Five years after that he finally retired. His biographer, Dick Francis, once asked him how long he would have gone on if he could have stopped time. "A thousand years," said the master. And a thousand more.

Normal service is resumed. Piggott and O'Brien conspire, plotting another victory. Words were scarcely necessary; each knew what the other wanted. Actions always spoke louder.

June 1993

Ball of the century

Shane Warne exploded into Ashes cricket with his first ball. It was an extraordinary delivery. It didn't just undermine England in that game, it sent them spiralling into long-term decline. It also saw the resurrection of a long-despised art, leg-spin bowling. Warne, pudgy and peroxided, was always an unlikely hero. Yet his place in cricket history was assured.

SIMON WILDE

The ball Shane Warne bowled to Mike Gatting on the afternoon of Friday June 4 1993, in the first Test between England and Australia at Old Trafford, is beyond doubt the most replayed, most talked about and most famous delivery ever set in motion. Television and Warne's own phenomenal career have seen to that. Whether we would still marvel at it had he never taken another wicket is open to question. It was, though, a sensationally good cherry. Sensationally good for a loosener for sure. It was Warne's first ball of the match, his first in an Ashes Test. Not for him a gentle opener – never was, never will be. This is a trait little remarked upon. Warne bowls the deliveries others regard as unimportant as though his life depends on them.

"Spectacular things like that have happened throughout my career," he told me. "It's been one of the things about my game that I've really enjoyed. What's going to happen that first ball, that last ball, of the day?" It is the sign of a supreme sportsman glorying in his gifts, as much in thrall to them as any bystander.

Two years later, Warne bowled Basit Ali, of Pakistan, in a Test at Sydney with a similar ball, a big leg-break that took off, only the result was even more humiliating for the batsman. On its way to the stumps, the ball darted through Basit's legs; not the way for the next Javed Miandad – which is what Basit fancied he was – to be out. It was the last ball of the day.

The Gatting ball was even more pregnant with meaning. Warne regarded Ashes Tests as the ultimate challenge and was unwilling for his arrival to go unnoticed. He succeeded beyond his wildest imaginings. "It was a ball that changed my life," he now concedes. More importantly, it changed cricket's course.

Leg-spin bowling was in the doldrums. It appeared to have little relevance to Test cricket, which was dominated by pace. The side strongest in fast bowling, West Indies, had not lost a series for 13 years. In the right conditions, spin could be decisive, but it was an unreliable weapon. Abdul Qadir beat a lonely drum for leg-spin but his record outside Pakistan was poor.

When he came to England, Warne, 23, had spent 18 months in and out of the Australia side, just another rookie spinner trying to hang onto the cliff face of Test cricket. Martin Crowe's claim that Warne was the best leg-spinner in the world was both a compliment and a reflection on the dearth of alternatives. Nor could he expect much from English conditions. Australian leg-spinners had historically struggled to adjust to the softer, slower turf. But Warne was lucky, for Allan Border, his captain, believed leg-spin could unsettle English nerves, and Border shielded him in the build-up to the first Test. Warne was kept away from the one-day internationals, took cheap wickets in county games and the only prospective England batsman he bowled to was Graeme Hick at Worcester. Border instructed him to show nothing but leg-breaks. Hick

The hand of history: Warne's fist clenched in an "unseemly" celebration, as one journalist sniffily wrote, as wicketkeeper Healy congratulates him. Gatting still doesn't know what's going on.

struck 187. Warne's confidence wavered but Border's did not.

Thus, before Old Trafford England had given little thought to Warne. The complacency was evident in the failure to select a left-handed batsman, the classic counter to leg-spin. "We had heard about him, but knew little," said Gatting, acknowledged as England's best player of spin. "All we knew was that he was a promising leg-spinner and that he was a bit of a larrikin. We did not know what to expect."

This was a serious error, for Warne was highly unorthodox. He bowled a lot from round the wicket and attacked batsmen's legs with his stock leg-break, sharply spun. It was a clever strategy, for it frustrated opponents who, if they knew anything about leg-spinners, knew that they were usually good for a few free hits. Dickie Bird, who stood at Warne's end for the Gatting ball, was struck by the novelty: "Warne was not like Abdul Qadir, who pitched it leg and middle. Warne attacked leg stump and just outside. I had never seen a bowler like it before."

Warne was lucky in another respect. The Old Trafford pitch took an unusual amount of turn. When Australia batted first, and were dismissed for 289, Peter Such and Phil Tufnell took eight of the wickets, so Warne had reason to feel optimistic when Border, after two hours, called on him to bowl from the Warwick Road End. After a good start by Graham Gooch and Michael Atherton, England were 80 for one. With Atherton just gone, Gatting was the new man at the crease.

Warne was apprehensive. On handing over his sweater and white floppy hat, he was asked by Bird: "Are you feeling a bit nervous?" Warne replied: "Yes, I am a bit. The fingers are twitching. I'll be okay when I get into my rhythm." While he prepared to start from over the wicket, Gatting, 20 yards away, was feeling cooler: "I'd been in a while and was happy facing leg-spin, having faced Abdul Qadir before. There was nothing insurmountable."

Where's the ball? Gatting doesn't know it but he's just played his inadvertent part in cricket's mythology. Not until umpire Ken Palmer pointed out the sorry truth to the stunned Englishman with a simple "Well, Gatt, you're out," did the truth begin to sink in.

Warne walked a few paces, skipped and ripped his fingers across the ball's seam: "All I tried to do was pitch on about leg stump and spin it a fair way. As it left my hand it felt just about perfect. When a leg-break works really well it curves away to the leg side in the air before pitching and spinning back the other way. The curve in the air comes from the amount of spin on the ball and in this case I had managed to put quite a lot of purchase on."

Gatting's first movement was forward, but when he saw the ball swerve down the leg side he began to lose interest. "I was more worried that it was going to bowl me round my legs. I was not really worried about anything else. Maybe I should have been." Fatally, the ball's late dip pulled him off balance, exposing the off stump. The ball, pitching on a rough patch and, skewing back past an inert bat, brushed off stump two inches from the top. "I saw it spin and thought it had missed everything because of the amount it had turned," said Gatting. "Ian Healy [the wicketkeeper] was appealing and I thought it was for a stumping, so I looked at him and said, 'What are you doing?' He said: 'Look, the bail is on the floor'. I said: 'So what?' "

Gatting was still transfixed when Ken Palmer, the square-leg umpire, came in to replace the bail. "He just stood there, looking where the ball pitched," said Palmer. "He was obviously thinking, 'Well, I can't believe this'. Healy did not knock the bail off, I had seen that. He'd been bowled as clean as a whistle. They were all celebrating. Healy said, 'Great delivery Warney! Great delivery mate!' The bail was on the floor and as I picked it up I said, 'Well, Gatt, you're out.' He just walked off. He didn't say anything."

An air of amazement hung over the ground. Healy's face alone told that something extraordinary had happened. Gooch, at the non-striker's end, turned to Bird open-mouthed, saying with classic understatement: "That was a good delivery, Dickie." Bird, equally laconic, replied: "Aye it were, mate, aye." As he mooched off, Gatting, like a mathematician who had just discovered that two plus two did not, after all, equal four, kept looking back at the giant replay screen, seeking enlightenment.

In the BBC radio box at the Stretford End, confusion reigned.

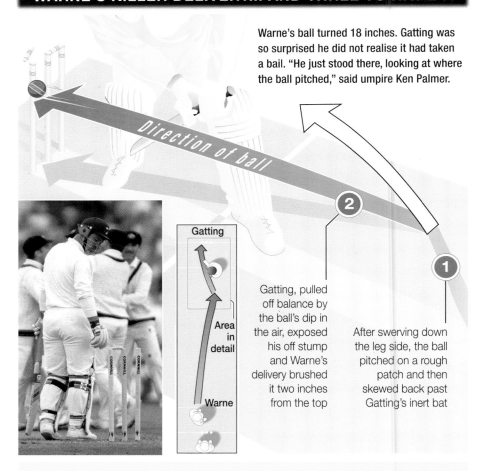

WARNE'S KILLER DELIVERY... AND THREE TO RIVAL IT

Warne's ball turned 18 inches. Gatting was so surprised he did not realise it had taken a bail. "He just stood there, looking at where the ball pitched," said umpire Ken Palmer.

Direction of ball

Gatting

Area in detail

Warne

2 Gatting, pulled off balance by the ball's dip in the air, exposed his off stump and Warne's delivery brushed it two inches from the top

1 After swerving down the leg side, the ball pitched on a rough patch and then skewed back past Gatting's inert bat

V F Trumper b S F Barnes 3.
Australia v England, Sydney, Dec 1907
The supreme bowler of his and probably any other day, Sydney Barnes accounted for Victor Trumper, the finest batsman of the period, with a ball that swung away before breaking back off the pitch. Charles Macartney, the non-striker, described it as "the sort of ball a man might see if he was dreaming or drunk".

D G Bradman b A V Bedser 0
Australia v England, Adelaide, Feb 1947
The ball the incomparable Donald Bradman thought the best he received surely ranks high among the finest ever to be bowled. This was it, a quick inswinging leg-break from Alec Bedser.

G Boycott b M A Holding 0
West Indies v England, Barbados, March 1981
Not just a tremendous ball but a tremendous over, nigh on unplayable. West Indian Michael Holding stepped up his pace with each delivery until the sixth, an inswinger of full length, burst past Geoffrey Boycott's still upraised bat and sent the off-stump flying.

Jonathan Agnew, at the microphone, had never seen Warne before and, to add to his troubles, his view was obscured by Gatting's ample frame and Healy's standing up to the stumps. He was unsure what had happened.

"At first the ball looked as though it was going to pitch on leg, then it began to drift. It dipped and went so fast, that was the killer. My commentary did not sound at all definitive but then that was how it was. It was a case of, 'Bloody hell, what's happened here?' "

Warne was euphoric, but his show of delight – restrained though it was by the standards of his later days – did not escape censure from those still coming to terms with peroxide blond hair on a cricketer. "Unseemly though it was in a slow bowler," one critic wrote, "Warne clenched his fist and charged down the pitch ... "

"Bloody hell, Warney, what happened?" Gatting was still fretting the next morning

"He was very confident for a young man," said Palmer. "You could see he fancied his chances. You have to be very talented to be like that. He kept on shouting, bawling and enquiring. I thought, 'We've got a new boy here, then'." Warne did not appreciate how extraordinary the delivery was until he saw a replay during tea. When he went in, he was feeling just as pleased about the wicket of Robin Smith, claimed with the first ball of his second over.

He denies that the Gatting ball gave him confidence to believe he could do anything, but surely it was not coincidence that in his very first over after the interval he bowled two terrific deliveries to Gooch. Seemingly mesmerised, the England captain drove the next, a full toss, tamely into the hands of mid-on. England ended the day on 202 for eight, destined to concede a significant deficit.

One of the first people into the Australian dressing room that evening was Gatting. "Bloody hell, Warney," he demanded, "what happened?" He was still fretting the next morning. Agnew found him inspecting the pitch before play: "Gatt was shaking his head. He felt he should have got further forward and padded it away. We got the groundsman over and started measuring how far it spun. I think it was 18 inches." Gatting is philosophical: "If I'd known what it was going to do I suppose I could have put my foot down and had a sweep, but who knows what would have happened? We shall never know."

Australia went on to win the game by 179 runs and Warne, with eight wickets, was man of the match. His grip over English minds was secured and his side set up for the summer. They won the series by an emphatic margin and Warne claimed 34 wickets, the most by an Australian leg-spinner in England. Gatting was dropped after the second Test and Gooch resigned as captain after the fourth. It was a rout, the edifice of English confidence fractured from the instant Warne detonated his first ball.

His success created a furore. Not only was he an unusual and brilliant bowler, but he had all the credentials of the Aussie rebel. He liked beer, burgers and beaches, and had even been kicked out of Australia's cricket academy. "Everyone wanted to talk about the Gatting ball," he said. "The

fuss went on for days and off the field a lot of things started to happen. That Test match consolidated me in the side. When I look back at it now I think that ball definitely changed my life."

It may have been the most replayed, most talked about, most famous ball ever bowled, but was it The Ball of the Century? This phrase was coined in *The Sunday Times* by Robin Marlar two days after the event. He wrote an article about what he felt was the significance of the ball – the shattering of England's self-belief, the revival of leg-spin, the emergence of an extraordinary talent: "The ball of the century, we can safely call it . . . Television repeats are bound to be frequent. The ball will become a myth . . . This is the stuff to bring back interest in cricket." Others took a narrower view. They described it as a "freak", a "wonder ball", the "ball of the decade" and "the ball from hell". But it was Marlar's phrase that stuck.

Warne, whose concerns are technical rather than historical, is unsure that it is even the best ball he has bowled. He holds it in special affection because of what it led to, but he

expressed reservations about it in his autobiography. He wrote: "The thing about the Gatting ball was that it came from nowhere – a great thrill but not quite as satisfying as setting up a good batsman, working a tactic out to counter his technique then bowling the right ball to get him out."

For this kind of killing, he cited Alec Stewart's wicket in the second innings of that same Test, and Stewart again at Brisbane 18 months later. Also in this category come the ball that bowled

Warne's grip over England was secure. Australia were set up for the summer

Gooch behind his legs in the Edgbaston Test of 1993 – another that turned fully 18 inches – and the one that rounded wickedly on Shivnarine Chanderpaul, the West Indies left-hander, at Sydney in 1997.

When I asked him whether the Gatting ball was his best, Warne at first said no, the two he bowled to Gooch directly after tea the same day were better. Then, after a moment's thought, he backtracked. Gatting's wicket was his "favourite ... Yes, it is probably my best ball, followed closely by Chanderpaul." Warne, it seemed, had realised it was pointless fighting the tide of popular opinion.

Still unable – or unwilling – to believe the evidence of his eyes, Gatting can only stand dumbfounded and stare at the stumps. The Australians knew what had happened, though.

June 1995

Rainbow Warriors

For South Africa, the 1995 Rugby World Cup was more than just a sporting tournament. It was a symbol of a nation reborn. Rugby was the game of the old white ruling elite, a symbol of discrimination. But with apartheid banished, the whole nation was swept up in a frenzy of emotional support for the Springboks.

STEPHEN JONES

"Amabokoboko". The headline appeared in June 1995 in *The Sowetan*, daily newspaper of that seething urban sprawl near Johannesburg, where millions of black South Africans were once confined by apartheid and then by economics. It meant, simply, "Wonder Boks".

For black newspapers to cover the World Cup at all, still more to enthuse about the Springboks, was remarkable enough. To whites in South Africa's polyglot society, rugby is a massive sport, a religious pastime. But to non-whites it had always been every bit as significant a symbol of apartheid as the police or the army. Untold grief and controversy had been caused by the efforts of rugby's conservative administrators, inside South Africa and elsewhere, to maintain rugby contacts in the face of boycott and inhumanity, old smug chums acting insufferably.

Since apartheid had been dismantled, the obvious backward yearning of elements of South Africa's rugby union had soured relations between rugby and Nelson Mandela's new ANC government. These culminated in the notorious decision, inspired by Louis Luyt, the formidable and controversial president of the South Africa Rugby Football Union (Sarfu), to play *Die Stem*, the Afrikaner anthem, before the very match which marked the official return of South Africa to the fold – against New Zealand at Ellis Park, Johannesburg, in 1992.

The World Cup began with a stunning opening ceremony at Newlands in Cape Town. The world watched, glued not only to the sporting efforts of the 16 competing nations, but to the backdrop provided by the Rainbow Nation. Not even the old guard could fail to grasp the possibilities. Sarfu had appointed as chief executive a young man of English descent, Edward Griffiths, an author and journalist who appreciated the public relations opportunity that the World Cup brought.

It was an inspired choice. "Rugby as it is today cannot survive in South Africa," Griffiths said. He launched a One-Team, One-Nation campaign in which Sarfu and the Springbok squad did their best, in PR gesture and genuine actions, to drag the country behind them, to make reparations for the past and to foster rugby in the disadvantaged areas. Chester Williams, the

Rarely can a gesture have been so eloquent – or meant so much. It was to Pienaar's credit just as much as it was to Mandela's that he understood how the World Cup could help heal the scars of apartheid.

Joy unconfined: South Africa are world champions. For the players, it may been no more than a stunning sporting victory. But for the country it meant much, much more.

coloured wing who played brilliantly in the tournament and whose image was used in poster campaigns across the country, was a godsend. Another ally was François Pienaar, the wise and plain-speaking captain, who banished memories of grim, tongue-tied Bok captains of old, played well, conducted himself impeccably and spoke beautifully. Pienaar's personal friendship with Mandela was to form the rock of the new South African rugby.

"One of the things we wanted to do was have all the boys singing *Nkosi sikelel' iAfrika*, the anthem," Griffiths recalled. Of course, these were all

Pienaar's relationship with Mandela formed the rock of the new South African rugby

merely gestures, but they were potent and as far as can be judged came mostly from the heart. "The object was not to find five Chester Williamses," he said of the investments in non-white rugby. "It was to give access to rugby to the mass of the nation's people who had been denied it by our policies."

So the event kicked off, with South Africa defeating Australia, the holders, in the opening match. In an era when defences ruled, it was not to be a glorious World Cup for rugby spectacle. But it did produce one great side in New Zealand – though they did not win the tournament – and one player of staggering size, ability and glamour – Jonah Lomu.

New Zealand, led by the charismatic and ferocious Sean Fitzpatrick, were easily the outstanding team. South Africa, well coached by Kitch Christie, were worthy and massive but nothing like as good or as entertaining as the All

Blacks. The signature of the team was Lomu, every defender's nightmare come true. Lomu was 6ft 6in and over 19st but could run the 100m in 10.3sec.

His build-up for the World Cup had been fractured because his fitness was suspect and, at 20, he was callow. By the time the team arrived in South Africa, he was ready. He scored two barnstorming tries against Ireland in the opening Pool match; throughout the tournament he either blasted tackling aside or simply carried defenders on his back, massive thighs pumping. He became rugby's biggest individual sensation. Ever.

The semi-final clash with England was staggering. Lomu blasted the English half-way back to Heathrow. He scored four tries, beginning with a thunderous run through three would-be tacklers. In that match, he showed footballing ability as well as naked, terrifying power. Tony Underwood, his marker, was engagingly frank: "We spoke all week about what we had to do, but in the end, we were dealing not with a player, but a phenomenon.

Moment of destiny: Stransky drops the winning goal against the All Blacks. It was the triumph the whole country had waited for.

All you could do was try to hang on to him until help arrived." Lomu's profile was to become astronomical, even if his battle with illness would later drag him back towards playing mortality.

It was not just on England that Lomu made his mark. Only six days after the match, the three major southern hemisphere unions signed a huge television deal with Rupert Murdoch's News Corporation, one which set up the Tri-Nations series, the Super 12 and, more to the point, dynamited the last vestiges of amateurism. By all accounts, Murdoch watched Lomu's match on TV and was entranced. According to Peter FitzSimons, the Australian journalist, Murdoch rang a lieutenant after the match. "That's the most incredible thing I've ever seen," he said. "We have got to have that guy." They got him.

Even before South Africa won through against the unlucky French, in a semi-final in Durban played in torrential rain, the evidence of a nation coming together, of *The Sowetan* cheering on the boys, took the breath away. It reached a massively emotional high on the day of the final at an electrified Ellis Park.

The match had a mighty intensity. South Africa beat New Zealand when Joel Stransky, their fly-half, dropped a goal in extra time to take it to 15-12. The final whistle of Ed Morrison, the English referee, signalled that South Africa were champions of the world. Rarely can a mere drop kick have had such significance.

Mandela had been raucously cheered at South African rugby grounds for some time. For the final, he sat in the stands wearing the green and yellow jersey of the once-hated Springboks. It bore No 6, Pienaar's number. As the stadium celebrated, he walked out on to the field and mounted the podium for the presentation, his dignity all-enveloping. He and Pienaar greeted each other joyously and, as Pienaar held the trophy above his head, Mandela danced alongside, caught up in the the joy of the moment. There has never been an image in rugby to match it, nor anything so elo-quent of the joy of winning the Rugby World Cup – nor of the depth of human forgiveness. Given everything that had gone before, it was an amazing sight.

"When he gave me the trophy," Pienaar remembered, "he thanked me for what I had done for South Africa. I thought that no one had done as much for South Africa as the president." Pienaar was asked how it felt to have the 65,000 people in the stadium behind him. "There were 43 million behind us," he replied. Movingly, he meant the whole country.

That evening, we drove out of Ellis Park through the normally dark and threatening no-go areas of Johannesburg. People were on the streets, celebrating, blowing horns, flourishing Springbok favours. These were streets where, normally, people skulked. South Africa TV jumped frantically around the country, to bars and

In the semi-final, Lomu blasted the English half-way back to Heathrow

gatherings in white, black and coloured areas. Joy was unconfined.

It may have been just a day release for some. Certainly, doubts surfaced later as to whether the old guard had been subdued, especially when the ludicrous Luyt dismissed Griffiths within a year. Griffiths had spoken prophetically at the time of the World Cup: "If there is to be a relationship between rugby and the black majority, the World Cup has done no more than cause their eyes to meet. There will have to be a long courtship before there can be any thought of marriage." Luyt's old guard had one more throw, as Griffiths was to discover.

Certainly, too, one sporting success when set against years of neglect and inhumanity meant little. But it was still the five weeks of our lives. To spend time among the sporting clamour, the shifting political landscape, the day-to-day dangers and the sheer size and spectacle of the country assaulted the senses. The World Cup final was a day of profound and lasting significance. To find tears flowing when attempting to dictate the story of the day down a telephone line, as Mandela danced, was testimony enough for me.

One section of the global community was not celebrating. Whatever happened to the All Blacks at Ellis Park? According to their coach, Laurie Mains, foul play. Two nights before the game, the All Blacks started dropping like flies. "When I put my head on the pillow, the room started to spin," recalled Ian Jones, the All Black. He was frequently, copiously sick. At 2am he went to the team doctor, Mike Bowen. He found a queue. "You are number 22," Bowen told Jones grimly.

"We were in great shape going into that final week," Jones said. "We were ready, physically and psychologically." But the illness, diagnosed as food poisoning, changed all that: "At the training session we were the most disorganised rabble you've ever seen. There was a sickly smell in the air." Only two players, Robin Brooke and Zinzan Brooke, were not affected. They were the only players who had not attended a buffet at the Crowne Plaza Hotel on the Thursday.

To this day, Laurie Mains, the coach, believes that the team was deliberately

The World Cup final was a day of profound and lasting significance

poisoned: "It was all too much of a coincidence, and there was so much at stake for South Africans." He claims knowledge that a waitress named Suzie had spiked tea and coffee at the hotel buffet. Hotel authorities denied that Suzie existed and blamed bottles of chilli sauce which the team had brought in from the outside. The team were recovering, but still well below their best, on match day. Jeff Wilson started the game but could not go on. Was the poisoning deliberate? In my view, possibly. Did it affect the outcome of the 1995 World Cup? Definitely.

To those who watched on television it would not mean much, but anyone present at Ellis Park would also unquestionably remember The Jumbo. As part of the pre-match show, a South African Airways

747 flew over the stadium. At least, just about. You could see it approaching from a blimp camera on the giant screens, but it suddenly arrived with a thunderous roar, seemingly about two feet above the stand, and appeared to dip into the bowl of the stadium before it lifted and flew onwards. Underneath was painted the message "Good Luck Bokke". No one will convince me that it was was meant to be that low, and people were chilled, as well as elated, when it flew on. We met the pilot at the post-match dinner and enquired after the long period of preparation he must have put in. Blithely, he explained that he'd only done the manoeuvre in a light plane.

It was a whole five weeks of stunning sights and sounds, and play and politics. Perhaps it was just as well that belief had already been suspended when the giant aircraft made its hairy pass – and when President Mandela jigged for joy.

A phenomenon: Lomu in the semi-final against England. The giant All Black was simply devastating that day, running in four tries. The English didn't have a prayer.

Magnificent seven

In September 1996, at the tail-end of an injury-plagued season, Frankie Dettori achieved a wildly improbable clean-sweep at Ascot. In an atmosphere of mounting hysteria, he won every single one of the day's seven races. For the bookies, it was little short of meltdown; for the punters it was simply unforgettable.

JONATHAN POWELL

Frankie Dettori, normally so full of zest, was unusually muted when he arrived at Ascot on September 28 1996. Diamond Dance, the 7-4 favourite in the opening race at Haydock the previous day, had finished only third for Dettori and from there his afternoon had only deteriorated : six rides, six losers.

But if Dettori's career has told us anything, it is that his highs and lows are rarely far apart. Ten weeks earlier, on June 12, the most charismatic jockey of our times had won six races in a day for the first time, split equally between Yarmouth and Kempton; the next afternoon, he had a horrifying fall at Newbury which saw him out for two months in the heart of the season.

Having missed Royal Ascot and Glorious Goodwood, Dettori was still making up for lost time when he arrived at Ascot for the opening day of the Festival of British Racing. Few held out much hope of an upturn in his fortunes. In *The Sun*, Templegate tipped only one of Dettori's seven rides. Thunderer, in *The Times*, could not see any of them winning. There was, though, a vote of confidence from one of the *Racing Post*'s tipsters: of the four Dettori horses tipped by Newmarket,

The previous day, Dettori had lost all six races he rode. He came to Ascot less than optimistic

the most unlikely was Fujiyama Crest, an outsider in the last race of the day.

The gifts that Dettori brings to the arena are not confined to his brilliance in the saddle. By 1996, his natural, infectious ebullience was familiar to many with only the flimsiest interest in the sport of kings. Born in Italy, the son of a champion jockey, Dettori moved to England as an apprentice and became the first jockey since Lester Piggott to ride a century of winners as a teenager. At 23, he became champion jockey for the first time with a prodigious 223 winners. A retainer for racing's most powerful owner, Sheikh Mohammed, soon strengthened his hand, and on that tumultuous afternoon at Ascot it was for the sheikh's Godolphin team that Dettori, riding Wall Street, won the opening Cumberland Lodge Stakes. As Wall Street, the 2-1 favourite, passed the post in front, Dettori's natural high spirits were immediately restored.

Dettori had won before on Lucayan Prince, the 15-8 favourite in the next race, the Racal Diadem Stakes over six furlongs, but Godolphin required his presence on Diffident. When sprinters are jostling for position, races are won and lost in a split-second, and if Walter Swinburn had found an opening a moment sooner he would certainly have prevailed on Lucayan Prince. Instead, it was Dettori who seized the initiative on Diffident as Swinburn searched frantically for a gap. By the time Swinburn found daylight, inside the final furlong, Diffident had swept to the front. Two strides past the line Swinburn's horse was in front. Diffident, the winner by the shortest of short heads, was returned at 12-1. "That was probably the luckiest winner of the year for me," Dettori recalled. "I saw Walter coming, but he was just too late."

In her room at the Holiday Inn in Mayfair, Mary Bolton, a Somerset housewife, turned away from her television with a smile. In London to celebrate their 19th wedding anniversary, John and Mary Bolton had decided on a whim to back Dettori in all seven races. They worked out a complicated bet involving 21 £9 doubles and a £5 each-way accumulator, found the nearest Ladbrokes and invested a total of £216.91p, including betting tax. Once the result of the second race was announced, Mary set off on a shopping expedi-

tion; her husband, a farmer and cattle dealer, was already at Ascot as Dettori and Diffident entered the winner's enclosure.

At 3:05 Dettori marched to the paddock for the third race, the Queen Elizabeth II Stakes. In the ring, bookmakers were offering 100-30 against his mount, Mark of Esteem. The favourite, Bosra Sham, was a truly gifted filly, but as she and Pat Eddery set sail for home, Dettori was stalking them with intent. Bosra Sham stretched two lengths clear, maybe more, before Dettori pounced on Mark of Esteem. It was an electrifying display of controlled energy. Bosra Sham in full flight was considered invincible. Mark of Esteem swept past her as if she was standing still. "I didn't want to go too early and burn up all my fuel," Dettori remembered. "When I did ask him, the delivery was like the kick-in from a fuel-injection car. It almost knocked me out of my saddle."

At the line the little jockey in vivid blue silks raised his right arm in a salute of triumph. A stone-hearted official moved alongside to warn Dettori against performing his trade-

Trademark Frankie: standing up in the saddle, whip aloft, and screaming, screaming and screaming as Fujiyama Crest makes it seven out seven.

mark flying dismount. At first Dettori agreed, but he is an unashamed showman and when the moment came he launched himself into the air. Three out of three.

Race four. A year earlier Dettori had finished second on Decorated Hero in the Tote Festival Handicap. This time a 5lb penalty left him carrying top weight of 9st 13lb, a for-

No one, least of all Dettori himself, held out much hope for the last race

midable burden. In addition he was unfavourably drawn in the middle of the course in stall 22. The horse started at 7-1, which scarcely reflected his jockey's pessimism: "I thought it was an impossible task." But he waited with clinical patience at the rear before launching Decorated Hero on a thrilling charge that took him into a decisive lead with a furlong to run. This time Dettori returned with four fingers raised. John Gosden, the trainer who has been his most loyal supporter, stepped forward to shake his hand. It was a very English reaction amid the celebrations already breaking out over the course.

In the fifth, Dettori rode Fatefully for Godolphin in the Rosemary Rated Stakes Handicap. By now the doubles, trebles and accumulators around the country on Dettori's mount ensured that Fatefully started a heavily backed 7-4 favourite, but as the field bunched near the stand rails soon after half-way Dettori was forced to sit and suffer for a few tense seconds and hope a gap would present itself. On another day he might have waited in vain. Not this time. When Ninia, ridden his by close friend Jason Weaver, weakened a furlong out, Dettori dashed his mount through the opening that briefly appeared. As he did so, Weaver called out "Go on Frankie, go and get 'em!" At the line

Fatefully had won by a neck from Abeyr. Godolphin had now completed a remarkable four-timer but their jockey's achievement was even greater. There followed a brief crisis as the stewards inquired into an incident when Fatefully brushed against Pat Eddery's mount, Questonia, who finished fourth. "My filly did drift a bit left and interfere with Pat's horse for a second but it was accidental and made no difference," Dettori said. The stewards agreed.

By this stage you could feel the high-voltage buzz running through the crowd. Many of us felt we were on the verge of witnessing a defining sporting achievement as Dettori cantered to the start of the Blue Seal Stakes on Lochangel, the 5-4 joint-favourite. News of Dettori's achievement was not confined to a corner of Berkshire. On BBC1, Grandstand's coverage of Ascot had ended after the fourth race, but in an impromptu piece of scheduling the producers returned for the sixth race.

Dettori planned to hold up his big filly for a late challenge but she jumped out so quickly that she immediately led. Dettori let her run.

Surging for home in the third on Mark of Esteem. Dettori would later say that his horses's acceleration "almost knocked me out of my saddle". Pat Eddery on Bosra Sham was left helpless in his rival's wake.

"I did not begin to understand what had happened. It was too much, too much"

Lochangel led throughout and held Pat Eddery on Corsini by three-quarters of a length. Six out of six, and Dettori punched the air, but as Lochangel was led in he was already discounting his chances in the seventh race: "I thought there could not be a fairytale ending – it was impossible to win another race. There was so much emotion I even forgot what I had ridden in the first race."

Jockeys who have finished their work tend to rush away from the racecourse to beat the traffic. Not this day. "Nobody was going to leave while Frankie had a chance of going through the card," recalled Dettori's valet, Dave Curry. "By the end they were all rooting for him. It was pandemonium in the weighing room." Amid the mayhem, Dettori found time for a typically flamboyant interview with the BBC's Julian Wilson: "I warned Julian not to touch me because I was red-hot."

By now there was blind panic in the ranks of the country's bookmakers. Several already faced ruin, but logic dictated that Dettori could not win the seventh race on the blinkered Fujiyama Crest. In the morning he was freely on offer at 12-1. Now an avalanche of money forced his odds down to 2-1. It was an absurd price for a horse at the top of the handicap. Sentiment is not one of the bookmaker's guiding principles and in the ring Gary Wiltshire was one of several layers who saw the chance of a lifetime. It was a decision that would cost him more than £500,000. "Fujiyama Crest was a 10-1 chance at best and I had the opportunity to lay him at 2-1," he said. "The odds were miles wrong. I laid all comers. I would do it again tomorrow."

In the paddock, Dettori handed his saddle to Fujiyama Crest's trainer, Michael Stoute. "If this one gets beat, I'm going to blame you," he joked. He decided on aggression, however hopeless the cause: "Although I could not see him doing it, I decided I was not going to let defeat spoil my day."

John Bolton, by now thoroughly dazed, took up his postion on the grandstand steps, close to the finishing line. He had watched the odds on his final selection tumble, but could not begin to work out the implications for his bet. He and his wife had already won a handsome sum. But the real jackpot was riding on Fujiyama Crest. At the first bend, Dettori had managed to

cajole his mount into the lead. There they remained until, turning for home, Northern Fleet emerged from the pack, driven with grim determination by Pat Eddery. Twice before that afternoon he had finished runner-up to Dettori. For Eddery, one of the most competitive sportsmen in any arena, it was becoming personal. Few jockeys have tried harder in defeat. In full, furious flight, whip cracking, arms pumping, backside thumping into the saddle, there is nobody stronger in a finish. But every time it looked certain that Northern Fleet would overhaul Fujiyama Crest, the leader found a little more. "It's a desperate finish!" cried the BCC's John Hanmer. "In the final furlong I was praying for the post to come in time," Dettori recalled. "The weight was beginning to tell. Fujiyama Crest was so weary he was only just managing to put one leg in front of the other."

Slowly, inexorably, thrillingly, Northern Fleet closed on Fujiyama Crest. Time seemed to stand still as he narrowed the gap inch by inch. An advantage of more than a length entering the final furlong was reduced all the way to the line. Against outrageous odds, he held on by a neck. Dettori, by now beside himself, stood up in his irons and started screaming: "I did not begin to understand what had happened. It was too much, too much. I wish I could go back and relive it all again and milk it."

The full impact was yet to come. Fujiyama Crest and his jockey returned to unprecedented hysteria in the winner's enclosure. Racegoers rushed headlong to acclaim him. Predictably, we were treated to one more acrobatic flying dismount: "the highest I have ever managed," suggested Dettori. There were emotional embraces from Michael Stoute and Dave Curry before Jason Weaver stepped forward to hold up his great friend's arm in the style of a champion boxer. Dettori made an impromptu speech from a balcony before spraying champagne over the massed ranks of racegoers. Finally, he tossed his goggles to the crowd.

John Bolton estimated he had won around £300,000 and waited for almost an hour to thank Dettori personally. The jockey looked as pleased as if he had won the money himself. Bolton rang his wife with the news: she

The punters' delight – and the bookies' nightmare. Dettori still can't believe what he's just done. Some bookies would be counting the cost for years.

had not even thought to check the last five results. Later, they would find John had miscalculated. The cheque they received from Ladbrokes was for £500,000: it would have been £900,000 but for limits. Later still, the Boltons would give the jockey a more tangible expression of their appreciation in the shape of a solid silver calendar.

It was a black Saturday for bookmaking, their equivalent of the Stock Market crash. Those punters who had put together all seven winners in an accumulator were rewarded with combined odds of 25,095-1. William Hill's spokesman said it for all of them: "The fifth was expensive, the sixth disastrous and after the seventh it was time to put the lights out." Ladbrokes paid out £10m. The total cost to the industry was upwards of £30m. A few independent shops were forced out of business. Other bookmakers, like Gary Wiltshire, are still feeling the pain: "It

has been incredibly hard but people have pulled together to help. I could have walked away without honouring my debts but that is not my way, even though I will not recover for years. We are all still paying but I don't blame Frankie. I hope he rides a winner for me one day."

Ultimately, it was the quality of Dettori's achievement, more than the

"I wish I could go back and relive it all again and milk it"

statistics, that made it historic. In Italy, Gianfranco Dettori called up the Ascot results one by one on BBC World Service Teletext. Until his son telephoned after the last race, Dettori senior was convinced there was something wrong with the results service.

The following morning a newspaper reporter knocked on Dettori's door and marched in without waiting for an invitation. The jockey's life would never be the same again.

May 1999

Glory, Glory Man United

Manchester United's 1999 Treble of Premiership, FA Cup and European Cup was one of the most extraordinary feats in English football. But for Teddy Sheringham, it meant not just success but a kind of redemption. Sidelined for most of the season, he came back at the death to play a key role.

DAVID WALSH

Ears deaf to the chants of their still loyal fans, eyes blind to the journalists who will write their obituaries, the Bayern Munich players move through the tunnel from their dressing room at the Nou Camp stadium to the team bus. Their spirit has left before them. Dead men walking. For Germans, especially footballing Germans against footballing English, it isn't meant to end like this.

Someone asks the midfielder Stefan Effenberg how he feels: "I don't have the words to describe such a sickening moment. It is too brutal." Mehmet Scholl files past. Scholl could have won the European Cup with a chip that hit the post, and as he nears the bus the dam inside his head bursts. "S***, this is unbelievable, this is unbelievable," he laments. "I should have won this."

Overhearing the anguish, some journalists approach Scholl and he tells them how badly he feels. Watching from his seat in the bus, Bayern's goalkeeper, Oliver Kahn, quickly moves to end it. "What are you doing?" he asks Scholl as he pushes away the reporters. How different it is when Manchester United's players come through the same tunnel.

A red rose in their lapels, a gold medal around their necks and 1968 – the year of United's other European Cup triumph – no longer on their backs. They are unusually keen to stop and talk. Such a strange ending that no one is quite sure where to begin. This tapestry could only be understood by first unravelling it.

"Jaap, Jaap, a few words?" Stam, the big Dutchman, ambles towards the steel barrier and those crushed behind it. "Yah, when we scored the goal, you think, 'Maybe there's time for another one'." "Gary, Gary, will everyone in England now love Man United?" "After what we've done and the way we've played, people will have to admire us, even if they don't like us," says Neville. "Nicky, Nicky, you must be knackered?" "It was the lap of honour that got me," Butt says. Roy Keane, the suspended skipper, has to be coaxed into conversation. "Won without me tonight," he says. "It'll probably cost me when I renegotiate my contract. Seriously, the top teams come back and win these trophies again; that's what I want us to do."

Solskjaer scores and United take the lead. It was already deep in injury time and United had just equalised through Sheringham. Then as Beckham's wickedly struck corner came over, Sheringham flicked it on to the unmarked Solskjaer. His instinctive strike sent United surging to delirious victory.

And there's Teddy Sheringham with his little boy, Charlie. Charlie was at Old Trafford to see his father play against Spurs when the championship was won. Six days later he was at Wembley to see him score in the FA Cup final against Newcastle. And now, on this extraordinary evening in Spain, he is again beside his dad. One day, when Charlie is old enough, Teddy will recount the story to his son.

It could begin three months earlier, on a winter's evening in February. It was around nine when Sheringham got back to his home in Manchester and zapped his television on. Arsenal were battering one of the Premiership's lesser lights at Highbury. Even though he only watched the game in parts, Sheringham could tell Overmars and Bergkamp were on song, but the song which made him sit up was familiar.

"Oh Teddy, Teddy – went to Man United and you won f***-all!" Arsenal's fans refused to forget he was ex-Tottenham and enjoyed reminding the football world that in Sheringham's first season at Old Trafford he won nothing. "Have they got nothing better to sing?" he would say to himself before laughing it off. The phone rang and he couldn't stop himself saying "Did you hear? They were singing my song again tonight." But this second season at United was tough. He spent most of it in the treatment room at The Cliff, United's training ground. First his right knee, then his left; in all, the injuries cost him four months. But being a good footballer,

Sheringham spent most of the season in United's treatment room

he knew, was a matter of character, not talent. Arsenal's fans could sing to their heart's content; he would not lose faith in himself.

From the treatment room, he could watch his team-mates train and their performance always excited him. Amongst them, he took it for granted but from afar he could appreciate it. "Am I really a part of this?" he asked himself. To while away the time, he played games – Manchester United v England, which was the better team? No matter who he picked for his country, he couldn't find 11 better than United's best. He heard that Middlesbrough wanted to buy him but no one broached the subject with him. To Sheringham, it didn't matter where he went; if he agreed to go it was an admission that he wasn't as ambitious as before. As the season wore on and the team got closer to their targets, one

Sheringham turns away in delight after pulling back Bayern's lead in the European Cup final. Suddenly the tide was all flowing United's way. The Germans began to crumble, their nightmare at hand.

of the physios or the coaches would say, "Don't worry Teddy, you're going to get your medals this season", and he would bristle at the suggestion that medals were enough.

"I actually said to them, 'I don't want medals if I don't play'. It's the same for every footballer. If you don't play you don't feel part of it – you can't get away from that. I thought about the celebrations that would follow United's victories. If I hadn't contributed I would have to endure them. I didn't want that."

The story, Teddy will tell Charlie, was no fairytale. The injuries cleared and the sharpness returned, but he couldn't get from the periphery to the centre of the team. In a few games he came on as a substitute and then, in a memorable FA Cup semi-final against Arsenal, he played the entire match. But always he was there because others were rested. In the final League game against Spurs he was taken off at half-time. He was left out for the FA Cup final, even though all the guys at Old Trafford who thought they knew told him he would start.

Roy Keane's ankle injury in the early minutes of the Cup final offered Sheringham an opportunity he never expected. How he seized it: having scored the important goal, he went on to be easily the best player on the field. He thought that performance would get him into the team for Barcelona but on the Monday morning before they left for Spain Alex Ferguson came to see him and told him he hadn't made it. Character, Teddy reminded himself, is what makes a footballer.

"Teddy, if things don't change in the first 10 or 15 minutes of the second-half I'm bringing you on – make sure you're ready," Ferguson said to him at half-time in Barcelona. For 20 minutes after the restart he did not know what team to cheer for. "We were one down and one minute I was thinking, 'We've got to get back into it' but I didn't want it to happen without me."

Introduced with 23 minutes to go, Sheringham did well on the left side of United's attack, but Bayern remained in control. The Germans should have extended their one-goal advantage

but Scholl's shot came back from the post and Effenberg's volley ricocheted off the crossbar. Like many United players, Sheringham considered those escapes important, as if the gods were still undecided.

If the gods were uncertain, they were the only ones. This was Bayern's night. For all their energy and determination, United had created little. Three minutes from the end, one of the security men assigned to Uefa president Lennart Johansson suggested it was time to move. The president made his way to the back of the stand and into the lift which would take him to ground level. He rehearsed what he would say to the winning captain, Bayern's Kahn.

As the ball rises and shakes the net, Bayern's players fall as if machine-gunned

A night to remember: champions of Europe. United's celebrations were as uninhibited as their victory was improbable.

On German television, commentator Marcel Reif felt an urge he knew he should resist. "Maybe I shouldn't say it but football, as Gary Lineker once said, is a simple game; 22 men chase a ball for 90 minutes and at the end the Germans win." As Reif succumbed, the ball had found its way into the hands of a hairy Hungarian. Birka Tibi had travelled from Budapest to support United and there he was hurriedly tossing the ball to Gary Neville, who would restart the game with a throw. The clock struck 90 minutes; the game was expiring, United almost gone.

Neville throws the ball deep into the Bayern area. It is half-cleared before Effenberg slides it out for a corner. Beckham notices the cup being carried down to the pitch, sees Bayern's colours on it and then places the ball by the corner flag. From the other end of the field Peter Schmeichel troops forward. "Can you f***ing believe him?" Ferguson says to his assistant, Steve McClaren. After every other last resort, there is Schmeichel. He jumps for the corner, causing a little confusion in the Bayern defence. The ball beats every-one and lands near Dwight Yorke at the far post.

Yorke heads it tamely inside, but Thorsten Fink mistimes his clearance and the ball comes to Giggs on the edge of the area. He doesn't catch his shot cleanly but the mishit finds Sheringham, alone and onside: "As it comes rolling towards me, I can see the goalkeeper out of the corner of my eye and I want to smash it, to make sure of it. I still don't know whether I half pulled out of it to slide it into the corner or whether I've miskicked it. I don't get perfect contact, but it's enough to alter the line of the ball. I just guide it into the net."

Sheringham thinks the team shouldn't do anything silly; they have extra time. But the game has spun out of control. McClaren tries to get Ferguson to change his 4-3-3 forma-tion to a more conservative 4-4-2, but the manager feels something is hap-pening. Ferguson sees devastation in the Germans' body language and reju-venation in every red jersey. His sharks have seen blood in the water.

Twenty-three seconds after Bayern's kick-off, Denis Irwin plays a long ball down the left to Solskjaer, who wins a corner off Sammy Kuffour.

Sheringham senses a winning goal: "As soon as we get the corner I think, 'While they're still panicking, we can nick another'. David whips in great balls but the way he whips them in, you can't determine where they're going – it's just a matter of getting across your man and being there if it comes your way." It comes Sheringham's way and, reacting quicker than Thomas Linke, he glances a header diagonally across the goal and sees it fall for Solskjaer.

"I think if it had fallen to anybody else we might not have scored. Ole is the best natural finisher at the club. He just always hits the target and the moment it hit the roof of the net – that is pure ecstasy."

Bayern have contributed to their own destruction, for at the last moment Kahn pushes Kuffour out of the six-yard area and leaves Solskjaer unmarked. It is the last mistake of a

Inconsolable: Bayern's Carsten Jancker sees his world come to an end. Team-mate Thomas Helmer tries to comfort him.

long night. As the ball rises and shakes the net, Bayern's players fall as if machine-gunned. Many have no wish to carry on. Mercifully, referee Pier Luigi Collina ends the match just 10 seconds after restarting it.

Just then Johansson walks through the tunnel leading to the pitch: "The lift takes time to come, then we have to go through a long hall, down steps, through different rooms, through the dressing room area and because we are inside, we never hear a thing. At the end, we must explain to five stewards and a policeman that we are who we say we are. I can now see out onto the pitch and I'm confused. 'It cannot be,' I think, 'the winners are crying and the losers are dancing'."

And Teddy Sheringham got his medals. February evenings watching Arsenal will never be the same. But these are medals he can live with, medals he helped Manchester United to win. When he hears the full story, Charlie will think that's what mattered to dad, being a proper part of the success. And Charlie will be wrong. "On the open-top bus coming back through Manchester," says Teddy, "it wasn't anything said between Charlie and me, it was just the way our eyes both lit up at the same time as we looked at all the people who had turned out to welcome the team home. We just looked at each other and the look said 'Bloody hell'. I'm just so glad he was there, that we could expe-rience it together. That's the bit I'll remember."

Father and son: Sheringham and Charlie back in Manchester with David Beckham – and the European Cup.

June 2000 – April 2001

The Tiger Slam

The sense of inevitability that attended Tiger Woods's extraordinary achievement in winning four consecutive Majors is unlikely ever to be repeated. For ten months, Woods held the game by the throat, overwhelming both his rivals and our sense of what was possible. It was at once the most inconceivable and predictable event in golf.

DAVID WALSH

This is the part your grandchildren will not understand. On the Sunday afternoon that brought his fourth consecutive Major title, Tiger Woods walked up the 18th fairway at Augusta National and the acclaim was merely respectful.

It was the expectation, bordering on certainty, that struck those present and is now speared into the memory. Woods stood on the 18th tee one shot ahead of David Duval, knowing par would be good enough. In golf's history, no player had previously held the Masters, US Open, Open Championship and US PGA titles at the same time. Woods was within four strokes of that achievement and, dutifully, we waited for history to unfold.

The last hole would be a coronation, not a contest; a conclusion not a climax

Let us not miss the point here: this was Augusta, home of the Masters. At 4.30am that Sunday morning 70 or 80 people queued outside Gate 3, determined to claim the best greenside seats. But by 4.30pm, well before the end of the tournament, quite a number were filing through the exits. Those wishing to beat the traffic already knew, as we all did. Easing down the Bobby Jones Highway and

out of Augusta, they could listen on their radios certain that the last hole would be a coronation, not a contest; a conclusion, not a climax.

The 18th at Augusta used to be a fine closing hole, a tough tee shot through a narrow corridor of pines that had to move a little to the right to avoid the enormous bunker on the left. Fourteen years before, Greg Norman messed up his 4-iron approach and eventually lost in a play-off to Larry Mize. But, now, as his caddie Steve Williams crouched behind the bag and Woods himself stood over the ball, that kind of denouement seemed like something from a distant past.

Woods hit his drive 330 yards, cutting it precisely to miss the bunker and find the middle of the fairway. From there, he had 75 yards to the pin. His gently-struck sand wedge pitched close to the hole and ran 15 feet by. After the gallery's respectful acclamation, Woods studied his putt. With a one-shot lead, he didn't need a birdie, but Tiger's wants have long outstripped his needs.

He rolled the putt into the middle of the hole and then retreated to a quiet corner of the green to allow Phil Mickelson to putt out. For a moment, Woods quietly considered what he had done. "I walked over to the side," he would say afterwards, "and I started thinking, 'I don't have any more shots to play. I'm done. I just won the Masters'."

We could applaud the achievement, be thankful that we were there to witness but, somehow, Woods's sustained excellence had dulled our sense of wonder. This had started with

his 15-shot victory in the US Open at Pebble Beach. To find something resembling it, historians had to exhume Old Tom Morris, who beat about a dozen competitors by 13 shots to win the 1862 Open Championship.

After Pebble Beach, Sir Michael Bonallack, the former secretary of the Royal and Ancient, said: "If he doesn't win the Open Championship, there should be a stewards' inquiry." Bonallack is a man from whom you might have expected restraint but, in fact, he spoke for us all.

In the final round at St Andrews, David Duval's run of birdies – seven in the opening 10 holes – catapulted him into a share of leadership, but there would be only one result and everyone seemed to know it. Reason never entered into it, the sense of inevitability was there. And there it was, the final leg in Tiger's Slam, at once the most inconceivable and predictable event in golf.

At the peak of their powers, the greatest players make it look easy. Maradona slaloming through England's mesmerised defence, Muhammad Ali taunting George Foreman, Michael Jordan knifing through the Utah Jazz for that basket: in these moments, the gifted redefine our sense of what is feasible. Woods is another story. He didn't bewilder us with one performance, nor entrance us with an extraordinary shot. For a run of four straight Majors, he overwhelmed our sense of what was possible.

Driving home: Woods tees off on the 18th at St Andrews, his swing tempo perfect, his mastery of the field complete

Before Woods, golf was a game of chance, teeming with cruel possibilities and beyond the power of one human being to dominate. Oh, yes, Bobby Jones, Ben Hogan and Jack Nicklaus all had periods when they stood on the summit. But though they were the greatest players, they were not greater than the game itself. Theirs was a streak of supremacy, an escape from the purgatory of not knowing whether next weekend would be heaven or hell.

Yet for that run of four straight Majors and an accumulated winning margin of 25 shots, Woods changed all that and had the game by the throat. Now, with normalcy restored, we can better appreciate the achievement and maybe agree that, in our lifetimes, it is not likely to be repeated.

It all began in June 2000, on the putting green at Pebble Beach, California. A necklace of humanity circled the small practice area and though Woods was relaxed, chatting all the while to his coach, Butch Harmon, he was still at work. With clear blue skies and oppressive heat, no one casually chooses to spend the afternoon in the sun. Woods practiced there for two hours, working on his posture and his release of the putter.

This was the same Woods who, after his runaway victory in the 1997 Masters, his first Major, watched a recording of his triumph and could see his swing was too fast. With so much speed comes a reliance on perfect timing and Woods knew it would not do for the long-haul career he envisaged. It wasn't broke, but he decided to fix it. Then, not long after that, he looked at his entourage and didn't like what he saw.

On the golf course "Fluff" Cowen, his shaggy-dog caddie, barked a little too loudly at fans. Hughes Norton, his man at the sports management company IMG, committed Woods to events and tournaments that the player himself would have avoided. And then there was Earl Woods, the devoted dad, who couldn't stop himself when it came to his gifted son. Tiger, said Earl, would be this generation's Gandhi; he would have more influence than any other human being in history.

Tiger, the guy who played the shots, realised he was no longer calling them. He had decisions to make and when Fluff was sacked the writer Frank Deford wrote it was "like shooting

Lassie". Woods suggested to IMG that Norton be taken off his case and that was it. Norton was history. Then there was Earl: "I asked him, 'Do you want me to be around more?'" recalled Woods senior. "I hadn't been going to too many tournaments. I wanted to know if he needed me at them. And he said, 'I'll be alright, Pop.' Those words hit me. He was saying, 'I'm grown up.' He was declaring his freedom."

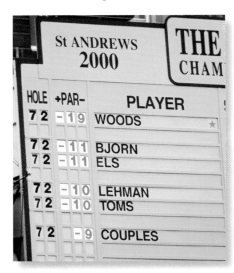

A class apart: Woods's dominance writ large on the St Andrews leaderboard

The young man grows. With so much desire, Woods had often struggled to control his emotions on the golf course. But what was the benefit of growing older if not an increase in wisdom? His fist-pumping lost little of its passion but it became a more personal, less public gesture. On Sundays, he changed his shirt from blood-red to an almost understated burgundy. These changes were made seamlessly, without fanfare. But they demonstrated Woods's desire to remain in control. So he spent an extra two hours on the putting green at Pebble Beach on the day before the 100th US Open began.

Practice made for a game almost perfect as Woods shot 65 in his first round, with just 24 putts. On the ropes after only 18 holes, the opposition was knocked out at the end of round three, with Woods 10 shots clear. The difficulty for Ernie Els, Miguel Angel Jimenez, Thomas Bjorn and the other competitors was they could not simply fold their tents and get the hell out of the Monterrey Peninsula. On Sunday they were at once in front of him and in his wake, at once in pursuit of him and

imprisoned by him. An enormous television audience watched Sunday's conclusion but then armchair spectators do like a coronation. Woods strolled to his first US Open title and left us with the impression that all he had to do was turn up at St Andrews and collect for the first time the claret jug. Preposterous as the impression was, it turned out that way. Always in control of the Open, he won by eight shots. The master of Pebble Beach, the master of St Andrews and, in both tournaments, the master of suspense. Not in the Hitchcock sense, but in the way he drained the hope from his rivals. The dead men walking the fairways on both Sundays should have been the opposition.

Numbed by this unprecedented mastery, we could hardly remember one shot from Pebble Beach or St Andrews. Rather, there are details that remain because they convey a sense of the total performance: over four days at the US Open, Woods did not once three-putt. At the Open, he did not once find a bunker. On the Sunday evening, Woods said it was down to luck and as the jaded nods expressed disbelief, he listed the five shots that were the lucky ones. Like the schoolchildren and their master in Oliver Goldsmith's Deserted Village we marvelled "that one small head could contain all he knew".

The dead men walking the fairways on both Sundays should have been the opposition

Such was the distance between Woods and his rivals, it was hard to imagine him ever again in a battle. Four weeks later, in the US PGA Championship at Valhalla, Woods and an unsung member of the Tour, Bob May, fought out the mother of all battles. On Sunday afternoon Woods played the final 12 holes in seven under par. And that simply to get him into a play-off with May.

The turning point came on the 15th green; May, leading by one, had a six-

footer for birdie. Woods had 15-footer to save par. This was the putt to stay in the tournament, and Woods stalked it as if he had waited all of his life for the opportunity. He made the putt and the hole shrunk for May, who missed. Another nerveless putt on the 18th helped, and a birdie on the first of the three play-off holes clinched it, but Woods won an extraordinary contest with that putt on the 15th.

But frozen in the glare of Woods's greatness, even the masters of yesterday forget themselves

"Someday I'll tell my grandkids I played in the same tournament as Tiger Woods," Tom Watson said at Valhalla. No, Tom. Tell them first about that even greater head-to-head when you beat Nicklaus at Turnberry for the Open in 1977. But frozen in the glare of Woods's greatness, even the masters of yesterday forget themselves. When it came to the Masters and Woods's shot at a fourth consecutive Major, it was expected he would go down to Georgia and roll over all those guys. But you saw him arrive at the clubhouse around noon on the Sunday, leader by one shot but with a tournament on his mind, and you thought again.

Driven to within 10 paces of the locker-room door, he politely refused the kids who waited for autographs, bid good day to old Bill Thibideau, who stood sentry at the door, and breezed inside. At the the putting green, his eyes avoided contact with those between him and his destination. He spent 25 minutes putting, then 55 minutes on the range. With Harmon, he envisaged the shots he would have to hit in that final round and practised them. Then, back to the putting green where he had one last rehearsal with the most important club in his bag. From there out past the clubhouse, by the sprawling and twisted oak tree on the lawn where Kultida, his mum, sat and wished him well as he passed.

After his birdie on the 18th hole at Augusta, Woods retreated to a quiet corner of the green to consider his achievement

Zoned in, he didn't turn his head, didn't seem to hear and from that point to his triumphal walk onto the 18th green, he would make eye contact only with his caddie.

Such focus could be deemed unnatural, even robotic. Or it could be that it reflected Woods's sense of what it would take for one human being to win his fourth consecutive golf Major. That understanding was as important to his unique accomplishment as his gift for the game.

So momentous was Woods's achievement that a number of his fellow professionals were not content to watch the last shots from the clubhouse. Rather, they stood around the 18th green, faces in the crowd, clapping like everybody else. Elite sportsmen are not easily reduced to fans. "We knew we were watching something that would never happen again in golf," said Woods's fellow professional, Rocco Mediate. "That is, unless he decides to do it again."

The Ultimate Olympian

Steve Redgrave's achievement in winning gold medals at five successive Olympics was monumental for many reasons. During the long and torturous build-up to Sydney, Redgrave had come close to abandoning his dream, but courage and resilience carried him all the way to unforgettable glory

NICK PITT

The moment of truth for Steve Redgrave came shortly after nine o'clock on a calm bright morning on Penrith Lakes in the shadow of the Blue Mountains west of Sydney.

Olympic gold medals for rowing, as Redgrave knew better than anyone, are not won in the final, the six minutes of fury that take a craft 2,000m from the start to the finish, but in the four years of toil that precede them. Yet for Redgrave, sitting on the start line in the number two seat of Britain's coxless four, along with Matthew Pinsent, Tim Foster and James Cracknell, was when reality caught up.

For four years, every action and consideration had been tailored to being ready, subordinated to the objective.

Four years for six minutes. He was used to that, for he already had four gold medals from four Olympics. But this time there was a difference. Previously, Redgrave had been protected by confidence bordering on certainty. At Sydney, he did not know he was going to win. There were question marks, and they were all about him.

"By Christmas I had to train alone and felt very isolated"

"Those two minutes, when we're waiting on the start line, will be, bar none, the longest two minutes of a lifetime," Redgrave had said on his arrival in Sydney. "It's the worst sort of slow-motion hell. I'll still see and hear. I'll know where I am. People will think I'm in a trance but I'll still know what's going on. You're in a boat, in your element and in control, but I know exactly at what point I'll wish someone would shoot me, as I begged after the Atlanta Games – between 500m and 700m. The bad news is that it's a race over 2,000m."

As if training to compete in a fifth Olympics as a 38-year-old had not been sufficiently Herculean a trial, Redgrave had been given a further handicap, the late onset of diabetes. At first, he seemed to be able to cope by changing his diet and taking relatively small doses of insulin, but gradually his performances in training deteriorated until he was brought to despair.

"At Christmas in 1997, I was in a very bad way," Redgrave said. "In fact I was pretty close to jacking it all in. I was training hard but not performing. I know how hard it is to be at the top and I didn't know if I could get back to it. The other guys in the four were way ahead of me and by Christmas I had to train alone and felt very isolated. I went awol for two weeks, which is something I've never done before. I just went off skiing, going pretty mad down the black runs."

Redgrave went back to his pre-diabetes diet and took larger doses of insulin. His training performances improved, but he was worryingly erratic. Sometimes, when racing on a bicycle as a variation in training, he would trail in 10 minutes after the others. His times over 2,000m and 5,000m on the static rowing machine,

Pain brings gain. The British coxless four in action during their first heat in Sydney

which is the most accurate method of measuring power output and stamina, were some way from his historic best. In domestic trials, which were rowed in pairs, Redgrave and Matthew Pinsent, who had been all but invincible for a decade, were beaten. And since Pinsent was without question the best athlete in the British squad, it seemed that Redgrave had become a weak link.

Most worrying of all, on the threshold of the Olympics, the British coxless four, who had won three consecutive world championships, were beaten in the last international regatta before the Sydney Games. At Lucerne, the four were narrowly defeated in their semi-final and humiliatingly left trailing in fourth place in the final, six seconds off the pace.

"There have been times when I thought I wouldn't be here," Redgrave said in Sydney. "I prided myself on consistency over the years and what worried me over the past three years was that the consistency wasn't there. That has been very difficult to cope with mentally. At times I've gone and had meetings with Jurgen, shaken my head and said, 'I'm giving this up, I'm not going to make it,' but he would always come up with some words that would keep me going for another few days, another week."

Uncertainty and vulnerability were unfamiliar companions for Redgrave as he waited for the starter's signal in the Olympic final, but there were substantial comforts on the other side of the ledger. Physically, he could still produce the goods when it mattered most — at the very start, and the finish. It was an extraordinary tribute to his ability that in one training exercise, 12 strokes flat out, he remained the best in the squad. Mentally, his competitive fires burned as strongly as ever, even more strongly after defeat in Lucerne. And he also knew that in just over six minutes time, he would never have to race again. Once more, only once, with everything committed.

If anything marked out Redgrave, even in the company of champions, it was commitment. Born in 1962, the son of a builder, he attended Marlow Comprehensive School, leaving at 16 with one GCSE, in woodwork. He was later diagnosed as dyslexic. At first, it was his physiology that marked him as a potential champion. He grew to 6ft 4in and 16st 7lb, and possessed

Fabulous fifth: Redgrave with the spoils of victory. "I'll remember it for the rest of my life," he said

Physically, he could still produce the goods when it mattered most – at the very start, and the finish

exceptional heart and lung capacity. With long levers and a big engine, he was built for rowing.

He was stubborn, too, with a monumental, almost incomprehensible will to win and willingness to work to win in a particularly torturous sport, suited to obsessives. One might imagine that superfit athletes feel on top of the world, but here is Redgrave describing the effects of the training regime he followed for 49 weeks a year for two decades: "I go round feeling knackered all the time. I have no energy and I'm fighting the margins of being ill and not being ill. I go to dinners and fall asleep. I'm pushing back the boundaries all the time, and training so hard takes a toll on the body. If you feel fit and strong then there's something wrong. You're not training hard enough."

And if training is pain upon pain, as dull and deadening as a long prison sentence, racing is a concentrated, exquisite form of self-punishment. Long before halfway on a 2,000m course, lungs and legs scream for mercy; but the brain must deny and ignore them, for each stroke, although wrenched with furious effort, has to be sweet and in harmony.

Anyone who wins an Olympic gold medal in rowing, therefore, has challenged the accepted bounds of nature, mental and physical. By winning four and attempting five, Redgrave had stretched achievement into a personal, unknown realm.

The race itself, which produced such tension among the thousands of onlookers and millions of viewers (in Britain 7.5m stayed up into the small hours to witness it), was for Redgrave relatively straightforward. "We moved into a comfortable lead after 200m, and at that point I knew we would win," he said.

If so, he was almost alone, for despite their wonderful start, the British boat was forced to fight off a series of challenges down the course, first with determination, later with mounting desperation. Most tena-cious among the challengers were the Italians and the Australians. Both crews had beaten the British boat in Lucerne two months earlier. "We are very desperate when it counts," said Bo Hanson, the Australian stroke. "We threw 100% at it."

The Italians, who won in Lucerne, were not surprised by Britain's explosive start. "We knew it would happen and we reckoned they would pay for it," said Carlo Mornati. By 1500m, it appeared that the British four were on cruise control with almost a full-second advantage. As planned, Redgrave, who controlled race strategy, called for a push. It came, but the Italians pushed harder, closing significantly. Redgrave had planned to wait for the 200-metre mark before calling for the final push, but he saw the danger and called early.

"In the water," was Redgrave's call, meaning that whatever power was left to the four must be "attached" to the water through the blade and not wasted.

Every last reserve of strength and will-to-win was required from every member of the British boat, not to go faster, but, even more difficult, to maintain speed as their bodies screamed. "It got very painful and gutsy," said Pinsent. "When you dig deep after going flat out for five

All over now: Pinsent, left, leads the celebrations as Redgrave feels agony and ecstasy. "Steve's the ultimate Olympian," the younger man said

minutes, it's going to hurt. Hurt in the legs, the arms, the lungs."

Cracknell, in the bow seat, could see the danger. The Italians were closing stroke by stroke. "You're not supposed to look around when you sprint to the line, but I like to know what's going on," Cracknell said. "We had to give a lot."

Foster, sitting behind Pinsent, was an experienced, world-class oarsman, yet he had not anticipated quite what he would have to give in the last 500m. "They told me if we won, it wouldn't hurt," he said. "They lied."

Fatigue at the finish was too intense for any immediate celebration

Thousands of British supporters were in the stands and the chorus of gasps and exhortations on all sides was replaced by a great cheer as the four held off Italy and Australia to cross the line ahead. Another 50m, or, one might say, another year on Redgrave's 38-year-old life, and it might have been defeat.

The British four won in 5min 56.24sec, which gave them a margin of just 0.38sec over Italy, with Australia a further second in arrears. The split times told the story: the British four were easily fastest over the first 500m, but only fourth fastest over the final 500m. But as Grobler remarked, "it was enough".

Fatigue at the finish was too intense for any immediate celebration, although Pinsent managed to hold his arms aloft. All four had pulled for their lives. For a moment, Redgrave seemed in some distress. None of them could speak. At length, Pinsent, aware of the achievement of his partner in racing and training for a decade, clambered down the boat to embrace Redgrave. The incalculable debt each owed to the other was shown to the world. And then, as an antidote to sentimentality, Pinsent allowed himself to tumble into the water.

"I know I will remember it for the rest of my life," Redgrave said once he had made dry land. "It has echoes of my first Olympics, 16 years ago. I remember everything from waking up, to rowing through the finish line for my first gold medal. Far from being a blur, it has an extra clarity to it."

Matthew Pinsent, after clambering down the boat, embraces Redgrave in the moment of victory and the world sees the incalculable debt each owed to the other

The celebration of Redgrave's achievement in particular was universal. "Earlier in the week, there was a New Zealander, an old boy, who came up to me and said, 'You're rowing against my son, but I still want you to win,'" Redgrave said. But it was Pinsent who understood better than anyone what Redgrave had done, and who led the tributes to the first athlete of the modern era to win five Olympic gold medals at successive Games. "Steve's the ultimate Olympian," he said.

Some months later, when the next Olympic cycle had begun, without Redgrave, Grobler gave a hint of just how close Redgrave and his crew had come to failure. "Steve had some terrible times leading up to the Games, and sometimes he was in despair. But believe me, what he did in that final was unbelievable. In all his years of rowing, all his honours and achievements, that was his greatest performance."

Wild day at Wimbledon

Three times a beaten finalist at Wimbledon, Goran Ivanisevic looked a busted flush when he was made to sweat on a wild-card entry into the 2001 Championships. But what nobody knew – including the mercurial Croat himself – was that Ivanisevic was mentally ready to play the most inspired tournament of his life.

NICK PITT

When Wimbledon's Order of Play Committee met in a large room adjacent to the referee's office at 2pm on Tuesday June 12 2001 for the business of selecting wild cards, little did they know that they were about to set in train a chain of events that would lead to the most dramatic and unlikely climaxes in the tournament's long history.

The denouement, almost a month later, was a Monday final in front of a wildly passionate crowd, in which Goran Ivanisevic, who had started as a 125-1 outsider with dreadful form and an injured shoulder, took the title and climbed into the stands for a tearful embrace with his father (who seconds before had thought he was about to suffer a heart attack as his son squandered a second match point against Pat Rafter with a second double fault). Three years after losing his third Wimbledon singles final, after which he said he wanted to die – three years in which he sank ever lower – Ivanisevic, the first ever wild-card champion, was declaring that he didn't care if he never won another tennis match in his life.

Wimbledon's greatest story began with sober detachment. Mike Hann, the chairman of the seven-strong Order of Play Committee, asked Alan Mills, the tournament referee, to tell the meeting which "interesting" overseas players had applied for a wild card. The first name mentioned was Goran Ivanisevic.

"Goran's career was on the way down," Hann recalled, summarising

the debate that followed. "He was not given a wild card at the Australian Open and he hadn't played the French Open. But we were well aware that he had played in three Wimbledon finals. He has always been popular with our public, and he has never complained about anything here. Last year, he attended the champion's parade, which earned him a lot of Brownie points. In fact, not one voice was raised against Goran. He was our first wild-card choice."

While the committee decided his fate, Ivanisevic was in west London, at Queen's Club, waiting to go court to play a first-round match in the Stella

Missile launcher: Ivanisevic serves against Henman in their epic semi-final

Artois tournament, against Cristiano Caratti, a veteran Italian clay-courter with a weak service. Ivanisevic was nervous – not because he hadn't played for a month, nor because he feared the pain of serving with his sore left shoulder, and certainly not because he feared Caratti. He was anxious to know whether his request for a Wimbledon wild card had been successful. Several times, Ivanisevic rang Andy Fyfe, a friend who handles his affairs in Britain, until at last Fyfe could tell him that Alan Mills had

Centre Court eruption: Ivanisevic celebrates victory over Rafter in the final

called to confirm he was in the draw.

Technically, Ivanisevic needed the wild card because his ranking had plummeted to 125th in the world, precluding direct entry, which is reserved for the top 108 players. Emotionally and physically, he also needed a lift. If he had to play the qualifying tournament, there was no guarantee he would make it through. At the Australian Open in January, he had lost in the first round of qualifying – "I tanked it," he admitted.

Hearing that he had a wild card was a mighty relief for Ivanisevic, but it had little immediate effect on his form. He played an awful match, losing easily to

Caratti. "That was a concern," said Hann. "It wouldn't have looked good for us if he'd then lost easily at Wimbledon in the first round."

What nobody knew — and that includes the mercurial, erratic Ivanisevic himself — when the gates opened on the first Monday of the championships, was that although he had lost in the first round in 2000, and although his form and recent record were dire, Ivanisevic was mentally ready to play the best and most consistent tournament of his life.

It was largely a matter of personal liberation, of the merciful kind

sometimes granted to those who sink close to the bottom. "All my life I played for someone else," he explained. In the past, he had played to make his parents proud; to pay for the medical bills when his sister Srjdana fought a three-year battle with leukaemia; to show his patriotic allegiance to Croatia; to raise money for his own children's charity.

"After I lost in the Australian qualifying, I decided I would either stop playing or I would just play for Goran," he said. "Only for Goran."

Actually, it wasn't quite that simple. The day before the championships began, Ivanisevic's father, Srjdan, who had only watched his son play once in 18 months, but who had an inkling that it might be worth watching him at Wimbledon, brought him some Croatian newspapers. One carried a poster-sized photograph of Drazen Petrovic, the Croatian basketball star who

"If someone wants to beat me here, they have to play better. No pressure."

died in a car crash in 1993. Ivanisevic, who was a good friend of Petrovic, attended his funeral shortly before that year's Wimbledon, and intended to dedicate that tournament to his memory, but he lost in the third round.

Eight years later, Ivanisevic cut his friend's portrait from the newspaper and stuck it on the wall. "This must be destiny," he said. "This is it."

For destiny to work, its beneficiary needs more than a little faith in it, and also needs to contribute. Ivanisevic armed himself with a series of superstitious practices. His father (a lucky supporter) could attend Wimbledon despite a worrying heart condition and against doctor's orders, but his mother (unlucky, because she had attended all three finals he lost) could not. He would not shave during the tournament. He would stand up before his opponents at every changeover. He would make sure he didn't step on the lines when walking around the court. He would pick up his bag at the same time each day and listen to the same Croatian songs on his Walkman.

With the assistance of a service-action that delivers tennis balls like a sidewinder missile-launcher, and which clicked into mechanical perfection from the start, despite the pain, it worked. In Round One, Ivanisevic beat Fredrik Jonsson in straight sets. "I just pray every night," Ivanisevic said. "I just try to toss the ball, hit the serve, and not to feel the pain. I'll just go on until my shoulder drops off and I have to stop. Last year, I didn't leave Wimbledon proud. This year, I want to leave here proud of myself. If some-body wants to beat me here, they have to play better. No pressure."

In Round Two, Ivanisevic beat Carlos Moya in four sets. "Today I served 35 aces," he said. "Whoever comes, you know, you just have to consider how I play, not how the other guy is playing."

In Round Three, Ivanisevic served 41 aces as he beat the hot young American Andy Roddick in four sets on Court One, and threw his shirt to the crowd in the ecstacy of victory. "That was a lesson on how to serve and how to play on grass," said the big-hitting Roddick, who often didn't move as Ivanisevic's serves flashed by. "He made my serve look like a schmuck serve."

Ivanisevic had reached the second week of the championships, and he was managing to maintain an unusual state of equanimity, thanks, he revealed, to the presence of a third Goran. To explain his contradictory nature and tumultuous emotions, Ivanisevic used to refer to the two Gorans, his inner and outer selves, and their struggles for supremacy. Now the third Goran, a kind of referee, was at hand if needed.

Serving for the match against Roddick, Ivanisevic froze and almost blew it. "Both Gorans were nervous," he said. "One was rushing and the other was rushing more. Then the third one came and said 'Guys, relax. It's a lovely court, relax. Just calm down.' The third Goran is the brain man, for emergencies. He came on deuce. I calmed down. Two aces, thank you."

Thus, in a flurry of aces and a succession of post-match interviews marked by his engaging sense of humour and his growing sense of destiny, did Ivanisevic prosper. In the fourth round, Greg Rusedski fell in three sets; in the quarter-finals, Marat Safin succumbed in four. "I'm very quiet, very focused," Ivanisevic said. "It's really peace inside me. It's like great story, you know. They gave me wild card, I am in the semis. Who knows what can happen?"

What happened was further assistance, temporal and divine. Despite a forecast of rain in the late afternoon of

Power and the glory: Ivanisevic's service-action clicks into mechanical perfection against Rafter

Ivanisevic's prospects of actually winning the thing had moved from impossible, through amusing and unlikely, to very real

men's semi-finals day, the Order of Play Committee scheduled Ivanisevic's match against the Great British Hope, Tim Henman, as second on court after Pat Rafter versus Andre Agassi, a match which predictably went to five sets.

That decision effectively undermined Henman's cause. When play was halted on the Friday evening, Henman, who Ivanisevic said had begun "to play like God", led by two sets to one and two games to one.

If that interruption was hard on Henman, worse was to come. When the fourth set was resumed on the Saturday, another rainy day, Ivanisevic played like a novice. His returns were going everywhere but in; his volleys were dumped in the bottom of the net. For that set, Ivanisevic was a player with one shot, but that shot was the serve, the deadly weapon that exemplified the lottery that grass-court tennis can be. Henman, superior throughout the set, lost it in the tie-break. Along with the set went Henman's conviction, and ultimately the match.

Ivanisevic's prospects of actually winning the thing had moved from impossible, through amusing and unlikely, to very real. With the exit of Henman, as well as the defeat of Agassi, who was unfortunate to lose to Rafter, they had achieved a strange inevitability. It really was Goran's year. "Now I'm in the final," he said. "If somebody told me that two months ago, I would tell him, 'Man, you're crazy, you're not normal.'"

Naturally, it was no ordinary final. It was played a day late, on Monday, and not in front of the usual Centre Court crowd. Ten thousand fans, many of them Australian and many Croatian, either by birth or temporary allegiance, had queued through the early hours to pay £40 each on a first-come-first-serve, cash-only basis.

Sweet victory: the Champion's finest hour

After three hours of thumping serves and swings of fortune, each cheered with good-humoured abandon, it came down to this: Ivanisevic, having broken Rafter's service to lead 8-7 in the fifth and final set, had to serve for the match. At 40-30, match point, Ivanisevic served a double fault, the second serve two yards long. A second match point followed, and another double fault.

For Ivanisevic's father, it was almost too much, almost heart-stopping. He had first felt a pain in his chest, and then his back, after the Safin match. He put a pill under his tongue and lay down until the pain passed. "Then after the second match point in the final, I feel pain in the chest again," Srdjan Ivanisevic said. "You can imagine what I was going through. So I took another pill and was okay although Niki Pilic, sitting next to me, said afterwards he was sure I was going to die."

He survived to see Rafter save a third match point with a fine lob, and for his son to finally fulfil his life's ambition with a second serve that Rafter put into the net. Ivanisevic, who had so frequently looked to the heavens for help, fell to the ground.

"I don't even care now, you know, if I ever win a match in my life again," Ivanisevic said. "If I don't want to play, I don't play again. This is it. This is the end of the world. My dreams came true. Whatever I do in my life, I am always going to be Wimbledon Champion."

PICTURE CREDITS

The following abbreviations have been used: (t) top; (b) bottom; (r) right; (l) left.

pp. 1-2 Action Images; p. 7 Associated Press; p. 8 Allsport; p. 9 (l) Hulton Getty, (r) Allsport; p. 10 Hulton Getty; p. 11 (l) Allsport, (r) Popperfoto; p. 12 (t) Hulton Getty, (b) Popperfoto; p. 13 Popperfoto; p. 14 (t) Alpha/Sports General, (b) Sportsphoto/Stewart Kendal; p. 15 Hulton Getty; p. 16 (t) Popperfoto, (b) Colorsport; p. 17 Hulton Getty; p. 18 (t) Empics, (b) PA; p. 19 (t) Graphic Photo Union, (b) Alpha/Sports General; p. 20 (t) Hulton Getty, (b) Allsport; p. 21 (t) & (b) Allsport; p. 22 (t) Alpha/Sports General, (b) Camera Press; p. 23 PA; pp. 24-7 Allsport; pp. 28-31 Corbis; p. 32 (t) Hulton Getty, (b) Corbis; pp. 33-4 Hulton Getty; p. 35 Associated press; pp. 36-9 Corbis; p. 40 Roger Mann; pp. 40-1 Allsport; pp. 42-3 Roger Mann; p. 44 (t) & (b) Fox Photos; p. 45 Associated Press; pp. 46-7 Allsport; p. 48 (t) & (br) Hulton Getty; p. 49 Popperfoto; p. 50 Times Newspapers; p. 51 Hulton Getty; p. 52 (t) PA, (r) Hulton Getty; p. 53 Popperfoto; p. 54 Times; p. 55 Topham; p. 56 (t) Corbis, (b) Corbis; pp. 56-7 Corbis; p. 58 Corbis; p. 59 Corbis; p. 60 Hulton Getty; pp. 60-3 Hulton Getty; p. 64 -7 Popperfoto; p. 68 Hulton Getty; p. 69 Popperfoto; p. 70 Hulton Getty; pp. 71-4 Popperfoto; p. 75 Times Newspapers; p. 76-8 Alpha/Sports General; p. 79 Allsport; p. 80 Topham; pp. 80-3 Popperfoto; p. 84 Alpha/Sports General; pp 84-5 The Age, Melbourne; p. 86 Alpha/Sports General; p. 87 Hulton Getty/ Central Press; p. 88 (l) Associated Press, (r) Katz/Time; pp. 89-90 (t) Associated Press; pp.90 (r)-91 Hulton Getty; p. 92 PA; p. 93 Topham; p. 94 (l) & (r) PA; p. 95 Popperfoto; p. 96 PA; p. 97 Popperfoto; p. 98 PA; p. 99 Associated Press; p. 100 (t) Allsport, (b) Topham; p. 101 Sunday Times; p. 102-3 Topham; p. 104 Hulton Getty; p. 105 Topham; p. 106 Apex Picture Agency; p. 107 Hulton Getty; pp. 108-9 Hulton Getty/ Central Press; p. 110 Universal Pictorial Press; pp. 111-4 Times Newspaper; p. 116 Associated Press; p. 117 Allsport; pp. 118-9 Associated Press; p. 120 (t) Andrew Varley, (b) Popperfoto; pp. 121-3 Andrew Varley; p. 124 (t) Southland Times, Invercargill, (b) Peter Bush/Visual Impact; pp. 124-5 Peter Bush/Visual Impact; p. 126 Southland Times, Invercargill; p. 127 Peter Bush; pp. 128-9 Associated Press; pp. 130-1 Sports Illustrates/Colorific; p. 131 Michael Brennan; p. 132 Mike Brett; p. 133 Times Newspaper; p. 134 Mike Brett; p. 135 Alpha/Sports General; p. 136 (t) Alpha/Sports General, (b) Popperfoto; p. 137 Popperfoto; p. 138 Hulton Getty; p. 139 Alpha/Sports General; p. 140 Associated Press; pp. 140-1 Sports Illustrates/Colorific; p. 142-6 Associated Press; p. 147 Chris Bott; p. 148 (t) Sports Illustrates/ Colorific, (b) Allsport; p. 149 Sports Illustrates/Colorific; p. 150 Orange County Register; p. 151 Sports Illustrates/Colorific; p. 152 (t) Michael Cole, (r) Allsport; p. 153 Allsport; p. 154-5 Michael Cole; pp. 156-8 Allsport; p. 159 Michael Cole; p. 160 (t) Patrick Eagar, (b) Sporting Pictures; p. 161 Patrick Eagar; p. 162 Times Newspaper; p. 163 Patrick Eagar; pp. 164-7 Picthall Picture Library; p. 168 Daily Mail; p. 169 Trevor Smith; p. 170 Daily Mail; p. 171 Trevor Smith; p. (t) & (r) 172 Phil Sheldon; p. 173 Associated Press; pp. 174-5 Phil Sheldon; pp. 176-8 Popperfoto; p. 179 Allsport; p. 180 (t) Allsport, (b) Times Newspaper; pp. 181-2 Allsport; p. 183 Can Press; p. 184 Allsport; pp. 184-5 Colorsport; p. 186 Allsport; pp. 187-91 Colorsport; p. 192 (t) Allsport, (b) George Selwyn; pp. 193-4 Trevor Jones; p. 195 Allsport; pp. 196-9 Graham Morris; p. 200 (t) & (b) Empics; pp. 201-2 Allport; p. 203 Today; pp. 204-207 Hugh Routledge; p. 208 (t) Popperfoto/Reuters, (b) Times; p. 209-10 Action Images; pp. 211 (t) Popperfoto/Reuters, (b) Allsport; pp. 212-214 Empics; p. 215 Allsport; pp. 216-23 Empics

Front cover: Empics (Roger Bannister, Goran Ivanisevic, Tiger Woods, Steve Redgrave), Reuters (Teddy Sheringham), AP (Muhammad Ali)

Back cover: Empics (1966 World Cup, Francois Pienaar), Allsport (Pietro Dorandi)

Ancient
MYTHS,
LEGENDS, and
SUPERHEROES

Dr Steve Kershaw

OXFORD
UNIVERSITY PRESS

Great Clarendon Street, Oxford OX2 6DP

Oxford is a registered trade mark of
Oxford University Press in the UK and in certain other countries

© Oxford University Press 2023
Text written by Dr Steve Kershaw
Illustrated by Geraldine Sy and Ana Seixas

Designed and edited by Raspberry Books Ltd

The moral rights of the author and artist have been asserted
Database right Oxford University Press (maker)

First published 2023

All rights reserved.

British Library Cataloguing in Publication Data:

ISBN 978-0-19-278289-2

1 3 5 7 9 10 8 6 4 2

Printed in China

Paper used in the production of this book is a natural,
recyclable product made from wood grown in sustainable forests.
The manufacturing process conforms to the environmental regulations
of the country of origin.

Acknowledgements

The publisher and authors would like to
thank the following for permission to use
photographs and other copyright material:

Cover artwork: Geraldine Sy and **Ana Seixas**:
Photos: Pavlo S/Shutterstock; Aleksandr
Bryliaev/Shutterstock and author. **Inside
artwork:** p1: Pavlo S/Shutterstock; p14:
MMCez/Shutterstock; pp28-29: notsuperstar/
Shutterstock; p42: Pino Tage/Shutterstock;
p52: Audrey Snider-Bell/Shutterstock; p60:
Eric Isselee/Shutterstock; pp60-61: Roman
Marusew/Shutterstock; p61: Sveta Aho/
Shutterstock; p68: Mila_ls/Shutterstock;
pp70-71: Hoika Mikhail/Shutterstock;

p74(l): Drakuliren/Shutterstock; p74(r):
Plateresca/Shutterstock; pp78-79: bluehand/
Shutterstock; Jingjing Yan/Shutterstock;
42pixels/Shutterstock; pp82-83: Paolo Gallo/
Shutterstock.

Artwork by **Geraldine Sy**, **Ana Seixas**,
Ekaterina Gorelova, Adam Quest, Aaron
Cushley, and Raspberry Books.

Every effort has been made to contact
copyright holders of material reproduced
in this book. Any omissions will be rectified
in subsequent printings if notice is given to
the publisher.

Images are to be used only within the context of the pages in this book

Contents

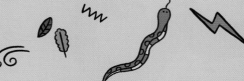

Chapter 1

Myths and Legends Matter

People have been telling myths and legends featuring superhero superstars for thousands of years, and we are still reading them today.

Myths and legends are **fantastic** stories with **wondrous characters,** but there's much more to them than that. Humans tell myths because they help to make sense of what the world is like, how it works, where people came from, and why they live and think the way they do.

The stories are also full of **messages** which give us lots of important things to think about, although they don't always give us obvious answers. In the world of myths and legends even gods and heroes can behave badly, and people who make good choices don't always live happily ever after. With myths and legends, we need to **think for ourselves!**

Speak like a mythologist

MYTHOLOGIST

A mythologist is a person who studies legends, myths, and mythology. 'Mythology' can mean a collection of stories, as in 'tales from African mythology', or the study of those stories.

MYTH AND LEGEND

'Myth' comes from a Greek word, *mythos*. It means a story, or something you say. 'Legend' comes from the Latin *legenda*, 'things to be read'. Myths can be hard to define, but most people agree that they are shared narratives which help to give a community a sense of identity, and create meaningful ways of understanding the world. Myths are very important to the members of the society they belong to, and they most often deal with subjects that relate to the **divine**, or the sacred.

Myths change all the time

Very often there are **several versions of the same story** told for different reasons by different people in different places at different times. A lot of tales were originally **passed around by word of mouth,** so they were always being retold and reworked. Once they were written down, they were preserved for generations to come, but even then people still told them in new ways. While a little book like this can't tell you about every version of every myth or legend, in this *Very Short Introduction to Myths, Legends, and Superheroes*, you will be introduced to some of the best known and most interesting ones.

The names of mythical characters come from many cultures and languages. This means there are many ways of spelling them. The Greek Akhilleus is known as Achilles in English, and some of the Greek gods and heroes are given Roman names too. Artemis is known as Diana, Zeus as Jupiter or Jove, and Odysseus as Ulysses.

In this book, you'll discover why these **incredible stories** have stood the test of time and are still told all over the world.

Find out about . . .

how a **spider** gained all the **wisdom** in the world

wolves that swallow the sun and moon

how to **travel through the mist** in a magical south-pointing chariot

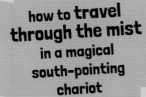

the Lord and Lady of Death who **drank pus porridge** from skulls

how the world began, and how it will end

Read on, and be swept away by some of the **oldest, strangest,** and **most important** stories ever told.

7

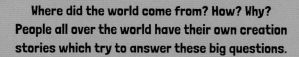

Chapter 2

How the World Began

Where did the world come from? How? Why? People all over the world have their own creation stories which try to answer these big questions.

Everything comes from nothing

Ancient Egyptians had many different creation myths and here is one of them. The creation god **Atum**, known as 'The All' emerged from Nun, which is the 'Ocean of Non-being.' He then sneezed out Shu, representing air, and spat out Tefnut, representing moisture. Atum made his right eye the sun and put it on his brow in the form of a cobra so that he could rule the world for ever. He made the waters recede, so that he had an island to stand on. Shu and Tefnut then had two children, Geb and Nut. To create room for life between earth and sky, Shu trod on Geb (god of dry earth) with his feet and pushed up Nut (god of moist sky) with his hands.

In the Jewish and Christian traditions, everything was dark until **Elohim**, also known as the Christian God, 'the Supreme One', said: **'let there be light'.**

Then He made heaven, gathered the seas together, and made dry land appear. After plants and trees began to grow, He created the **sun, moon, and stars**. Finally, He populated the world with birds, sea monsters, fish, all kinds of land animals, and a man and a woman. This took Him six days, and He rested on the seventh.

Atum, ancient Egyptian creation god

The **Islamic** tradition, recorded in the Qur'an and the sayings of the Prophet Mohammed known as the Hadith, follows a similar pattern. **Allah** said, **'Be',** and created the world so that He might be known. It took Allah just **six days** to create the dark and the light, the heavens and the earth, the astral bodies, animals, a man and a woman. He also created **Hell** for those who choose to reject Him as their God rather than accept him.

Many people believe these creation stories today. They give their god a capital letter when they use His pronoun, as a sign of respect.

Everything comes from chaos

In a poem called the *Theogony*, the ancient Greek poet Hesiod says that everything started with **Chaos**, which is the name of a god, but also describes a gaping, empty mess.

Then **Gaea**, goddess of the earth, emerged out of Chaos, along with the gloomy underground region of Tartarus and the love-god Eros.

Gaea

HEROES OF MYTH AND LEGEND

GAEA

(also known as Gaia or Ge)
The great mother goddess in
ancient Greek mythology. She was
parent of all living things, and
granted humans children
and fertile land.

Nyx, goddess of Night, and Erebus, god of darkness,
were then born from Chaos, and in their turn gave
birth to Day and Bright Air. Next, Gaea created her
partner Ouranos (Sky), the hills, and the sea-god
Pontus, before giving birth to twelve more children.
One of them, Cronus, badly wounded Ouranos using
a mighty sickle, married his sister, Rhea, and became
king of the gods. The sun, moon, stars, rivers, and
winds all now appeared.

Because of a prophecy that Cronus would be
dethroned by his own son, **he swallowed all his
children at birth,** but when Rhea gave birth to
Zeus, she disguised a stone as a baby and gave that
to Cronus to swallow instead. So, Zeus grew up,
overthrew his father and became king of the gods.

☀ Speak like a mythologist ☀

EPIC POEM

A poem about the exploits of legendary heroic characters. Many epic poems were originally passed down by word of mouth from generation to generation. They were memorized and recited by poets and singers, and they were eventually written down.

Everything comes from a dismembered body

One of the world's oldest creation stories is told in the Babylonian **epic** poem *Enuma Elish.* The poem, which was written in Ninevah, Iraq, in the language of Akkadian, is still preserved in clay tablets today.

In a time when even the sky and the earth had no names Apsu, god of Sweet Water, and Tiamat, goddess of Salt Water, **mingled their waters** and created the first gods. These new gods were so noisy that Apsu plotted to destroy them, but the wisest god, Ea, killed Apsu first.

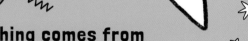
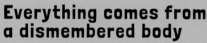

Tiamat wanted revenge. She created dragons, a horned serpent, a rabid dog, a scorpion-man, and other demons. The gods were terrified, but Ea's son Marduk fought back, killed Tiamat, and created the world **by slicing Tiamat's body in two**. One half of her made the heavens, the other made the earth. Marduk used Tiamat's eyes to make the Tigris and Euphrates rivers, and created the city of **Babylon** to be the home of the gods. Human beings were created from the blood of Tiamat's lover Qingu, so that the gods could have servants.

Tiamat

Marduk

Earth-diving and cosmic eggs

Right across the world there are tales of how a creator sent an **'earth-diver'** into the primal waters to bring up little bits of mud and sand, which gradually formed dry land. In the oral tradition of the Ainu people of Japan, one variant of the creation story says that the earth-diver was a type of bird called a water wagtail.

It used its wings to splash the waters and reveal little patches of ground, which it packed down using its feet and tail to form the islands where the Ainu live.

a water wagtail

In other creation stories, everything emerged from a cosmic egg. A story from Tahiti tells of a massive egg-shaped shell floating in nothingness at the dawn of time. The feathered god Ta'aroa lived inside the egg until he decided to crack it open and create life.

He pushed up half of the broken shell to form the **heavens** and used the bottom half to make the **earth**.

Then Ta'aroa made soil from his own skin, clouds from his insides, oceans, lakes, and rivers from his tears, mountain ranges from his bones, trees from his feathers, sea creatures from his guts, and the colours of the sky and rainbows from his blood. Finally, he created children who hung the sun, moon, and stars in the sky, and helped to make more plants and animals. Ta'aroa then made the first people.

Ta'aroa

These creation stories are **how people from various cultures explained how the world** began. In the next chapter we can explore some intriguing tales that tell us how the gods made human beings.

Chapter 3

Where Did Human Beings Come From?

How were we made? Did human beings evolve?
Were we created? Who or what created us?
Across the world there are extraordinary stories
which give mythical answers to the origin of life.

Askr and Embla

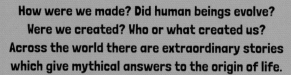

A lot of what we know about **Norse** mythology comes
from the **Poetic Edda** and the **Prose Edda.** In the *Prose
Edda*, the god Odin was strolling along the beach with
his brothers Vili and Ve. They found two pieces of
driftwood and shaped a man and woman from them.
They named the woman **Embla** ('Elm' or 'Vine') and
the man **Askr** ('Ash Tree'). Askr and Embla were given
Midgard ('Middle World') at the base of a mighty ash
tree called Yggdrasil, which grew right in the middle of
the cosmos and held the eight Norse worlds together.
There Embla gave birth to the first humans. The gods
then **created their own world of Asgard** in the
sky and joined it to Midgard with a fiery Rainbow Bridge

called **Bifrost,** which humans often see, but only the gods could cross.

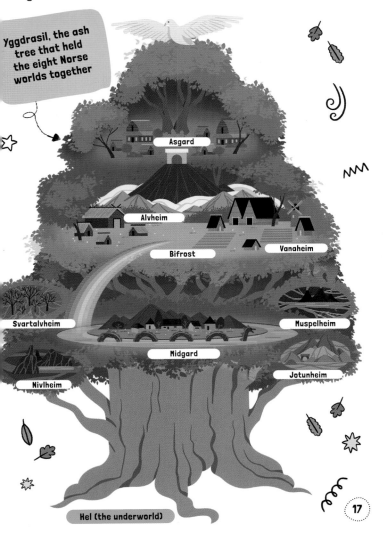

Yggdrasil, the ash tree that held the eight Norse worlds together

Asgard

Alvheim

Bifrost

Vanaheim

Svartalvheim

Muspelheim

Midgard

Nivlheim

Jotunheim

Hel (the underworld)

The Popol Vuh story of the K'iche' Maya

The *Popol Vuh* (meaning 'Book of Advice') of the **K'iche' Maya** people from Guatemala was handed down by word of mouth until it was written down in around **1550 CE.** It told how the gods wanted to be remembered, but the animals couldn't say their names. So, **Tz'aqol** and **B'itol**, along with **Xmucane** and **Xpiyacoc,** created a human out of soil from the earth. Unfortunately, it went all mushy and dissolved when it got wet.

The gods made a second version out of wood. These creatures looked and talked like humans, but they had no blood, no sweat, and no souls, and did not remember their creators. Then, the god **Huracan** sent down a Great Flood, and the wooden people were attacked by Chisellers of Faces, Death Knives, jaguars, dogs, cooking pots, and tortilla grinders.

The gods succeeded on their third attempt. They discovered maize, and created four humans from that. These people had wisdom and understanding, could see through mountains and seas, and respected the gods. But the humans were **too godlike,** so the gods tweaked them, making sure they couldn't become divine. The gods gave the people partners, and the people's hearts were filled with joy. They had children, planted crops, and praised the gods.

Speak like a mythologist

PATRIARCHY

Most ancient societies were patriarchies. This means men had the power. In many creation stories the men were made first, and then the women, to be their companions and helpers. The men didn't want to share their power, so they often invented myths in which women caused trouble for everyone, whether accidentally or on purpose. As you read the stories in this book, think about how they reflect these patriarchal societies and their beliefs.

This illustration is similar to the ones of Tz'aqol and B'ital in the *Popol Vuh.*

Adam and Eve

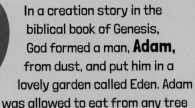

In a creation story in the biblical book of Genesis, God formed a man, **Adam,** from dust, and put him in a lovely garden called Eden. Adam was allowed to eat from any tree except the Tree of the Knowledge of Good and Evil. God used one of Adam's ribs to make a woman, **Eve.**

Unfortunately, there was a **crafty serpent** in the garden who told Eve that if she ate the forbidden fruit, she would gain knowledge of good and evil. Eve wanted to gain wisdom, so she **ate some fruit,** and gave some to Adam. They instantly realized they were naked, covered themselves up with fig leaves, and tried to hide from God. God told the couple that their lives would now be full of hard work and pain, and banished them from the Garden of Eden.

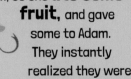

Eve means 'living' because she would become the mother of all living people.

Abuk and Garang

The Dinka people of South Sudan tell of **Abuk,** the first woman, and **Garang,** the first man. The Creator god Nhialic moulded them out of clay and put them in a large pot where they grew into human beings.

Nhialic gave them one seed of grain a day to eat, but they were hungry, so Abuk decided to eat one grain on alternate days, plant the other one, and grow her own crops. Nhialac wasn't happy about this. He cut the rope that tied the earth to his heavenly home, and from that moment humans have **had to experience work, sickness, and death.** Despite being the one who upset the Creator, Abuk is still celebrated by the Dinka people.

Pandora

In **Greek mythology,** Prometheus, whose name means 'Foresight', stole fire from Zeus and gave it to men. But Zeus hated being cheated, and ordered the creation of the first woman, Pandora. **Pandora was loved by everyone,** but she was also a cunning liar.

Zeus introduced Pandora to Prometheus's brother Epimetheus ('Hindsight'), along with a gift of a **large jar** that contained all the world's troubles. Epimetheus forgot he'd been told never to accept any gifts from Zeus, and now it was too late: Pandora opened the jar and **the troubles escaped,** leaving only Hope still trapped inside when she **slammed** the lid shut. Is there now no hope, because Hope is shut in the jar? Or do we at least have hope, if nothing else?

Pandora

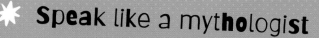

Speak like a mythologist

PANDORA'S BOX

The modern expression 'to open a Pandora's box' means to do something that will cause lots of problems that you haven't thought about. In the original story, Pandora didn't have a box. She had a jar called a *pithos* in Greek, but a sixteenth century CE scholar called Erasmus made a mistake when he was doing a translation, and her container has been called a box ever since.

The world was a much more interesting place with human beings in it. But the gods didn't necessarily love the humans, and the humans would often try to trick the gods as they worked out how to deal with all the challenges that life brought them.

In the next chapter, we will explore the rich stories of some of the **most amazing humans** who lived in this world of myth and legend.

Chapter 4

Superheroes

Today's superheroes, such as Batman, Power Girl, Superman, and Wonder Woman, have extraordinary powers. They are inspired by ancient heroes' miraculous births, magical weapons, and brilliant skills. Superheroes can also be complex characters who show strength and loyalty, and can excite fear, love, and pity.

RHIANNON

Cunning hero Rhiannon features in the *Mabinogion*, a collection of Welsh myths.

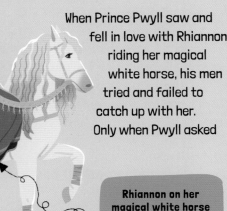

When Prince Pwyll saw and fell in love with Rhiannon riding her magical white horse, his men tried and failed to catch up with her. Only when Pwyll asked

Rhiannon on her magical white horse

her to stop, did she wait for him. Rhiannon declared that she was betrothed to Gwawl but would rather marry Pwyll. The prince was delighted.

But at a grand feast, Gwawl turned up in disguise and tricked Pwyll into giving up Rhiannon. Rhiannon came up with a clever plan. She gave Pwyll a magic bag and told him to arrange another feast in Gwawl's honour. Pwyll disguised himself and asked to fill his bag with food. Gwawl agreed but no matter how much food was put into the bag, it never filled up. Rhiannon encouraged Gwawl to stamp the food down and when he stood in the bag, Pwyll pulled it shut and tied it closed.

Rhiannon instructed Pwyll to release Gwawl from the bag on the condition that he agreed not to seek revenge, and Pwyll and Rhiannon were finally united.

 Speak like a my**tho**lo**gi**st

THE *MABINOGION*

A collection of eleven medieval Welsh tales, full of heroic and supernatural elements, about the legendary past of the British Isles. Based on the spoken tradition of storytelling, they are preserved in written form in the *White Book of Rhydderch* (1300–1325 CE) and the *Red Book of Hergest* (1375–1425 CE).

Mami Wata

Mami Wata ('Mother Water') is an unpredictable figure who can be mysterious, protective, and dangerous all at the same time. The legend originated in Africa and between the 16th and 19th centuries CE and was spread to the Americas by enslaved African people who valued her strength and support. Mami Wata is celebrated today in over 20 African countries, as well as the African **diaspora**.

Mami Wata

Mami Wata is often like a **mermaid**. She has the upper half of a woman and lower half of a fish, and she often carries a snake. She is a nurturing figure who looks after people's physical, spiritual, and mental health, and many who respect her are healers or leaders.

Mami Wata can bring good or bad fortune in the form of money, which can be a blessing or a curse, and her followers are both attracted to and scared by all the hopes, fears, risks, and rewards that she can bring.

Louhi and her daughter

Shape-shifting Louhi was the ruler of the northern land of Pohjola in the Finnish epic poem, the *Kalevala*. The first man, Väinämöinen, set out from Kalevala to marry Louhi's daughter. Louhi would only agree if Väinämöinen got the blacksmith Ilmarinen to make the *sampo*, a mysterious tool that could grind flour, make salt, and create gold out of thin air.

We never learn the name of Louhi's daughter, but she too gave tasks to Väinämöinen, including building a boat from the splinters of a spindle. He failed her tasks but Ilmarinen did forge the *sampo* out of white swan feathers, the milk of virtue, one grain of barley, and the finest lambswool. Ilmarinen gave the *sampo* to Louhi, who hid it under a hill in Pohjola.

Some time later, Väinämöinen sailed to Pohjola to steal the *sampo*. He used the jaw of a massive fish to make the *kantele*, a magic **zither** that sent everyone to sleep while he sailed off with the *sampo*. Louhi woke up, turned into a giant eagle, and swooped after him . . . but as they fought, the *sampo* fell into the sea.

Louhi was furious: she sent nine plagues against the people of Kalevala, but Väinämöinen cured them all. When she sent a bear to **attack** their cattle, Väinämöinen defeated it. Louhi confiscated fire, but Väinämöinen caught a fire-fish and got it back. Then she hid the sun and the moon in iron-banded caves, but Väinämöinen made her put them back in the sky. So the world went back to how it was.

Speak like a mythologist

THE *KALEVALA*

The *Kalevala ('Land of Heroes')* is an epic poem first told orally. It was written down from old Finnish songs and poems by a doctor called Elias Lönnrot in the 19th century CE.

Antigone (*pronounced* An-**ti**-guh-nee)

In Greek mythology it is sometimes necessary to make **impossible** choices. In a tragic play by Sophocles, written in around **441 BCE**, Antigone's brothers, Eteocles and Polynices, had both died fighting each other over who should become king of **Thebes**. Antigone's uncle Creon, now the king, decreed that Polynices' corpse should be left to rot and that anyone trying to bury him should be put to death.

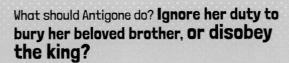

What should Antigone do? **Ignore her duty to bury her beloved brother, or disobey the king?**

She respected the laws of the gods more than the laws of humans, and so gave Polynices the traditional funeral rites. Creon decreed that she should be entombed alive, but then changed his mind. By then, though, Antigone had ended her own life. Creon's son Haemon, who was in love with Antigone, was so distraught he also ended his life. Creon's **heartbroken** wife Eurydice killed herself too, laying terrible curses on the devastated king.

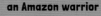

an Amazon warrior

Her story has inspired the English playwright Shakespeare and the French playwright Anouilh to write powerful plays about her.

The Amazons

In Greek and Roman stories the ultimate mythological powerful women were the Amazons, athletic and colourfully dressed warriors. The Amazons were challengers of men and could fight at long-range with their bows and arrows, or at close quarters with their spears and shields. They gave away male babies and only brought up the females. They also removed their right breasts to stop them getting in the way when they threw their javelins. These legendary women were the inspiration for **Wonder Woman** in the DC Comics, who was sculpted from clay by her Amazon mother Hippolyta and given superhuman powers by the Greek gods.

Speak like a mythologist

HERO

'Hero' is derived from the Greek word, *heros*. A modern real-life hero is usually someone who is respected for doing or achieving great or brave things. A mythological hero is someone who often has a divine parent and superhuman powers, but is still very much like us. Heroes suffer the joys and pain of human life, can be wise or foolish, and can do both good and bad things.

The Twelve Labours of Heracles

The **mightiest** Greek hero was Heracles. He's most famous for completing twelve impossible-sounding Labours, though there are different versions of the myth. One story says that the goddess Hera hated him, and made him kill his family. To make amends, Heracles had to complete twelve tasks set by his enemy, King Eurystheus. **And they were very hard tasks . . .**

7 Capture the Cretan Bull.

8 Steal the Mares of Diomedes.

killer horses

9 Fetch the queen of the Amazons' belt.

10 Capture Geryon's cattle.

Geryon

11 Fetch the Apples of the Hesperides.

golden apples

12 Fetch Cerberus from the underworld.

✴ Speak like a my**tho**logist ✴

HERACLES OR HERCULES?

Heracles means 'Hera's Glory' in Greek, but people most often use the Roman form, which is Hercules. Which one is correct? They both are!

As the favoured son of Zeus, Heracles became a god after his death.

Cúchulainn

The Irish Cúchulainn was the son of the god Lugh and the mortal Deichtine. He got his name when, as a child, he killed the blacksmith Culann's guard dog, but promised to take its place as the 'Hound of Culann', which is what Cúchulainn means in Irish.

When Cúchulainn was seven years old he heard a **druid** prophesy that anyone who picked up weapons and got ready to fight that day would have eternal fame. So, Cúchulainn asked his uncle Conchobar of Ulster for his weapons. But he had not heard the rest of the prophecy: the warrior would live a very short life, just like Achilles, who we will meet later on.

Aged seventeen, Cúchulainn fought against Queen Mebd of Connaught, who wanted to steal the Brown Bull of Cooley. He slaughtered Mebd's troops with the deadly Gae-Bolg ('Spear of Mortal Pain'), but of course he could not escape the druid's prophecy. Shortly after the battle, Cúchulainn himself was fatally wounded by a magical spear. He tied himself to a stone so that he would die standing up.

Sigurd

When a hoard of gold, including a cursed ring, was stolen by the venomous dragon-serpent Fafnir, Norse hero Sigurd swore to kill the thieving monster.

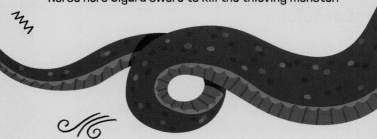

He hid in a trench near the beast's lair and, as Fafnir slithered over it, he thrust his sword into the serpent's belly and killed it. But the curse of the ring passed on to Sigurd as he took the treasure.

The curse of the ring came true when Sigurd was travelling some time later. He awakened the **Valkyrie**

Brynhildr from a sleeping spell and promised to marry her, but then drank a potion of forgetfulness and married the princess Gudrun instead. Gudrun's brother married Brynhildr and killed Sigurd, then Brynhildr ended her own life.

Sigurd in battle with Fafnir

✳ Speak like a mythologist ✳

THE *VÖLSUNGA SAGA*

The *Völsunga Saga* is a thirteenth century CE poem written in the Old Norse language. It tells of the rise and fall of the Völsung clan, who were descended from the god Odin. Sigurd is the main character in the story.

✳ Speak like a mythologist ✳

MAGIC RINGS

Sigurd's story inspired the composer Richard Wagner's mighty opera *The Ring of the Nibelung*, and J. R. R. Tolkein's *The Lord of the Rings*. Magic rings also appear in Harry Potter's world.

Mythical heroes are brave, sometimes flawed, talented, determined and often have superhuman qualities. Some heroes have fateful weaknesses, but they can do things that ordinary humans might never dream of—facing unimaginable dangers, making terrible mistakes, and achieving astounding feats in their **quest** for eternal glory or to make the world a better place. Read on to hear how following a quest or making a remarkable journey is an essential part of many hero stories.

Chapter 5

Mythical Journeys and Quests

Awesome journeys and quests appear in the myths and legends of nearly every people in the world.

Stories like this, where the hero heads off, encounters fabulous forces, and wins a wonderful victory, are often called 'the Hero's Journey'. We see these story patterns in *Star Wars*, *Toy Story*, *Frozen*, *Harry Potter*, *The Hunger Games*, *The Lord of the Rings*, and countless other tales, as well as in ancient legends.

Speak like a mythologist

THE HERO'S JOURNEY

There are patterns in many hero stories. When the adventure starts, the heroes might need someone to help them begin their journey. They meet friends and enemies, and, as they approach their goal, they have to face a big test. When it looks like they will succeed, they must deal with even more problems. Finally they return home in triumph, having learned things and matured during their journey.

The *Odyssey*

On his **amazing** voyage home to Ithaca after the **Trojan War**, the cunning Greek hero Odysseus had to face all sorts of incredible challenges. It took him **ten years,** but he made it home in the end.

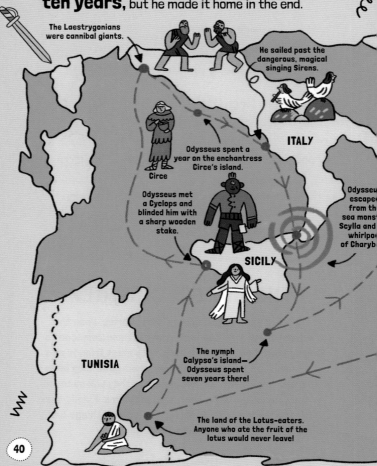

The Laestrygonians were cannibal giants.

He sailed past the dangerous, magical singing Sirens.

ITALY

Odysseus spent a year on the enchantress Circe's island.

Circe

Odysseus met a Cyclops and blinded him with a sharp wooden stake.

Odysseus escaped from the sea monster Scylla and whirlpool of Charybdis

SICILY

The nymph Calypso's island— Odysseus spent seven years there!

TUNISIA

The land of the Lotus-eaters. Anyone who ate the fruit of the lotus would never leave!

40

This map of Greece and parts of Turkey, Italy, and Tunisia charts where some of Odysseus's **fictional voyages** might be in the real world—though many of the lands in the story aren't on any actual map.

Troy

The island of the Phaeacians. They took him home in one of their ships.

GREECE

Odysseus fought in the Trojan War.

TURKEY

ITHACA
Home at last!

Mediterranean Sea

Odysseus' journey

Speak like a mythologist

THE *ODYSSEY*

The *Odyssey* is a Greek epic poem that tells of the hero Odysseus's ten-year journey home after the Trojan War. 'Odyssey' has become the word for a long trip full of different and exciting adventures.

HEROES OF MYTH AND LEGEND

HOMER

The name given to the author of two Greek poems, the *Iliad* and the *Odyssey*, which had been memorized and repeated for hundreds of years before they were written down in around 750 BCE. It is a mystery who Homer was, where he came from, whether he wrote both poems, or whether each poem was created by just one person. But the poems are still being read and studied today.

Sindbad the Sailor

The *Odyssey* inspired the adventures of Sindbad the Sailor in a collection of stories known as the *Thousand and One Nights* or *The Arabian Nights*, which was written down in Arabic in the fifteenth century CE.

Sindbad was a merchant from Baghdad who made **seven fantastic journeys** that made him very rich. On his first voyage, he landed on an island that was actually a whale and was almost drowned when it dived into the sea. On his second trip, Sindbad used a **huge** mythical bird called a Roc to help him collect diamonds.

Sindbad and the Roc

Sindbad's next adventures remind us of Odysseus. He met a Cyclops-like giant who ate several of his sailors before he blinded it with red-hot iron spits. Like Odysseus with the Laestrygonians, during his fourth trip, Sindbad was shipwrecked among cannibals, but **again he escaped.**

On Sindbad's other adventures he survived being buried alive, attacked by more Rocs, shipwrecked, and captured by the Old Man of the Sea. His final voyage took him to the farthest corner of the world, where the local people turned into birds and Sindbad flew above the clouds on one of them. These bird-people were in fact devils, but when Sindbad praised Allah, they dropped him on a mountain-top. He returned home, and never went to sea again.

Xuanzang, Sun Wukong, and the 'Journey to the West'

The sixteenth century CE Chinese novel *Journey to the West* by Wu Cheng'en is inspired by myth and legend and features a clever trickster, the Monkey King Sun Wukong, who was born from a magic stone egg.

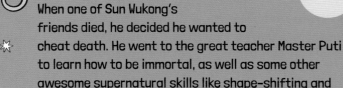

When one of Sun Wukong's friends died, he decided he wanted to cheat death. He went to the great teacher Master Puti to learn how to be immortal, as well as some other awesome supernatural skills like shape-shifting and somersaulting over clouds. When Sun Wukong got home, he stole the Dragon King's magic weapon, fought off the ambassadors from Hell, and rubbed his own name off the *Register of the Living and the Dead.* This made him immortal.

The supreme god, The Great Yu, decreed that Sun Wukong should be moved to heaven, where he could keep an eye on him. But Sun Wukong caused havoc there, and even ate the Peaches of Immortality that belonged to the Heavenly Queen Mother.

Sun Wukong

So, Sun Wukong was imprisoned underneath a mountain until, 500 years later, Guanyin, the goddess of mercy, had him released on the condition that he went to India with a monk called Xuanzang on a quest to fetch some sacred *sutras*—teachings of the **Buddha**.

After eighty-one adventures among demons, evil wizards, raging rivers, and uncontrollable monsters, Xuanzang and Sun Wukong got the sutras from the Buddha himself. Sun Wukong was rewarded with the title 'Victorious Fighting Buddha'.

HEROES OF MYTH AND LEGEND

WU CHENG'EN

A writer of the Chinese Ming Dynasty in the sixteenth century CE. His writing was inspired by myth and folklore though *Journey to the West* was based on a real trip to India made by the monk Xuanzang in the seventh century CE.

On their journeys and quests, heroes often have to face **terrifying** creatures of various kinds if they are to make it safely home. So let's meet some of the scariest creatures, and discover how to deal with them.

Chapter 6

Monsters and Monster-Slayers

Myths and legends are crammed with fire-breathing, snaky, flesh-eating, turn-you-to-stone creatures. Others are harmless, but people still fight against them.

Medusa

Medusa was one of the three Gorgons. Anyone who looked at her turned to stone.

staring eyes

writhing snakes on her head

tusks

The Greek hero Perseus was given the seemingly impossible task of bringing back Medusa's head. So, he set off armed with a pair of winged sandals, a special bag, the cap of invisibility, and a sickle made of adamant, the hardest metal in myth. To avoid looking at Medusa directly, he used a bronze shield to reflect her image while he chopped off her head. Then he stuffed it into his bag, put on the cap of invisibility, and flew away.

✸ Speak like a mythologist ✸

APOTROPAIC

The Greeks and Romans often hung carvings of Medusa's head on buildings. These were believed to be 'apotropaic', meaning they could avert evil forces and keep bad luck away.

The Minotaur

The Minotaur, which means **'Bull of Minos',** was thought of as a monster. People were scared of someone who looked so different, with the body of a human and the head and tail of a bull. The Minotaur was named after King Minos of Crete, who was so horrified

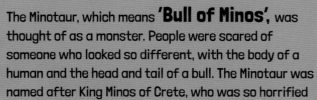

the Minotaur

by the creature that he shut it up in the Labyrinth, a specially made underground maze that it was almost impossible to get out of.

Minos also forced the king of Athens to send a tax of seven young men and seven young women every year as food for the Minotaur. One year, the king's son, Theseus, was chosen to be one of these 'Minotaur victims'. Theseus intended to terminate both the Minotaur and the tax. When he arrived in Crete, Minos's daughter Ariadne **fell in love with Theseus.**

Ariadne gave Theseus a **ball of thread** to unwind as he went down into the Labyrinth, where he and the Minotaur fought to the death. Theseus won and used the thread to find his way out again.

HEROES OF MYTH AND LEGEND

THESEUS

Ancient Greek minotaur-slaying hero.

The Qallupilluit

The Inuit who live in the Arctic regions of Alaska, Canada, Siberia, and Greenland tell stories of the terrifying Qallupilluit. The Qallupilluit are human-shaped creatures that live in the icy waters where the land meets the sea. They have green, slimy, scaly skin, with claw-like fingernails, and long hair. They lure young children

a Qallupilluit

50

onto thin ice and snatch them when it breaks, then carry their victims away in a pouch. Inuit adults tell these scary stories to make sure that children don't wander off on their own onto the dangerous ice.

HEROES OF MYTH AND LEGEND

EDWARD W. NELSON

An early American ethnographer who collected information about Inuit myths and folktales.
An ethnographer is a person who studies different cultures, often using first-hand observation and interviews.

Kut-o-yis

Some heroes sacrifice themselves to overcome evil beings. The **Indigenous American Blackfoot** Nation have a hero called Kut-o-yis ('Blood-clot Boy').

An old man stole a big clot of blood from the carcass of a buffalo which he and his stingy son-in-law had hunted. The son-in-law never allowed him any meat from their hunting, so the old man and his wife **boiled the blood clot** in a pot to make soup. They were amazed to hear a noise like a child in pain, so they opened the lid and found a little boy. They named him Kut-o-yis, Blood-clot Boy, but told their daughters the baby was a girl.

After just four days Kut-o-yis had grown into an adult. He took revenge on the son-in-law for being so mean to the old man, before heading off to kill all the bad things in the world.

He despatched a rattlesnake, and then went into the mouth of the people-swallowing Wind Sucker, stabbed

it in the heart, and freed everyone inside. After defeating two women who terrorized travellers, Kut-o-yis came to the **great Man-Eater**. He allowed the monster to kill, cook, and eat him four times, but every time Kut-o-yis was reborn, and he finally killed the Man-Eater by throwing it into its own cooking pot.

Beowulf and Grendel

Beowulf is the hero of an **Anglo-Saxon** poem. He went to Denmark to help King Hrothgar fight the

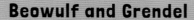

giant demon Grendel.

Grendel was a 'shadow-walker', a cursed descendant of Cain, the first murderer in the Christian **Bible**. Grendel hated the joyful sounds that came from Hrothgar's feasting hall, and every night he terrorized the partying Danes.

But when Grendel tried to devour Beowulf, the unarmed hero ripped off the demon's arm, and Grendel ran away and died in his marshy lair.

In his relentless fight against evil creatures, Beowulf also fought a brutal battle with Grendel's vengeful mother, slaying her with an ancient sword he found in her underwater hall. After that, Beowulf had to confront a **fire-breathing** dragon that was ravaging his kingdom of **Geatland**.

He entered its den and killed it, but not before it had sunk its fangs into his throat. And so Beowulf died, fighting to save his own people.

Beowulf

Speak like a mythologist

BEOWULF

The hero of a poem of the same name that was written in Old English somewhere between **975** and **1025 CE**, although we don't know who wrote it. *Beowulf* is **3,182** lines long and there is only one copy of it, in the British Library in London, UK.

Caipora: guardian of the rainforest

Tales from the South American **Tupí-Guaraní** peoples' mythology were first written down in the sixteenth century CE. A popular character is the Caipora, whose name means 'forest inhabitant'. The Caipora is described in many different ways by the separate peoples.

The Caipora often appears as a small human-shaped creature with a long mane of flame-coloured hair and red eyes, riding on a **peccary** and shaking a short spear.

This is one interpretation of what the Caipora could look like.

All the stories agree that the Caipora is as *fast as a gust of wind*, and that it protects the forests and animals. If hunters do not respect the rules of fair play, it whips them or confuses them, makes them have bad luck, and gets them lost in the jungle. The Caipora imitates animal noises, leaves false tracks, scares off the hunters' prey, and can even bring animals back to life.

The Caipora has inspired modern writers too. In the world of Harry Potter the Caipora are mischievous, furry spirit-beings who protect the Wizarding Castle of Castelobruxo in the Brazilian jungle. In DC Comics, Caipora is a companion of the second Wonder Woman, Yara Flor, and is a guardian of the Amazon rainforest.

If you are going to deal with a mythical creature, you will need **strength** and **courage**, and possibly a **magic weapon** and help from your companions. But even this might not be enough. You will need to be cunning and crafty, and some of the most entertaining legendary characters are brilliant tricksters, as we will see . . .

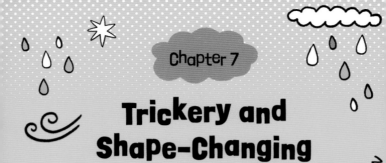

Chapter 7

Trickery and Shape-Changing

Trickster characters appear frequently in myths
and legends, bringing unpredictability, chaos, and fun.
They can be thieves and liars, destructive or helpful,
often have no morals, and almost all
of them can change shape.

Coyote

The story of Coyote is told by many Indigenous
American peoples. He is usually male and human-shaped,
although he can have fur, pointy ears, a tail, yellow
eyes, and claws like a wild **coyote** dog. Coyote is
both cunning and thoughtless, does harm and
good, and doesn't care about right and wrong.
He can even play tricks on himself.

In one White River **Sioux** story, Coyote and his trickster
friend Iktome the Spider-man found a storytelling
rock called Iya. Coyote gave Iya his beautiful blanket,
but when the weather became stormy, he took it
back again.

Iya was offended, and although Coyote thought he'd got away with it, he hadn't. After the storm passed, the great rock suddenly came hurtling straight at Coyote and Iktome. They ran for it and then swam across a river, but the rolling stone just kept coming, smashing down the trees in its way. Iktome changed himself into his spider form and scurried down a hole, but Iya caught Coyote, squashed him flat like a rug, and took the blanket.

Some time later, a man came past and thought Coyote really was a rug, and took him home. However, the next morning the 'new rug' **ran away.**

Coyote could **always** come back to life.

Speak like a mythologist

METAMORPHOSIS

Metamorphosis means the change of something or someone into a completely different form. Many tales of supernatural transformation are told by the ancient Roman poet Ovid in a poem called the *Metamorphoses*, published about 8 CE. Ovid is one of the most popular authors about myth in European literature.

Ananse

Ashanti people of West Africa have a tale in which the sky god Nyame owned all the stories and knowledge. The trickster, Ananse the Spider, wanted to buy this information. Nyame would sell it in return for the Python, the Leopard, the Hornets, and a **Fairy**.

Ananse found the Python. 'I wonder whether the Python is longer than a palm branch,' he said. The snake stretched out, offering to be measured, and Ananse tied him to the palm branch and delivered him to Nyame. Next Ananse dug a hole and covered it over with leaves. When the Leopard fell into the trap, Ananse pretended to help him, but tangled up the Leopard in his spiderweb, and then the Leopard was hauled off to Nyame too.

There are many different interpretations of how Ananse looks.

Ananse caught the Hornets by creating a pretend rain shower and offering to keep them safe in his **gourd**. When they flew into it, he plugged up the hole and carried them back to Nyame. Finally, Ananse made a wooden doll covered with sticky gum, and put some **yams** in its hands. One of the Fairies ate some of the yams, but ended up stuck to the gum, and Ananse carried the captured Fairy to Nyame.

Nyame was impressed and gave Ananse the stories. Ananse put all the world's wisdom into his gourd, but **accidentally** broke it, and so everyone in the world was able to share the knowledge.

Loki

The Marvel character Loki, **god of mischief,** was inspired by the Norse trickster god Loki, who could change shape and gender at will. Norse Loki became a fly, a salmon, and a mare that gave birth to an eight-legged wonder-horse called Sleipnir.

Through mischief and trickery, Loki helped the gods to acquire Gungnir, the spear that never missed its target, Skidbladnir, the ship that could carry all the gods but could be folded up into a pocket, and Thor's hammer, Mjölnir.

Loki was charming and funny, but they were also a cunning, cowardly, selfish liar, and was jealous of Odin and Frigg's popular son Baldur. When Baldur had dreams that prophesied his own death, Frigg made every living thing promise not to harm him,

Loki

but overlooked the mistletoe plant. When the gods played a silly game where they threw things at Baldur without harming him, Loki tricked the god Hod into hurling a mistletoe spear, which hit Baldur and killed him instantly.

Hel, goddess of the underworld, agreed to release Baldur if everyone would weep for him. Everyone did, apart from the cold-hearted Tokk, who was actually Loki. So Baldur had to stay in the underworld, but the gods took vengeance for Loki's many crimes. They used the entrails of his son, Narfi, to tie him to a rock underneath the jaws of a serpent that dripped venom on to his face, causing earthquakes as **he writhed in agony.**

HEROES OF MYTH AND LEGEND

THOR

The thunder god of Norse mythology who rode across the sky in a goat-drawn chariot. His most famous possession was his hammer, Mjölnir, which means 'Lightning'.

Māui

In the culture of the **Polynesian** islanders, Māui is a cunning trickster. Tales about him were told for hundreds of years, and first recorded around 130 years ago.

The Islanders tell many different stories about Māui. In some of them he created the islands of Hawaii and New Zealand by fishing them out of the sea using a magic fishhook made from his grandmother's jawbone.

There are also amazing stories about how, in order to steal fire from the gods, he recited a poem that opened the gateway to the underworld, and then shrank himself and hid inside a red pigeon, which flew to the fire god Mauike.

Māui

Back in human shape, Māui won a fight with Mauike, and made the god teach him how to make fire. He grabbed two fire-sticks, hid inside the pigeon, and flew back to the upper world, where he shared the secret of fire with humans.

The days were too short because the sun god Tama-nui-te-rā moved across the sky too quickly. So, Māui captured Tama-nui-te-rā and threatened him with the enchanted jawbone until he promised to move more slowly.

Finally, Māui tried to win eternal life from the death-goddess Hine-nui-te-pō, but she crushed him to death. Māui still lives on in stories and in the Disney film *Moana*, where Moana, a chief's daughter, meets him in her quest to save her people.

Tricksters often use their powers to try to help humans, as well as playing tricks on them. Because they break rules, they often get into fights with the gods. But as we are about to discover, there were other mighty conflicts involving gods, heroes, and humans that were fought in stories all across the world.

Chapter 8

Mythical Wars

War stories are always compelling, and the legendary battles of gods v gods, heroes v heroes, gods v mortals, or Good v Evil are some of the best ever told.

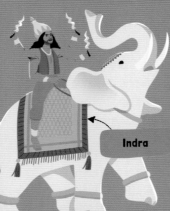

Indra

Indra v Vritra

The *Rig Veda*, the ancient Hindu scriptures, are written in **Sanskrit** and date from about 1500 BCE. They tell of how Indra, king of the gods, faced a gigantic challenge from the serpent-dragon-demon Vritra. The monster had coiled himself round a mountain, built ninety-nine fortresses, and blocked up the rivers, causing a terrible drought. So, Indra went to Tvastar, the maker

Vritra

of divine weapons,
who created the
vajra, which was
as indestructible
as diamonds and
as irresistible as
thunderbolts.

Indra fortified
himself by drinking
three sacred beakers of

soma, the plant juice
of immortality, and stormed into battle.
Vritra collapsed under Indra's onslaught and crushed
all the fortresses as he fell. The dragon still fought on,
though, until Indra finally smashed him between the
shoulders with his *vajra*. As Vritra lay in lifeless pieces,
Indra set the rivers free, and their waters rushed
down like bellowing cows. Indra then gave life to the
sun, dawn, and heaven, and slew Vritra's mother Danu,
bringing order to the world and earning the title of
The Great Impetuous Many-Slaying Hero.

Troy

The story of the Trojan War is about a conflict between heroes, although the **Olympian gods and goddesses** also joined in. The story sounds like a real war, and some people think it might have really happened.

Speak like a mythologist

THE *ILIAD*

Homer's *Iliad* is an epic poem telling the story of the Trojan War and the hero Achilles, who was disrespected, sulked, lost his best friend, and killed his worst enemy. In the end he realized that there was more to life than revenge, and more to adulthood than slaughtering other people.

Trojan prince Paris was made to decide which goddess should be given a golden apple bearing the words 'for the fairest'.

For the fairest

He chose Aphrodite because she promised him Helen, the most **beautiful** woman on earth, and the war began when Paris kidnapped Helen, who was already married to Menelaus.

Helen of Troy

The Greeks sent an army on a fleet of 1,106 ships to get Helen back. Their best fighter and *fastest runner* was Achilles. His goddess mother wanted to make him immortal, so she dipped him in the **River Styx** as a baby, making him totally invulnerable everywhere except for his heel, where she had held him.

At Troy, the Trojan warrior Hector slew Achilles' best friend Patroclus (some scholars think that Achilles and Patroclus were lovers). Achilles knew about a prophecy that he would die if he rejoined the battle, but he didn't care. He went into battle, fought against a river god, and drove all the Trojans except Hector inside their city.

Hector

Achilles

Hector tried to run for safety, but Achilles chased him three times around Troy's walls before slaying him. True to the prophecy, Achilles was killed soon afterwards by an arrow that struck him in his heel.

With Greece's finest fighter lost, another warrior, cunning Odysseus, had the idea of building a **huge wooden horse**. The Greek army pretended to sail away, and despite being told to 'beware of Greeks bearing gifts', the curious Trojans dragged the horse into their city to see what this mysterious present was.

Greek warriors hiding inside it jumped out and opened the city gates to let in the waiting Greek army

The Greek army burned Troy to the ground, massacred the men, enslaved the women and children, and sailed home with Helen.

HEROES OF MYTH AND LEGEND

ACHILLES

Ancient Greek hero. Achilles was given the choice between a long but unremarkable life or a short, glorious one. He chose glory. Because of the way he died, some people now use 'Achilles heel' to describe a vulnerable point or a weakness. In your body, the Achilles tendon connects your calf muscles to your heel bone.

Emperor Huang Di v Chiyou

One of the **most famous** figures in Chinese mythology and culture is Huang Di, who was honest, clever, and wise. He lived to be **300** years old.

Huang Di was challenged by Chiyou, a creature who had eighty brothers with animal bodies, bronze heads, iron brows, and who ate sand and stone. Chiyou was also a blacksmith. He made weapons and attacked Huang Di with an army of fierce creatures on the plain of **Zhuolu**.

Both sides used magic, and when Chiyou enveloped the battlefield in supernatural fog, Huang Di's warriors made their way through the mist using Fang, a miraculous south-pointing chariot that had a wooden person with a magnetic hand fixed to it.

Huang Di ordered the dragon Yinglong to do battle with Chiyou, but when the dragon gathered up all the water, Chiyou unleashed Feng Po, the hideous Wind Master, and the Rain Master, Yu Shih.

Huang Di called on his daughter, Ba the Drought-Ghoul, to descend, and she stopped the wind and rain. Eventually Chiyou was killed, and Huang Di was carried up to heaven on a dragon and became a god.

The **Han** people, who make up about 90% of China's population and 19% of the world's population, are still seen as the descendants of Huang Di.

Huang Di

The great mythological wars could cause destruction to humankind, but so could natural disasters. As we shall see in the next chapter, the gods could attack humans with devastating floods.

Chapter 9

Flood Myths

All over the world there are tales about a Great Flood. Even though there probably never was one enormous cataclysm, the details of these stories can be amazingly similar.

There is often conflict between the gods and humans in which nearly all mortals are destroyed, but sometimes humans are given a second chance and bounce back stronger than before.

Noah, Atrahasis, and Ut-napishtim

In the Jewish and Christian Bible story of the Great Flood, God told Noah to build a **large** ship known as the Ark. Noah and his family and pairs of different animals went aboard the Ark and were saved from the flood.

They knew the world was drying out when a dove Noah sent out returned with an olive leaf, and then finally didn't return at all.

There are similar tales in the **Mesopotamian** *Epic of Atrahasis* and the Babylonian *Epic of Gilgamesh*, in which the heroes Atrahasis and Ut-napishtim tell how they survived the flood.

In the *Epic of Atrahasis*, the gods sent the flood because humans were too noisy. In both stories one of the gods warned the hero, telling him to build a boat, abandon possessions, and save lives. So, Atrahasis and Ut-napishtim both built

≥ enormous ≤

cube-shaped boats and sailed off on them with their families and various animals.

The gods sent down showers of bread, wheat, birds and fish, and then started a countdown to the deluge on a water clock.

✳ Speak like a mythologist ✳

THE *EPIC OF GILGAMESH*

The Babylonian *Epic of Gilgamesh* was composed around 1100 BCE and survives on twelve clay **cuneiform** tablets in the Akkadian language. It is about the adventures of the young King Gilgamesh who is seeking immortality. When Ut-napishtim tells him this is impossible, Gilgamesh focuses on becoming a good king instead.

As the weather got worse the storm gods **roared,** the boats started to float, the sky was torn apart, the land was smashed like a broken pot, and everything went dark. Even the gods themselves were frightened by what had happened. The storm lasted seven days.

In the *Epic of Gilgamesh*, after Ut-napishtim's boat ran aground on Mount Nimush in Iraq. He released a dove and a swallow, both of which came back, followed by a raven which did not.

Speak like a mythologist

THE *EPIC OF ATRAHASIS*

The Mesopotamian *Epic of Atrahasis* was written down during the reign of King Ammisaduqa of Babylonia around 1600 BCE. It contains a creation myth and a flood myth that probably influenced the story of Noah.

Then he made a sacrifice to the gods, and the weather god Enlil decreed that Ut-napishtim and his wife should become like the gods.

In the *Epic of Atrahasis* the gods got hungry because there were no more farmers, and no one was sacrificing any more. They realized that they needed human beings, so when they discovered that Atrahasis had survived, they decided that the human noise was OK within limits but made sure that not too many humans would be born in future.

Plato's Atlantis

In works called *Timaeus* and *Critias*, the fourth century BCE Greek philosopher Plato invented an amazing flood myth about the island of Atlantis, which was in the Atlantic Ocean and seemed like a wondrous paradise. The wealth of its kings was **astonishing,** every kind of animal lived there, the cities were exquisite, and the earth produced everything they could ever wish for.

But Atlanteans still wanted more. After they tried and failed to conquer the city of Athens, Zeus punished them with a **cataclysmic** natural disaster. Atlantis disappeared under water in one awful day and night.

Plato's message in the story is, 'Keep it simple and modest, don't ask more for than you need, and don't be like those imaginary Atlanteans because it will only end badly.' Did Atlantis ever really exist? It was certainly just a story with a moral, although that has not stopped people searching for Atlantis ever since.

✳ Speak like a mythologist ✳

CATACLYSM

The floods are literally cataclysmic! The ancient Greek word *kataklysmos* means 'flood'.

None of these Great Floods destroyed the whole of humanity. All the ghosts of the people who were drowned in these terrible events were believed to go

down to the **underworld,**

but the survivors were all given a second chance. And as we are about to find out . . . the underworld was a strange place, and there were other ways in which the end of the world would come.

Chapter 10

The Underworld and the End of the World

Most mythologies divide the Universe into three levels: the heavens, where the gods live; the earth, inhabited by humans; and an underworld, sometimes known as Hell.

Different cultures have diverse ideas about life after death, and about how the world itself might end. Some people see time as a straight line, with a beginning and end, while others see it as cycles of creation and destruction, with each cycle ending in an apocalyptic battle or natural disaster.

Speak like a mythologist

APOCALYPSE

Today we use 'apocalypse' to mean an event that causes destruction on a massive scale, and 'Armageddon' for a terrible conflict that could wipe out humans. In the Christian Bible the *Book of Revelation* (aka The Apocalypse) tells the final battle between the forces of Good and Evil will be fought at a place called Armageddon in ancient Palestine.

Duat, the Egyptian underworld

The ancient Egyptians believed that there was a vast underworld, the *Duat*, beneath the earth. The *Duat* was ruled by the god Osiris, and every night the sun god Ra would sail through it on his night boat, the *Mesektet*, and be reborn in the morning.

The dead made a similar journey and had to get past gods, mysterious creatures, and demon gatekeepers, although they had *The Book of the Dead* to guide them, and the jackal-headed god Anubis made sure they didn't get lost.

sun god Ra

When they reached the Hall of Judgement, the dead had to appear in front of forty-two divine judges. *The Book of the Dead* helped them to say all the right things, even if they were not totally innocent. But then came the 'Weighing of the Heart'.

Everybody's heart recorded everything they had ever done. So, it was placed on one side of a balance, with a single feather of Ma'at, the winged goddess of truth, on the other.

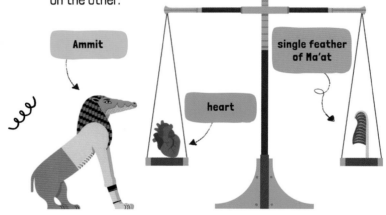

Ammit

heart

single feather
of Ma'at

If the heart weighed more than the feather, it was fed to Ammit, a demon who was part hippopotamus, part wild cat, and part crocodile, and the dead person would simply disappear for ever. But if the scales balanced, they had passed the test, and Osiris would welcome them into the afterlife.

✴ Speak like a mythologist ✴

EGYPTIAN *BOOK OF THE DEAD*

The Book of Coming Forth by Day, also known as *The Book of the Dead*, is actually a huge collection of spells. The spells were usually written on a papyrus roll that was placed with the dead person, but sometimes they were inscribed or painted on the walls of their tomb.

details of the ancient *The Book of Coming Forth by Day*, also known as *The Book of the Dead*, (1070 BCE), Thebes—Egypt

83

Milu, Hiku, and Kawelu: the Hawaiian underworld

The Hawaiian chief Milu became god of the underworld, known as Lua-o-Milu, after he disappeared in a surfing accident. In his kingdom under the sea, he organized sports and games like the ones that his ghostly subjects enjoyed when they were alive.

In a Hawaiian legend recorded in the nineteenth century CE, Hiku and Kawelu were a newly married couple. They had a terrible argument and Kawelu ended her own life leaving Hiku heartbroken. Hiku decided to go to Lua-o-Milu to bring Kawelu back from the dead. To get to the underworld, a priest told him, he must paddle his canoe into the middle of the ocean, and let down one end of a vine into the water.

Hiku did as he was told and climbed down the vine into the underworld. He began to swing on the vine, and the spirits all jumped on to play on it too. Even Milu joined in. Eventually, Kawelu's ghost joined in the game, and straight away Hiku called to the people on his canoe to pull up the vine, while he held on tightly to Kawelu.

Hiku brought Kawelu to their home, where her dead body lay. He pushed her spirit back into her body from the feet upwards, and Kawelu crowed like a cockerel and was restored to life. She and Hiku went back to living as husband and wife.

Milu, god of the underworld

85

Mictlan

The people of the Aztec Empire, who lived in what's now Mexico, believed that there were thirteen levels in the heavens and nine in the underworld, which was called Mictlan.

In Aztec mythology, unlike the myths of ancient Egypt and Greece, what happened to people after death did not depend on how they had lived, but on the way they died. Warriors and women who died in childbirth went to the land of the sun god Tonatiuh; those who died by drowning, certain diseases, or being hit by lightning went to the mansion of the Rain god Tlaloc; but adults who died of other causes went to Mictlan and young children went to Xoxchatlalpan (place of abundance and flowers).

The descent through the nine levels included passing through the Place of the Obsidian-bladed Winds, where the air cut their skin like a knife, the Place Where People are Killed by Arrows, and the Place Where People's Hearts are Devoured.

Finally, they reached the Place That has no Outlet for Smoke, and met the Lord and Lady of Death, Mictlantecuhtli and Mictecacihuatl, who fed on a diet of feet, hands, **beetle stew**, and a **porridge made of pus** which they drank from skulls.

Mictlantecuhtli wore a headdress of owl feathers, a necklace of **human eyeballs**, and his clawed hands carried a knife to remove people's hearts.

Mictlan was the place of ultimate disappearance, but there is no record of how the Aztecs believed the dead spent the rest of time.

This is one interpretation of what Mictlantecuhtli and Mictecacihuatl could look like.

Ragnarök

In the Norse *Prose Edda*, the end of the world is Ragnarök. Three severe winters, full of war, will be followed by The Great Winter, which will engulf the world in ice for three years. The wolves Sköll and Hati will swallow the sun and moon, and earthquakes will rock the earth. Loki and his son, the terrifying wolf Fenrir, will break their chains and Hel's guard dog Garm will snap the rope that tethers him.

The seas will spill over the land as the serpent Jörmungandr slithers ashore, and Naglfar, the ship made from the finger- and toenails of corpses, will slip its moorings, captained by Hrym, the leader of the army of Frost Giants.

Hrym captaining the ship Naglfar

Fenrir's jaws will reach from the earth to the sky;

Jörmungandr will belch poison; Surt, the leader of the
Fire Giants, will lead them across the Rainbow Bridge
between the earth and the sky, and it will shatter
beneath them. After Asgard's guardian Hiemdall
has summoned the gods with the loud-sounding
horn called the Gjallarhorn, Odin will ride to the Well
of Knowledge to seek advice, and the cosmic tree
Yggdrasil will tremble. The gods will march from Odin's
heavenly hall of **Valhalla**, and battle will be joined on
the field of Vígrid.

Odin, in golden armour and wielding his magical spear
Gungnir, will duel with Fenrir, but the wolf will swallow
him. Thor will slay Jörmungandr but die from the
serpent's venom. Freyr, the god 'hated by none', will
lose to Surt. Garm and the war god Tyr will kill each
other, and so will Loki and Hiemdall. Odin's son Vidar
will kick Fenrir's jaws open with his **magic shoe**
and thrust his sword into his heart.

Finally, Surt will send fire through all the Nine Worlds,
putting an end to humans, gods and goddesses,
giants, **elves**, and **dwarves**, before the world sinks
beneath the waters. However, in the *Poetic Edda* this
is not the end of the story. Baldur will eventually lead
a number of gods back to Asgard, and a new green,
bright, fertile world will emerge from the waves.

Chapter 11

Myths, Legends, and Superheroes in the Modern World

These myths and legends are hundreds, sometimes thousands, of years old, but there is no sign of them fading away. The exciting plots and fascinating characters in these enchanting and inspiring stories still entrance us with their magic.

We can travel back in time on our own journeys of discovery, sail the Seven Seas with Sindbad, watch the world come into being, and rid it of dangerous and mysterious creatures. And we can see the ancient characters morphing into today's superheroes, as the Norse Thor wields his magic hammer Mjölnir in the **Marvel Universe**, the Amazon Wonder Woman saves the world from chaos and destruction, and Percy Jackson traverses a gloriously reimagined world of Greek gods and goddesses.

We can find our own special hidden meanings in these stories too, although these won't be the same for all of us because myths and legends speak to everyone in different ways. They can be totally illogical, and yet they make perfect sense. They are full of truth. They change all the time, but they are fixed for ever. And they explain things that can't really be explained.

There is no end to the power of brilliant storytelling.

Glossary

Allah Arabic word for God among Muslims

Anglo-Saxon earliest recorded form of the English language, spoken in England and parts of Scotland in around 450–1150 AD

Babylon rich and powerful ancient city on the River Euphrates in what is now Iraq

BCE stands for 'before common era'

Buddha Siddartha Gautama, the 'awakened' or 'enlightened' one, who renounced his wealth and family and taught everybody who came to learn from him. He founded the religion or philosophy called Buddhism

CE stands for 'common era'

Christian Bible Christian is the name originally given by the Greeks and Romans to the followers of Jesus. The Bible is the sacred writings of the Christian religion

coyote North American wild dog, rather like a wolf

cuneiform very early writing system that uses wedge-shaped characters

DC Comics one of the oldest American comic book publishers. The imaginary DC Universe features superheroes such as Superman, Wonder Woman, and Batman

diaspora people who have been dispersed from their homeland

divine like a god or goddess

druid celtic ancient priest, magician, wizard, or soothsayer

dwarves mythical Norse creatures. They live underground, and are brilliant blacksmiths and craftspeople

elves god-like beings in Norse mythology who are more beautiful than the sun

epic long poem about the exploits of legendary heroic characters

ethnographer a person who studies and describes the customs and behaviour of human cultures, often using first-hand observation and interviews

fairy supernatural being in human form, usually represented as small, clever, and playful, with magical powers

Geatland Beowulf's kingdom in what is now southern Sweden

gourd hard-shelled fruit that can be dried and used to make containers and other useful objects

Greek mythology the group of stories about gods, goddesses, heroes, and creatures of ancient Greece. These are some of the most well-known and long-lasting tales in the world

Han the largest ethnic group in China

Islam related to the Muslim religion. In Arabic 'Islam' means submission to the will of God

K'iche' Maya people who flourished in Mexico and Central America between about 300 and 900 CE.

Marvel Universe a modern fictional universe produced by Marvel Comics and Marvel Studios that is full of characters with superhuman powers, who are dedicated to protecting humanity

mermaid a mythical creature with the upper body of a woman and the tail of a fish

Mesopotamia the ancient region between the Tigris and Euphrates Rivers, now in Iraq. Mesopotamia means 'the place between the rivers'

Norse a word that describes the ancient Norwegians and Scandinavians and their language and culture

nymph a spirit of nature in the form of a woman who inhabits rivers, pools, woods, seas, and mountains

Olympian gods and goddesses Zeus, Hera, Poseidon, Apollo, Artemis, Athena, Aphrodite, Hephaestus, Dionysus, Hermes, Ares, and Demeter—the Greek divinities whose home is on Mount Olympus in Greece

peccary a medium-sized pig-like mammal, also known as a javelina or skunk pig

Poetic Edda collection of anonymous poems from the eighth to eleventh centuries CE, which records many tales of Norse mythology

Polynesia an area of islands between Hawaii, New Zealand, and Easter Island in the Central and South Pacific Ocean

prose writing that isn't poetry

Prose Edda Norse textbook written in Iceland during the early thirteenth century CE by a scholar called Snorri Sturluson

quest long or difficult search for something or someone

River Styx mythical river that divides the earth from the underworld

saga long story of heroic deeds, especially one told in Old Norse or Old Icelandic

Sanskrit the ancient language of South Asia, and the sacred language of Hinduism

Sioux an alliance of tribes of Indigenous American peoples from the South and Midwest USA

Sirens musical enchanters who bewitched sailors and lured them to their deaths

Thebes important city in central Greece that featured in many Greek myths. Not to be confused Thebes on the River Nile, the capital of the kingdom of Egypt in its heyday

Trojan War mythical ten-year siege of Troy by the Greeks after the Trojan prince Paris kidnapped Helen from her husband Menelaus

Tupí-Guaraní South American Peoples who mainly inhabit rainforest areas around the River Amazon

Valhalla great hall ruled by Norse god Odin, where warriors go if they have died fighting

Valkyrie attendants of Norse god Odin. They decide the outcomes of battles and take the souls of slain warriors to Valhalla

yam vegetable that you can boil and mash, or fry, roast, or bake, common in West African countries

Zhuolu region of northern China

zither musical instrument played with the fingers and a plectrum. It has a flat wooden sound box with about forty strings stretched across it

✿ 🌿 Index ⚡ ✦